Information Systems and Technology in the International Office of the Future

IFIP – The International Federation for Information Processing

IFIP was founded in 1960 under the auspices of UNESCO, following the First World Computer Congress held in Paris the previous year. An umbrella organization for societies working in information processing, IFIP's aim is two-fold: to support information processing within its member countries and to encourage technology transfer to developing nations. As its mission statement clearly states,

> IFIP's mission is to be the leading, truly international, apolitical organization which encourages and assists in the development, exploitation and application of information technology for the benefit of all people.

IFIP is a non-profitmaking organization, run almost solely by 2500 volunteers. It operates through a number of technical committees, which organize events and publications. IFIP's events range from an international congress to local seminars, but the most important are:

- the IFIP World Computer Congress, held every second year;
- open conferences;
- working conferences.

The flagship event is the IFIP World Computer Congress, at which both invited and contributed papers are presented. Contributed papers are rigorously refereed and the rejection rate is high.

As with the Congress, participation in the open conferences is open to all and papers may be invited or submitted. Again, submitted papers are stringently refereed.

The working conferences are structured differently. They are usually run by a working group and attendance is small and by invitation only. Their purpose is to create an atmosphere conducive to innovation and development. Refereeing is less rigorous and papers are subjected to extensive group discussion.

Publications arising from IFIP events vary. The papers presented at the IFIP World Computer Congress and at open conferences are published as conference proceedings, while the results of the working conferences are often published as collections of selected and edited papers.

Any national society whose primary activity is in information may apply to become a full member of IFIP, although full membership is restricted to one society per country. Full members are entitled to vote at the annual General Assembly, National societies preferring a less committed involvement may apply for associate or corresponding membership. Associate members enjoy the same benefits as full members, but without voting rights. Corresponding members are not represented in IFIP bodies. Affiliated membership is open to non-national societies, and individual and honorary membership schemes are also offered.

Information Systems and Technology in the International Office of the Future

Proceedings of the IFIP WG 8.4 working conference on the International Office of the Future: Design Options and Solution Strategies, University of Arizona, Tucson, Arizona, USA, April 8–11, 1996

Edited by

Bernard C. Glasson
Curtin University
Perth, Western Australia

Douglas R. Vogel
University of Arizona
Tucson, Arizona, USA

Pieter W.G. Bots
Technical University of Delft
Delft, The Netherlands

Jay F. Nunamaker
University of Arizona
Tucson, Arizona, USA

SPRINGER-SCIENCE+BUSINESS MEDIA, B.V.

First edition 1996

Originally published by Chapman & Hall in 1996
MyCopy version of the original edition 1996

DOI 10.1007/978-0-387-35085-1

A catalogue record for this book is available from the British Library

Printed on permanent acid-free text paper, manufactured in accordance with ANSI/NISO Z39.48-1992 and ANSI/NISO Z39.48-1984 (Permanence of Paper).
www.springer.com/mycopy

CONTENTS

Preface

It is our pleasure to introduce these proceedings of the International Federation for Information Processing (IFIP) Working Group 8.4 working conference on the *International Office of the Future: Design Options and Solution Strategies*. IFIP's mission is to be the leading, truly international, apolitical organisation which encourages and assists in the development, exploitation and application of information technology for the benefit of all people. IFIP Technical Committee 8 (TC8) in turn aims to promote and encourage interaction among professionals from practice and research and the advancement of concepts, methods, techniques, tools and issues related to information systems in organisations. IFIP TC8's working group 8.4 (WG 8.4) field of interest within TC8 is the study of information systems that impact office work.. This includes the analysis, design, development, implementation and evaluation of office systems and associated technology support for office work. These systems may either be intra-organisational or inter-organisational.

Historically the focus of office systems has been intra-organisational. The field addressed concerns that were for the most part dealing with same-place, same-culture and often same-time situations. More recently there has been a shift in interest towards different-place, different-time and different-culture situations. The office systems focus has shifted towards inter-organisational systems. The computer and telecommunications enabled globalisation of business, internationalisation of trade and the increasing prevalence of multi-cultural interdisciplinary teams are beginning to redefine the nature of office work. Different-time/different-place/different-culture teams will become the norm. Same-time/same-place/same-culture workgroups will become the exception. The International Office of the Future (IOF) will be a dramatically different environment than that which exists in the majority of today's organizations. Whether this has been caused by a computer and communications technology push or by the demand pull of global business is a not important here. What is important is that the globalisation of business through the so-called "information superhighway" brings with it many opportunities and challenges for those interested in office systems - more particularly inter-organisational systems but these have impacts in intra-organisational systems too.

WG 8.4 responded to this shift in interest by asking the question - *what will be the international office of the future*? It went further and arranged a series of three events to help answer this question. The first event, "The International Office of the Future: A Problem Analysis", took place in 1994. The second event "The International Office of the Future: Design Options and Solutions Strategies", is the subject of these proceedings. The third and final event in this trilogy is planned for September 1997. "The International Office of the Future: Working Apart Together" will be a globally distributed conference in which the participants will live the experience of working in a setting that emulates a possible future office (see "Global Inc: An Experiment Across Time and Space" in these proceedings). The focus of this working conference however was "design options and solution strategies" open to organisations contemplating a computer and telecommunications enabled global future.

Prospects for the IOF give rise to numerous questions. What are the salient issues? What design options or solution strategies exist to address these issues? How might these design options be best implemented? What are their implications? The purpose of this conference was to provide a forum and prototype environment in which researchers and practitioners could interact. Electronic meeting technologies and facilities were available for participant use and evaluation. Specific topics included: the IS and IT infrastrucure to support distributed work; multi-cultural team productivity; real-time conferencing alternatives; CSCW; GSS; multi-media; global telecommunications; effective use of the internet and the information highway; international business systems and processes; office architectures; and social/political implications. This was truly a working conference. A feature of it was the formation of work teams to develop prototype designs for a future office environment. These designs will be used to guide the development of "Global Inc", the mythical organisation that will provide the setting for the final conference in this series to be held next year. They will also be of general interest to others in the field.

We would like to thanks those that made this event possible. First to the contributors. We received approximately forty five responses to our call for participation. After a strict "blind reviewing" process we came down on a final program of twenty three full submissions; seven extended abstracts; and six panels. Second we would like to thank the program committee who carried out the blind review. Their cooperation in meeting out tight deadlines made our task more easy and their helpful comments to the authors let to an improvement in the quality of the submissions. Third we would like to thank the support staff who have helped bring this event to fruition. In particular we would like to thank the program chair's assistant, Francesca Vallini who compiled these proceedings, and the organising chair's assistant, Melissa Glynn, who took responsibility for local arrangements. Fourth we would like to thank the University of Arizona for hosting the event. Last but not least we would like to thank all who accepted our invitation to attend the conference. As this was a truly working conference which attracted people from some 25 countries. Their active participation will have a significant impact on the eventual working conference outcomes.

Researchers and practitioners who would like to join the IFIP WG8.4 electronic mailing list and be kept informed of the group's activities should subscribe to the WG8.4 list server service. The procedure is to e-mail the account **Majordomo@IOF.curtin.edu.au** with nothing in the subject line and the command **subscribe IFIPWG84,** and nothing else, in the body of the message. The group's next principal activity will be the global working conference "The International Office of the Future: Working Apart Together" in September 1997.

Bernard C. Glasson

Douglas R. Vogel

Pieter W. G. Bots

Jay F. Nunamaker

Conference Committee

General Chair:

Jay Nunamaker, University of Arizona, USA

Program Chair:

Bernard Glasson, Curtin University, Western Australia

Organizing Chair:

Doug Vogel, University of Arizona, USA

Program Committee:

Fran Ackermann University of Strathclyde, UK
Rob Anson Boise State University, USA
Allan Baird Digital Corporation, Australia
Jim Brancheau University of Colorado, USA
Bob Bostrom University of Georgia, USA
Pieter Bots Delft University of Technology, Netherlands
Lynn Daniel The Daniel Group, USA
Pal Danyi Technical University of Budapest, Hungary
Annette Easton San Diego State University, USA
Brent Gallupe Queens University, Canada
Terri Griffith Purdue University, USA
Michiel van Genuchten Eindhoven, Netherlands
Joze Gricar University of Maribor, Slovenia
Jonathan Grudin University of California Irvine, USA
Judy Hammond University of Technology, Sydney, Australia
Judith.R. Holt JRH Associates, USA
Steve Horn ANDRULIS Research Corp., USA
Trevor Housley Housley Computer Communications Pty Ltd, Australia
Hiroshi Ishii MIT Media Laboratory, USA
Leonard Jessup Indiana University, USA
Helmut Krcmar University of Hohenheim, Germany
Klaus Lenk Universitaet Oldenburg, Germany
Ting-Peng Liang National Sun Yat-sen University, Taiwan
Petri Maaranen University of Jyvaskyla, Finland
Ben Martz Ventana Corp, USA
Jonathan Miller University of Cape Town, South Africa
Ken Myers Minnesota Technical College System, USA
Ken Moen Wright Patterson AFB, USA
Beatriz Morales ITESM, Mexico
Joline Morrison University of Wisconsin Eauclaire, USA
Juzar Motiwalla Institute of Systems Sciences, Singapore
Bill Olle T William Olle and Associates, UK
Otto Petrovic Karl-Franzens University of Graz, Austria
Carol Pollard University of Calgary, Canada
Petko Ruskov University for National and World Economy, Bulgaria
Peter Saalmans AARNET, Australia
Jeff Sacks Coopers and Lybrand LLP, USA

Bill Spano National Cryptologic School, USA
Ralph Sprague University of Hawaii, USA
Phillip Stone Harvard University, USA
Margaret Tan National University of Singapore, Singapore
Roland Traunmueller University of Linz, Austria
Jeff Trulsen Cornell University, USA
Joe Valacich Indiana University, USA
Rick Watson University of Georgia, USA
Alma Whitely Curtin University, Australia
Ginny Wilkerson Chevron, USA
Pak Yoong University of Wellington, New Zealand
Ilze Zigurs University of Colorado, Boulder, USA

Local Organisers

Melissa Glynn, University of Arizona, USA
Katie Rodda, University of Arizona, USA
Anne Rodda, University of Arizona, USA
Jeanette Gonzales, University of Arizona, USA

Program Committee Secretary

Francesca Vallini, Curtin University, Western Australia

PART A

Scope and Aims

1

Global Inc: an experiment across time and space

B. C. Glasson
School of Information Systems, Curtin University,
GPO Box U1987 Perth 6001, West Australia, Phone +619 351 7685; Fax +619 351 3076; Email Glasson@BA1.curtin.edu.au
D. R. Vogel
Department of MIS, 430EE McClelland Hall, University of Arizona, Tucson, AZ 85721 USA, Phone +520 621 4475;
Fax + 520 621 2433; Email Vogel@bpa.arizona.edu
P. W. G. Bots
Department of Systems Engineering and Policy Analysis, Delft University of Technology, PO Box 5015, NL-2600 GA Delft,
The Netherlands, Phone +31 15 782 948; Fax +31 15 783 429;
Email Bots@sepa.tudelft.nl

Abstract

Recent and rapid developments in electronic commerce enabled global trading have raised many questions about future office work. In the light of these questions IFIP WG 8.4 has organised series of events which will culminate with the running of a globally distributed working conference in September 1997. The September 1997 conference will focus on "Global Inc". Global Inc is a mythical organisation. Global Inc in its first incarnation will run for some 50 hours around the clock in three countries to simulate the 24 hour-a-day operations of a globally distributed organisation. It will serve three purposes. It will provide a forum through which researchers and developers can report and discuss IOF research outcomes. It will allow participants to live the experience of working in a globally distributed, 24 hour-a-day "organisation". And it will provide a "laboratory" through which to conduct experiments in future office technologies, processes or work practices.

Key words

Electronic Commerce, Future Office, Global Trade, International Business, Distributed Teamwork, Inter-organisational Systems, Computing and Communications Technology

1 INTRODUCTION

This papers discusses the third in a series of related research activities focussing on the international office of the future (IOF). This trilogy of IOF events has been devised and managed by IFIP WG 8.4. The International Federation for Information Processing (IFIP) exists to encourage and assist in the development, exploitation and application of information technology for all people. It operates through a number of technical committees (TC's). The TC's in turn comprise a number of working groups (WGs). WG 8.4 has the responsibility within IFIP for promoting research, development, application, education and information dissemination in the field of office systems.

In 1993, WG 8.4 forecast the rapid development and expansion of electronic commerce (Vogel 1993). The maturation of network technology and the commercial interest in the internet seemed to be providing the supply-side technology push for a new era of electronic commerce (eg. (Piel 1991)). At the same time the forces of globalisation seemed to be providing the demand-side pull (eg. (Tapscott 1993)). These supply and demand forces foreshadowed a new era of computing and telecommunications enabled international business - an era of global business based on global information technology bringing with it a number of opportunities and challenges (eg. (Ives 1991)). Hence the question - *what would be the international office of the future (IOF)?* This overall question spawned many sub-questions. Will the future office be a place or a space? Are the technologies sufficiently mature to support effective inter-organisational systems - and if not, what development work needs to be done, and if so, how best do we diffuse them? How do we manage inter-group synchronous and asynchronous communication? How do we manage multi-cultural and multi-disciplinary teams? How do we change business processes to adapt to, or capitalise on, a global trading environment? What would be the worker, work-place, organisational and even societal outcomes of the IOF? And these broad questions in turn generated many more detailed ones. As a consequence WG 8.4 agreed on a plan of research focussing on the IOF which culminates with a living experiment called "Global Inc".

2 GLOBAL INC

Distributed Working Conference

Global Inc is a mythical organisation. It is a concept rather than an entity. Some would call it a virtual organisation. Its line of business is IOF research, development, application, education and information dissemination. Its reason for being is to enable researchers and developers with an interest in any aspect of the IOF to work for a short while in a globally distributed organisation. In September 1997 Global Inc will run as a globally distributed working conference around the clock in three geographic regions over a period of two consecutive days. The theme of the working conference is "The International Office of the Future: Working Apart Together". Each region will take responsibility for a particular conference track. Each track will probably comprise two sessions. Each session will be made up of presentations, panels, birds-of-a-feather sessions or experiments. The Asia /Pacific region will run the organisational aspects track. The European region will run the business processes track. And the Americas region will run the technology track. Interested researchers and developers will be invited to participate in the work of Global Inc by physically attending at one of the regional centres. It is assumed participants will either choose the region running the track which is of most interest to them or the region that is closest. All the regions will be linked by technology of various levels of sophistication to facilitate information exchange and to enable collaboration.

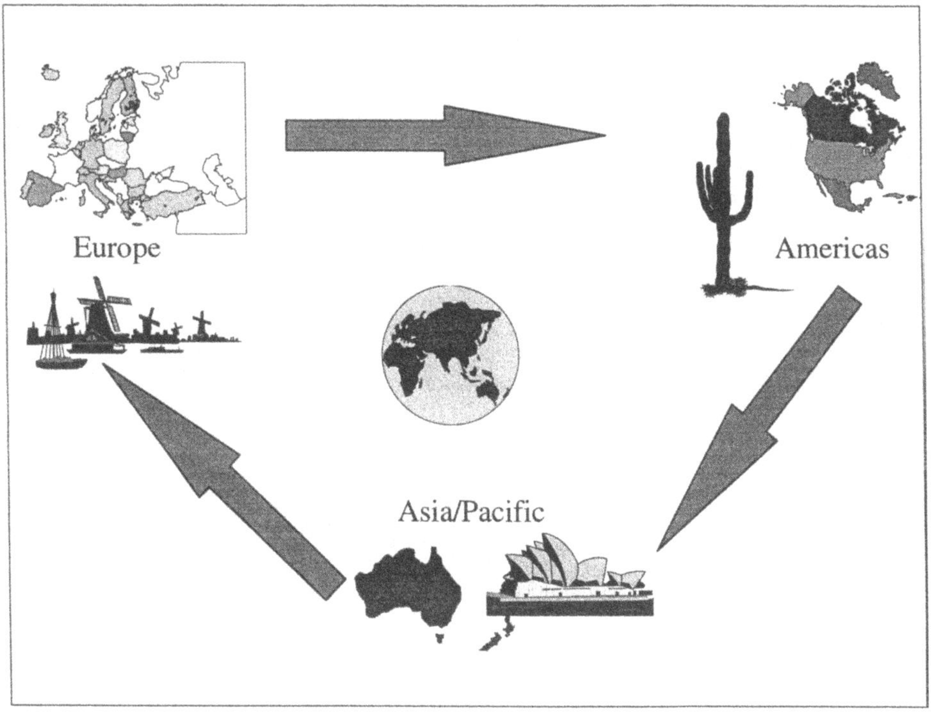

Figure 1 Global Inc Work Flow

At any one time each region will either be "in session", "on-line" or "off-line". When "in session" the region will be holding same-time, same-place, face-to-face activities for its local participants. It will also be responsible for distributing its work to the other two sites. When "on- line", the region will be linked to the "in-session" region to allow for same-time but different-place interaction. When "off-line" a region will not be engaged in Global Inc work. Work done at either of the "in-session" or "on-line" regions will need to be accessed by the "off-line" region later in a different-time, different-place mode of working.

Around the Clock

Global Inc will commence its Asian Pacific operations at (say) 1900 hours local time on Thursday September 25 1997 at Curtin University in Perth, Western Australia. It will commence its European operations some 8 hours later in The Netherlands at the University of Delft. And it will commence it Americas operations at the University of Arizona in Tucson, USA approximately 8 hours after that. Once operational it will run on a 24 hour basis for some 50 hours (ie until 1700 hours local time in Tucson Arizona USA, Saturday, September 27 1996). The "baton" would start in Perth. The Asia/Pacific region would close its first working day with a "keynote" address or panel which would be shared by the European centre via video link. At the conclusion of the Asia/Pacific keynote address the "baton" would pass to Delft. Similarly the European centre's closing session would be shared with the Americas and the America's closing session would be shared with Asia/Pacific. The

Table 1 Prototype Work Schedule

Project Time	Regional Centres Day, Approximate Local Time and Activity Approximate times and 8 hour blocks are used here for illustration purposes only. The "baton" holder is shown in **bold.** The baton holder region will be "in session". The two other regions will either be "on-line" (ie participating in the active regions session synchronously via a link) or "off-line" (ie will have access to outputs from the active region's session asynchronously). Shading indicates a two-way video link					
Start Time minus "n"	All regions could be involved in some pre-conference collaborative research project set-up activities					
	Perth		**Delft**		**Tucson**	
Evening before local Start Time	Local Welcome	Thu 2000	Local Welcome	Thu 2000	Local Welcome	Thu 2000
Start Time 01 Hrs	**Session 1**	**Fri 0800**				
08 Hrs	**Keynote**	**Fri 1600**	On-line	Fri 0800		
10 Hrs	On-line	Fri 1800	**Session 2**	**Fri 1000**		
16 Hrs	Off-line		**Keynote**	**Fri 1600**	On-line	Fri 0800
18 Hrs	Off-line		On-line	Fri 1800	**Session 3**	**Fri 1000**
24 Hrs	On-line	Sat 0800	Off-line		**Keynote**	**Fri 1600**
26 Hrs	**Session 4**	**Sat 1000**	Off-line		On-line	Fri 1800
32 Hrs	**Keynote**	**Sat 1600**	On-line	Sat 0800	Off-line	
34 Hrs	On-line	Sat 1800	**Session 5**	**Sat 1000**	Off-line	
40 Hrs	Off-line		**Keynote**	**Sat 1600**	On-line	Sat 0800
42 Hrs	Off-line		On-line	Sat 1800	**Session 6**	**Sat 1000**
48 Hrs	On-line Over breakfast	Sun 0600	On-line After dinner	Sat 2400	**Closure** Followed by dinner	**Sat 1600**
50 Hrs	End of event					
End Time plus "n"	Write-up of conference related collaborative research activity					

"baton" being passed to the next region after the baton-holder's closing session for the day (see Figure 1, Global Inc Work Flow above).

One *possible* arrangement of work is shown in Table 1, Prototype Work Schedule above. We stress possible because one of the aims of this conference is to set the level of ambition for the 1997 event and to agree the work arrangement (see Conference Format below).

Format

Global Inc will run as a three track working conference with a difference. There will be the usual submissions, panels, and birds-of-feather sessions. What will be different is the time and space dimension. Global Inc will run for 24 hours a day across three continents. This will provide an opportunity for participants to "walk the talk" and experience around the clock work. It will also provide the opportunity for experimentation given rich variety of work modes being used.

Participants may work in one of several modes. The variables determining the mode of work being place, time, face-to-face, interaction type, and action type (see Table 2, Some Work Type Variable Alternatives below). An important coordinating resource will be the Global Inc "Project Clock". The local time at each regional centre will need to be linked to the "Project Time". As the project time advances, the possible work types the participants in each region might experience will change.

Table 2 Some Work Type Variable Alternatives

Variable	**Alternative**	**Explanation**
Place	Same	Participants are at the same location.
	Different	Participants are at a different location
Time	Same	Participants are working at the same project time - but the local time may well be different
	Different	Participants are working at different project times
Face-to-face	Yes	Participants have eye contact
	No	Participants do not have eye contact
Interactive	Yes	Participants can interact in real time (Full Duplex)
	No	Participants must communicate in turn (Half Duplex)
Action Type	Initiates	This region initiates the work activity
	Reacts	This region responds to work initiated by the active region
	Observes	This region observes the work outcomes of others

Experimentation

WG 8.4 sees the Global Inc working conference as making a contribution to the field in three ways.

First, the subject matter is timely and important. The concept of an "information superhighway" changing the way we do business and impacting the way we live is as topical as it is potentially significant. Therefore the contributions made through the traditional working conference submissions will add to our knowledge of the field.

Second, Global Inc will enable those of us interested in the IOF to truly experience working in an around the clock "organisation". As this mode of work is novel for most of us, Global Inc will be for many a unique experience.

Third, it will provide a living laboratory for experimentation. In calling for participation in the 1997 Global Inc working conference, WG 8.4 will be particularly interested in receiving submissions proposing experiments that can be conducted during the Global Inc conference. They may be experiments involving joint authoring or collaborative writing; they may be short studies requiring

Delphi; they may be observations of one or other of the conference activities (eg a distributed panel); or they may propose short laboratory type experiments with control groups and experimental groups using different modes of work (eg a six team management game with two teams made up of participants from a single region, two teams made up of participants from two regions, and two teams with participants from all three regions). Conference participants would be encouraged to take part in these experiments as part of the Global Inc experience.

3 TRILOGY

The 1997 Global Inc working conference will be the culmination of three WG 8.4 activities. The two earlier sets of activities have, or will have, an important part in shaping the eventual Global Inc event. One set of activity took place in September 1994. The second is the subject of these proceedings.

The focus of the 1994 activity was "The International Office of the Future: A Problem Analysis". It was an attempt to define the opportunities and challenges facing any organisation contemplating engaging in computing and telecommunications enabled global business activities. Those opportunities and challenges were surfaced in a series of workshops. The outcome gave some insight into the issues that would need to be addressed in running Global Inc (Bots 1995).

The second activity is the subject of these proceedings. This working conference on "The International Office of the Future: Design Options and Solution Strategies" has brought together researchers and practitioners with an interest in proposing, testing or discussing design options and solution strategies for dealing with key technological, business process and work practice issues of the IOF. The conference has two aims. First it aims to make a contribution to the field through the published submissions. The second aim is to develop socio-technical infrastructure requirements for Global Inc. The first aim will be achieved through the publication and dissemination of these proceedings. The 30 full submissions or extended abstracts address a range of IOF issues and will make a contribution to the field in their own right. How we intend to achieve the second aim needs some explanation.

4 CONFERENCE FORMAT

The focus of this conference is Global Inc. Our secondary aim for this 1996 event is to develop a set of socio-technical infrastructure specifications for WG 8.4's 1997 global conference which we are referring to as the Global Inc Design. These specifications will guide the organising and program committee members as they bring Global Inc into being. In this sense this IOF Design Option and Solutions Strategies event here at the University of Arizona will truly be a working conference. These specifications will be developed over the course of the conference by the participants working in designated teams.

The conference will begin with two plenary sessions. In the opening plenary session we will attempt to develop the Global Inc "vision". The process will use stakeholder input to develop a shared vision of Global Inc which will serve to give the various working activities of the conference a focus. The second plenary session involves presentations of three different distributed environments - three views that might give insights into how the Global Inc socio-technical infrastructure might be developed.

These opening plenary sessions will be followed by a number of parallel paper and panel presentations which will run from the afternoon of the first day of the conference until mid-afternoon of the second. Each paper or panel relates directly or indirectly to an aspect of Global Inc that will need to be considered by the Global Inc design teams. Topics groupings include organisational aspects; technology aspects; culture; group support; international business; technology transfer, diffusion and adoption; video and computer conferencing; IOF work and workers; team facilitation; office architectures; and an array of IOF research issues.

Mid-way through the second day, participants will be arranged into multi-disciplinary Global Inc design teams. The teams will first meet over a working lunch to decide their modus operandi. The last session of that second day will be given over to Global Inc design workshops. Each team will be asked to develop a suggested design for Global Inc that is in line with the agreed vision based on the design options and solutions strategies raised during the conference to date. In the morning of the final day of the conference these "designs" will be presented in plenary session. These designs, separately or collectively will be used by the 1997 conference committee to develop Global Inc. And while the focus of the designs will be Global Inc, this will not be the exclusive focus of the conference. We anticipate that aspects of these designs will have general application.

The conference will close with a plenary panel which will explore IOF futures. The panel will look beyond Global Inc both in terms of issues and time horizon.

5 CONCLUSION

Global Inc is an attempt by WG 8.4 to replicate the workings of a globally distributed organisation operating around the clock. The success or otherwise of Global Inc will depend to a large part on the insight, enthusiasm and input of those participating in this years IOF conference here at the University of Arizona. We see Global Inc as great opportunity. We hope you do as well.

6 REFERENCES

Bots, P.W.G., Glasson, B.C and Vogel, D.R (eds) (1995) *International Office of the Future: A Problem Analysis*, Technische Betuurskunde, Delft University, Delft, The Netherlands

Ives, B. and Jarvenpaa, S.L. Applications of Global Information Technology: Key Issues for Management, *MIS Quarterly* March 1991

Piel, J. (Ed) (1991) Communications, Computers and Networks, *Scientific America* Special Issue Vol 265 No 3, September 1991

Tapscott, D. and Caston, *A. Paradigm Shift: the New Promise of Information Technology*, McGraw Hill NY, 1993.

Vogel, D.R., Marshall, P.H., Glasson,B.C. and Verrijn-Stuart, A.A. (Eds) (1993) Local Area Network Applications: Leveraging the LAN, *IFIP Transactions A-31* North-Holland, Amsterdam, 1993

7 BIOGRAPHY

Bernard Glasson is chairman of IFIP TC8 and program chair for this conference. **Doug Vogel** is chairman of IFIP WG 8.4 and the organising chair of this conference. **Pieter Bots** is vice chair of IFIP WG 8.4. Glasson, Vogel and Bots jointly developed the IOF trilogy concept and are taking various active roles in its implementation.

PART B

Full papers

2

Working with groups using groupware: electronic problem structuring and project management support for face to face and dispersed organisational groups

F. Ackermann
Department of Management Science,
University of Strathclyde, 40 George Street, Glasgow
Tel +44 141 552 4400, Fax +44 141 552 6686
Email Fran@mansci.strath.ac.uk

Abstract

This paper uses experiences gained from working with both senior and middle managers in organisations to describe a number of 'observations' identified concerning the impact technology has upon groups using Groupware in a face to face environment. These observations along with two case studies describing different instances of dispersed group working (one focusing on electronic problem structuring, the other project management support) are then considered alongside the impact dispersed working has on facilitating groups using Groupware. Both the observations and the facilitation discussion focusing on providing facilitation to dispersed groups are aimed at providing researchers and users with insights into some of the potential difficulties experienced when implementing groupware systems.

Keywords

Groupware, facilitation, problem structuring, project management, dispersed group working, face to face group working

1 INTRODUCTION

For a large number of people the question "what *is* Groupware?" immediately comes to mind when either confronted with the numerous articles (Byte 1993; PC Week 1994) or books (Johansen, 1988; Lloyd, 1994; Coleman and Khanna, 1995,) written on the subject. One definition given by

Watson (1994) states that groupware is "about people and processes first; technology and systems second" whereas Coleman (1995) asserts that Groupware " impacts the way people communicate with each other" and Opper and Fersko-Weiss (1992) note that groupware "must in some way facilitate and promote group interaction". All three of these definitions focus on the issue of *groups communicating and working together* placing the role technology plays at a lower level.

One means of distinguishing groupware from other Information Systems is that groupware allows groups to work at anytime and in anyplace. As such group members are able to contribute to discussions and take responsibility for the implementation of actions regardless of their location, and work schedules - an attractive proposition to organisations working in different cities or countries looking to increase their effectiveness. For the majority of groupware packages, the concepts behind them are not new, Engelbart in the 1960 and 70s (Engelbart 1963; Engelbart et al 1973) suggested the idea of computer based networks for communication. However with the availability of fast, inexpensive and reliable networks (including ISDN and Internet links) within and between organisations the idea of electronic communication and working has become a reality for both business and business education (Alavi et al 1995).

A number of Groupware systems have already been developed to support group working at various levels and on different tasks. One of the most well known is Lotus Notes which, using an E-mail and text based format, provides a valuable means of communication for group members working together. However, while Lotus Notes and others help with communicating on structured, coordinated and well understood tasks, they are not as effective in supporting groups working on messy, complex, unstructured problems. One reason for this is that these systems structure information in a predominantly linear style whereas people, when working on complex problems, think beyond simple sequential text. N-dimensional structures which encourage the "properties of the whole" as well as the detail to emerge, provide a powerful basis for the sharing of ideas and expertise. Therefore, in considering the adoption and usage of a groupware system, it is worth ensuring that an appropriate system is adopted. Briggs and Nunamaker (1995) provide a useful framework for determining the different levels of information technology support.

This paper commences with a brief exploration of the background to Group Support Systems leading into a review of the impact technology and computer support has had on face to face working with Groupware. This review, it is asserted, is necessary as many of these impacts are considerably amplified when working in a dispersed environment and others give rise to potential questions and dilemmas. Using the findings of the review and observations from two case studies, the paper then moves onto investigating the impact dispersed working has on facilitating groups using Groupware as well as other opportunities to be had, before concluding with a reflection on the current state of understanding and suggesting further research angles. This focus on facilitation is due to the role of facilitator being seen as critical to the support of groups (Bostrom et al, 1993; Ackermann, 1996; McGoff and Ambrose, 1991), particularly those groups working on messy, complex and unstructured problems.

2 BACKGROUND

It is worth considering, however, what the underlying effects are of these groupware packages and their attendant information technology infrastructure. One question worth addressing is "what does this introduction of technology do to group working and dynamics?" Considerable research has been undertaken into the use of Group Decision Support Systems(GDSS)/Group Support Systems (GSS) - systems which in the main have relied on the same time/same place mode of working

(Johansen 1988), i.e. face to face. It is notable from the findings that they are by no means conclusive in their verdict. Dennis and Gallupe, (1993) in a review of the history of GSS note "the results of early experiments can be summed up in one word: mixed. Some experiments suggested that GSS improved decision quality whilst others showed no effect or worse decision quality for groups using a GSS". According to Dennis and Gallupe, later field studies showed more positive findings with possible explanations being a) the size of group(increased), b) type of task (real and complex) and c) the inclusion of a facilitator. Nevertheless, it becomes obvious - we are still learning and will require more experiments, field studies etc before we can accurately predict and design such systems.

Groups working together are a complex aggregate of personalities, politics and power issues, content and substance. As such the systems employed need to be able to deal with all of these aspects rather than focus on one or two to the detriment of others. Laboratory studies offer valuable insights into individual components or sets of components but by their nature do not address the holistic superstructure - often a critical element. Field studies (McGrath 1984) however allow "testing" of such systems but are subject to criticisms (rightly so) of single case/uniqueness and subjectivity - although it is this author's contention that even lab studies suffer from subjectivity and designer bias.

3 OBSERVATIONS OF THE IMPACT TECHNOLOGY AND COMPUTER SUPPORT HAS HAD ON GROUP WORKING

So what have we learnt from our examinations of groups using such systems? What may be some of the impacts of technology to a group's decision making process? If we are to seriously consider extending computer support to dispersed group members, it stands to reason that we review how technology affects groups working in the same time/same place mode (Johansen 1988).

The following observations are gained from working with numerous organisational groups using the SODA/COPE multi-user system (Ackermann and Eden 1995a and b). The current software is designed to allow *structuring* and synthesis of the reasoning of many people, in a manner that can, through analysis, reveal important properties of combined wisdom. The process, provides significant productivity gains, better quality solutions, significantly higher levels of ownership of agreements made, and importantly group and organisational learning. Whilst the IT context has been primarily that of a single software user - the facilitator/analyst for the group, two years ago this single user group decision support was extended to enable multiple participants/ group members to interact with the software thus capitalising on the additional benefits of anonymity, fast data entry, and increased control over the expression of ideas/assumptions/assertions.

To provide group members with this interaction or 'direct entry' into the model, the software was extended to run on a network of PC's with each participant within the group being able to contribute, at the same time, to the problem structuring, evaluating and project management/ monitoring effort. This was achieved through "electronic brainstorming and linking", "electronic voting" in relation to desired *and* "no-go" options and "electronic rating" to determine either leverage (level of impact upon a particular variable) or progress. Observations of groups using this direct entry facility have shown that group productivity and participation is, on the whole increased.

This facility currently allows groups to work in the same place at the same time, building on rich communication protocols (non verbals). This mode of working can be instigated at various points during the collaboration. For example, to capture ideas, explore and negotiate a way forward, learn more about one another's roles and skills, and finally provide an organisational memory. This may be the first step in a meeting, allowing members to become familiar with one another and the technology. As such the multi-user allows;

- ideas to be entered directly into the system but in a graphical manner rather than linear. The relationships (linkages) between ideas can also be entered.
- voting on preferences where the original context is preserved, multiple criteria can be considered, and the results either hidden or displayed to the groups depending on the requirements (See figure 1 for the results of a voting session)
- rating to determine leverage or performance/ bench marking (used predominantly for evaluation of progress) (See figure 2 for a participant's screen when rating)

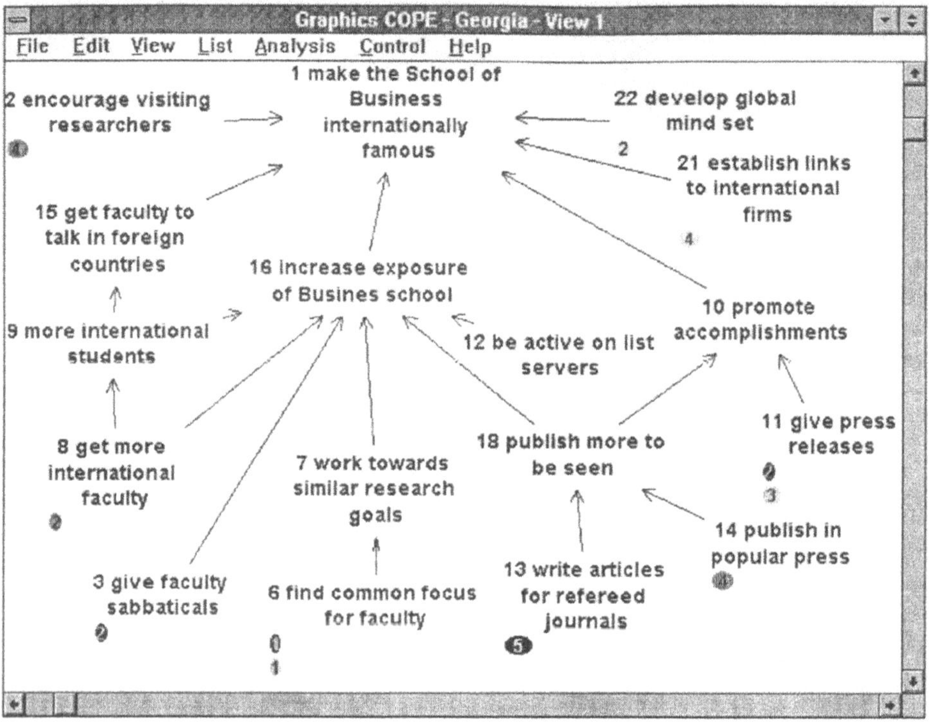

Figure 1 Results of voting exercise.

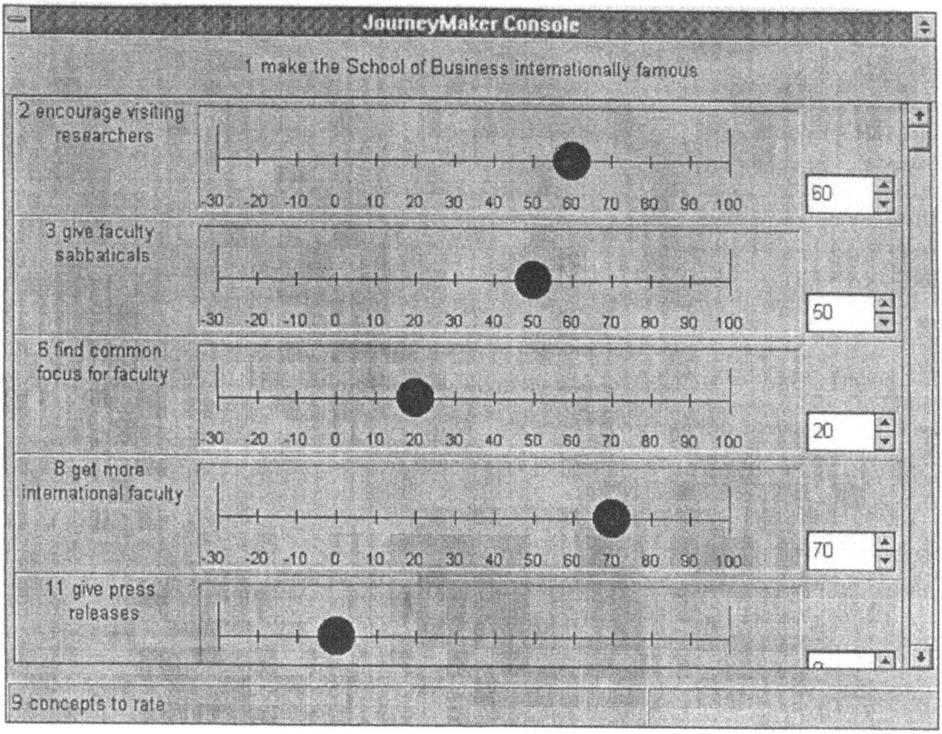

Figure 2 Example of the rating system

Along with

- the ability to switch between user entry and facilitator control over the model's contents. This facility is powerful as it allows the group members to develop a shared understanding of the content through moving between divergence (direct entry) and convergence (facilitator controlled)
- a monitoring system to detect generation, voting and rating patterns (see figure 3 below)

The observations were:

3.1 Dealing with personality or status issues

Dominant members (usually senior officers) often felt hobbled by the process of equality as they missed their ability to sway people or persuade their colleagues. Whilst this need to control the meeting may not be conducive towards increasing the creativity of group members or their ownership of the outcomes, it does raise issues relating to the ongoing nature of the group, ie can it continue to work together (a requirement of GDSSs according to Huber 1984) as well as the political feasibility of the outcomes (Eden 1991). If these, often powerful, people reject the process, it is going to be more difficult for others to support the outcome, thus diminishing the chances of implementation.

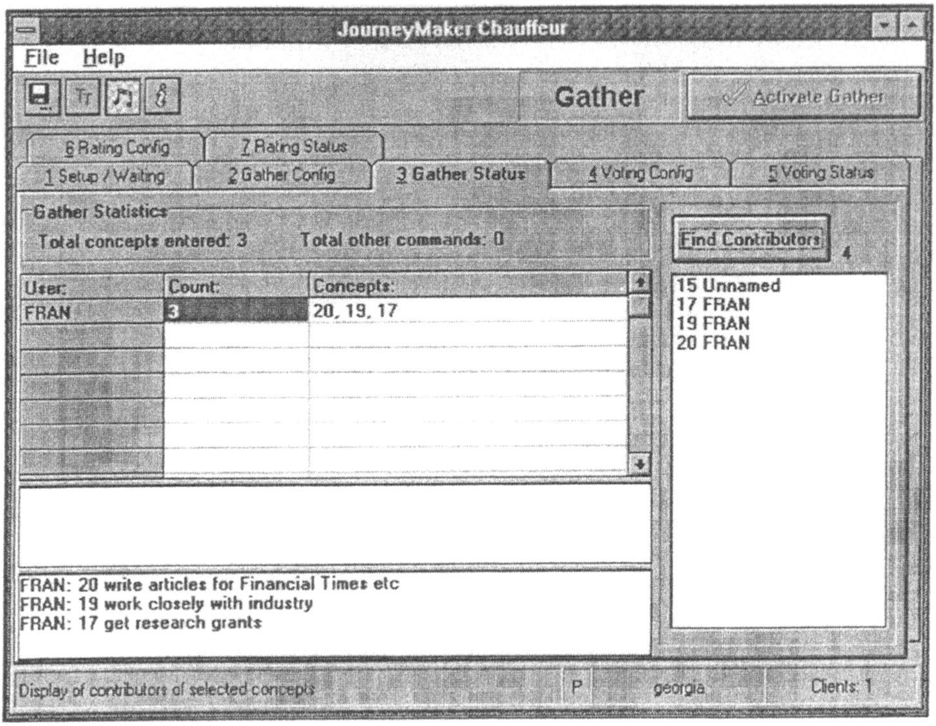

Figure 3 Example of the monitoring facility showing contribution levels etc.

This difficulty with equality is also evident when discussing the meetings with the 'client'. Organisations on the whole are not cooperatives, and to state implicitly or not that all members have an equal say in the decision, results in clients feeling uncomfortable if not threatened (Ackermann 1991; Ackermann and Eden 1995). Informing the client that through the monitoring system (figure 3) it is possible to determine the generating, rating or voting patterns (for example have a large number of people placed one vote on an issue or one person placed a large number of votes, or when gathering ideas has one person contributed lots of ideas or are they well spread). This ability, easily managed when working with manual systems as it is possible to observe the patterns, may go some way to reassuring clients who rely on the facilitator to ensure that the outcomes are those they will act upon, i.e. politically feasible. Whilst dealing with dominant or status issues is not necessarily a technology problem it is seen to be more pervasive when using technology and steps taken to resolve it.

Alongside issues concerning the management of dominant or powerful members, it has been noted that 'quieter' members do not necessarily contribute more with technology - nor for that matter does direct entry lead to quality ideas. In one case when working with a management team it was observed that a number of them entered very few ideas into the system. When gently questioned about this (by a colleague inside of the organisation) a number of them commented that in areas where they did not have direct experience or in depth knowledge they felt more comfortable remaining 'silent' and learning from their colleagues (Yeates, 1996). However they did appreciate that this 'silence' was not obvious to the group.

3.2 Mixing manual, single user and multi user modes of working

Having the ability to use a variety of support systems rather than just direct entry was seen to have the edge over just using multi-user/direct entry. This was partly to the variety providing a sense of mental refreshment. Looking at the screen all day was noted to be tiring particularly if the room being worked in had to be darkened to allow the projection device to work properly. Whilst it is acknowledged that projection devices through increases in resolution and power now perform better in daylight conditions, this requirement for mental refreshment continues to be an issue particularly if the meetings last one or two days.

Another benefit from having the different modes of working is that systems that support one task well may not be effective in supporting a different task. For example, the ability to allow group members to directly enter their ideas into the system provides the group with anonymity and the benefit of fast entry of ideas 'talking simultaneously" (Nunamaker et al, 1988). However, once this initial generation has been completed, moving to the single user mode (facilitator driven) allows the group to begin to discuss the ideas that have emerged, and so begin to reach a common understanding about the issue/problem and how ideas, assumptions etc relate to one another (Ackermann and Eden 1995b). Relying on the facilitator to manage the system also frees up the group members, allowing them to concentrate on the task at hand, and avoiding them from having to learn how to operate the system and adhere to the rules (Ackermann 1996).

3.3 Avoiding being reliant on technology

Whilst great improvements have been made, both to the software and hardware available, it is never absolutely reliable. Through having a manual or single user backup an alternative is available should it become necessary - as well as providing the benefits listed above. In those circumstances where the system suddenly ceased to work (sometimes through no fault of the system, e.g. power failures) it was noted that the ongoing discussion was interrupted, often fatally, that the group members enthusiasm was diminished resulting in a sense of demotivation and that sometimes all the positive benefits of working electronically were wiped out.

However, working to avoid being reliant on technology may place extra effort on the facilitator. Not only does he or she have to be familiar with the direct entry system, but also with the manual or single user modes of working. Whilst this may not be a problem to a skilled facilitator who is used to working with different techniques, where the facilitator is the leader of the group who has only learned to use the direct entry supported system, this may result in either the meeting being postponed or even the system being rejected. It may be that where the GSS being used replicates existing and well known manual techniques eg listing ideas and categorizing them (eg Group Systems 1988) this transition between modes is easy, however, where the system is underpinned by a new methodology, for example SODA or Decision Conferencing (Quinn et al, 1985), then the transition is more complex.

3.4 Using portable rather than desk top machines

Through working with a portable network, not only can the system be taken to the group's preferred location but also the above observation of moving between different modes of working is supported. Portables, by their very nature are easy to pick up and put down, and the system can easily be tailored to the number of group members rather than working in a room too large or too small. Furthermore, due to their size they avoid any visual clues from being blocked. However, they do have disadvantages in that there is a real danger of having the network connections terminated through cables being uncoupled from the computer and the number of machines available being dictated by the network setup.

3.5 Working with groups familiar with the process compared with those new to the support system

The group's familiarity with process was seen to have a significant effect on the way that the GDSS/GSS was introduced. Groups unfamiliar with technology in general (particularly the case with one organisation where over 60% were computer illiterate) experienced a sense of apprehension and wariness. This situation may be compounded when using portable systems as the 'spaghetti' like nature of the cabling raises group member anxiety. Not only are members faced with operating the computer but also with a new way of working, one that is unfamiliar to them. Where the groups begin working with a manual system, becoming acquainted with the particular way of capturing and structuring information, and then move to the technology the transition becomes more natural and less obtrusive. Even so, reassuring those members who are concerned that they might 'crash' the system is still important.

Once group members had become more expert with the system a different issue emerged - how to manage groups where a large number were experienced with the system but one or two required further attention. Those members comfortable with the direct entry mode and computers in general were impatient to start working whereas those new to the process were faced not only with a new way of working but also a set of colleagues eager to get started. Reminding these seasoned group members that they too had experienced the same concerns helped in managing the group dynamics.

4 USING GROUPWARE WITH DISPERSED GROUPS

To support groups working with more qualitative and subjective issues, for example strategy development and implementation, and noting the above observations of face to face work, a research project has been set up to develop a unique, and powerful means for enabling group members who may be in different locations to work effectively. One focus is to develop the methodology to enable group members to make decisions based upon ideas and comments entered into a model at different times and from different locations using an "electronic conversation" or "*electronic problem structuring*" process. Not only would this ensure that when the group members got together to finally decide on a course of action, the meeting was as effective and efficient as possible but also allow members to contribute at more conducive times rather than being forced to be creative at a set times (Case Study 1). The second focus concentrated on using an existing model (perhaps developed during a face to face series of meetings) for *project management* or reviewing progress (Case study 2).

In both different place/different time situations, the software's ability to capture both ideas and their relationships along with its extensive analytical facilities provided the means for examining the *holistic nature* of the issue rather than just the individual parts. This allowed group members to begin to explore and play with the model (Eden 1993) thus increasing their understanding of the issues and associated ramifications. However, in order to begin to explore electronic problem structuring conversations and project management a number of changes had to be made to the software. These were:

- Simultaneous access to the system. This was to allow multiple group members to be able to conduct an electronic 'problem structuring conversation' discussing issues and options or to discuss the operationalisation of agreed actions. Through using network protocols to 'lock' ideas and relationships, thus ensuring that several users do not manipulate the same part of the model at the same time, group members would be able to view the same material and work together. Not only would this ensure that the meeting was as effective and efficient as possible but would also allow members to contribute at appropriate times rather than being forced to be creative at a set time.

- Support for sharing ideas and data between group members. By using a bulletin board to alert members to specific issues of interest, and creating shared/global views (argumentation supporting a particular point of view) group members can begin to share ideas around a specific topic. This facility also aids project management as it allows group members to jointly develop the system of ideas, and consequently take ownership of the outcomes discussed. In addition, they can implement these outcomes with reference to the agreed direction. Changes made can then be entered into the system with those responsible being able to track and monitor progress.

4.1 Case study 1

The particular organisation involved a number of senior executives engaged in a complex strategy development issue. All of the executives were extremely busy people, often spending more of their time outside of the office than at their desk. As such finding time to get together was problematic and when they did meet they wanted to ensure that the time was spent as effectively as possible. Using the dispersed mode of working over a period of two weeks, the executives used the system to discuss the complex issue, spending short bursts of time entering ideas as they occurred to them, browsing through the material suggested by their colleagues and adding new comments prompted by other's material and raising questions. The structuring element of the system allowed the material to be managed effectively through showing how options could have both positive and negative effects, displaying feedback loops and demonstrating key or 'busy' ideas. In some instances the time actually spent entering ideas and exploring the model's contents only lasted 10-15 minutes - fitted in between other meetings when ideas or issues germane to the topic occurred to them.

Following this asynchronous discussion, a face to face meeting was held using the resultant model. Within 30 minutes the group had managed to resolve the issue and agree upon a set of actions. The dispersed mode of discussion had allowed them to 'speak', 'listen', 'comment' and reflect in their own time so that when they came to the meeting, they were already familiar with the material and its nuances. Consequently the process had maximised the efficiency of their time when getting together as a group (Bedgood, 1993).

4.2 Case study 2

The second organisation used the system in reverse. Through working together in the face to face mode the senior managers had developed a system of ideas (the model) reflecting the strategic direction that they hoped to take along with the associated actions necessary to achieve the direction. They had involved a large number of staff members in the process (to gain ownership and understanding) and had even incorporated key clients (to ensure that the resultant strategy was not in conflict with the client's aims and aspirations). Once the strategy model had been agreed upon by the management team, the individual team members agreed to take responsibility for particular issues and associated actions. To support the implementation process, the model containing all of the actions and their rationale was placed on the network for easy access. As the actions were started, substantially progressed or completed they were categorised accordingly - the categories being in the form of colours denoting progress (Ackermann et al 1992). In addition, to support the implementation further, job descriptions and roles were changed to match the strategic direction moving away from a traditional structure to one more suited to the strategic direction and future of the organisation.

Through enabling the management team access to the model and facilities to record progress, the Chief Executive was able to track progress on all the actions, promulgate successes and nudge those falling behind. When alterations were necessary due to changes in either the internal or external environment, they could be made in the light of the model/strategic direction as a whole. By sharing views and alerting one another to changes through an electronic message facility, new actions could be introduced that not only supported the area in question but also had benefits for other parts of the organisation - thus acting both corporately and synergistically. Members could share their views and post electronic messages (Miller and Ackermann, 1994).

5 PROVIDING FACILITATION TO DISPERSED GROUPS WHEN WORKING ANYTIME/ANYWHERE

One of the issues that has emerged from these two case studies, the observations of same place same time groups and reading the literature is the importance of facilitation. It has been noticed that when working on predominantly structured tasks with clearly defined roles groups are reasonably able to manage themselves. However, when the issue or problem is more unstructured, complex and has political ramifications for the group members facilitator assistance is often needed and sought. This belief that the inclusion of facilitators is important to the success of GDSSs has been supported in reports regarding face-to-face work, for example McGoff and Ambrose's statement that "experience continues to confirm that the quality of the group session is predominantly dependent on the facilitator" (1991) and when a facilitator is present to "manage both process and the content" (Phillips and Phillips 1990; Eden 1990; McGoff and Ambrose 1991). Translating this facilitation support to dispersed working however, raises a number of issues hitherto unexplored as the group working becomes fragmented, sporadic and less coordinated, and as such the question arises as to which or whether many of the skills/ procedures adopted by face to face facilitators can be utilised.

Some of the guidelines provided by researchers discussing facilitation, for example, providing clear objectives and an agenda for the process, agreeing upon who should be involved, prompting participants to perceive themselves to be equal for the event can probably be accepted without much hesitation. For these guidelines a slightly different packaging might be all that is needed. However from observations gained from the two cases studies noted above and conversations with other groupware researchers there appear to be other significant facilitation issues that need to be addressed, some of which include;

* developing methods for helping groups work with the large, complex structures they develop,
* keeping the model (or discussion) up to date and relevant,
* ensuring that related areas are adequately linked together rather than disconnected,
* finding ways to prompt members, keep the energy flowing and test assumptions, and
* building in some form of model review and maintenance.

Whilst some of these new facilitation issues are already being examined through reviewing current groupware projects, many of these are reactive rather than proactive - a not surprising finding given the newness of the field. Nevertheless, further research into group dynamics, facilitation methods and the impact distributed working will have on groups will require considerable attention and carefully conceived research design both in laboratories and in field studies. Furthermore, as these systems do become more prevalent and are used by groups working globally further complications in the light of facilitating multi-cultural groups will arise linking the research into cultural collaboration with group working and electronic support.

One avenue to consider when investigating how to support groups using groupware is through disaggregating the skills and techniques used by a facilitator. It has been argued that a number of the tasks undertaken by a facilitator could be automated (for example linking tools eg from brainstorming to voting) and that tasks such as prompting for the relationships between ideas, requests for elaboration, and reminders to contribute could be introduced into the groupware system. Another means of circumventing the difficulty is to design carefully tailored 'help' packages where the group members themselves become more self reliant and work to manage the group's effort. Both of these options however, tend to focus on tasks that are to some extent structured and where the political ramifications are small.

Nevertheless, in many circumstances the facilitator is brought in to a) provide a different perspective, or content expertise to the group, b) as a means of having a relatively unbiased person guiding the meeting, or c) harnessing a specialised set of skills. All three of these rationalisations defy automation or training. Firstly an outside facilitator not only brings new perspectives but can force a group to question their 'world taken for granted', the established practices (Ackermann 1996), prompting a fresh look at the issue or problem in question. Secondly, when using sophisticated modelling systems in order to structure the information particular coding rules apply. Ensuring that group members conform to information capture guidelines, not only to ensure the consistency of 'coding' data, but also to enable the various forms of analysis to be used as effectively and accurately as conceived, requires additional energy and commitment on the part of the members. The final point, that of bringing a relatively unbiased perspective is virtually unresolvable.

6 OTHER OPPORTUNITIES

For much of the groupware literature, readers could be forgiven for assuming that on the whole Groupware was used for either face to face meetings (Same Time, Same Place) or dispersed asynchronous meetings (Different Times/Different Place). However the two intermediary quadrants also provide powerful incentives. If groupware systems can be developed to support group working in all four of the quadrants, thus freeing up groups to work when and how they like then groupware will become a powerful system. One of the commonly asserted characteristics of Groupware is that the system must be 'seamless' (Malone 1992). This seamlessness may be the transfer of information between the different working modes as evidenced in the case studies, or the development of easy and intuitive to use interfaces (adopting existing ways of working and tapping well established routines). Given industry's often shy behaviour around information technology introduction, it is probably worth addressing both of these forms of seamlessness so as to quickly buy people into the benefits without any of the difficulties often associated with software.

Taking this request to address all four quadrants seriously, it is worth considering some of the instances where it can be conceived that the COPE groupware system may be applied to support the other two quadrants:

Different Time/Same Place

a) the organisational memory (the resultant model developed by the group) can be continually monitored for progress (either by group members or the Managing Director) and progress reports provided for departments, organisations, steering groups etc.

b) new members joining the organisation can quickly and easily determine the strategic direction, identify how the different parts of the company work together, explore areas relating to their sphere of influence and therefore be able to contribute more effectively

Same Time/Different Place

a) members in different locations will be able to discuss possible alternatives and co-responsibilities while viewing and expanding a joint representation of the issue. This development will help increase understanding through providing context whilst also ensuring that any alternations are made within the context of the overall direction of the collaboration. The model may be used as a means of exploring the issues, structuring the dialogue, visualising the different ramifications whilst maintaining communication through a standard phone conversation. In addition the resultant image provides a form of artefact - a transitional object - that the two group members can refer to at any time.

b) any new actions/ideas can be assessed to ensure that they support rather than conflict with existing work.

7 CONCLUSIONS

If groupware is to reach its full potential then many of the above issues do require investigation. One of the ways we can increase the chances of groupware systems being used by dispersed groups is to reflect upon the observations noted from face to face groups and try to determine how they relate and impact on dispersed working. The first observation, dealing with personality or status issues, appears to continue to be relevant with senior or dominant members either avoiding using groupware systems or struggling with more apparently equal modes of working. In an environment where non verbals are not available through group members being in different locations, it is easy to conceive of group members expecting an even greater degree of equality and freedom. Thus it becomes more important to make clear the distinction between being able to influence the direction and having a clear decision making prerogative.

Being able to mix manual, single user and multi-user modes of working to stimulate and refresh members does fail with dispersed working. However, to some extent it becomes replaced with the freedom to contribute when conducive. One of the important factors present in both of the case studies was the fact that the group members were familiar with the method of working and had used the software, albeit in single user mode, already. This familiarity appears to be a key factor in the adoption of groupware systems (as reflected in the observations) with novice groups potentially balking at having to learn new methods, software systems and ways of working together.

The two observations focused on technology have radically different ramifications. If groups are going to work in a dispersed mode using groupware then inevitably they are going to be reliant on technology and so the need for robust software becomes imperative. However whilst reliance on technology may well be seen as a potential danger, it may also provide some benefits. For example, group members using portable computers are able not only to work with them as 'desk top' machines (by connecting them to an external monitor, keyboard and office network) and therefore contribute to dispersed, asynchronous work but also use them for working in a same time/same place environment. This 'portability' may well contribute towards making the groupware process more seamless as moving between modes of working (any time/any place) becomes effortless.

As mentioned earlier the issue of group facilitation also requires attention as groups working at different times and places demand additional support. One particular demand is the increased need for monitoring the group's progress - during the discussion, evaluation and implementation stages. Models for automating facilitation must be investigated, but these impersonal aids often result in as many disadvantages as advantages. Automation often results in constraints as group members have to work within the parameters set by the automation. As such exploration in the field of artificial intelligence may provide some clues as to how a system can be developed that 'grows' with the user and can be tailored to meet the different styles of group members - a common requirement for Decision Support Systems (Sprague and Carlson, 1982). Teaching group members how to be self facilitators also raises concerns as for many of the potential users finding the time and energy is a problem - as is a concern about whether they will recoup the effort put into learning how to use the systems in productivity and effectiveness increases.

Finally, the question of whether organisations and their staff actually want to work remotely must be examined. For many of these systems to work successfully a change in organisational working practice must take place. It will become necessary to develop a means where a) collaborative working is accepted, b) sharing of information is seen as acceptable and necessary and c) decision makers consider the strategic development of the collaborative project as paramount. For many organisations this openness is both new and radical and as such avoided. Nevertheless there is a growing belief that sharing is necessary, that in order for teams to become empowered and collaborative and through the introduction of techniques like Business Process Reengineering (Hammer and Champy 1993) systems such as groupware offer rich opportunities.

8 REFERENCES

Ackermann, F. (1991) 'Consideration of a Specific Group Decision Support Methodology in the light of the Group Decision Support Systems Literature' Phd thesis, unpublished PhD thesis

Ackermann, F. (1996) 'Participants Perceptions on the Role of Facilitators using Group Decision Support Systems', *Group Decision and Negotiation,* 5 93-112

Ackermann, F. and Eden, C. (1995a) 'Visual Interactive Modelling: using multiple workstations for problem solving and action programming' Presented to TIMS/ORSA conference, Los Angeles, April.

Ackermann, F and Eden, C. (1995b) Contrasting GDSS's and GSS's in the context of strategic change - implications for facilitation' proceedings of the Inaugural *America Conference on Information Systems*, Pittsburgh, August

Ackermann, F. and Eden, C. (1994) 'Issues in Computer and Non-Computer Supported GDSSs' *International Journal of Decision Support Systems*, 12 pp 381-390

Ackermann, F., Cropper, S. and Eden, C. (1992) 'Moving between Groups and Individuals using a DSS' *Journal of Decision Sciences* pp 17-34

Alavi, M., Wheeler, B.C., and Valacich, J.S. (1995) 'Using IT to Reengineer Business Education: An Exploratory Investigation of Collaborative Telelearning', *Management Information Systems Quarterly, 3* 293-312

Bate, J.S. and Travell, N. (1995) *Groupware: Business success with computer supported cooperative* working. Alfred Waler, Henley on Thames.

Bedgood, D. (1993) 'An assessment of networked Graphics COPE as a groupware tool for Shell International' MSc in Operational Research thesis, Strathclyde University

Bostrom, B., Anson, R. and Clawson, V. (1993) 'Group Facilitation and Group Support Systems'. In L. Jessup and J. Valacich (eds) *Group Support Systems: New Perspectives.* Van Nostrand Reinhold, New York .

Briggs, R. and Nunamaker, J. (1995) 'Getting a grip on Groupware' in P. Lloyd (ed) *Groupware in the 21st Century.* Adamantine Press Ltd, London.

Byte (1988) *In Depth Groupware*, edited by J. Morill, 242-282

Coleman, C. and Khanna, R. (1995) *Groupware; Technology and Applications.* Prentice Hall, Engelwood Cliffs, NJ

Coleman, D. (1995) 'Groupware Technology and Applications; An Overview to groupware' in *Groupware; Technology and Applications* in C. Coleman and R. Khanna, (eds). Prentice Hall, Englewood Cliffs, NJ; -38

Dennis, A and Gallupe, B. (1993) A History of Group Support Systems Empirical Research: Lessons Learned and Future Directions. In L. Jessup and J. Valacich (eds) *Group Support Systems: New* Perspectives. Van Nostrand Reinhold, New York .

Eden, C. (1989) 'Using cognitive mapping for strategic options development and analysis (SODA)'. In J. Rosenhead (ed) *Rational Analysis for a Problematic World,* Wiley, Chichester

Eden, C. and Ackermann, F. (1992) 'Strategy Development and Implementation - the role of a Group Decision Support System' in S. Kinney, B.Bostrom and R. Watson (eds) *Computer Augmented Teamwork: A Guided Tour.* Van Nostrand and Reinhold, New York.

Eden, C. (1993) 'From the Playpen to the Bombsite: The Changing Nature of Management Science,' *Omega*, in press

Eden, C. (1991). "A Framework for Thinking About Group Decision Support Systems (GDSS)", *Group Decision and Negotiation, 1,* 2, 199-218

Engelbert, D.C. (1963) 'A Conceptual Framework for the Augmentation of Man's Intellect'. In P.W. Howerton and D.C Weeks (eds) *Vistas in Information Handling* Vol 1, Spartan Books, Washington DC 1-29.

Engelbart, D.C., Watson, R.W., and Norton, J. (1973) 'The Augmented Knowledge Workshop' in *AFIS Conference Proceedings*, Vol 42, National Computer Conference and Exposition, June 4-8, New York City. AFIPS Press

Hammer, M and Champy, J. (1993) *Reengineering the Corporation: A Manifesto for Business Revolution*. Nicholas Brealey Publishing , London.

Huber, G. (1984) 'Issues in the Design of Group Decision Support Systems', *Management Information Systems Quarterly* 8 195-204

Johansen, R. (1988) *Groupware; Computer support for Business Teams*. Free Press, New York

Lloyd, P. (1994). *Groupware in the 21st Century; Computer Supported Co-operative Working toward the Millenium*. Adamantine Press Ltd, London.

McGoff, C.J. and Ambrose, L. (1991) 'Empirical Information From the Field: A Practioners' View of Using GDSS in Business', in the Proceedings of the *24th Annual Hawaii International Conference on System Sciences*, Vol 3, Society Press, Los Alamitos, CA 1991

McGrath, J. (1984) *Groups: Interaction and Performance*. Prentice Hall, Englewood Cliffs NJ.

Malone, T. (1992) Defining Groupware - The History and Functionality of Groupware from both Theoretical and Commercial Perspectives'. *Network World - Groupware Today*, September.

Miller, A. and Ackermann, F. (1994) 'Soft Focus Re-Engineering' Presented to the Strategic Planning Society/Operational Research Society conference on 'Recipes for Re-Engineering, London May

Nunamaker, J.F., Applegate, L.M. and Konsynski, B.R. (1988) 'Computer-aided Deliberation: Model Management and Group Decision Support, *Journal of Management Information Systems*, 3 5-19

PC Week *(1991) Groupware; The Teamwork Approach*, PC Week supplement, October 14 Vol 8 No 41

Phillips, L.D. and Phillips, M.C. (1990) 'On Facilitating Groups' Working Paper, Decision Analysis Unit, London. London School of Economics and Political Science

Quinn, R.E., Rohrbaugh, J. And McGrath, M.R (1985) Automated Decision Conferencing: How it works', Personnel, 62 pp 48-55

Sprague, R.H. and Carlson, E.D. (1982) Building Effective Decision Support Systems. Englewoord Cliffs, NJ: Prentice Hall

Yeates, D. (1996) 'Developing and Implementing a Strategic Direction for Govan Initiative Ltd using SODA' unpublished MBA these, Strathclyde Graduate Business School

9 BIOGRAPHY

Fran Ackermann is a lecturer in the Department of Management Science at Strathclyde University. Her main research interests are focused around the areas of Group Decision Support Systems, Strategy Development and Implementation and Facilitation. Within the GDSS field itself, specific research projects include exploring and enhancing the links between group and individual work, developing methods for group members to enable them to contribute to discussions operating in a 'different time/different place' paradigm, and investigating how to aid managers working with complex qualitative problems. She has written numerous papers on the subject and is President of the European Group Decision Support Working Group. Her research has involved supporting decision making groups on messy, complex problems and has included working with organisations such as Shell International, AMEC Process and Energy Ltd, and the National Health Service using a methodology developed by herself and others at Strathclyde - namely SODA.

3

The information superhighway: an on-ramp to global markets for Austrian corporations?

L. Alkier
Vienna University of Economics and Business Administration
Department of Management Information Systems
Augasse 2-6, A-1090 Vienna, Austria
phone: +43-1-31336/4444, fax: +43-1-31336/746
e-mail: alkier@wu-wien.ac.at

Abstract

Global networks and the Internet in particular are major drivers for the globalization of markets and new types of organizations. User-friendly services transform the Internet into a viable business place and cause impressive growth rates in the numbers of users as well as access and service providers. This paper discusses how the Internet as a business place has developed in Austria over the last years and outlines various possibilities to take advantage of the Internet for international business purposes. International market research, communications and coordination with business partners and customers abroad, public relations, advertising, and on-line sales stand out as the most promising business uses of the Internet in a global context. Finally we show how the Internet evolved in Austria and present the first results of a survey of Austrian Web sites to outline how Austrian businesses are preparing for electronic commerce on the Internet.

Keywords

Information Superhighway, Internet, global markets, business strategy, electronic commerce, Austria

1 INTRODUCTION

Although global business is still mostly associated with multinational enterprises, global competition is changing drastically. E.g. in the US small and medium-size enterprises already account for more than half of the $548 billion in exports of manufactured goods (Business Week, 1995a). Information technology can and will be an important factor in helping smaller firms overcome many obstacles they experience in competing with their large multinational counterparts.

Especially global telecommunications, namely the Internet, is regarded as an enabling technology for the global marketplace. Besides being used as a fast and cost-effective means for competitive intelligence it enables new business processes, on-line marketing and sales opportunities, as well as new types of flexible, networked organizations that would not be possible otherwise.

In this paper we will first give a brief overview of relevant Internet demographics and usage trends. We will then discuss how businesses use the "Information Superhighway" in general and especially with regard to the global marketplace. Finally we will present a short survey how Austrian corporations are using the Internet for global electronic commerce.

2 INTERNET DEMOGRAPHICS

The government initiatives in the US or the EU show that the construction of the Information Superhighway is well under way. However, while the basic telecommunications infrastructure exists in industrialized nations, multi-gigabit links that are needed for multimedia applications between households and businesses, government agencies, and other organizations are still far away in the future. The concept closest to the intentions of the Information Superhighway today - in terms of its global reach, its openness, its heterogeneous user groups, and the enormous business expectations - is the Internet. In contrast, on-line services (e.g. America Online, or Prodigy in the US) or public videotex systems (e.g. Minitel in France) mostly target national audiences. Furthermore all major on-line services either provide Internet access already or are in the process to do so. We therefore assume that the distinction between on-line services and Internet services will further diminish and will focus our discussion solely on the Internet.

The numbers of Internet participants rise exponentially and open up enormous business opportunities. In January 1996 Network Wizards (1996) reported that the number of Internet hosts reached 9.4 million, compared to 2.2 million hosts in January 1994. While this number can be determined quite accurately, experts disagree on the number of Internet users. Estimates vary from 30 million active users worldwide to 10 users per host, which would account for more than 90 million users.

After several years of use mainly within the scientific community, businesses already run more than half of the networks connected to the Internet. Enhanced user-interfaces for basic network services like telnet, ftp, or electronic mail and new navigational, indexing and search tools were able to broaden the interest. Aside from many other improvements the one service that profoundly changed user demographics on the Internet, is the World Wide Web (also called Web or WWW). Browsers such as NCSA Mosaic or Netscape Navigator allow users to access information on distributed Web servers just by clicking on predefined links. The concept of the Web allows not only to present static information of various types (text, graphics, pictures, audio, video) but also allows to attach forms, transfer files, query databases, use remote application programs and other Internet services from within the Web. Businesses and non-commercial organizations soon recognized the Web's ease-of-use. Within two years after the introduction of the Web the number of servers that could be accessed from around the world approached 30,000, while it was just 100 in mid 1993.

With these large numbers of novice users, and the many new business offers announced every day, tools that assist users in finding the "right" information become a necessity. Agent-based search engines like Alta Vista (http://altavista.digital.com), Web Crawler (http://www.webcrawler.com), Lycos (http://www.lycos.com), and Harvest (http://harvest.cs.colorado.edu) or meta-lists of Web sites such as Yahoo (http://www.yahoo.com), a collection of links to World Wide Web sites, allow easy access to distributed resources.

According to surveys by the Michigan Business School (Gupta, 1995) and Georgia Tech's GVU Center (Pitkow and Recker, 1995) the demographics of Web users are changing rapidly. The 1994 survey showed a mostly male US-based Web audience with high participation rates of technical professionals and the scientific community. In 1995 these characteristics shifted significantly towards affluent business and private users, typically highly educated males in their thirties. More than half of all Web users get on the Internet through access providers, the majority of them use IBM-compatible PCs. They are concerned about security and quality issues; as a result they tend to use the Web rather for browsing than for shopping on-line.

The demographic changes in the user community show that the Internet already made the transition from the predominantly academic and research setting into businesses and households. With the necessary security enhancements for business transactions and electronic payment processes and additional investments into high-capacity telecommunications infrastructure the Internet will become a global electronic marketplace that is easily accessible through all kinds of access and service providers.

3 BUSINESS USE OF THE INTERNET

Despite many inspired Internet-related projects and the impressive overall growth of the Internet most companies have not yet decided upon their strategies in dealing with the Internet. Many different ways of incorporating electronic communications into internal business processes or customer related activities are being explored in companies of all sizes, from small start-ups who find new business opportunities to large corporations that use Internet-technology for cost advantage. While the expectations are highest for on-line marketing and sales activities, many technical and security issues still have to be solved to make business transactions on the Internet reliable enough for a broad consumer base. But although on-line sales do not meet the expectations of most businesses yet, firms are already aware of the cost and time advantages of the Internet for internal use. Business Week (1996) reports that many firms already experience considerable cost reductions by distributing internal documents, directories, manuals, or newsletters to employees worldwide via Web servers.

Kambil (1995) identified six categories of Internet use for cost or competitive advantage:

1. for process reengineering or enterprise-wide information systems, to reduce the costs of software distribution, gain more hardware independence and make information available throughout the firm via "intranets",
2. for customer support and product information on Web sites,
3. for creating electronic marketplaces and bypassing traditional intermediaries through electronic shopping malls and direct on-line sales via Web sites,
4. for new business opportunities, e.g. information brokers like Yahoo,
5. for easier market segmentation and information targeted at specific user groups,

6. for access to worldwide resources without geographical constraints and with lower barriers for small businesses.

According to a survey by the Yankee Group (Business Week, 1995b) the main reasons for corporations to use the Internet are communications purposes. 30% of all firms surveyed use the Internet for internal communications, and 49% for external communications, especially with suppliers and contractors who can track inventory or project schedules. But the biggest growth rates in Internet activities are expected in advertising and selling products on the Internet. While only 8% of the firms currently advertise on the Internet, 33% have plans for the future. Direct selling to consumers is expected to rise from 5% today to 35% of all firms in the near future.

Recent studies by Maier and Traxler (1995) and Kiessling, Schweeger and Sporn (1996) show that many of these expectations are shared by Austrian corporations currently on the Internet. In an on-line Web survey done by Maier and Traxler (1995) cost savings and competitive advantage through fast and cheap worldwide communication with business partners, reduction of geographical constraints, international cooperation, internationalization of research and development, and better and cheaper customer service were mentioned as the most important objectives for Austrian businesses in joining the Internet community. Kiessling, Schweeger and Sporn (1996) report that more than half of all firms not yet on the Internet plan their presence within the next three years, their main objective being marketing reasons and reaching new customer segments rather than high expectations in soaring on-line sales. It is not surprising that small and medium-size enterprises are the ones most interested in electronic commerce. They can expect better and cheaper access to global markets while at the same time they are able to react faster to market and technological changes and are more flexible in implementing new organizational structures.

Similar developments are reported for Germany and Switzerland by Bohr (1996) and Sieber (1995). Most businesses regard the Internet as a valuable tool to access and disseminate information, and to communicate with customers. On-line sales and revenue growth are not seen as immediate benefits whereas firms hope that the Internet will become an important new marketing channel and will allow them to attract new customer segments.

New technologies for the Internet - according to Kambil (1995) especially software agents inexpensive cost settlement and payment processes, and transaction templates ("EDI over the Internet") - will have a major impact on business processes and will be able to lower transaction costs considerably. At the same time consumers become more powerful since they can use the same media as firms to express their discontent with products and services. For businesses this means that they have to find appropraite strategies for communications with customers on the Internet.

4 INTERNATIONALIZATION VIA THE INFORMATION SUPERHIGHWAY

MCI chairman Bert Roberts predicts that on the Information Superhighway "...you can have access to millions of customers. Products and services can be sold 24 hours a day. And since transactions are handled electronically, sales and distribution can be done much more cost-effectively" (Edupage, 1995). This statement describes not only the domestic opportunities that businesses have on the Internet, but includes an international business perspective that has not been widely exploited yet. A survey of German firms on the Internet shows that they still regard Switzerland and Austria as their preferred foreign markets (Bohr, 1996). It can be expected that in the future electronic commerce on the Internet will increasingly cross country borders. We will therefore now take a look at the Internet from an internationalization perspective and discuss, in which ways the Internet can be used for the entry in a new market.

4.1 The Internet as a global information source

The Internet can provide firms with information about a variety of issues important to the entry into new markets, such as general information about foreign countries, regulatory information about exports and imports, Internet characteristics of foreign markets, consumer demographics, industry-specific information, information on foreign competitors and products, potential business partners, distributors, and customers etc.

Given its roots in the academic setting the Internet provides a strong knowledge base especially for the *IT industry* and other technology-rich disciplines such as biology or medicine. The computer industry is one of the most visible business sectors on the Internet, and computer science and information systems researchers discuss all kinds of issues in worldwide mailing lists and newsgroups. *Internet-specific information* covers the most recent developments and ideas and is indispensable for businesses considering to apply new Internet-based technologies. Companies interested in on-line business with foreign customers can directly observe how the Internet is used in the target countries and directly investigate the usage characteristics, cultural differences, attitudes towards security issues, data privacy, transborder data flow issues, and much more. Research projects such as Hermes (Gupta, 1995) regularly survey Internet users and gather this type of information. They help to identify shifts in usage patterns, give insight into attitude changes towards critical issues of electronic commerce as the usage of the Internet progresses and provide Internet demographics. So far, most surveys concentrate on US Internet users and may therefore not be directly applicable to other regions of the world.

The Internet also provides potential exporters with *general and import/export oriented information* about foreign markets. Newsgroups discussing foreign countries or regions, Web sites of government agencies, foreign trade associations, international organizations like the OECD or the UN, or foreign news services on the Web provide country-specific information from which further investigations can be made. Specific information for exporters and importers is increasingly being made available on the Web. Several institutions provide links to sites with information on legal and administrative issues, such as export permissions, import quotas, export/import procedures, legal responsibilities, financial support for exporters, customs declarations etc., all issues that have to be thoroughly researched before making strategic decisions about an engagement in a foreign market. An example for such a server is "David", the Web site of the Austrian Foreign Trade Commission for their Austrian members. It contains an extensive database on the Internet with country profiles, economic statistics, export control lists, market reports etc. While basic information is freely accessible, offers or inquiries from foreign firms and calls for tenders are restricted to registered members.

Although the Internet will certainly not replace personal contacts and traditional market research it is a valuable additional information source that can be accessed anytime and at low cost. Access to most of the information mentioned so far is provided through different Internet services: newsgroups, Web or ftp servers, freely accessible databases, on-line publications and archives, library information systems, gopher servers, and WAIS servers all over the world are possible sources. Locating relevant information within reasonable time is therefore becoming increasingly important. "Right now it is like an enormous library with no card catalog. People look around and leave." (Forbes, 1995) is a common observation. An impression of the amount of information available on the Web gives Alta Vista, the powerful Web agent by Digital that was already mentioned earlier. It provides a full text index of 21 mio. Web pages and handles approximately 5 mio. HTTP requests daily. To make these amounts of information available to interested users, personalized software agents and Internet directories will become even more important.

4.2 The Internet as an international marketing and sales instrument

Its global reach makes the Internet an ideal tool for international marketing and sales activities beyond traditional sales channels in an information society. The rapid deployment of commercial Web sites all over the world shows the importance of this cost-effective possibility for businesses to present themselves in a global marketplace.

Despite this embrace by many industries on-line business is still in an early evolutionary stage. Many innovative ideas how to take advantage of the Information Superhighway are being tested and firms of all types and sizes are setting up Web sites and develop applications for electronic commerce. The earliest and most active industry sectors to become involved (beyond the computer and telecommunications industry) were the entertainment sector, the publishing industry, the financial sector, and the retail industry.

But even with extraordinary investments into application development for electronic commerce actual on-line sales lag far behind expectations. "People don't want to pay for anything. I guess it's all part of the culture", a disappointed on-line book vendor expresses the feelings of many (Forbes, 1995). Besides this "everything for free" attitude that will change gradually as the number of business participants and consumers grows, firms also have to take into account different consumer attitudes towards distance shopping in foreign countries. A recent study of European consumer behavior indicates that Europeans show very different shopping interests than US customers, especially in "...what are considered 'precursor behaviors' to interactive television use, such as video rental, mail-order purchasing and home delivery of take-out food" (Wall Street Journal, 1995). Another reason for consumers to use Web sites for browsing rather than shopping are the security and privacy concerns associated with transferring sensitive data over the Internet.

While most money on the Internet is currently made by Internet access and service providers, the hardware and software industry, and Internet consultants, industry analysts have no doubts about the future of electronic commerce. Blanning and King (1995) report that on-line shopping did not play a significant role in 1994 with sales of only $200 million, but forecasts for 1998 predict this market to grow to $4.8 billion. Another analysis by Goldman, Sachs & Co. (Business Week, 1995) estimates the Internet market - including software, hardware, and services - to rise to $4.2 billion until 1997.

Because of the media interest in on-line shopping the Internet is often perceived mainly as *the* tool for on-line sales. But the possibilities of the Internet also encompass pre-sales activities such as public relations and advertising, and post-sales customer service. Corporations will therefore have to examine at what stage of their customer contacts the Internet can be used successfully.

Public relations and advertising

The prospect of reaching millions of potential customers worldwide at very low cost and with relatively little effort by sending advertising messages over the Internet may be tempting at first thought. But according to the Internet etiquette advertising messages by e-mail to individuals or newsgroups ("spamming") are considered offensive. Firms therefore have to use other ways of communicating their products and services to Internet users.

The most subtle approach is to *participate in discussions* that relate to a firm's products, services, or other areas of expertise. Examples in the computer industry show that these activities can help to build a positive image for a firm, e.g. by participating in discussions, offering solutions for customer problems, answering questions, reporting about new developments, or providing some other sort of information. A corporation that addresses customer problems fast and effectively, and offers useful and up-to-date information is certainly leaving a positive impression on the newsgroup's subscriber base. On the other hand incompetent or rude behavior on the Internet is likely to fire back, since many Internet users communicate their experiences with firms to relevant newsgroups.

Advertising and image-building through participation in on-line discussions and by providing informal on-line support offer good chances for international recognition. Newsgroups are distributed to many countries and most of them use English as the common language. Nevertheless firms will often find additional local discussion groups in their target markets and should therefore carefully observe the newsgroups available and join them according to their internationalization plans.

For many products or services this type of interaction with the public is not a viable alternative. The most common alternative to attract immediate attention is to set up a virtual storefront on the Internet. Since Internet users are very technology-minded word about new interesting sites is spreading rapidly within the Internet community. Many sites maintain links to "cool" places on the Web and new design ideas are often discussed in traditional news media as well. While extraordinary design is one way to attract attention, unique information - even if it is not directly business-related - is another reason for visiting a Web site frequently. For a bookstore that might be links to foreign language magazines and newspapers available on-line or to on-line dictionaries, while a hotel chain might provide links to weather forecasts, foreign currency exchange rates, airline or car rental information, museums, city information, etc.

To get the desired public attention businesses have to plan their Web presence as thoroughly as any other advertising or public relations campaign. They have to decide which user groups the Web site should address, if the Web presence should be designed for a local user community or as a first step into international markets, and if it should serve as an advertising medium only or offer on-line shopping possibilities. Furthermore the layout and the contents have to be professionally designed. From what we can observe the first prototypes of Web sites are often set up by interested individuals who experiment with new technologies and give more thought to the technical details than to the potential domestic or international impact. Eventually those Web sites become the firm's electronic link to the public without getting the same attention as other forms of advertisements. We frequently find Web sites carrying notes that they are still under construction and what to expect in the future. This may not have posed problems in early experiments with the Web, but meanwhile the Internet is too mature to allow an unprofessional attitude or serious flaws in Web-based advertising. While the Internet is surely a more informal medium than traditional TV or newspaper, a halfhearted Web presence certainly creates a negative image of a firm and will not attract users to check the site again.

Direct marketing and on-line sales

Using the Internet for direct marketing and on-line sales is an interesting opportunity beyond the domestic market. In the home market the Internet as an additional distribution channel enables firms to address new customers and to offer extended shopping hours while at the same time speeding up the ordering and shipping process. In an international setting the Internet can further expand a firm's reach to theoretically more than sixty countries without the cost of setting up subsidiaries abroad.

As exciting as this may sound, not every product can be successfully sold over the Internet - or at least not yet - as many businesses are currently experiencing. While advertising and public relations seem to get immediate attention, for many firms the numbers of on-line sales are far from meeting even modest expectations. The examples of 1-800 Flowers which reported about 30,000 daily hits of its Web site, but only 25 on-line orders, or a small German translating service that did not receive a single on-line order within three months from setting up a Web site show that the Internet may not be the right medium for a number of products.

But there are also encouraging examples from the retail as well as the service industry: record stores are selling CDs on-line, publishing houses offer books and magazines, especially technology-related literature, home shopping networks and mail-order businesses offer consumer electronics products, computer companies sell hardware and software, car rental companies accept on-line reservations, international express delivery services enable tracking of parcels over the Internet, and banks offer on-line banking over the Internet. It may be questioned if fast food orders via the Internet have any advantage over telephone orders and if customers will really order jewelry over the Internet, but in general self-explaining, standardized and relatively low-priced merchandise is considered well suited for being sold on the Internet. Mail-order merchandise typically meets these criteria well. We already see several examples of mail-order firms opening up Internet branches where customers can browse catalogs on-line and place orders via the Internet. So far, most firms explicitly exclude international sales or refer browsers to customer service representatives for further inquiries about foreign shipping.

To achieve an *immediate presence* in a foreign market, businesses should consider joining well-established electronic shopping malls abroad that attract many visitors or to join forces with other businesses that offer products and services for similar consumer segments and build specialized *international shopping malls*.

Another approach for *linking international business partners* electronically is to offer specialized services for international business operations. A few such services like the Trade Point Network and World Trade Center Network are already in use. Another service, the International Business Exchange (IBEX), has been announced by the US Chamber of Commerce in September 1995. IBEX is a joint effort of AT&T who provides the network, Dun & Bradstreet as the database provider, SHL Systemhouse who builds the systems, the Global Business Alliance who distributes IBEX, and GE Information Services, who provides the electronic data interchange component (Information Week, 1995). IBEX will eventually offer intelligent agents to match buyers and sellers automatically throughout the world.

To stay technologically ahead of the competition firms could join research projects about the Internet as a marketplace like CommerceNet, a consortium sponsored in part by US government research grants but also by its industry members. Its members are leading Internet proponents who are actively involved in all kinds of electronic commerce projects, from transaction security to design-to-manufacturing integration.

While the capabilities of the Internet for on-line selling to consumers are enthusiastically explored many features to *support traditional business procedures* do not get the attention they deserve. Businesses can use the Internet's communications capabilities to establish and to maintain long- or short-term alliances and business networks, to work with local distributors and/or to communicate with subsidiaries in foreign countries. Quick solutions for a single purpose might rely on basic Internet services like e-mail and file transfer for non-standardized communications, while in a long-term business relationship access to the partner's order processing and logistics systems, or EDI can be added as needed. Web-based groupware like the new version of Lotus Notes will enable firms to even better coordinate their internal operations as well as their cooperation with foreign partners, international customers, distributors, international and local carriers, customs authorities and other government agencies.

Post-sales customer support

A 1994 IDC survey of the computer industry reports significant changes in customer service. Respondents named customer contact, especially technical support for their customers (87%), and software updates and patches (59%) as the most important reasons for on-line access by their companies (Levitt, 1995). While the computer industry has been a pioneer in electronic communications, the Internet now offers the same potential for more industries and a growing number of private customers. The growing numbers of private homes and businesses with access to the Internet slowly makes on-line customer support an alternative to traditional means in a growing number of industries.

High-quality customer support for consumers usually has high manpower requirements that can often not be met by small firms on an international basis. Especially for companies with worldwide customers who cannot afford a local support structure electronic mail is an excellent communications tool, both in terms of costs and timeliness. Services and products that need scheduled maintenance, need to be upgraded regularly, or manuals and technical documentation - in general technical products and services - are good candidates for on-line support. Services can remind customers of scheduled maintenance intervals, or offer databases with frequently asked questions about products. As mentioned earlier participation in discussion groups with prospective buyers and actual customers is an effective way of combining customer support with advertising. Many companies offer ftp-servers for downloading software upgrades or even make new hardware and software accessible on the Internet for benchmarking (Jarvenpaa and Ives, 1994).

Firms can make all kinds of existing support applications available for customers to increase their responsiveness without worrying about hardware platforms and installation procedures of dial-in solutions. Always an excellent example of innovative IT use is Federal Express who in 1995 launched a Web-based application where customers can track the status of expected deliveries (http://www.fedex.com). Similar applications such as querying replacement parts inventories, (re)scheduling deliveries or maintenance appointments, and many other tasks can be offered to customers over the Internet. These applications can be cost-effective and easily accessible alternatives to common practice.

5 AUSTRIAN CORPORATIONS ON THE "HIGHWAY" TO GLOBAL MARKETS?

After discussing the business use of the Internet in general and in an international setting we will now concentrate on Austrian corporations and their use of the Internet. We will first give an overview of Austria's present telecommunications situation and the most recent Internet statistics, and will then present a survey of Austrian Web sites and their focus on an international clientele.

5.1 Telecommunications infrastructure

The telecommunications sector in Austria is still regulated by the federal government and will remain largely under government control until 1998. By then EU law requires the full liberalization of telecommunications services in all member countries. The Austrian government is starting this process in 1996 by transforming the Austrian PTT into a separate business entity that will remain 100% government-owned until 1998. For many years telecommunications has been the only profitable business division of the Austrian PTT, while mail services and the public bus transportation system are both heavily subsidized.

During the last years there have been considerable investments into fiber trunks and digital technology by the PTT. By the end of 1994 the PTT had switched about two thirds of all telephone lines to digital service, in urban areas the availability is almost 100%. Although ISDN is now available on a broad basis, the actual number of users in December 1995 was less than 16,000. While the monthly ISDN surcharge of approximately $30 for a private customer is rather low, the high overall tariffs prohibit intensive Internet usage.

Table 1 compares regular Austrian calling rates (rates are displayed in ATS) internationally:[1]

Table 1 Telephone rates in selected countries

Country	*Local calls* (*per hour*)	*Long-distance calls, nationwide, >100 km* (*per minute*)	*Intercontinental calls to USA* (*per minute*)
Austria	40.0	5.3	12.6
Germany	16.5	4.7	14.1
Switzerland	31.0	12.6	8.5
Great-Britain	36.3	1.6	9.5
USA	1.0 (per call)	2.1	7.5

[1] The current exchange rate for 1 US-$ is app. ATS 10. All data except the calling rates for the US are from Profil (1995). The US data were taken from the author's Nynex and AT&T telephone bills in January 1995 and reflect the average cost of local calls within New York City, long-distance calls to Boston and international calls to Austria.

Table 1 shows that on average European telephone rates are considerably higher than in the US. Austria is in the top ranks of the countries listed: it has not only the highest rates for local calls, but also ranks second in the other two categories. These high rates are the most important reason why the use of telecommunications services in Austria, and in Europe in general, is notably lower than in the US.

A similar situation as shown above for the more casual user exists for leased line needed by businesses that want to provide services on the Internet. Leased lines are priced according to capacity and distance: a 64 Kbps line costs about $80 per kilometer and month within a local calling area, but in rural areas rates run much higher, creating considerable cost advantages for urban areas. As an Internet access provider, Telecom, a partnership between the PTT and industry partners founded in 1994, charges $2,700 per month for a 128 Kbps leased line ($5,400 for 256 Kbps), if the line is within 5 km of an access point, which is usually the case in urban areas. In contrast the US consortium CommerceNet charges $150 per month for a 128 Kbps line (Bayer, 1994). For high capacity networking the Austrian PTT offers a 34 Mbps country-wide Metropolitan Area Network connecting all nine state capitals in Austria. Since fall 1994 the PTT also uses an ATM network to link the three largest Austrian cities, Vienna, Graz, and Linz (155 Mbps), as well as Austria with Germany, Switzerland, and Italy.

Austrian state-owned utility companies that already have an extensive terrestrial infrastructure in place, and the Austrian Railroad have intensified their exploration of new business opportunities, especially by providing telecommunications services through their already existing networks.

Domestic and international joint ventures are working on projects to provide terrestrial telecommunications services, mobile telecommunications services in the upcoming European GSM network, cable TV, interactive TV, and other services. One of two GSM network licenses in Austria was acquired by ÖCall, a joint venture of Austrian and mostly German telecommunications equipment manufacturers and media corporations. Cable and satellite TV infrastructure already reaches 67% of all Austrian households and cable companies may therefore become additional competitors in urban areas.

In 1994 several state governments together with the PTT and future telecommunications providers started projects to build regional fiber-optic "data highways" that will connect businesses at low cost to world-wide networks. One recent project in Salzburg aims at attracting businesses to rural areas by providing network access at local calling costs for about 80% of all private and commercial customers in the state of Salzburg. These improvements to the infrastructure of rural areas are supposed to attract high-tech companies and the service sector that do not have particularly high traditional infrastructure requirements.

5.2 Austria's presence on the Internet

Austria's Internet activities started in the late 1980's with universities and other research institutions forming a nation-wide research network (ACOnet). Since 1994 the strong international media attention for the Information Superhighway and the Internet made Austrian entrepreneurs and managers increasingly aware of new business opportunities and attracts a growing number of private users.

Reports of the number of computers connected to the Internet vary somewhat: For January 1996 the RIPE DNS host count[2] reported 60,320 Internet hosts in Austria, while Network Wizards reported 52,728[3]. The latter report puts Austria in the 17th place worldwide as shown in Table 2.

---

[2] Source: ftp://ftp.ripe.net/ripe/hostcount/RIPE-Hostcount, March 10, 1996

Assuming five to ten users per host the current number of Internet users in Austria is somewhere between 250,000 to 500,000. Under the most favorable conditions this means that as of spring 1996 17% of all Austrian households have access to the Internet.

Table 2 Host distribution by top-level domain name (Source: Network Wizards)

Rank	*Domain*	*Hosts*	*Domains queried*	*Percent missed*	*Country*
	TOTAL	9,472,224	240,520	34%	
1	com	2,430,954	132,216	45%	US Commercial
	edu	1,793,491	10,081	8%	US Educational
	net	758,597	9,054	24%	US Networks
	gov	312,330	1,873	16%	US Government
	org	265,327	11,823	23%	US Organizations
	mil	258,791	866	15%	US Military
2	de	452,997	6,302	6%	Germany
3	uk	451,750	9,979	16%	United Kingdom
4	ca	372,891	5,909	11%	Canada
5	au	309,562	5,608	6%	Australia
6	jp	269,327	7,584	6%	Japan
7	us	233,912	5,405	18%	United States
8	fi	208,502	1,337	8%	Finland
9	nl	174,888	1,808	6%	Netherlands
10	se	149,877	3,007	9%	Sweden
11	fr	137,217	2,439	6%	France
12	no	88,356	2,084	1%	Norway
13	ch	85,844	1,401	4%	Switzerland
14	it	73,364	2,669	6%	Italy
15	es	53,707	1,255	4%	Spain
16	nz	53,610	804	5%	New Zealand
17	at	52,728	1,169	9%	Austria

Table 3 compares the Austrian numbers with other European countries and the US. It shows that Austria's Internet usage is certainly comparable to other countries within the European Union. While Switzerland comes closest to US standards within our comparison, Austria has almost the same penetration rate as the UK and a higher Internet density than Germany. Still the overwhelming percentage of users (experts estimate more than 50%) are associated with research institutions, but business and private users are the fastest growing segments.

[3] Source: http://www.nw.com/ Zone/WWW/report.html, March 10, 1996

Table 3 Internet density in selected countries (March 1996)

Country	*Internet hosts*	*Households (in mio.)*	*Population (in mio.)*	*Hosts/households (in 1000)*	*Hosts/population (in 1000)*
Austria	52,728	3.0	7.9	17.6	6.7
Switzerland	85,844	2.6	7.0	33.0	12.3
Germany	452,997	35.7	81.0	12.7	5.6
UK	451,750	23.0	58.1	19.6	7.8
US	5,819,490	97.6	260.7	59.6	22.3

Together with increasing user numbers new Internet access and service providers joined the one pioneer corporation that is in the market since 1992. In March 1996 more than 30 Internet service and access providers offer a broad range of servives. Few of them have their own national/international network infrastructure in place, most are resellers and specialize in Web site design, shopping malls, consulting, etc. The service range starts with limited access by e-mail only, targeted at the private customer market, and includes full Internet access mostly for corporate clients. Prices for limited Internet access by e-mail start at $10 per month, and run higher for full Internet access (starting at $60 per month plus volume charges above a certain limit). While the number of Internet access and service providers grew rapidly the number of on-line service providers is still very small (CompuServe and Europe Online).

Businesses on the Internet

Subsidiaries of multinational corporations were the first commercial users in Austria. The second notable user segment are Austrian multinational corporations like OeMV, Zumtobel, AVL List, or VOEST who use the Internet mainly for internal communications purposes (Trend, 1994). But lately the user-friendly graphical browsers for the World Wide Web attract new business and private users to explore the Internet. There are still few commercial Web sites in use that are beyond the experimental stage, and seem to be professionally designed and maintained.

Table 4 Austrian commercial Web sites (March 1996)[4]

Area of business	*Sites*	*Percentage*
Tourism, entertainment, lodging, culture	119	20%
Providers, web agencies	37	6%
Broadcasting, publishing	64	11%
Banking, insurance	20	3%
Commerce	360	60%
All commercial Web sites	600	100%

In the first half of 1995 about 20 new Austrian Web sites were announced on the Internet per month[5] with the total number of Web sites estimated by the author as of May 1995 below 200. Until March

[4] Source: http://harvest.Austria.EU.net/Server-in-AT/commercials.shtml, March 23, 1996

1996 the most comprehensive list of Web sites in Austria showed considerable growth, especially in the commercial sector, as can be seen in Table 4.

5.3 International marketing and sales activities on the Web

We will now discuss how Austrian corporations make use of the international business opportunities on the Internet. We will concentrate on marketing and sales activities via the Internet that are visible to prospective clients (business and private users) who are "surfing the Web". We will not comment on the use for information purposes, communications, and collaboration via e-mail, mailing-lists, and other more informal means of communicating, as this requires more in-depth knowledge about a firm's internal usage characteristics. This question is part of an Internet survey currently under way in all Austrian corporations that are present on the Internet. There we ask businesses in detail about their intra- and interorganizational use of various Internet services.

For our purpose we looked at Austrian WWW sites (top level domain "at") from the perspective of a potential international firm or private customer. We checked all commercial WWW servers that we found in the most complete list of Austrian commercial sites available on the Web as of January 29, 1996.[6] This list distinguishes four groups of Web sites: (1) computers and telecommunications, (2) media and publishing, (3) shopping and business (commerce), and (4) tourism. Within these Web sites we concentrated on groups (3) and (4). We excluded group 2 (media and publishing) because of the limited interest of German-language publications for international readers. Group 1 was excluded from our survey because of the special status of this industry in an IT-related context.

Within the two remaining groups there were 223 Web sites. 43 sites (19%) were unreachable, even when tried at least 3 times within one week. This leaves 180 sites that we could include in our further analysis.

We used the following three criteria to characterize a Web as targeted towards international customers:

1. We determine *language* (German, English, others) to be a major factor in addressing global markets. We therefore examined every site for the languages that could be chosen from the home page. We use the home page, because it does not seem reasonable to offer this choice later.
2. Another indicator for internationalization efforts of businesses on the Web are the *areas of operation* of Web sites and the customer groups that are explicitly or implicitly addressed. To figure out the targeted customer group (domestic, international, or both) we looked at (a) the home page for specific statements, and (b) additional information such as price, payment, or delivery information.
3. We measure the *commitment* towards electronic commerce on the Internet by distinguishing sites that offer information only, with or without the possibility of sending e-mail for additional information, from sites that allow on-line ordering.

---

[5] The data were gathered by the Vienna University's Computing Center and can be accessed at http://www.ifs.univie.ac.at/austria/new.html. While it can be assumed that organizations are interested to announce their Web-servers on this page, this listing is not necessarily complete.

[6] Source: http://www.public.co.at/public/dir/sbt.html#ShopBusiness (February 29, 1996).

In addition we checked all Web sites whether they were offering goods and services of domestic firms or if the Web sites were set up by foreign firms using the Internet as a marketing and sales instrument for reaching Austrian customers.

Language

Although Web sites in German offer sales and marketing possibilities beyond the Austrian home market, additional information in other languages can open up international market opportunities. Table 5 shows the distribution of languages offered on Austrian servers:

Table 5 Languages of Austrian Web sites

Reachable sites	*All sites* 180	*Commerce* 145	*Tourism* 35
German only	62%	66%	46%
English only	15%	14%	20%
German and English	18%	15%	28%
Multiple languages	5%	5%	6%

The overwhelming majority of all Web sites uses German as the only language (62%). The other important language is English; 15% of all Web sites are presented only in English, another 18% offer a choice of German and English. Only 5% of the sites give more than these two choices, not one site is presented solely in languages other than German or English, and no combinations of German with some other language could be found.

In the tourism industry the number of servers that support more than German is higher than average. Although almost half of all tourism-related servers are available strictly in German, 28% are available in both English and German, 20% are available only in English, and 6% (which is only 2 servers) offer additional languages. It does not surprise that in the tourism industry foreign language support is higher than on other commercial servers, since Austria's travel industry is an important economic factor. It surprises for the tourism sector that languages other than German and English are so far not well established. Additional offers in Italian, Spanish or French might be interesting, while the overall telecommunications infrastructure and the Internet availability in Eastern European countries will for some more time not justify additional offers in those languages.

Areas of operation

Besides the language being used, Web sites sometimes contain explicit statements, in which areas they operate. For a local grocery with delivery service or a Pizza shop that maintains a Web site for on-line ordering this policy certainly makes sense. In many other cases such a statement is missing and a potential customer needs to check several Web pages to figure out that a product is only sold domestically or that the firm might be willing to ship goods abroad.

In most cases foreign languages and other indicators for international business transactions coincide, but not always. Tables 6 and 7 show in some more detail how the surveyed Web sites position themselves on their Web pages.

Table 6 Areas of operation of Austrian Web sites

Reachable sites	*All sites* 180	*Commerce* 145	*Tourism* 35
Domestic business	66%	72%	40%
Domestic and foreign business	34%	28%	60%

Table 7 Areas of operation of Austrian Web sites and languages offered

Domestic and foreign business	*All sites* 62	*Commerce* 41	*Tourism* 21
German only	15%	15%	14%
English or German/ English	70%	68%	76%
Multiple languages (incl. German, English	15%	17%	10%

Overall, two thirds of all servers are obviously designed to meet domestic needs. As already seen with the language indicator, tourism sites have a stronger interest in foreign markets. Only 40% of all tourism sites do not mention e.g. reservation procedures for foreign guests or quote rates in foreign currencies. Within the commercial group this number is much higher (72%). In both groups there is a small percentage of firms that obviously target only German speaking countries (15%), whereas most internationally oriented sites combine German pages with English (24%) and another 15% with additional languages.

Commitment towards electronic commerce

As a measure for the Internet commitment of Austrian corporations we used on-line shopping as a way to interact with customers. The assumption is that many - especially smaller businesses - can easily find a service provider or mall operator who sets up several pages that can be browsed by potential customers. In the case of on-line ordering a stronger involvement of the firm is necessary, and a strategic decision for joining the Internet beyond a mere "trial period" can be assumed.

Table 8 On-line ordering versus browsing

Reachable sites	*All sites* 180	*Commerce* 145	*Tourism* 35
On-line ordering	19%	20%	14%
Information only	81%	80%	86%
On-line ordering for international customers	4%	3%	11%

The data for on-line shopping on existing Web sites seem to emphasize the general ambiguity against transferring sensitive data over the Internet and distance shopping in general. Across all surveyed Web sites on-line shopping is only offered by 19% of all firms and almost non-existent for foreign customers.

There seems to be no big difference in the attitude of the tourism sector: we could argue that tourism is rather consulting-intensive and therefore most customers will not book hotel rooms over the Web, but in many other tourism-related areas customers and firms are simply not ready for on-line transactions.

Incoming business

While not directly a part of our main question we were also interested in incoming business, namely foreign firms that present services or goods via Austrian Web sites to potential customers. While this somewhat contradicts the Web's general design approach it can be useful for businesses who want to enter a foreign market by acting as a local firm. Another reason - at least for some more years - could be the mere technical advantage of faster access to graphics-intensive Web pages. While we are lacking the direct comparison of Austrian firms presenting themselves abroad (e.g. in foreign electronic shopping malls), the number of firms that offer goods and services directly on Austrian servers is minimal. In the tourism industry we found only one site that combined Austrian and foreign offers. For the commercial sites the numbers were slightly higher: 10 foreign Web sites (7%) offer goods and services to Austrian customers and seven sites (5%) combine Austrian and international offers.

6 CONCLUSION

Business opportunities on a global scale have developed rapidly as improved services on the Internet become available and the numbers of commercial and private Internet participants explode. Nations all over the world are initiating infrastructure programs to improve their competitive position in the global marketplace.

In this paper we discussed a broad range of possible Internet uses for international business activities. The Internet's communications capabilities combine cost-effectiveness and productivity gains with open accessibility by business partners worldwide. While the Internet already supports distributed intra- or interorganizational teamwork with simple solutions like e-mail or mailing lists, the future use of groupware on the Internet will enhance the coordination of dispersed workgroups further.

Using the Internet for international marketing and sales offers the greatest opportunities but also the biggest challenges. For small countries like Austria with mostly small and medium sized enterprises the Web can be an excellent opportunity to export goods and services at a cost-advantage. Our survey of Austria shows that the number of Internet business participants is rising fast. So far the typical Austrian Web site is designed to advertise goods and services to German-speaking, mostly domestic Internet users. On-line electronic commerce is still in its infancy and businesses and consumers are skeptical about security and privacy issues. Especially on-line business with foreign customers is almost non-existent yet. While the languages of Web servers indicate interest in foreign markets, we can assume from the overwhelming use of English that businesses tend to target foreign markets in general, and do not specifically set up Web sites for customers of a certain nationality. Beyond the numbers about international Web activities in Austria it was noticeable when we accessed all the sites that most foreign language Web sites seemed to have a foreign-language complement rather than being designed specifically for non-German speaking customers.

This survey does only provide descriptive data about some international characteristics of Austrian Web sites. To help businesses plan their internationalization strategies via the Information Superhighway we will have to investigate in more detail which Internet services work for Austrian firms internally, externally, in a domestic or international setting, which products or services can be marketed successfully on the Internet, or which countries offer the most interesting on-line business perspectives. Since the pioneer days of the Internet are over, Austrian firms have to make a conscious choice for international activities on the Internet, and clear objectives about the role of the Internet within the international operations of a firm have to be set - ranging from the use as a strategic weapon in international competition to the use as a productivity tool. These objectives have to be part of the company's strategic IT and business plans and need the full commitment and support of top management.

7 REFERENCES

Bayer, R. (1994) Plädoyer für eine Nationale Informations-Infrastruktur. *Informatik-Spektrum* 17, 302-208.

Blanning, R. and King, D. (1995) *Internet and the Information Superhighway.* Tutorial, 28th Hawaii International Conference on Systems Sciences, Maui.

Business Week (1995) Planet Internet. April 3, 1995, 118-124.

Business Week (1995a) It's a small (business) world. April 17, 1995, 51-56.

Business Week (1995b) Business on the Net? Not yet. June 26, 1995, 100-101.

Business Week (1996) Here comes the Intranet. February 26, 1996, 46-54.

Bohr, D. (1996) *Deutsche Unternehmen im Internet: Eine empirische Untersuchung* Arbeitsbericht Nr. 75, Institut für Wirtschaftsinformatik, Universität Bern, Bern.

Edupage (1995) MCI calls Internet the "Next Commercial Frontier". Available from http://educom.edu/edupage.old/edupage.95/edupage-02.05.95

Forbes (1995) Where's the money? January 30, 1995, 100-108.

Gupta, S. (1995) *Consumer Survey of WWW Users.* Michigan Business School, 1995. Available from http://www.umich.edu/~sgupta/hermes.htm.

Information Week (1995) Agent-based service joins electronic trading lineup. April 10, 1995, 32.

Jarvenpaa, S.L., Ives, B. (1994) *Digital Equipment Corporation: The Internet Company (A).* Available from CIS-FSERV@ube.ubalt.edu, filename: CASES.DIGITALWWW.

Kambil, A. (1995) Electronic Commerce: Implications of the Internet for Business Practice and Strategy, in: *Working Paper Series, New York University*, Stern #IS-95-22, New York.

Kiessling, U., Schweeger, T. and Sporn, B. (1996) *Der Nutzen des Internet für österreichische Unternehmen.* Eigenverlag, Wien.

Levitt, L. (1995) Commercial Use of the Internet. *Proceedings of INET '95*, Honolulu, Hawaii, June 27-30, 1995. Available from http://inet.nttam.com/HMP/PAPER/128/txt/paper.txt

Maier, G. and Traxler, H. (1995) *The Emergence of the Virtual Enterprise? How Austrian Companies Use the Internet.* Presented at the 35th European Congress of the Regional Science Association, Odense, Denmark, August 22-25, 1995.

Network Wizards (1996) Host Distribution by Top-Level Domain Name. Available from: http://www.nw.com/Zone/WWW/report.html (retrieved on March 10, 1996).

Pitkow, J.E. and Recker, M.M. (1995) *Using the Web as a Survey Tool: Results from the Second WWW User Survey*. Available from http://www.cc.gatech.edu/gvu/user_surveys/

Profil (1995) Der Störfaktor Kunde. No. 5, January 30, 1995, 40.

Sieber, P. (1995) *Schweizer Firmen im Internet: Eine empirische Untersuchung*, Arbeitsbericht Nr. 72, Institut für Wirtschaftsinformatik, Universität Bern, Bern.

Trend (1994) Rein ins Netz. No. 11, November 1994, 66-72.

Wall Street Journal (1995) Interactive offerings have less appeal in Europe than in U.S., survey says. June 20, 1995, A7A.

8 BIOGRAPHY

Lore Alkier is Assistant Professor of MIS at the Vienna University of Economics and Business Administration (WU). Her research interests include information management in multinational corporations, strategic and long term information systems planning, corporate strategy and information technology, and information management at universities. In 1994 and 1995 she was a Visiting Scholar at the Leonard N. Stern School of Business at New York University. Besides her research interest she served as Director of the WU Computing Center for several years and works as a management consultant, especially in the area of strategic IT planning. She has been teaching post-graduate, graduate and undergraduate MIS courses at WU, and in the joint International MBA program of WU and the University of South Carolina.

4

An IBIS-based model to support group discussions

G. Bellassai[1]
Universidad Católica de Asunción, Paraguay
M. Borges[2]
Santa Clara University, USA[*]
D. A. Fuller[3]
Pontificia Universidad Católica de Chile, Chile
J. A. Pino[4]
Universidad de Chile, Chile
A. C. Salgado[5]
Universidade Federal de Pernambuco, Brazil

Abstract

In this paper, an extension of the IBIS argumentation model is presented to support pre-meeting activities. The data model of a system called SISCO is introduced, and a case example is presented. This system allows remote and asynchronous collaboration to do the work of meeting preparation.

Keywords

CSCW, IBIS, pre-meetings.

[1] Laboratório de Electrónica Digital, Asunción, Paraguay, gbellas@ledip.py
[2] Object Technology Laboratory, School of Engineering, Santa Clara, CA 95053, USA, fax: + 1 408 554-5474, Phone: + 1 408 554-2139, mborges@otl.scu.edu
[*] On leave from:Universidade Federal do Rio de Janeiro, Brazil., mborges@nce.ufrj.br
[3] Depto. de Ciencia de la Computación, Casilla 306, Santiago 22, Chile, dfuller@ing.puc.cl
[4] Depto. de Ciencias de la Computación, Casilla 2777, Santiago, Chile, jpino@dcc.uchile.cl
[5] Departamento de Informática, Recife, Brazil, acs@di.ufpe.br

1 INTRODUCTION

The use of computer systems to intermediate and facilitate human interaction has been expanding very fast. CSCW (Computer Supported Cooperative Work) is an emergent area that examines how computers can assist several people working together (Khoshafian and Buckiewicz, 1995). In its various proposals, people can be at the same or different places. It also matters when the human interactions are synchronous (same time) or asynchronous (different time). Among the main applications developed so far we can mention meetings support, workflow, and cooperative editors.

The support of meetings is very appealing for business in general. Systems that support meetings aim to increase efficiency by speeding the decision process and by generating automatic documentation. Besides, if the meeting is geographically distributed there is also a reduction of traveling costs and time.

Several systems have been designed to support meetings on their various forms (Nunamaker et al., 1991). An alternative idea is to provide a tool for the preparation of a pre-meeting (Bellassai, Borges, Fuller, Pino and Salgado, 1995).

In SISCO we provide a discussion environment where no decisions are made. Many times people are not prepared to discuss or, in some cases do not know about, the agenda items of the meeting they are invited to. This fact can produce very long and inefficient meetings. The purpose is to improve meetings productivity and to well inform meetings participants before the face-to-face meeting takes place. In SISCO we want to make meetings more efficient but we do not attempt to eliminate them because we believe that face-to-face meetings are essential for decision making.

To support group interaction such as in SISCO it is necessary to consider the varied aspects of collaboration. They include information sharing, communication among members of a group, and coordination of their cooperative activities.

In any group interaction there is a need for a repository of data. If all members are present, such as in a face-to-face meeting, the repository works more as a group memory, to where one can recall whenever it is needed to review topics discussed in the meeting. In this case however, it is assumed that a member is aware of the main elements of the discussion. On the other hand, if the interaction is asynchronous, the data repository plays a more active and comprehensive role. Besides playing the role of a group memory, the repository also serves as the mechanism for interaction and awareness to where group members recall when they want to update their knowledge of the meeting status.

The objective of this paper is to present a data model to support group discussions in a pre-meeting context assuming an asynchronous and geographically distributed interaction. The proposed data model is an extension of the basic IBIS argumentation model (Kunz and Rittel, 1970). The extension includes several elements to facilitate interaction and understanding of the discussion.

The paper is organized as follows. Section 2 presents some requirements for group discussion. The IBIS data model, with its characteristics and deficiencies, is discussed in Section 3. In Section 4 we present our proposed data model. An example illustrates our proposal in Section 5 and the conclusions are presented in Section 6.

2 GROUP DISCUSSIONS AND PRE-MEETINGS

Meetings are certainly an important activity people do within organizations (Jay, 1976), (Hackman and Kaplan, 1974) and a recent survey confirms that white-collar workers spend an average of 50% of their time in these meetings. Jay (Jay, 1976:43) adequately states that "*a meeting still performs functions that will never be taken over by telephones, teleprinters, Xerox copiers, tape recorders, television monitors, or any other technological instruments of the information revolution*".

This is not equivalent to saying that computers are useless for supporting meetings within organizations. Research has been done, for instance, in having face-to-face meetings with interconnected computers (Wagner, Wynne and Mennecke, 1993) and meetings done remotely with the help of multimedia systems (Streitz, Geibler, Haake and Hol, 1994) (Bergmann and Mudge, 1994).

Why meetings are so important? Jay (Jay, 1976) has identified six functions meetings perform, including group membership delimitation (who belongs to the group?), common knowledge, understanding of the collective aim of the group, and be a status arena. These functions are not directly tied to the subject of the meeting but are of a socio-psychological flavor.

Our approach recognizes the role of face-to-face meetings, especially for decision-making. We emphasize the preparation of the meetings with information technology tools as a way to make them effective and efficient.

The preparation of the meeting is crucial in various respects. First of all, it may help to make all members of the group gather valuable information. As Jay puts it: "*a solid basis of agreed-on facts is the best foundation to build any decision on*" (Jay, 1976:43).

Secondly, and even more significantly, a clarifying discussion held before the meeting may help to reduce both the equivocality and uncertainty of the meeting (Daft and Lengel, 1986). Equivocality in this case refers to the ambiguity and confusion concerning the agenda items: many times meeting members do not know or agree on answers to very basic questions, such as, why are we concerned with this matter?, what are the implications of this matter?, is this the right time to decide on this issue?, what is this matter, anyway?

Uncertainty refers to the lack of answers to questions and issues that need further elucidation, although there is already an understanding about their importance. Of course, meeting members do not identify the nature of their concern. In normal meetings, they just manifest them. But progress in the meeting will probably be reduced, reflecting the deep weakness in the common understanding, especially if most doubts are of the equivocality type.

A discussion held before a meeting then opens interesting opportunities for people to have a sound agreement on many aspects of the meeting. Our goal is to materialize such opportunities by facilitating the means of achieving the interchange of information, opinions, goals, etc. Is a face-to-face encounter needed for such interchange? It may be, but it can be complemented with work from everyone's office if a structured, simple-to-use mechanism is available. A distributed software system presents the benefits of keeping the familiar furniture plus easy access to physical and computerized files, and not requiring same-time availability (Ellis, Gibbs and Rein, 1991). Furthermore, if the discussion is done with computer help, it may be stored for later reference.

The social environment of the meeting is very important. If people do not want to collaborate with each other, there is no computer-based system which compulsively will make them effectively work together. We do not address the noncollaboration issue in this paper. Our assumption is that the group members will not try to hide information and have an open, collaborative approach to the group work. This environment is called "Le Canton style of cooperation" and is further discussed in a previous paper (Bellassai, Borges, Fuller, Pino and Salgado, 1995).

Will there be incentives to spend time with the computer simply preparing a meeting? In reality, users interact with the computer but also with the other users in our approach (Bellassai, Borges, Fuller, Pino and Salgado, 1995), and that could make a difference to some users. Also, we expect that the mere need to keep updated will motivate people to connect to the system to see what is new.

Finally, the system includes features to allow users to stimulate participation in the discussions through virtual rewards.

3 THE IBIS MODEL OF ARGUMENTATION

A constructive discussion consists of presenting ideas in an organized way with some supporting arguments that can be understood and revised by other members. In face-to-face meetings people use natural language to express their positions. Although rich by nature, a text or a speech are too ambiguous when not properly organized.

The organization of speech or text will depend very much on the capacity of the individual to put his ideas in simple, concise and objective ways. Even when this goal is attained, due to the various possibilities of speech organization, it may be difficult for another individual to separate the various elements of the speech in order to better understand it. If the speech is meant to be stored by a system, automatic interpretation and classification is even harder.

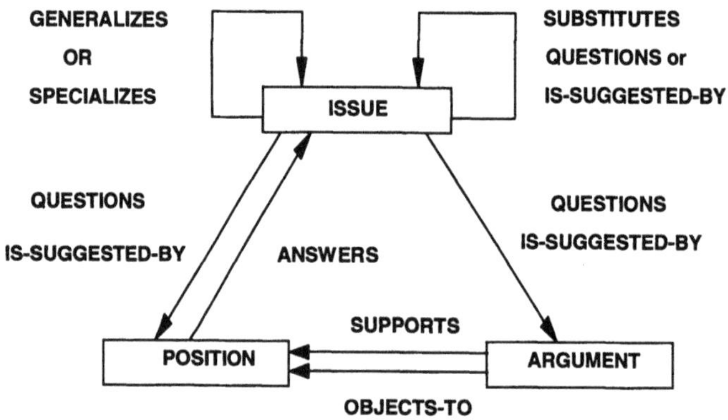

Figure 1 The IBIS Model (reproduced from Kunz, W. and Rittel, H. (1970)).

For example, a speech can mix several elements in different places. Sometimes it is difficult to recognize even more basic issues, like for example, if he is in favor or against a proposal.

In order to help organizing the discussion memory, authors suggest some classification on the statement, by separating it into different categories. In this way it is also possible to save time to introduce the subject. It is always possible that a participant may wrongly classify his statement or mix several categories under the same, like in a free speech. With the model however, one can always check and if it is the case, divide the statement in several parts to better represent the idea.

In 1970, Kunz and Rittel proposed a model called IBIS (Issue based information system) composed of three elements and nine relationships (Kunz and Rittel,. 1970). The model aimed to represent the main elements of a discussion allowing people to understand and easing additional contributions. The conceptual IBIS schema proposed by Kunz and Rittel is depicted in Figure 1. The IBIS model has been successfully applied in discussions (Conklin and Begeman, 1988). The main advantage of the model is its simplicity and intuitiveness.

In this way, an individual trying to put an argument to a position can write directly the argument text and link to the appropriate position with one of the possible relationships, that is, *in-favor* or *against*. The member is restricted to these three types of statements and the mutually exclusive nine relationships. Only a new issue can be inserted without any relationship. All others must take part in one relationship.

For the purpose of our system, we decided to extend the IBIS model to accommodate new types of statements. Each of these statements is explained below. On the other hand, we simplified the relationships by removing some of them.

- **Participant**
  We defined the concept of a discussion participant in order to identify the origin of the statements. However, we also provide anonymity as the relationships between participant and statements are optional. We have also defined the specialization of a participant related to the role of coordinator;
- **Pre-Decision**
  Although we decided not to make any decision during the pre-meeting, we thought it would be important to store decisions of previous meetings or assertions to a discussion in the form of pre-decisions. Pre-decisions can in some cases take the form of **constraints**.
- **Proposal**
  The proposal is a special kind of issue that is suggesting an action, such as the performing of a task, or a re-definition to the issue.
- **Task**
  As a result of a discussion we sometimes need to gather additional information to endorse or to help an argument. A task is the object that represents this job.
- **Remark**
  We felt that in a discussion there is a need for statements that cannot be classified by any of the IBIS elements. Therefore, in order to avoid distorting the basic elements we create the remark element that can accommodate any statement that does not fit in the original IBIS classification.

4 OUR PROPOSAL - THE DATA MODEL

In our approach, the central problem is to manage the discussion among participants in the preparation for a meeting, that means a pre-meeting. A common organized memory - called the discussion database - is provided to assure all participants can have access at any time to discussion elements.

Our database model is an extension of the basic IBIS argumentation model. It has the same basic elements: issue, position and argument; but it is enlarged with remarks and tasks. The data model also includes information about all participants, pointing out the coordinator of the pre-meeting, the agenda items with its objectives and some pre-defined constraints. It is further assumed that one can consult information outside the discussion process in an external repository.

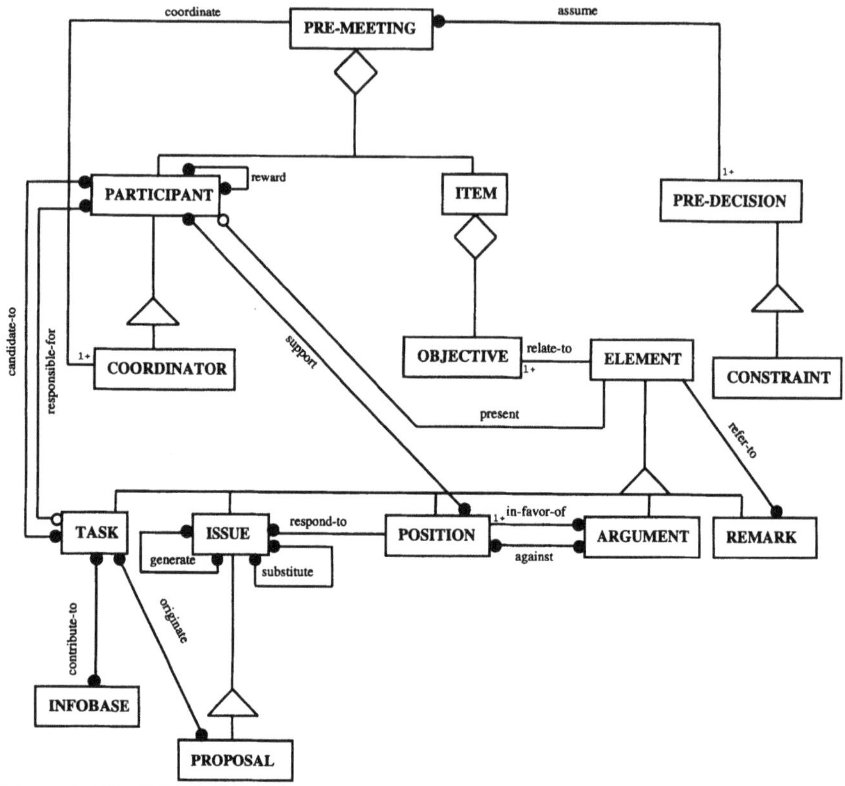

Figure 2 The SISCO data model.

Some basic assumptions are necessary to best define the data model. They are:

- A pre-meeting is a preparation for a meeting, where no decisions, concerning agenda items, are taken.
- At a creation of a pre-meeting, a coordinator is assigned. The coordinator specifies the list of participants, initial pre-decisions, constraints, agenda items and objectives.
- The pre-meeting process takes place with participants asynchronously interacting through the presentation of assertions (issues, positions, arguments and remarks).
- Some issues are classified as proposals and these may suggest a task to be performed.
- Participants may candidate themselves to carry out a task. One of these candidates is chosen by the coordinator to be responsible for the task.
- Tasks have deadlines that can only be changed by the coordinator.

The data model was completely specified using the Object Modeling Technique (OMT) (Rumbaugh et al., 1991). The relationship among the object classes defined are illustrated in Figure 2. In this methodology, aggregations are drawn like associations with a small diamond indicating the assembly end of the relationship and the notation for generalization is a triangle connecting a superclass to its subclasses. In what follows, the data model is described including the object classes, the relationships among them, some constraints, and the operations concerned.

4.1 Description of object classes

The basic class of the data model to the preparation for a meeting is the pre-meeting class, characterized by a title, a description and a deadline. The group members of a pre-meeting compose the participant class, characterized by user-id, name, affiliation, status and e-mail address. A subclass of the participant class is the coordinator class, representing the participant assigned to the coordination of the pre-meeting.

General topics that are part of a meeting agenda, supposed to be discussed in the pre-meeting, compose the item class, characterized by name, description, creation-date and priority. A goal pursued by the group as part of each item of the meeting agenda defines the objective class, with attributes name, description, status, creation-date and priority.

Assertions made by group members as part of a pre-meeting discussion are represented by the element class, characterized by type, creation-date and content. The element is a generalization of the classes: issue, position, argument, task and remark.

Assertions expressing facts are represented by the pre-decision class, characterized by a name, a description and a creation-date. It results from decisions or common agreements on a subject occurred outside the pre-meeting discussions. A pre-decision is not to be questioned and should work as an assumption during the pre-meeting. It can specialize to a constraint class, representing a restriction to be considered during a discussion.

A reference material for consultation of group members defines the infobase class, with attributes: file-name, directory and supporting application. It points to a repository of information generated by some application, including a previous pre-meeting discussion.

4.2 Description of relationships between objects

A pre-meeting is composed by agenda items and the group of participants, where one of them coordinates the pre-meeting, and it assumes pre-decisions or constraints to be considered during the pre-meeting. Items have objectives to be pursued. During the pre-meeting, a participant presents an element that represents an assertion to the discussion.

An element relates-to an objective, and may be an issue, a position, an argument, a task or a remark. An issue may substitute or generate other issues. A position responds-to an issue. An argument is presented either in-favor-of or against a position. A participant may support a position presented by another participant. A participant can make a remark that refers-to an element.

A proposal may originate a task. A participant may candidate-to a task. When candidating he has to tell the system why he is doing it and the deadline he proposes to accomplish the task. If accepted the participant will be responsible-for the task.

To motivate the pre-meeting discussion a participant may reward another participant, informing the reasons to do so.

4.3 Definition of constraints

Some constraints are the following. A task can only be presented by the coordinator, a participant cannot reward himself, an argument has to be either in-favor-of or against the same position, a participant cannot support a position he presented and only one coordinator can exist in a pre-meeting.

4.4 Description of operations

The objective here is to describe services which are provided to users of the system in order to run a pre-meeting session. Some services may not be required if the pre-meeting does not involve certain functions of the system. An interface should be designed for each type of service. There are also internal services. Services of the latter type are performed by the system but they are not visible to the user; they are not listed in this paper.

An insert function is associated to each object of the system. This can be considered a basic function of the system. The semantics associated to each function, however, is different for each service.

The first service of the system is the support to create a pre-meeting. A user requests the creation of a new pre-meeting to the system that responds to a creation of the database structure that will be the repository of all memory of the pre-meeting. The system also asks the user to define a coordinator of the meeting.

Some of the services available to a coordinator are inserting participants, creating agenda items, creating objectives, delegate coordination (to another participant), changing objective status (open for discussion or closed) and changing deadline of a pre-meeting.

A participant can start a discussion on how to reach an objective and what are the questions to be clarified regarding this objective by inserting issues. Issues are questions or proposals. The operations involved in the discussion process are associating issues (substituting or generating other issues), responding an issue (inserting a position), defining arguments (supporting or opposing positions), supporting positions, inserting remarks (associated to any element) and rewarding participants. A participant has a status, meaning the type of interaction he is prepared to carry out during a period of time and he may change it by doing a "change participant status" operation. Besides informing other participants, the system will use the status information to select events to be notified to each participant.

During the discussion a demand for additional information may occur. This generates a task that will later be assigned to a participant (assigning tasks). The creation of tasks is the responsibility of the coordinator by the creating tasks operation. The participant may only suggest a task, by means of a proposal. If the task is originated by a proposal, the coordinator sets up a corresponding link when inserting the task. A participant may offer himself to carry out a task by the operation candidating to a task. He also informs the deadline he is prepared to accomplish the task and the status of his work (informing the status of tasks).

Originated or not from a task, a participant can create an infobase by the "create an infobase" operation. Infobases store relevant information from other sources, including the memory of a previous pre-meeting. Each infobase has its own supporting application.

A number of views are provided by the system allowing users to access data without having to write a query. Views are different ways to see the objects of the system and can be obtained by doing "accessing views" operations. In the first version of the system, views are fixed, that is, the participant cannot define new views. New versions of the system will incorporate this service. Examples of views provided are listed below.

- List an element with its attributes;
- List an element with its attributes and connections;

- List of all issues with their positions and arguments, indicating the proponent;
- List of tasks opened with their responsible;
- List of objectives with their issues;
- List a participant with all elements presented by him;
- List of items with their objectives and pre-decisions;
- List of proposals with tasks originated from them.

5 AN EXAMPLE

In this section we show the most important concepts of our conversational model in terms of adapting a real example borrowed from Senn (Senn et al., 1991).

Sevco Industries is a company specialized in the design and production of parts and small electronics components. The company was born seven years ago to supply electronic parts to the automotive industry, aircraft, sound equipment, and others. Sevco Industries was founded by John Seversky, who serves now as its president. Harry Jacobson is the operations director, being responsible for the establishment of contacts with possible clients and the follow-up of negotiations between clients and Sevco representatives. He is also responsible for the company's "Costs and Benefits" centers. The leader engineer Jim Olson, in charge of the production operations , together with his two other employees, is responsible of all decisions related to scheduling and purchasing materials and products dispatching. Olson is also responsible for the design of products made by the company. Finally, Marjorie Carbo and her three assistants manage the accounts payables and accounts receivables.

The company grows at an average annual rate of 40%, but it is not always possible to hire appropriate people to match new production requests. The fast growth of Sevco Industries requires the revision of local processing of requests reception and invoicing, currently being done manually. There is a concern of loosing control of requests and accounts receivables as the result of the company growth. Jim Olson asked a study about the reception processes of requests and accounts receivables, used by the company to determine the convenience to automate this functions. Currently, only two employees take care of the requests reception and the control of accounts receivables. The solicitation was done to Joyce Handal, responsible for the Information Systems Department. Nowadays, only the functions of accounts payables and the accountancy of the company are automated.

5.1 The pre-meeting

The directors of Sevco Industries resolve to realize a pre-meeting represented as follows, based on the model proposed in this paper. Our purpose here is to identify the entities and relationships of the model, as well as their meanings related to the example. We do not worry, therefore, in showing all the interactions, but just those needed for the understanding of the model. Basic terms are shown in italics.

Jim Olson, assumes the role of *coordinator* of the pre-meeting, defining the following *participants* and *items* :

<u>Participants</u>
Jim Olson, John Severski, Harry Jacobson, Marjorie Carbo and Joyce Handal.

Items
- revision of the Requests Reception and Invoicing processes;
- hiring of new employees;
- new possible areas of business for Sevco Industries.

Some *pre-decisions* have already been taken:
- new employees can only be hired starting next year;
- the company does not intend to work in the microelectronics area;
- no new employees will be hired for the production area;
- the processing of Requests Reception and Invoicing must be done by the same employees.

Next, the group concentrates the attention on the first pre-meeting *item*: Revision of the processing of Requests Reception and Invoicing.

Jim Olson, as the *coordinator*, establishes the *Objectives* of the *item* in discussion:
- to study the performance of the actual system, based on the operational and expansion plans;
- to verify other experiences of automation;
- to define strategies to improve the Requests Reception and Invoicing processes.

For the first *objective*, the following *issues* have been pointed out:
- problems with the actual system, by Joyce Handal;
- effects generated by the problems with the actual system, by Harry Jacobson;
- importance of these effects for the final objective, by Harry Jacobson.

For the first *issue*, the following *positions* have been stated:
- We have problems to process all requests, by Jim Olson.
- The customer's information and the requests are not obtained as soon as necessary, by Harry Jacobson.
-

For the first *position*, the following *arguments in-favor-of* are placed (including the one placed by Jim Olson):
- the demand increased too much, by Jim Olson;
- by company policy, workers are not allowed to work overtime, by Marjorie Carbo;
- there are not sufficient employees to do the job, also by Marjorie Carbo.

and the following *arguments against*:
- we do not have problems, since the job is not being done the right way, by Harry Jacobson;
- at the moment, the requests manipulation occurs in acceptable way, by John Severski.

Analyzing the *position* and the *argument* placed early by Harry Jacobson, Jim Olson contributes with a *remark* :
- I cannot understand your *argument* considering the *position* placed by yourself earlier.

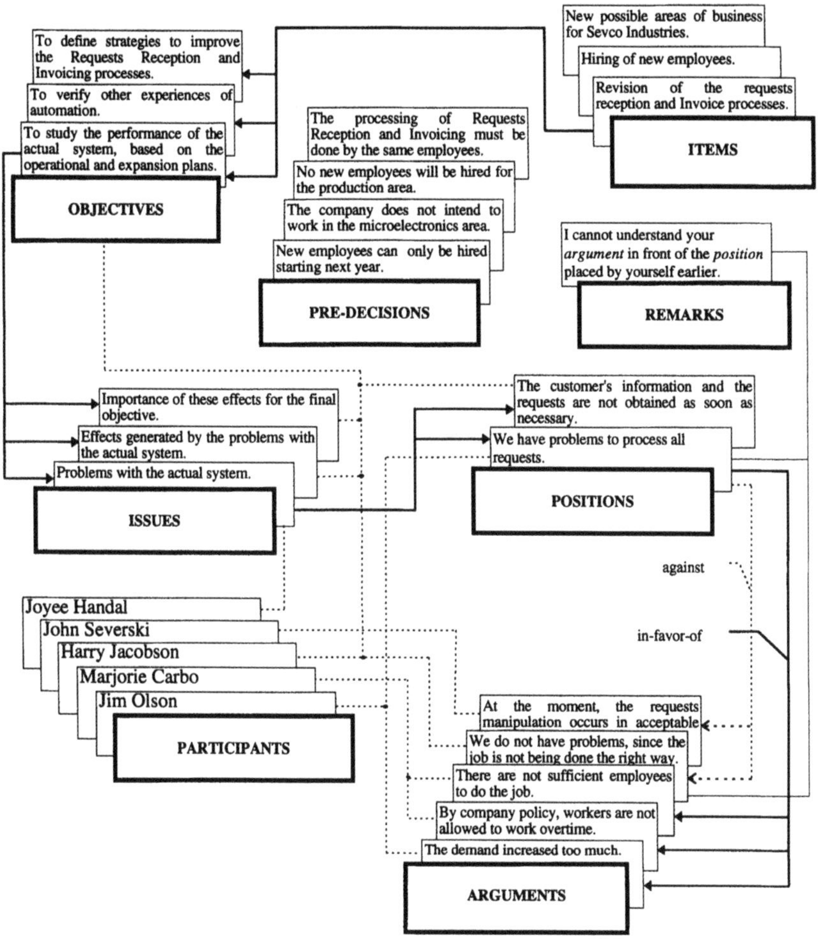

Figure 3 A conceptual view of the interaction using SISCO model.

In Figure 3 we present a conceptual view of the objects and relationships described so far.

Going back to the first *Objective*, the second *issue* would be the determination of the effects generated by the problems with the actual system. The *positions* below are presented:

- there is a customer's claim, by Jim Olson with the *argument-in-favor* that some requests are lost;
- causes the delay of other tasks, by Marjorie Carbo with the *argument-in-favor* that when the requests and invoicing are delayed, everybody needs to help to conclude that task.

Jim Olson's *position* is *supported by* Harry Jacobson, who agrees.

For the second *Objective*, to verify other experiences of automation, one *issue* is presented:

- are there other systems in the company that were automated, by John Severski.

who *substituted* it *by* the next one:

- what are the benefits to the company, obtained by the automated solutions, by John Severski;
- there are some solutions in other companies that could be analyzed, as a *proposal* that will *originate* a *task*, by Joyce Handal.

As responses, the following *positions respond-to* the *proposal* made by Joyce Handal:

- I think it is not necessary to look for external solutions, by Harry Jacobson, that concludes that Sevco Industries has a peculiar way to work;
- another company has used automated Requests Reception and Invoicing processing, by Joyce Handal with the *argument-in-favor* that the obtained results are positive.

Due to this *proposal*, Jim Olson as *coordinator* determines the realization of the following *task*:

- to obtain more information about the automated systems and their results.

Joyce Handal and Marjorie Carbo are *candidates to* execute the task. Jim Olson, as *coordinator* chooses Joyce Handal as the person *responsible for* the task. Joyce Handal will have to collect the information and save it in the *INFOBASE*, which will *contribute to* the execution of the task.

John Severski *rewards* Joyce Handal by her active participation and the quality of the presented issues.

In this way, the pre-meeting continues until the coordinator Jim Olson, determines its end. It is clear that this pre-meeting need not to be performed at the same room and at the same time if a proper software tool such as SISCO is available. Note that even in the same room, participants will have problems following the structure of the pre-meeting. Lack of concentration will very fast slow down the group work. Therefore, SISCO has great advantages in a pre-meeting: it can easily structure the conversation, allowing it to be followed at any time; the system is asynchronous and thus, participants can work on it as they feel or can, augmenting the overall productivity.

Once the pre-meeting is finished, the coordinator can call to a face-to-face meeting to take the decisions. In this way, we believe the meeting will be much shorter and productive than if a classical meeting was called at the beginning.

6 CONCLUSIONS

In this article we presented the data model of an information repository to support a pre-meeting interaction. The data model is an extension of the original IBIS model. The model is being used in a project named SISCO that aims to support members of a group preparing for a meeting.

As in IBIS, the evolution of an interaction is represented by objects ordered and shown in a chronological order. The semantics behind this decision is the assumption that a member is aware of the previous objects under the same hierarchy.

Our system's goal is to help the participants to reduce both the equivocality and uncertainty involved in the initial stage of a meeting. A subsequent face-to-face meeting is considered essential and it is not to be replaced by an electronic distributed meeting. The case example shows the complexity of a pre-meeting, which is extremely difficult to follow if proper tools are not available.

This may explain the lack of meetings performance, where participants loose concentration easily. With a system such as SISCO, we believe that participants will be able to easily interact among themselves and follow a discussion thread, provided an adequate user-interface is built. Since SISCO is a remote and asynchronous system, participants can work at their own pace. Also, they have access to common information and to the records of the pre-meeting.

The actual gain on performance could only be verified if the system is put to work in real-world situations. In order to enable such experiments some prototypes are being developed (Parra and Pino, 1995).

A number of open issues are still under investigation. A simple and intuitive interface, such as the one developed for GIbis (Conklin and Begeman, 1988) is called for. The problem of awareness in asynchronous interactions also requires further research (Borges and Jomier, 1995).

There is already a planned extension to the model. We intend to support hypermedia links and multimedia objects. With hyper links we will be able to point to other objects outside the data model. With multimedia objects we intend to allow group members to illustrate their argumentation with picture, sound and video objects.

Acknowledgments

This work is partially supported by the Chilean Science and Technology Fund (FONDECYT) grants No. 1950880 and 1940269, by the Brazilian Research Council (CNPq) grant No. 200919/94-6, and grants from RITOS (CYTED), UNESCO-Orcyt, Lotus-Paraguay, Synapsys S.A. and ORACLE Chile. We thank Maria Luiza Campos for her help in the data model.

7 REFERENCES

Bellassai, G., Borges, M., Fuller, D., Pino, J.A. and Salgado, A.C. (1995) SISCO: A tool to improve meetings productivity, in *Proceedings of the First Cyted-Ritos International Workshop on Groupware*, Lisbon, Portugal, 149-161.

Bergmann, N. and Mudge, J.C. (1994) Automated assistance for the telemeeting lifecycle, in *Proceedings of the ACM 1994 Conference. on Computer Supported Cooperative Work (CSCW 94)*, Chapel Hill, N.C., U.S.A., 373-384.

Borges, M. and Jomier, G. (1995) Using database versions to support awareness in group interactions, *Proceedings of the Workshop in Version Control at ECSCW'95*, Stockholm, Sweden.

Conklin, J. and Begeman, M. (1988) gIBIS: A hypertext tool for exploratory policy discussion. *ACM Transactions on Office Information Systems*, **6 (3)**, 303-331.

Daft, R. and Lengel, R. (1986) Organizational information requirements, media richness and structural design. *Management Science*, **32 (5)**, 554-571.

Ellis, C.A., Gibbs, S.J. and Rein, G.L. (1991) Groupware - Some issues and experiences. *Communications. of the ACM*, **34 (1)**, 39-58.

Hackman, J. and Kaplan, R. (1974) Interventions into group process: An approach to improving the effectiveness of groups. *Decision Sciences*, **5**,. 459-480.

Jay, A. (1976) How to run a meeting. *Harvard Business Review*, **54 (2),** 43-57.

Khoshafian, S. and Buckiewicz, M. (1995) *Introduction to groupware, workflow, and workgroup computing*. John Wiley and Sons, San Francisco.

Kunz, W. and Rittel, H. (1970) Issues as elements of information systems, Working Paper # 131, Institute of Urban and Regional Development, University of California at Berkeley.

Nunamaker, J.F. et al. (1991) Electronic meeting systems to support group work, *Communications of the ACM* **34** (7), 40-61.

Parra, R. and Pino, J.A. (1995) N-Sisco: A Notes implementation of SISCO, in *Proceedings of the First Cyted-Ritos International Workshop on Groupware*, Lisbon, 125-137.

Rumbaugh, J, et al. (1991) *Object-oriented modeling and design*. Prentice Hall Inc., Englewood Cliffs, N.J.

Senn, J. et al. (1991) *Analysis and design of information systems*. McGraw-Hill, New York

Streitz, N., Geibler, J., Haake, J. and Hol, J. (1994) DOLPHIN: Integrated meeting support across local and remote desktop environments and liveboards, in *Proceedings of the ACM 1994 Conference on Computer Supported Cooperative Work (CSCW 94)*, Chapel Hill, N.C., U.S.A., 345-358.

Wagner, G., Wynne, B. and Mennecke, B. (1993) Group support systems facilities and software, in *Group Support Systems - New Perspectives* (ed. L. Jessup and J.S. Valacich), MacMillan Publishing, New York, 8-55.

8 BIOGRAPHY

Geronimo Bellassai got a B.Sc. in Electromechanical Engineering at the Universidad Nacional de Asuncion, Paraguay in 1982. He specialized in Electronics at the Instituto Girolamo Montani de Fermo, Italy. He currently is Vice Dean and professor at the Universidad Católica de Asuncion (Faculty of Science and Technology). He is also chairman of the university's Laboratory of Digital Electronics.

Marcos Borges obtained a doctorate at the University of East Anglia (UK) in 1986. Since 1975, he is a consulting analyst for the Núcleo de Computação Electrônica of the Universidade Federal de Rio de Janeiro (UFRJ) and an Associate Professor at the Department of Computer Science of the same university. He has been a consultant for several companies in Brazil and in US. He is currently spending a sabbatical at Santa Clara University, California, USA.

David Fuller is professor in computer science at Pontificia Universidad Católica de Chile. His Computer Science Doctorate was obtained at the Imperial College of Science and Technology, UK in 1989. He currently is the Treasurer of the Chilean Computer Science Society and Executive Secretary of CLEI (Latin American Association of Academicians and Professionals).

Jose Alberto Pino obtained a M.S. and qualification towards a Ph.D. degree at the University of Michigan (USA) in 1977. He is a Professor at the University of Chile (Computer Science Dept.). He is a member of IFIP TC13 (Human Computer Interaction) and has participated in international Editorial Committees and Program Committees (such as the HCI Conference 93 and IFIP World Congress 92).

Ana Carolina Salgado obtained her Doctorate from the University of Nice (France) in 1988. She is Associate Professor at the Universidade Federal de Pernambuco, Brazil (Department of Informatics). She is the Coordinator of Undergraduate Studies in Computer Science at her university.

5

Measuring the impact of communication technology on group decision making

*Pieter W.G. Bots and Robert Jan Streng**
Faculty of Systems Engineering, Policy Analysis and Management
Delft University of Technology
P.O. Box 5015, NL-2600 GA Delft, the Netherlands
Voice: +31 15 2782948 Fax: +31 15 2783422
E-mail: bots@sepa.tudelft.nl

**The second author is presently working with BSO-ORIGIN Consultancy, Utrecht, the Netherlands.*

Abstract

This paper reports on a longitudinal experiment under controlled conditions that was conducted to measure the impact of communication technology on group decision making. Small groups of MIS students were observed while playing a series of rounds in a management game under three different conditions: face-to-face in one room, dispersed over four rooms with audio and video connection, and dispersed with audio connection only. Contrary to expectation, hardly any significant differences in task performance were found. Although the limitations of the study ask for cautious interpretation of the findings, it would seem that communication technology will not be a major obstacle on the road to effective international offices of the future.

Keywords

Communication technology, decision making, CSCW, impact assessment, management game

1 INTRODUCTION

If the different problem analyses in Bots *et al.* (1995) with respect to the international office of the future (IOF) hold any truth, then of all potential keys to this office, communication technology will be the easiest one to turn. Yet earlier literature on management and decision making in organizations points out phenomena that may impede adoption of this technology. For one, Daft *et al.* (1987) observed in practice that managers are reluctant to replace their conventional meetings by technology-based ones: "Executives continue to prefer oral, face-to-face communication for much of their work. The availability of teleconferencing and other electronic media has not reduced travel or face-to-face communications".

The question we address in this paper is whether decision makers are right in preferring face-to-face meetings: Do video-conferencing and telephone-conferencing indeed have such a negative impact on decision process and decision outcome that a skeptic attitude towards these technologies is justified?

To get a better understanding of the impact of communication technology on group decision making performance, we conducted a longitudinal experiment in which groups of students had to work on a particular decision making task under one of three different conditions: either a face-to-face setting, an audio-conference setting or a video-conference setting.

In the following section we outline the conceptual framework that we chose as basis for the experimental design. In section 3 we show how the problem of measuring the impact of communication technology on group decision making was operationalized into an experim-ental design. In section 4 we present the obeservations and discuss the outcome of the experiment.

2 CONCEPTUAL FRAMEWORK FOR THE STUDY

Assessing the impact of new technologies on current business practice is a rich and complex issue. In conceptualizing this research we made reductions along several dimensions:

- the characteristics to differentiate between levels of communication technology;
- the type of activity in which this technology is used;
- the impact area that is observed.

Differentiating characteristic: media richness

To classify communication media, Daft and Lengel (1986) introduced the concept of "media richness". In their theoretical framework, the richness of a communication medium is operationalized in terms of four factors: feedback capability, the capability of the medium to transmit multiple cues, the language variety, and the personal focus of the medium. In this framework, face-to-face meetings provide the "richest" communication medium, video-conferencing is "leaner" (reduced visibility of group members, no "touch and smell") and audio-conferencing is again "leaner" (no visual cues at all). No use of telecommunication technology would result in even "leaner" communication media, such as asynchronous communication by exchanging written memos.

McCarthy *et al.* (1991) and Chappell *et al.* (1992) use a different classification scheme: They distinguish between communication channels on the basis of four tasks that should be performed: synchronization of communication, maintaining conversational coherence, repairing conversational breakdown, and maintaining shared focus. Although these factors are quite different from the factors in the media richness framework, the classification outcome when applied to the three communication settings (face-to-tace, video and audio) is essentially the same.

Following amongst others Rice (1984), Kinney and Watson (1992), and El-Shinnawy and Markus (1992) we adopt the media richness terminology for this study. A "rich" communication medium is expected to have less impact on group performance than a "lean" communication medium. Thus, media richness is taken as the independent variable.

Activity: group decision making

DeSanctis and Gallupe (1987) define a decision making group as two or more people jointly responsible for detecting a problem, elaborating on the nature of the problem, generating possible solutions, or formulating strategies for implementing solutions. Jacob and Pirkul (1992) state that the key difference between an individual decision maker and a decision making group is the need for interaction between the group members during the decision making process.

The information processing model of organizations (Galbraith 1977) implies that there are two factors that influence this interaction: uncertainty and equivocality (El-Shinnawy and Markus 1992). Uncertainty refers to "the difference between amount of information required to perform the task and the amount of information already possessed by the organization". Equivocality refers to ambiguity and multiple, conflicting interpretations of situations (Weick 1979). Communication is considered essential in resolving issues that involve ambiguity. This makes group decision making in ill-structured or semi-structured situations an appropriate activity for studying the impact of communication technology on group performance.

Group performance in problem solving and decision making tasks under different conditions has been researched extensively (McGrath and Hollingshead 1994). The research on support for group decision making can roughly be divided into two main streams: supporting the process by means of information technology and supporting the process by means of communication technology. The definition of *electronic meeting systems* (EMS) as given by Dennis *et al.* (1988) covers both: "EMS are systems that use information technology to support the group work that occurs in meetings. EMSs combine the task orientation of GDSS and the communication orientation of CSCW." In their literature review, Dennis *et al.* show that the largest body of research on EMS is concerned with comparing the use of a decision room with situations in which no computer support is provided. Since our objective is to measure the impact of communication technology only, the level of (computer based) decision support available to the group is a variable that must be controlled in the experiment.

Impact area: quality of decision making

In their research on the benefits of expert systems, Oz *et al.* (1993) make distinction between three key factors in decision making: decision quality, decision making time and confidence in the decision. They remark that there are two important schools of thought on the quality of decision making: one emphasizes the process, the other mainly considers the outcome. We consider both aspects important for assessing the impact of communication technology on group decision making.

Based on a survey of the literature on decision making, Janis and Mann (1977) compiled a set of major criteria that can be used to determine whether the decision making process is of high quality. They state: "The effective decision maker, to the best of his ability and within his information processing capabilities,

1. thoroughly canvasses a wide range of alternative courses of action;
2. surveys the full range of objectives to be fulfilled and the values implicated by the choice;
3. carefully weighs whatever he or she knows about the costs and risks of negative consequences, as well as the positive consequences, that could flow from each alternative;
4. intensively searches for new information relevant to further evaluation of the alternatives;
5. correctly assimilates and takes account of any new information or expert judgment to which he is exposed, even when the information or judgment does not support the course of action he initially prefers."

To measure quality of decision *process*, these five aspects must be further operationalized in the context of the specific decision making task. Quality of decision *outcome* can be measured if there is a standard for comparison of task performance and adequate control for external influences on the variables that are identified to indicate success. In theory, appropriate experimental design can create such circumstances. Practice shows that such decision making tasks tend to become too artificial to allow for generalization to real-life decision making contexts (Van Schaik, 1988; Kottemann and Remus 1991; Sheffield 1995). With this caution in mind, quality of decision process *and* decision outcome is taken as the dependent variable.

At the conceptual level, we formulate the relationship between dependent and independent variables by these two hypotheses:

H1. When two groups of decision makers with equal skills are working on the same problem, the group that uses the "richer" communication channel will go through a better decision process, that is: they will consider more alternative courses of action and they will analyze these deeper than the group that communicates through the "leaner" communication channel.

H2. When two groups of decision makers with equal skills are working on the same problem, the group that uses the "richer" communication channel will make better decisions than the group that communicates through the "leaner" communication channel.

In the following section, we describe the experimental setting created to test these two hypotheses.

3 EXPERIMENT

We set up the experiment along the same lines that were followed by e.g. Van Schaik (1988), Kottemann and Remus (1991) and Oz *et al.* (1993). The decision making activity involves playing a round in a management game, where small groups of students each are to make their decisions under different conditions, in this case audio, video of face-to-face. We first describe how the different levels of media richness have been implemented. We then turn to the decision making task, outlining the management game and the information that is made available to the decision making groups. Next, we further operationalize hypotheses H1 and H2 in the context of the experimental setup. Finally, we describe the way in which experimental control has been implemented.

3.1 Implementing different levels of media richness

For the experiment we made use of the Laboratory for Work and Information Technology (the WIT-lab) at Delft University of Technology (Van der Velden, 1995). The laboratory consists of five sound-proofed test rooms and a control room, all interconnected by several networks, supporting audio, video and data transmission. The rooms are decorated to create a genuine "office atmosphere". At the time of the experiment, each test room feautured an Apple MacIntosh™ , a video camera/monitor combination, and a clip-on microphone and two audio speakers to allow synchronous (full-duplex) voice communication. Figure 1 gives an impression of the "office workplaces" the WIT-lab thus provides.

Figure 1 Impression of the work places as used in the experiment

The video equipment has been designed to preserve the impression of "eye contact" between group members: a video camera registers the image of the person facing the monitor via a one-way mirror positioned at a 45° angle as depicted in Figure 2. The images from four cameras are displayed on the monitor simultaneously by means of a video splitter.

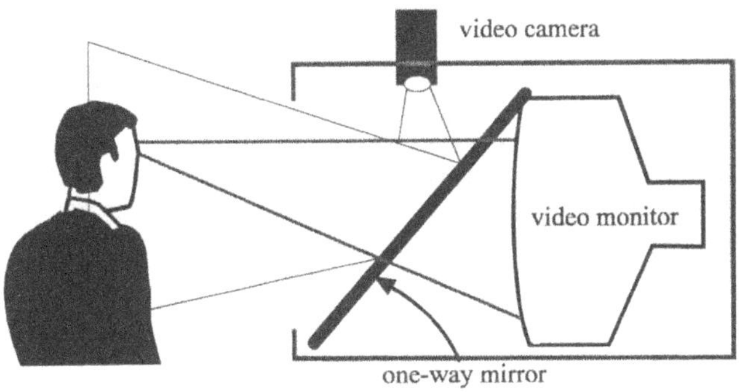

Figure 2 Mounting of video camera and monitor.

The computers in the test rooms all are connected with a server in the control room. The software used in the experiment runs on this server. Its output image is displayed on all computer screens using the MacIntosh Timbuktu™ software. This application also processes mouse and keyboard control from each of the computers.

The three different levels of media richness have been implemented as follows:

- *Face-to-face:* For this condition, we made use of the larger of the five rooms. Group members were seated on one side of the table on which the computer was installed, with a separate mouse available to each member. The audio and video equipment were not used.

- *Video:* The video-conferencing condition was implemented by dispersing the group over the four smaller test rooms. Here, each group member found him/herself in the position depicted by
- Figure 1.
- *Audio:* This condition was identical to the video-conferencing setting except that the video image was not displayed on the monitor.

3.2 The decision making task

To assess the impact of communication technology on group decision making, the decision making task should be sufficiently equivocal to require group members to interact to solve the problem at hand and yet sufficiently structured to allow the observers to measure the effectiveness of the decisions. Using a management game that is well-known to us and – at first – completely unknown to the student subjects seemed adequate to meet these two demands.

The management game we used in the experiment was developed at Delft University of Technology and has been used previously as a research implement (Van Schaik 1988; Bots *et al.* 1989). It is still being used in executive workshops on decision support systems. The game has two important characteristics:

- taking the decisions is experienced by players as an ill-structured task;
- there is sufficient evidence that systematic information gathering leads to a better score.

The decisions that have to be made concern the management of a firm that produces materials for housing construction. This firm competes with a number of other firms on a market that is sensitive not only to pricing and advertising policies of these firms, but also to such external factors as industrial production, interest rate and season – the number of housing starts tends to follow a seasonal pattern. A round in the game corresponds to a business period of three months. Each round, the players have to decide upon these six variables:

- selling price of their product;
- number of salespersons;
- amount of expense for publicity;
- number of production line workers;
- total production volume;
- number of new production lines to build.

Information regarding fixed factors such as the cost of labor, depreciation of equipment and investment in new production lines is available to the players in an 8-page instruction manual. Information regarding variable factors, including decisions made in prior game periods, are made available electronically at the beginning of the next round. Each round, players typically have one hour to browse through this information and make their decisions.

To be able to run the game on the WIT-lab equipment, the user interface was redeveloped using Apple's HyperCard™ software. Via this interface, players have access to information that is stored in a stack of "hypercards". The order of browsing through this stack is not enforced by the system; the players can freely move through the stack. As can be seen in Table 1, these cards conceptually fall into two categories: those supporting intelligence activities and those supporting design and choice.

Table 1 Two groups of cards

Intelligence	*Design and choice*
Balance information	Decision information
Profit statement	Notepad
Liquidity	
Market information	
Regression analyses	

As an example, Figure 3 shows four different cards: a balance, market information (competition and general economic outlook) and the decision input form. Balance, profit and liquidity data are presented in simplified accounting schemes. Information is organized per game period and players can click on "next" and "previous" buttons to browse through different game periods. In addition, the players can create scatterplots with linear regression lines and coefficients to examine potential relationships between 15 key variables, including period number and the six decision variables.

The balance sheet contains a gadget: The current state of the company is visualized using a face based on a paper by Chernoff (1973) and elaborated further by Korhunen (1991). The shape of the face is determined by the leverage ratio of the total debt and the equity. The curve of the mouth represents the net profit of the current quarter, resulting in a smiling face when profit is made. The size of the eyes is an indication for the cash flow. Although the information value of this representation is discutable, its intuïtive message is valid.

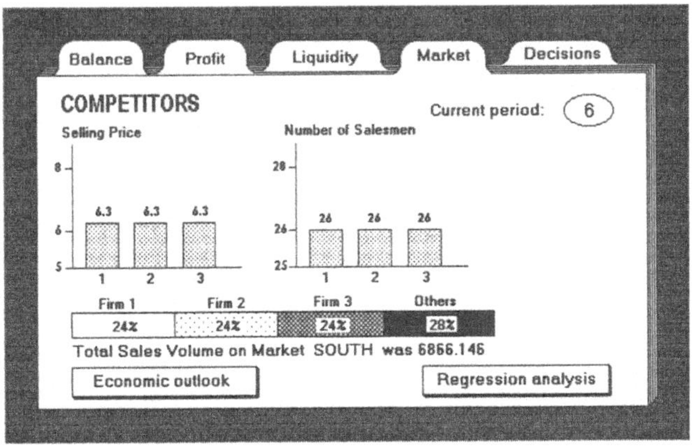

Figure 3 Examples of HyperCard cards used in the experiment

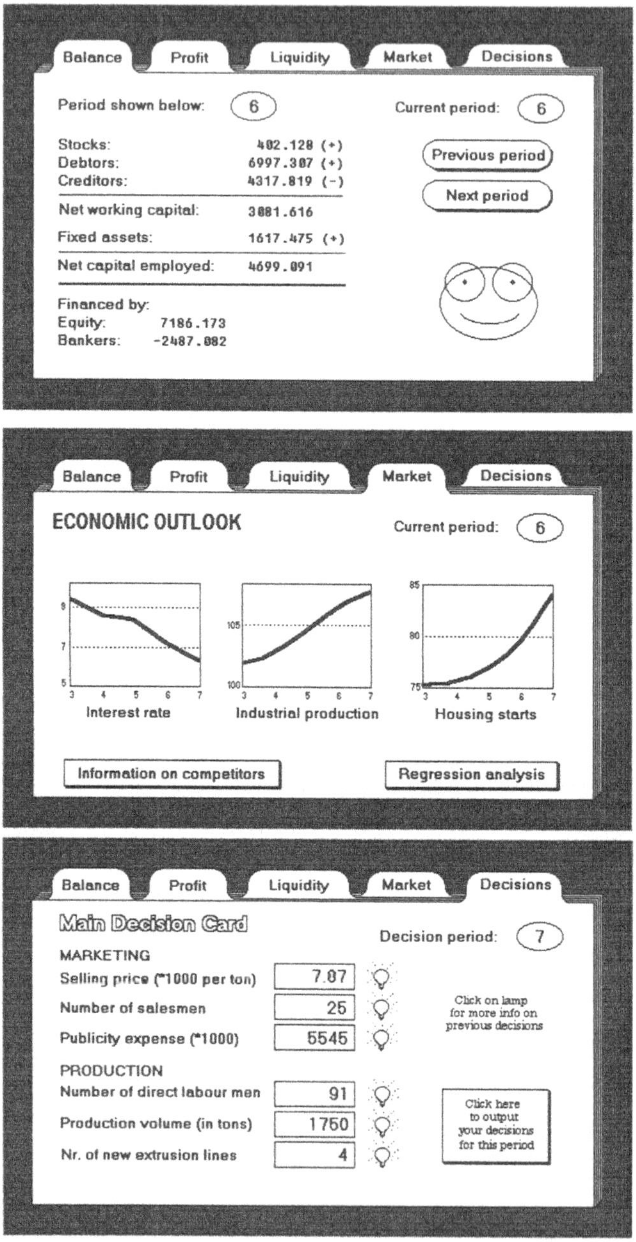

Figure 3 Examples of HyperCard cards used in the experiment (continued)

3.3 Operationalization

Figure 4 shows the basic scheme for the experiment. The unit of observation is one round in the game played by one group. The independent variable is medium richness. Group composition, decision making task and level of computer support must be controlled for.

Decision *process* quality has been operationalized in terms of the search for information studied and the number of alternatives considered. To measure the intensity of the search for information, the number of cards consulted during a session and the number of regression analyses made are counted. The number of alternatives considered is measured by counting the number of times key decision variables have been changed on the main decision card.

Decision *outcome* quality has been operationalized in terms of the amount of profit made (relative to the total profit made on the market in that period) and the market share realized in that period. Although these variables depend not only on the quality of the decisions made in that same round, they are suitable performance indicators when a series of rounds is played.

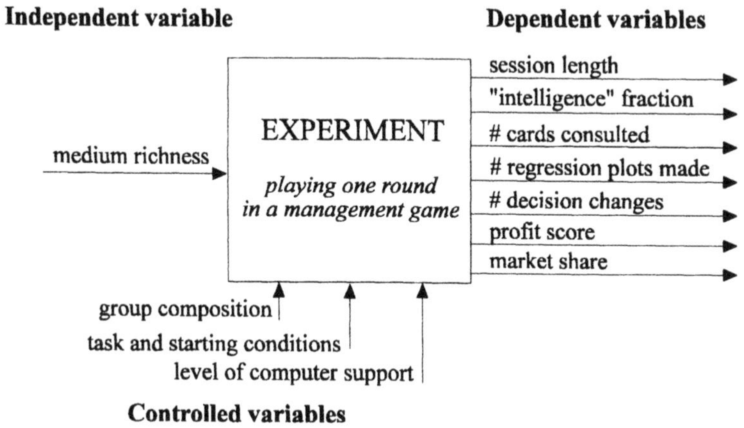

Figure 4 Experiment variables

Since groups would be playing a sequence of rounds, we anticipated a learning effect that might introduce a bias. Main indicator for a learning effect is the time required for decision making. Such time may possibly be influenced by medium richness. Fowler and Wackerbarth (1988) report that audio groups spend more time maintaining group organization than face-to-face groups do. However, this claim is not supported by Kinney and Watson (1992) who concluded that their hypothesis that the decision time for audio-supported groups would be longer than for face-to-face groups could not be proven. In view of these conflicting results, we choose not to use session length as an indicator for decision making performance, but only to check for possible differences in learning behavior. As a potential second indicator for learning behavior, we chose the fraction of time groups spend on "intelligence" activities. The rationale for adding this indicator is that as groups learn, they will require relatively less time finding and evaluating the information that is relevant, leaving more time for design and choice activities.

Operationalizing hypothesis H1 and H2 from section 2 in terms of the variables in Figure 4 leads to the following set of hypotheses:

H1.1. The number of cards studied will be higher for face-to-face groups than for mediated groups, and higher for video-groups than for audio-groups.
H1.2. The number of regression analyses made by face-to-face groups will be higher than by mediated groups, and higher for video groups than for audio groups.
H1.3. The number of decision changes by face-to-face groups will be higher than for mediated groups, and higher for video-groups than for audio-groups.
H2.1. The relative profit score for face-to-face groups will be higher than for mediated groups, and higher for video-groups than for audio-groups.
H2.2. The market share of face-to-face groups will be higher than for mediated groups, and higher for video-groups than for audio-groups.

3.4 Experimental control

The decision making groups all consisted of four participants: computer science students with only a basic background in management science. Participation in the game was mandatory to get credit for the MIS course it was part of. We controlled the group composition for any prior working relationships amongst students. The game was configured to allow 16 groups to play on four different markets: four groups on each market. Assignment of groups to markets was random. Each group played 10 rounds at a rate of one round per week. The students were asked not to discuss the game when not in session. With a single exception, this rule was observed.

To create uniform starting conditions, all groups started in game period 7 with up to that point identical firms. The players were made very clear that the objective was to realize both profit and market share. They were not instructed regarding their decision process, although they were told that the game tends to favor players that make good use of the available information. To increase motivation, we offered rewards ranging from $10 to $50 per student, depending on their final performance on their market. To control for "end of game" behavior – typically low performing groups that make "wild" decisions to chance for a last round success – the results of the last round were not included in the analysis.

For each market, the four groups were again randomly assigned to the different conditions: one audio, one video and two face-to-face. The second face-to-face group was placed in the video-conferencing setting after round 11 to see whether a switch to a "leaner" medium after working some time face-to-face would show a significant impact. With nine rounds, this could in theory yield 144 observations. The actual numbers deviate from this due to scheduling constraints imposed by availability of facilities and students. These irregularities should not introduce a systematic error in the observations, however.

4 EXPERIMENTAL FINDINGS

4.1 Checking for learning effects

As we remarked in section 3.3, different conditions might affect the groups in becoming proficient in the decision making task. We argued that a decrease in session length and the fraction of game time spent on "intelligence" activities can indicate increased proficiency. Figure 5 shows for each of the three conditions the average session length as a function of the game period. If we can discern any trend at all, it would be that the session length tends to decrease. Analysis of variance (see Table 2b) shows no significant difference between the conditions.

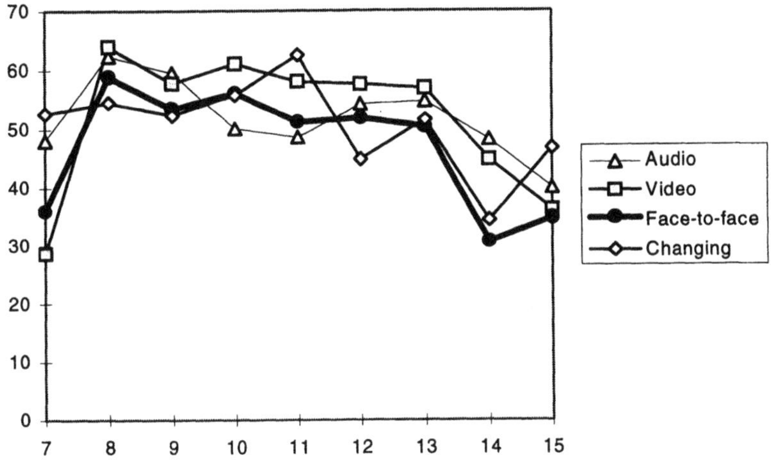

Figure 5 Session length (minutes) over periods 7-15 per condition

Table 2a Statistics on session length
Summary

Groups	*n*	*Sum*	*Mean*	*Variance*
Audio	30	1553.5	51.8	176.0
Video	34	1795.9	52.8	177.0
Face-to-face	32	1525.9	47.7	207.6
Changing	34	1720.7	50.6	247.4

Table 2b Statistics on session length (continued)
Analysis of variance

Source	*Sum of sq.*	*df*	*Mean sq.*	*F*	*P*
Among groups	479.0	3	159.7	0.787	0.503
Within groups	25543.3	126	202.7		
Total	26022.3	129			

Figure 6 shows for each of the three conditions the fraction of time spent on "intelligence" activities as a function of the game period. This fraction remains more or less constant, which suggests that the conjectured shift in focus towards design and choice does dot occur. Interestingly, however, analysis of variance (see Table 3b) shows a difference between the conditions that is significant at the 0.01 level. It would seem that face-to-face groups on average spend slightly more time discussing alternatives. The difference, however, is marginal (9 to 14% of game time).

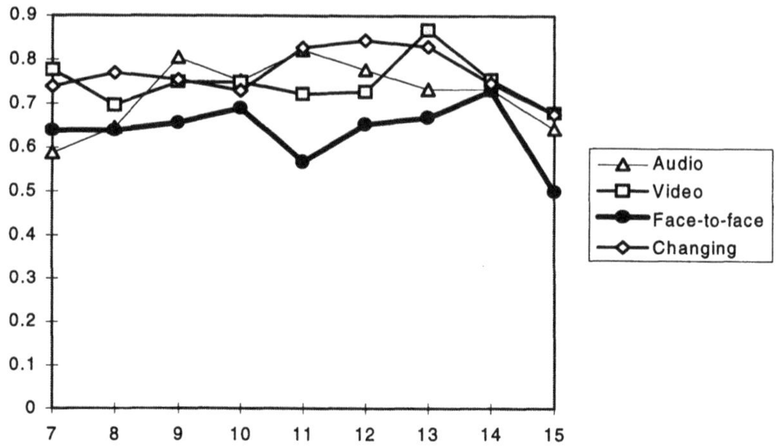

Figure 6 Fraction of "intelligence" time over periods 7-15 per condition

Table 3a Statistics on fraction of "intelligence" time
Summary

Groups	*n*	*Sum*	*Mean*	*Variance*
Audio	30	21.6	0.72	0.020
Video	34	25.5	0.75	0.010
Face-to-face	32	20.4	0.64	0.021
Changing	34	26.2	0.77	0.013

Table 3b Statistics on fraction of "intelligence" time (continued)
Analysis of variance

Source	*Sum of sq.*	*df*	*Mean sq.*	*F*	*P*
Among groups	0.330	3	0.1100	6.887	0.0002
Within groups	2.012	126	0.0160		
Total	2.342	129			

Given these observations with respect to session length and "intelligence" time, we see no reason to conclude that learning effects introduce a bias.

4.2 Decision quality: process

We operationalized the quality of the decision process in terms of three dependent variables: the number of cards consulted, the number of regression plots being made, and the number of times key decision variables have been changed.

As can be seen in the first section of Table 4, audio groups on average consult the least number of cards, whereas (initially) face-to-face groups consult the highest number of cards. Although this would seem to confirm the anticipated effect of medium richness, analysis of variance shows that the differences are not significant even at the 0.1 level.

Table 4 Statistics on number of cards consulted

Summary

Groups	*n*	*Sum*	*Mean*	*Variance*
Audio	30	1120	37.3	167.5
Video	34	1393	41.0	271.7
Face-to-face	32	1315	41.1	208.4
Changing	34	1526	44.9	335.9

Analysis of variance

Source	*Sum of sq.*	*df*	*Mean sq.*	*F*	*P*
Among groups	911.7	3	303.9	1.221	0.305
Within groups	31367.9	126	249.0		
Total	32279.6	129			

Table 5 shows the observations with respect to the number of regression plots made: again the audio groups score lowest, but this time the video groups show the highest average. Analysis of variance reveals this differences to be statistically significant at the 0.05 level.

Table 5 Statistics on number of regression plots

Summary

Groups	*n*	*Sum*	*Mean*	*Variance*
Audio	30	98	3.27	7.72
Video	34	193	5.68	13.38
Face-to-face	32	120	3.75	8.13
Changing	34	166	4.88	13.07

Analysis of variance

Source	*Sum of sq.*	*df*	*Mean sq.*	*F*	*P*
Among groups	115.2	3	38.4	3.586	0.016
Within groups	1348.8	126	10.7		
Total	1464.0	129			

Table 6 shows again a different picture: the differences between the three conditions with respect to the average number of changes made in key decision variables are quite marginal and not significant.

Table 6 Statistics on number of decision variable changes

Summary

Groups	*n*	*Sum*	*Mean*	*Variance*
Audio	30	158	5.27	4.13
Video	34	171	5.03	3.24
Face-to-face	32	180	5.63	2.89
Changing	34	177	5.21	6.74

Analysis of variance

Source	*Sum of sq.*	*df*	*Mean sq.*	*F*	*P*
Among groups	6.1	3	2.045	0.509	0.677
Within groups	505.9	126	4.015		
Total	512.0	129			

4.4 Decision quality: outcome

We have two indicators for the outcome of the decision: profit and market share. There were considerable differences in the total profits in each the four markets during the experiments. Taking the absolute profit value would give low-performance firms on a high-profit market an advantage above high-performance firms on low-profit markets. We therefore use a relative profit score in our analysis: the position relative to the highest and lowest profit score on the market. Best performing firms thus score 100, worst performing firms score 0. As can be seen in Table 7, the differences in profit scores between conditions are not significant.

Table 7 Statistics on profit scores

Summary

Groups	*n*	*Sum*	*Mean*	*Variance*
Audio	30	1377.3	45.9	2009.9
Video	34	2080.9	61.2	1393.5
Face-to-face	32	1774.4	55.4	1530.3
Changing	34	1706.1	50.2	1772.0

Analysis of variance

Source	*Sum of sq.*	*df*	*Mean sq.*	*F*	*P*
Among groups	4240.0	3	1413.3	0.847	0.471
Within groups	210186.2	126	1668.1		
Total	214426.2	129			

Table 8 shows a similar picture for market shares: again the video groups have the highest mean, but again the differences between groups are not significant. Note that the profit scores show a high variance. This is partly due to the scaling we applied. Although we cannot say that the two indicators are inconsistent, we consider market share to be the better performance indicator.

Table 8 Statistics on market shares

Summary

Groups	*n*	*Sum*	*Mean*	*Variance*
Audio	30	540.2	18.0	37.9
Video	34	679.6	20.0	101.9
Face-to-face	32	525.5	16.4	20.3
Changing	34	652.1	19.2	41.4

Analysis of variance

Source	*Sum of sq.*	*df*	*Mean sq.*	*F*	*P*
Among groups	236.0	3	78.7	1.536	0.209
Within groups	6456.5	126	51.2		
Total	6692.5	129			

4.5 Other observations during the experiment

Although the focus of this paper is on measuring group decision making performance, several other aspects have been measured systematically in the course of the experiment, for example the way subjects experienced different settings and perceived the quality of their decision making. We will not discuss these aspects here in detail, but summarize the observations by Van der Velden (1995) to add perspective to the observations with respect to performance.

Questionnaires filled out after each round by the subjects showed that – though all settings were rated as adequate for both task performance and group development – the face-to-face setting was perceived as most suitable for the task, and the audio-conferencing setting as least suitable. As more rounds were played, these differences in rating decreased. The shared screen facility was evaluated very positively by all groups. Also, all groups rated their motivation and group performance as high.

Analysis of a representative sample from the video recordings of the sessions revealed no differences in style of collaboration for groups that alternate face-to-face meetings with distributed meetings. Groups in the audio and the video condition showed more task-oriented behavior, and the social climate in the audio groups was less friendly than in the other conditions. These effects became stronger with time.

5 DISCUSSION AND CONCLUSION

The findings reported in the previous section seem to carry a single message: The experiment shows no significant impact of communication media on group decision making performance. None of the hypotheses H1.1 through H2.2 as formulated in section 3.3 is supported by our observations. The lack of impact may be explained by *adaptation:* the phenomenon that groups will develop styles of interaction behavior that compensate for the constraints imposed by communication media, thereby nullifying potential effects on task performance (McGrath and Kelley 1986). Face-to-face groups tend to be more "lively", which may explain the observed tendency of face-to-face groups to consult more cards, make more regression plots and spend some more time discussing and changing decision cards. Mediated groups, having less freedom of interaction, tend to be more "serious".

The question remains whether the experiment we described in this paper is appropriate for generalizing the conclusion that communication technology does not impact group decision making performance. We think that at least some mitigating comments are in order.

First, we must consider the decision making task that was studied in the experiment. Measuring decision making performance remains a tricky issue. In particular, correlation between indicators for the quality of the decision process and those for the quality of decision outcome is low (see Table 9).

Table 9 Correlations between decision quality indicators

Variables	*Profit score*	*Market share*
A. # cards	0.13	0.34
B. # decision changes	0.18	0.25
C. # regression plots	-0.22	-0.23

Secondly, it may be that in the artificial decision making context used in the experiment, the subjects rapidly develop what Rasmussen (1982) defines as problem solving at the rule-based level. This would mean that the results may not be generalized to problem solving at the knowledge-based level, i.e., decision making in unique, unfamiliar situations for which actions must be planned from an analysis and decision based on knowledge of the functional, physical properties of the system and of the various goals. Although the study was intended to measure the impact of communication technologies on group decision making in equivocal situations, it is questionable whether such conditions have indeed been achieved.

Although each of these considerations cautions us not to jump to optimistic conclusions regarding the feasibility of international offices of the future, the fact remains that in the situation as studied, students seriously working on a non-trivial excercise using "leaner" communication media showed no degradation in task performance. If anything, it is an intriguing indication that makes us look forward to seeing more empirical findings in this area.

Acknowledgments

The authors wish to thank Erik Andriessen, Jelle Atema, Henk Sol and Jeroen van der Velde for their respective contributions to this research.

6 REFERENCES

Adams, D.A, Todd, P.A., and Nelson, R.R. (1993) A comparative evaluation of the impact of electronic and voice mail on organizational communication. *Information & Management*, **24**(1).

Bots, P.W.G., Glasson, B.C., Vogel, D.R., eds. (1995) *The International Office of the Future: A Problem Analysis*, Technische Bestuurskunde, Delft University of Technology, Delft, The Netherlands. URL: http://www.sepa.tudelft.nl/~afd_sk/pb_iofapa.html.

Bots, P.W.G, Van Schaik, F.D.J. and Sol, H.G. (1989) A gaming environment for testing decision support systems. *Proceedings of the third European Simulation Congress*, Edinburgh, Scotland.

Canning McNurlin, B. (1989) Experiences with work group computing. *IS/Analyzer*.

Chappell, D.A., Vogel, D.R. and Roberts, E.E. (1992) The MIRROR project: A virtual meeting place. *Proceedings of the 25th Hawaii International Conference on System Sciences* (eds. J.F. Nunamaker and R.H. Sprague), volume IV.

Chernoff, H. (1973) Using faces to represent points in k-dimensional space graphically. *Journal of the American Statistical Society*, **68**, 361–368.

Daft, R.L. and Lengel, R.H. (1986) Organizational Information Requirements, Media Richness and Structural Design. *Management Science*, **32**(5), 554–571.

Daft, R.L., Lengel, R.H., Trevino, L.K. (1987), Message equivocality, media selection, and manager performance: implications for information systems. *MIS Quarterly*, **11**, 355-366.

Dennis, A.R., George, J.F., Jessup, L.M., Nunamaker, J.F., Vogel, D.R. (1988) Information technology to support electronic meetings. *MIS Quarterly*, **12**, 591-624

DeSanctis, G., Gallupe, R.B. (1987) A Foundation for the Study of Group Decision Support Systems. *Management Science,* **33**(5), 589-609.

El-Shinnawy, M.M., Markus, M.L. (1992) Media richness theory and new electronic communication media: a study of voice mail and electronic mail. *Proceedings of ICIS'92*, Dallas, USA.

Fowler, G., Wackerbarth, M. (1988) Audio Teleconferencing versus Face-to-Face Conferencing: A synthesis of the Literature. *Western Journal of Speech Communication*, **44**, 236-252.

Galbraith, J.R. (1977) *Organization Design: An information processing view*, Addison-Wesley, New York.

Janis, I.L., Mann, L. (1977) *Decision Making*, The Free Press, New York.

Kinney, S.T., Watson, R.T. (1992), The effect of medium and task on dyadic communication, *Proceedings of ICIS'92*, Dallas, USA, 107-117.

Korhonen, P. (1991) Using harmonious houses for visual pairwise comparison of multiple criteria alternatives, *Decision Support Systems*, **7**, 47-54.

Kotteman, J.E., Remus, W.E. (1991) The effects of decision support systems on performance. *Environments for Supporting Decision Processes* (eds. Sol, H.G., Vecsenyi, J.), North-Holland, Amsterdam.

McCarthy, J., Miles, V., Monk, A., Harrison, M., Dix, A., Wright, P. (1991) Four generic communication tasks which must be supported in electronic conferencing. *SIGCHI Bulletin*, January 1991.

McGrath, J.E., Kelley, J.R. (1986) *Time and human interaction: towards a social psychology of time*. Guildford, New York.

McGrath, J.E., Hollingshead, A.B. (1994) *Groups interacting with technology*. Sage library of social research, 194.

Oz, E., Fedorowicz, J., Stapleton, T. (1993) Improving quality, speed and confidence in decision making. Measuring expert system benefits. *Information Management*, **24**, 71-82.

Rasmussen, J. (1982) Human errors. A taxonomy for describing human malfunction in industrial installations, *Journal of Occupational Accidents*, **4**.

Rice, R.R. (1984) *The new media: Communication Research and Technology.* Sage, Beverly Hills, CA.

Sheffield, J. (1995) The Effect of Communication Medium on Negotiation Performance. *Group Decision and Negotiation*, **4**(2), 159-179.

Van Schaik, F.D.J. (1988) *Effectiveness of decision support systems*, Delft University Press, Delft, the Netherlands.

Van der Velden, J.M. (1995) *Samenwerken op afstand*, Delft University Press, Delft, the Netherlands (in Dutch).

Weick, K.E. (1979) *The social psychology of organizing*, Addison-Wesley, Reading, MA.

7 BIOGRAPHY

Pieter Bots is associate professor at the School of Systems Engineering, Policy Analysis and Management of Delft University of Technology, the Netherlands. He has a Master's degree in Computer Science from the University of Leiden and a Ph.D. in Information Systems from Delft University of Technology. His main research interest lies in the analysis and design of policy and decision making processes and supporting information systems in both public and private organizations.

Robert Jan Streng is consultant with BSO-ORIGIN Consultancy in Utrecht, the Netherlands. He has a Master's degree in Computer Science and a Ph.D. in Information Systems, both from Delft University of Technology. His expertise lies in business process reengineering, EDI and interorganizational information systems.

6

An internet realtime conference: design, experience and future applications

Ifay F. Chang, Ph.D., Li-Chieh Lin
Polytechnic Research Institute for Development and Enterprise
Polytechnic University
36 Saw Mill River Road
Hawthorne, New York 10532, USA
Tel: (914) 323-2061, Fax:(914) 323-2010
E-Mail: ifay@quasar.poly.edu

Abstract

This paper outlines the design of an Internet Realtime Conference (IRC) and reports on the experiences gained in running it. The IRC is believed to be the first ever full scale technical conference conducted over Internet in real time. The system architecture, software design and realtime conference procedure are illustrated. The first hand experience of running the conference and the conference attendees feedback are reported and analyzed. The technology issues and extensibility of IRC are discussed in view of encouraging results. Other possible applications based on the concept and system solution developed are pointed out.

Keywords

Internet Realtime Conference, Internet Applications, Homepage

1 INTRODUCTION

Internet has its roots in academic institutions and, for years, was principally used as a communications tool for researchers (Krol 1994). However, its recent rapid growth both in the number of nodes and in the number of users at non-academic institutions and organizations has stimulated many more applications. Numerous information services now appear on the Internet overshadowing the previous research and academic usage of the network.

While the new information service applications are valuable and interesting to the academic community, there are other possible applications on the Internet being developed by and for the academic community. In this paper, we report a new application of Internet, namely the Internet Realtime Conference (IRC). With rapid advances in sciences and technologies, there are many technical conferences being organized each year. These technical conferences are vital to researchers and professionals. Many need to participate not only in new specialty meetings but also in the meetings of overlapping disciplines. However, academicians, increasingly find it difficult to attend conferences due to the travel time and cost. This is a particular problem in the case of a global conference. In a global conference, the potential rewards are high but so are the costs. This dilemma caused us to develop an IRC model. The IRC can offer almost all of the features of a conventional conference yet is more economical in terms of cost and time.

One of the major benefits in attending conferences is the social interaction. One may argue that communication technology even with video bandwidth may never be able to provide the same experience as meeting colleagues face-to-face. However, while funds available for travel and meetings are shrinking and meeting organizers are under pressure to increase revenue by cramming a lot of activities in a few days, hence, expensive registration fees, it is difficult for conference attendees to justify the costs. Furthermore, an activity crammed conference does not give people much chance to engage in meaningful interaction in a leisurely manner. Therefore, the motivation behind the IRC is that we would like to use communication technology to simulate technical conferences with the hope that solutions may be developed to augment or even transform our present day costly and ineffective conferences. It is anticipated that Internet technology may be used to increase the participation of certain meetings both in frequency and duration and to moderate the need for attending other meetings, perhaps in part-time bases. We believe that the cost of conducting IRC can be very low, therefore, the above objective can be easily met. New communication technology may also provide new forms of interaction which can improve the effectiveness of a conference. For example, video conference technology has been used in a physical conference to link remote facilities. Internet web pages have been used to solicit conference papers. On-line post-conference forums have been used to strengthen interaction following a meeting.

In this paper, we report the first full scale IRC, which was sponsored by the Global Information and Software Society (GISSIC95, October 17-20, 1995) and supported by Polytechnic University (Polytechnic University 1996). The authors designed, participated and monitored the conference. The next section describes the conference system architecture and design, The details of our first hand experience with IRC is reported in section 3, section 4 discusses future extensions of IRC and possible other applications. Concluding remarks are given in section 5.

2 SYSTEM ARCHITECTURE AND DESIGN

World Wide Web (WWW) is an extremely effective mechanism for distributing and sharing information. The IRC system design takes full advantage of the Internet architecture. In the following, we describe the architecture and design of GISSIC95 - a virtual conference environment accessible via the Homepage. The basic idea of IRC is to build an environment, where conference preparation can be processed via Internet and attendees can investigate conference papers and discuss with authors or other attendees in realtime in the conference sense supported by multimedia and hypermedia technologies through the global network. Figure 1 gives the general system architecture with the Polytechnic University network system specifically defined. The client site can generally be a LAN supported site with or without a dedicated server for enhancing the system performance. At least, a dedicated HTTP (HyperText Transfer Protocol) server is required to store and fetch conference papers. The load may be distributed if multiple servers are linked to share the load. The HTTP server, located at New York, USA, runs on a Sun SPARC-20 with 128M RAM and RAID Level 3 disk subsystem. It connects to a 10 Mb/s Ethernet LAN and T3 link to the Internet. Papers are stored as separate HTML (HyperText Markup Language) files on local hard disk or machines over the network. Clients from different countries send requests to the server using HTTP protocol. The protocol provides very fast search and retrieval capability of ASCII text over a Telnet-style Internet protocol but for displaying images or video it requires extensive network bandwidth hence a time consuming task for users outside of the US. The more generic system architecture is a distributed system where multiple servers are distributed world-wide. A particular server may be selected to host a particular session of papers for operational ease as well as for balancing the information retrieval load. Digital library technology (Fox 1994) and Network Multimedia File System (NMFS) (Patel 1992) protocol will be very useful for multimedia presentation and system performance. However, these were not incorporated in the GISSIC95.

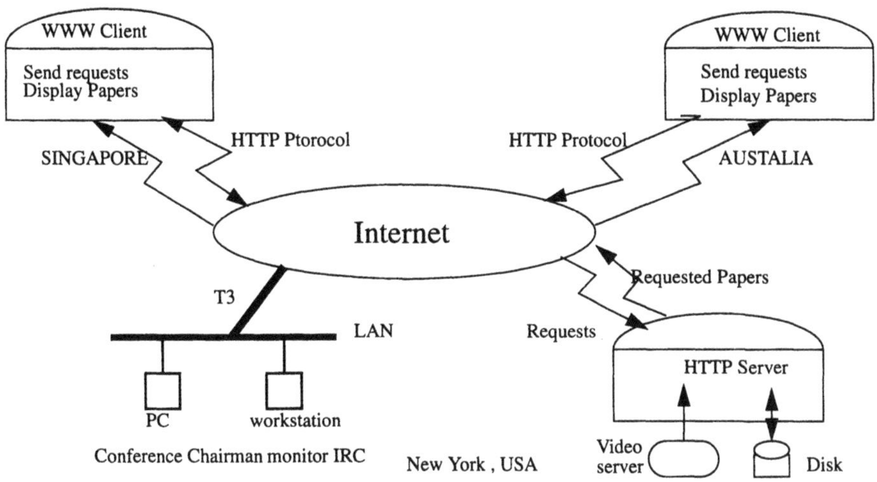

Figure 1 GISSIC '95 system architecture

On the user interface design, a number of alternatives were developed. The final choice was very much influenced by the size of the conference. Since the GISS conference is young and the IRC model is new, GISSIC95 did not get a large number of papers as desired. A simple user interface was adopted. The system provides an opening screen containing a list of paper titles with hyperlinks to full papers. The attendees can read HTML format papers (with ASCII text, images and even MPEG video clips, however, none of the conference papers provided video). HTML does not contain information about fonts and paragraph spacing which should be used for displaying the papers. On the one hand, this gives great advantage in that HTML format papers can be rendered successfully on whatever platforms they are viewed. On the other hand, the original author 's intended format is not guaranteed which sometimes annoys the readers and the authors. This is an issue deserving some consideration in future IRC; perhaps a user defined common standard should be adopted. To help navigating within the paper lists, the attendees use an interface matrix to link to a specific paper. During or after viewing the paper, attendees can access related information by clicking references (hyperlinks) if provided or can send questions or comments to authors by on-line

Q&A HTML forms. The HTTP server sends questions to authors using CGI (Common Gateway Interface) (CGI 1996) mail gateway. The authors send explanations back via e-mail which can contain textual data, images, WWW sites leading to other files, a bibliography or further references, etc. Listserv (Listserv Server 1996) is used by the conference organizers and attendees to distribute ideas, questions and answers or to organize fora. At GISSIC95, two post-conference fora were organized.

A conference program structure and its operating rules have been defined for the users to follow. Although they are specific for GISSIC95, they can serve as a reference for other IRC's. The GISSIC95 program consists of a keynote speech, invited papers and contributed papers. Papers are accessible during specified dates, over 24 hours per day with US Eastern Standard Time as the conference standard time. Authors of accepted papers are given specific time slots to receive questions and comments (limited to 1KB) and append responses to their papers (limited to a total of 10KB). The questions and responses must be addressed to the authors and session chairpersons and copied to the conference chairman. The session chairperson has the duty to monitor the Q&A process making sure it is properly and effectively done. On the last day of the conference, all Q&A will be accessible for review.

3 FIRST HAND EXPERIENCE WITH IRC

IRC is different from conventional conferences in that its conference structure and operational rules are implemented to make this conference intensively focused and efficient in information exchange and peer interaction. Preparation of the GISSIC95 took less than 6 months which is very efficient compared to a conventional conference taking about 12-24 months. (The six months included the delay caused by the author (IFC) moving from an industry position to an academic position, hence, the entire process may take even less time if no firewall had to be dealt with). As shown in Figure 2, the workflow of preparing & running a conference can be represented by a set of function modules. The first module is organizing the conference committee. The conventional way may take more than 2 months (phone calls, snail mails, even physical meetings may be required, of course rarely one can get everyone to agree on a singe date to attend the physical meeting) whereas GISSIC95 only took 3 weeks to organize the committee by sending and receiving HTML forms for confirmation. Due to the lack of a credible past for GISSIC95 as a viable conference in an IRC model, there was difficulty to organize an enthusiastic committee for the first time. This, in our analysis, is not due to the mechanism of the IRC model. They next module is publishing and distributing Call For Papers. The conventional way needs to schedule physical meetings to discuss themes, topics, sessions, schedule, etc. GISSIC95 used Listserv services to discuss those issues and took only one month. Instead of sending snail mail for registrations, all GISSIC95 registrations are done by on-line processing. Naturally, the conference may have missed some individuals who do not have access to the Internet. Naturally, the conference took the position that since the growth of the Internet users may exceed the population of the earth by the year 2000, according to its current growth rate, it is reasonable to assume that IRC can reach everyone. GISSIC95 is meant to be an experiment for assessing the effectiveness of the IRC model. The next module is paper submission where authors submit papers on-line and the system will automatically distribute papers to the proper committee members with an evaluation form for review. After reviewing, the committee members send back the evaluation forms and the system will automatically collect and rank scores for further review and confirmation. Unfortunately, GISSIC95 was not overwhelmed by paper submissions, hence the paper review and ranking process was not used.

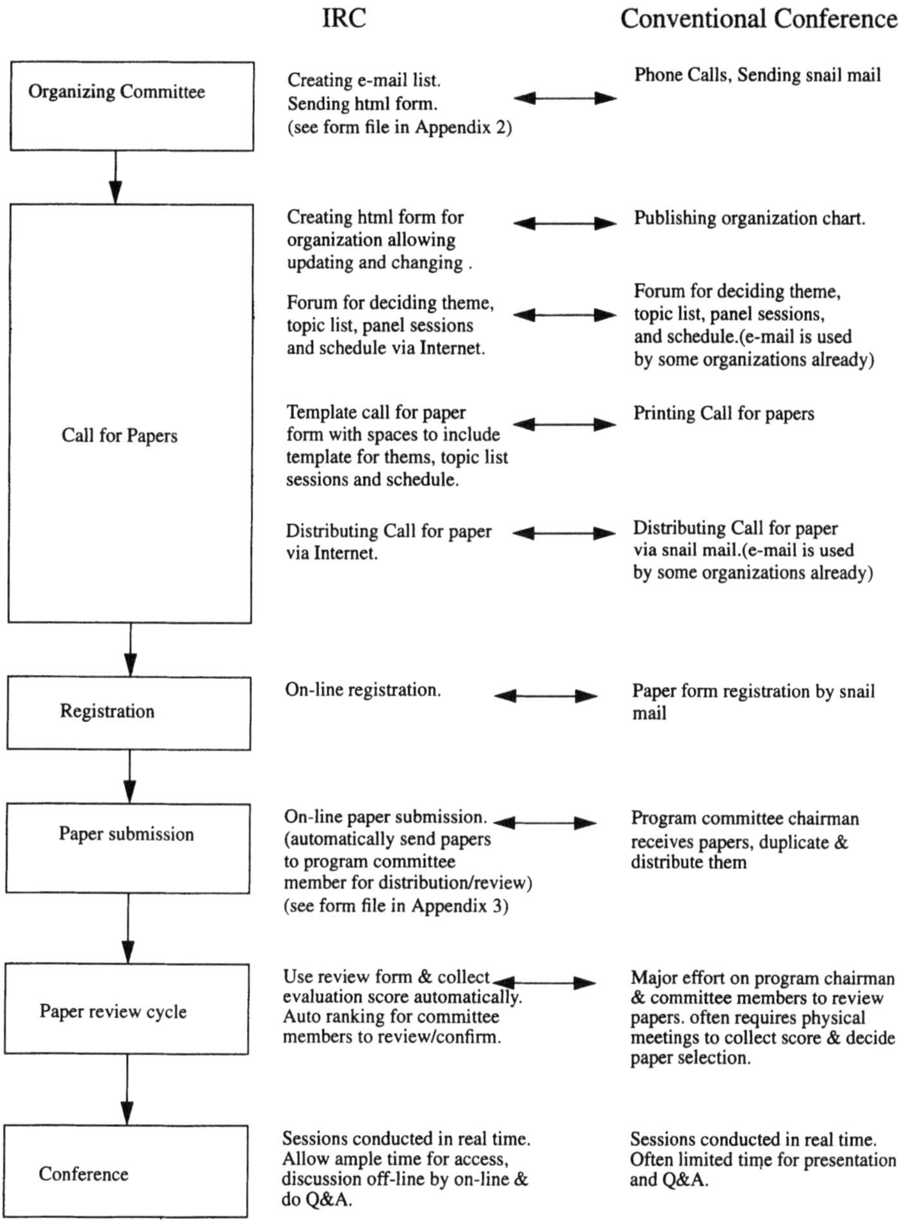

Figure 2 Workflow - IRC vs. conventional conference.

Both IRC and conventional conferences are conducted in realtime. In the conventional conference, there is a serious time limitation for both presentations and Q&A periods. IRC stretches its realtime procedure to allow detailed presentations to get ideas across and ample time for Q&A. In the conventional conference, authors have no way of sorting out questions by priority or refer to a co-author and other colleagues for giving meaningful answers. IRC accommodates multiple authors and cross references in dealing with Q&A. In the conventional conference, people are required to pay extreme attention to the presenter or to listen to the condensed speech. It is also extremely difficult to attend concurrent sessions and absorb everything. IRC allows attendees to take time to digest the paper and to hop across sessions without losing information perhaps even gaining correlated information. The paper proceedings of a conventional conference in a full paper version distributed at the conference would be useful for the attendees and could serve some of the purposes stated above, however, often they were too heavy to carry and too expensive to purchase and rarely in full paper version. The worst of it in a conventional conference is that one cannot easily identify the authors on site to shoot off a burning question. IRC e-mail is a good remedy to that.

There were more than 300 attendees from a dozen countries in the four-day IRC conference. There were more than 1800 browsers to the GISS homepage which links to the GISSIC95 conference. The four-day event ran smoothly except that some of the conference staff, including the authors, had to stay up late hours. (Well, we do that in conventional conference for different reasons). We were excited to know about what and how everything was going on. An official survey was conducted at the end of the conference. A lot of positive feedback was received even months after the conference. A summary of these comments, good and bad, stated below can certainly serve as a good guide for the future IRC's. Most attendees like this type of conference citing the following: 1) it is convenient to access updated information, 2) it fits in their time schedule (since the conference is 24 hours), 3) there is no reason to leave work (or office), 4) to know people in other countries working on the same topics (GISSIC95 had a strong Australian presence), 5) enjoyed the questions and answers posted behind the presentation and 6) the cost is low (GISS decided a registration fee of $20 but waived it after receiving an anonymous donation).

There were, of course, some negative comments as well. The most cited were 1) it loses the social aspect of meeting people (IRC encourages post-conference meetings for people to meet fact to face; even when video conferencing technology becomes affordable in a ubiquitous way; this requirement will still not be satisfied), 2) the response time of their systems are too long (these mostly come from outside the US. It is the network bandwidth issue, hopefully it will be improved as the global information infrastructure advances). Overall, the feedback is very encouraging. The authors are motivated to improve the system solution for future IRC's. Table 1 summarizes a list of Do's and Don'ts based on user feedback.

Table 1 Dos and don'ts list

Dos	Don'ts
Use distributed servers to improve system response time and balance system load	Avoid using too many images and graphics in the paper
Adopt standard paper format and user interface	Do not over use hyperlinks
Test system performance before conference begin	Do not have dead-end links
Encourage Post-conference meetings for follow up	Do not use browser specific enhancements

4 FUTURE EXTENSION AND OTHER APPLICATIONS

The first IRC conference offered a learning vehicle for defining a new conference paradigm and for developing appropriate groupware and software system for other applications. The first implementation had concentrated on interactive session activities to mimic a conventional conference's good features, to exploit the asynchronous characteristics of the internet and its future synchronous interaction possibilities. In a conventional conference, there is a standard set of audio-visual equipments and tools available to the presenters. These might include a whiteboard, projector, video play and sound system. The virtual conference environment can have equivalent equipment and tools using network-based software applications. Some of these tools are available and some are still emerging. Their potential use in a virtual conference environment is not yet understood which is definitely worthy of research. Some of the tools which may be considered for future IRC are:

- The whiteboard: the presenter will make use of a whiteboard for further clarification of a point. In an Internet environment the presenter may make use of shared whiteboard tools such as NCSA Collage (NCSA Collage 1996) and XTV (XTV 1996). Such tools allow images to be displayed, manipulated, annotated, and shared between two readers or among a group of people.
- The Video conferencing: Body language is one component of physical contact that is difficult to convert to pre-packaged text and still images. Incorporation of these might be accomplished in the future through video teleconferencing technologies over the Internet to achieve realtime effect. Work on the MBONE (Kumer 1994) and the CUSeeMee (Cogger 1994) have potential in this area.
- The Video/Audio Clips: Using video/audio clips managed by video servers (Chaney) can also achieve realtime effects or give demonstration support. They may be used in Keynote speech or vendor exhibits.
- The Forum/Panel discussion: An important part of any conference is the personal interactions as questions and answers discussed. Use of a listserv to redistribute e-mail questions or a usenet newsgroup are simple methods for sharing this interaction. A more dynamic period could be created using a chat session such as Global Chat (Global Chat Servers 1996). These, however, may require a different culture and a different interaction style. Although these communication styles are new but they may be more effective for large IRC's.
- The note: In a conventional conference, the attendees use pen or pencil to take notes on what is spoken. The presenter will use pen or pencil to jot down important points. The annotation capability with Netscape or Mosiac browsers is very limited. CoNote (Davis 1996) annotation system may be explored. The creation and use of audio-visual tools for IRC over the Internet are still problematic. The same functionality (or at least interpretability) must be available across all popular operating systems and graphic user interfaces. These are technical challenges for IRC designers. Java language (Java Programmer's Guide 1996) which is a machine independent and distributed Internet programming language may be used to build an interface for IRC.
- A graphical user Interface tool: A set of standards perhaps should be defined for IRC to facilitate the design of a common user interface for a particular IRC.

Although the present system does not have many of the function support discussed above, the system architecture is quite generic in that the new functions can be used for many other applications involving data transactions and data processing in a realtime application scenario. Examples may be Internet courseware for distance learning or conducting board meetings over the Internet or even running a university over the Internet. The non-education related applications are beyond the scope of this paper. We list only a number of educational applications in Table 2. The applications listed have been differentiated from one (teacher) to N (students) teaching style with low interaction to an M (teachers) to N (students) teaching style. The latter paradigm (M to N interactive teaching) is the basis for the CARE project, Cyberspace Assisted Responsive Education (Chang 1995). A virtual learning environment is being built for CARE which supports M (teachers) to N (students) teaching style and a non-linear learning style can certainly benefit from the IRC system.

Table 2 Characteristics of Applications

Application	Description	Data Flow	User Interaction	Duration
Boradcasting Services	One sender many receivers	1 -> N	None	Minutes to days
Seminar / Lecture	Lecture with discussion	1 -> N	Low	Hours
Internet Conference	Q&A from a subset of participants	M -> N (M << N)	Moderated	Days
Workshop / Forum	Group discussion	M -> N	High	Days
Courseware for distance learning	Group of students learn from group of teachers	M -> N	High	Weeks to months
Internet University or Care	Virtual campus or alliances of universities	M -> N	High	Years

It is envisioned that with proper system design, a realtime application scenario conducted over the Internet not only can achieve realtime responses (given sufficient network bandwidth and computer processing power) but also can obtain realtime computer compiled statistics to support the application, for instance, tallying scores, counting votes or executing Robert's rules.

5 CONCLUSIONS

We reported the design and experience of running an IRC. The IRC application models the conventional conferences and provides similar features and functions except each attendee participates in the conference at his or her computer, in office, in laboratory or at home via Inter access. A distributed server system is used to support the multiple sessions of the conference conducted in realtime. Homepages are programmed to serve as the user interface for conference participants. Functions of query, registration, paper submission and question and answer period for each paper are all conducted on-line with electronic form and electronic mail. Browsing of the news bulletin, registration of the conference and reading of each paper are tallied, hence at any given time, available as statistics at his or her fingertips (so to speak). The keynote paper can be either broadcast to a large mailing list or accessed the same way as the contributed papers. Session chairpersons are responsible for monitoring the paper sessions and have a duty to receive and transmit questions and answers between audience and authors. The Q&A sessions are posted for each paper and made reviewable at designated time periods. The conference encourages "off-site" or off-line on-line (in the jargon of Internet) correspondences of private discussions or organizing and conducting fora on some specific topics. A conference's content can only be as good as the organizers' effort to invite and/or solicit good papers. The entire process of organizing the committee, calling for papers and executing subsequent tasks is supported and conducted over the Internet.

The missing element of social (face-to-face) interaction in IRC is an issue that will not be solvable in the near future. Post IRC physical meetings may be used as a remedy. The advanced audio and video communication technologies may also be employed as partial solutions.

Based on our experience and user feedback discussed above, the authors believe that the model of an Internet Realtime Conference may very well be proven to be more effective than conventional conferences in many ways. Hence, the GISSIC95 experiment may trigger a paradigm shift in conferences especially those with a large global participation. People aided with computers are multi-tasking ever more than before. It is becoming increasingly difficult for people to drop everything else for a long period of time to attend a conference no matter how attractive the location may be. Hence a realtime event involving a large number of people from distributed places may be better off conducted on an Internet where flexible attendance and mutlitasking can be reasonably maintained. The first IRC was considered successful. The attendees' feedback are mostly positive. This encouraged us to consider further enhancement for IRC and to extend the system software to work for other applications.

The IRC support software developed by the authors can be licensed free of charge for non-profit usage per request basis. Please contact authors (ifay@quasar.poly.edu) for further information.

6 ACKNOWLEDGEMENT

The authors thank the Global Information and Software Society, for its generous support in conducting the first Internet Realtime Conference, and a number of colleagues, David Chang, Tony Monteiro, Wey Chang, Yu Zeng, T.W. Ma, Jintae Lee and P.S. Chang, whose encouragement and support are greatly appreciated.

7 REFERENCES

Ed Krol (1994) *The Whole Internet User's Guide & Catalog*, O'reilly & Associates, Inc.

GISSIC (1996) *Homepage*, http://quasar.poly.edu/~llin/GISS.

Polytechnic University (1996) *Homepage*, http://www.poly.edu.

Edward A. Fox, A. Abdulla, Ghaleb (1994) *Digital video for a digital library in computer science*, Proceedings of SPIE - The International Society for Optical Engineering v 2188.

S. Patel, G. Adbulla, M. Abrams and E. Fox, (1992) *NMFS: Network Multimedia File System Protocol* in Networking and Operating System Support for Digital Audio and Video: Third International Workshop, La Jolla, CA, Nov.

CGI (Common Gateway Interface) (1996), http://wwww.w3.org/hypertext/WWW/CGI/Overview.html

The Listserv Server (1996), http://www.earn.net/lug/server.html

NCSA, Collage (1996) http://www.ncsa.uiuc.edu/SDG/Software/XCollage/collage.html

XTV (1996) http://fiddle.ee.vt.edu/succeed/xtv.html

Kumer, V. Forum (1994) *The MBONE Information. Enterprise Integration Technologies* http://www.eit.com/techinfo/mbone/mbone.html

Cogger, D. (1994) *CUSeeMe*. Cornell University, http://www1.cern.ch/PapersWWW94/speh.ps

Alan Chaney, Ian Wilson, Andy Hepper, *The design and Implementation of a (RAID)-3 Multimedia File Server*, in Networking and Operating System Support for Digital Audio and Video: Fifth International Workshop

Global Chat Servers (1996) http://www.prospero.com/

Davis, J. Huttenlocher, D.(1996)*Annotation Homepage*, http://dri.cornell.edu/pub/davis/annotation.html

The Java Programmer's Guide (1996) http://java.sun.com/doc/programmer.html

Chang, Ifay F.(1995) *Paradigm Shifts in Education and A Future Education Solution (CARE)*, presented at GISSIC95 Oct. 17-20, on the Internet, to appear in Proceedings of GISSIRC'95

8 BIOGRAPHY

Ifay Chang is the Executive Director of Polytechnic Research Institute for Development and Enterprise and a professor at the department of the Computer and Information Science and the department of Electrical Engineering of the Polytechnic University. Dr. Chang received his BSEE from National Cheng Kung University and his MSEE and Ph.D. from University of Rhode Island. His present research interests include telecommunication and computer network technologies and applications, software technology and development, multimedia technology and media creation , and network-based applications such as information services, telemedicine, video on demand, distanceless learning and Internet Realtime Conference.

Li-Chieh Lin is a Ph..D student at Polytechnic University. His research interests are in distributed system, distance learning, Internet information services and WWW applications. He received his B.S. degree from National Chaio Tung University and M.S. degree from Polytechnic University.

7

Telecommunication and an information infrastructure in China

W. G. Chismar
University of Hawaii
College of Business Administration
2404 Maile Way
Honolulu HI 96822
(808) 956-7276 telephone
(808) 956-9889 fax
chismar@dscience.cba.hawaii.edu

Abstract

International telephony and computer networks now play a critical role in managing an international company. Unfortunately for companies doing business in China, reliable connections to these networks have only recently become available in the major cities and are non existent in most of the country. In response, the Chinese government has made telecommunications a priority in its efforts to promote economic development; but its efforts have been hindered by conflicting political and business interests. In this paper we look at the two aspects of the development of the information infrastructure in China: telecommunications development and the Internet. Currently the central government maintains tight control over telecommunications development, but this control is quickly breaking down. The Internet in China has been developing in a totally separate environment, largely out of the control of the central government. While control over telecommunications appears to be relaxing, control over the Internet has suddenly tightened. This paper presents the evolution of these policies.

Keywords

China, Telecommunications, Internet, Policy

1 INTRODUCTION

Access to information and connections to international locations are key to the development of the economy in China. In attempting to sustain very rapid economic development, China is luring in foreign companies at an amazing rate. Unfortunately for companies doing business in China, reliable connections to computer and telecommunication networks have only recently become available in the major cities and are non existent in most of the country. In response, the Chinese government has made telecommunications a priority in its efforts to promote economic development; but its efforts have been hindered by conflicting political and business interests.

The Chinese political system is based on a tradition of strong central control of information and a society closed to foreign influences. With Deng Xiaoping's reforms in 1979, China moved toward a more open door policy. As this policy created rapid economic growth in cities along the eastern coast and in the south of China, it became clear that China's telecommunication infrastructure was woefully inadequate. In addition, it was clear that the strict monopolistic control of telecommunications could not respond fast enough the demands placed on it. In the 1990's China began to reform its telecommunication policies, though it maintained strong regulations.

In contrast, the Internet in China evolved very rapidly in the 1990's, largely out of the control of the central government. Networks from academic and research organizations linked together and then opened gateways to the Internet. But the openness brought by the Internet would not long be tolerated by the central government. Recent policy changes have drastically changed the nature of the Internet in China. Control over the Internet is being placed in ministries traditionally in charge of telecommunications.

In the next section of this paper, we look at the recent development and structure of telecommunications in China. This is followed by a parallel presentation of the development of the Internet in China. The final section discusses the policies of the Chinese government and the merger of the Internet and telecommunications control.

2 TELECOMMUNICATIONS

The roles of the major players in China's telecommunication industry are undergoing a revolution of sorts. For many years, the Ministry of Post and Telecommunications represented the government's monopoly in three roles: the national public service provider; policy maker and regulator of telecommunications at the national, provincial, and municipal levels; and equipment manufacturing (Tan 1994). In the face of rapidly expanding demand for telecommunication services, the MPT, like so many other telecommunication monopolies, has been very slow to respond. Directly under the MPT are the provincial Posts and Telephone Administrations (PTAs). Reporting to the PTAs are the city Posts and Telephone Bureaus (PTB), which, in the face of the MPT's slowness to respond to market demands, have been exhibiting increasing degrees of independence from the MPT. Since 1978 they have been able to retain part of their revenue for reinvestment and encouraged to seek investments (Tan 1994). The southern PTBs of Guandong and Jiangsu are quite autonomous, driven by the greater economic activity in the south.

In addition to the MPT with its public networks, several ministries, notably those of railways (MOR), electronic industries (MEI), and power (MOP), and the People's Liberation Army (PLA) have been allowed to develop, own, and operate their own telecommunication networks. By law, they have been prohibited from providing public services over their networks. However, as it became clear that the MPT was unable to meet the telecommunications demands of China, the ministries, PLA, and PTBs began to enter the public telecommunications market. The MPT has shown a willingness to ignore or a political inability to counter these activities (Bien 1994).

In 1992, the Ministry of Electronics Industry (MEI) joined with the Ministry of Railways and the Ministry of Electronics to form a "united telecommunications company," Lian Tong, also known as Unicom and more recently, China Com. Lian Tong was formed primarily as a data network operator, but with clear intentions of competing directly with MPT on private networks (Tan 1994). In light of opposition from the MPT and the reiteration of MPTs monopoly by the State Council, Lian Tong got off to a very slow start.

In September of 1993, the MEI and Lian Tong formed a new company, Ji Tong. Ji Tong also has a list of minor shareholders consisting of about 20 Chinese companies. MEI, under the pro-telecom-reform leadership of Hu Qili, was positioning itself to confront MPTs monopoly by having Lian Tong established as the owner of a national data network and Ji Tong as the provider of services over the network (Business China, 9/19/94).

In December of 1993, it appeared that the State Council had given approval to Lian Tong to establish a second national voice and fax network. However, the MPT seem reluctant to accept a second national network and doubts grew over Lian Tong's long term viability. Despite this opposition, Lian Tong is clearly building a long distance network based on the railway ministry's existing network (Anonymous 1994).

When Lian Tong gained approval to compete with MPT, the need for Ji Tong reduced and Ji Tong lost the active support of the MEI (Business China, 9/19/94). With Lian Tong focusing on the bread-and-butter business of public voice and fax services, Ji Tong differentiated itself by focusing on more specialized services. In a rapid start, Ji Tong signed joint-venture agreements with foreign companies, including BellSouth for network planning and engineering services and IBM. It has undertaken some large projects, including the Golden Gate, an electronic data interchange network (EDI), the Golden Card, a national credit card clearing system, and the Golden Bridge, links among large national data centers. (Hendry 1994).

In 1994 China began a reorganization of the MPT which included the separation of roles of network operator and regulator. The Directorate General of Telecommunications, formerly under the MPT, is now the operator of China's public telecommunication networks, while the MPT it will remain the national regulator of the networks with the authority to license operators (Anonymous 1994). According to MPT's chief of information, the reorganization will lay the groundwork for setting up a national telecommunications service company with regional subsidiaries formed out of the existing PTBs (Hendry 1994).

3 THE INTERNET

China's computer networks and links into the Internet have been evolving since the late 1980's, mostly independent of the telecommunication networks and direct central government control. Most of the networks serve the academic and research communities, although commercial access to the Internet has recently become available. There are currently three major networks with access to the Internet: ChinaNet/NCFC, CERNET, and ChinaNET. In addition, several smaller networks are setting up links to the Internet.

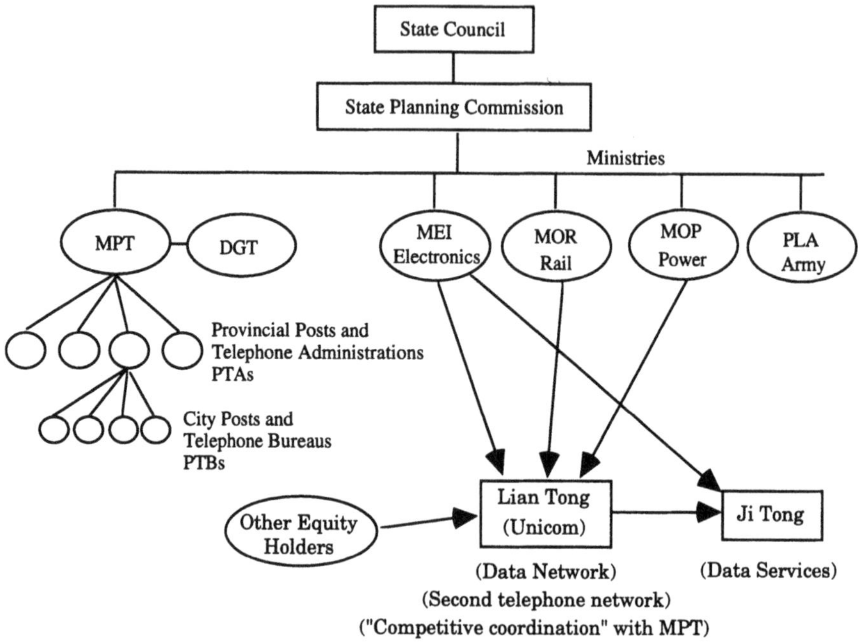

Figure 1 Telecommunications players in China.

3.1 ChinaNet/NCFC

In 1989 the World Bank and China's State Planning Commission funded development of the National Computing and Networking Facility of China (NCFC). Completed in 1993, the NFCF connected networks of the China Academy of Science (CASnet), Peking University (PUnet), and Tsinghua University (TUnet). In 1993, the IHEPnet (Institute for High Energy Physics), part of the CASnet, became the first Chinese regional network fully connected to the Internet via AT&T leased lines to the Stanford Linear Accelerator Center. In May of 1994, NCFC linked to NSFNET via a Sprint satellite link and got the country-level domain name ".CN".

While its original goal was to allow the three institutions to share computing facilities, NCFC became the core of ChinaNet, which connected the Beijing metropolitan area and other cities. Administration and operation of the ChinaNet is dominated by the China Academy of Science. In addition to NCFC, ChinaNet includes USTCnet (University of Science and Technology of China), SSTCnet (State Science and Technology Commission network), and some 20 other science-related networks. The Macau regional network and Hong Kong Chinese University network were also connected to ChinaNet.

3.2 CERNET

The China Education and Research Network (CERNET) is funded by the Chinese government and directly managed by the Chinese Sate Education Commission. With development starting in July of 1994, CERNET was modeled after the US. NSFNet project. Its goal is to link all of China's universities and eventually, other lower level schools. This includes some 1,200 universities, more than 39,000 middle schools, and 160,000 primary schools. If the proposed schedule is followed, CERNET will soon be the largest educational and research network in the world.

CERNET has a three-layer hierarchical structure: nation-wide backbone with international links, regional networks, and campus networks. The backbone nodes include ten key universities in Beijing, Shanghai, Guangzhou, Nanjing, Xian, Wuhan, Chengdu, and Shenyang. While its original link to the Internet was through NCFC, it now has an independent link to the United States, with two more soon to be added, one to Europe and one to the Asia Pacific region.

3.3 ChinaNET

China Internet (ChinaNET) is a nation-wide, general purpose public network managed by the MPT. It has links in more than 600 cities with plans to cover the country. ChinaNET evolved from the data and telephone networks of the MPT (CHINAPAC, CHINADDN, and PSTN) and began operating in the spring of 1995. Provincial telecommunication administrations manage the operation of the ChinaNET. The Beijing Telecommunication Administration manages the high speed fiber optic link among three gateways: Beijing, Shanghai, and Guangzhou. The link to the Internet is via SprintLink to the USA.

3.4 Other networks

Several smaller networks have also set up links to the Internet. The Beijing University of Chemical Technology (BUCT) connected to the Internet in September of 1994 through the Beijing Telecommunication Administration to the CAREN (Consortium of Asian Research and Education Network) and JVNCnet (John Von Neumann Center network). The Nanjing International Internet (NJNET) opened in April of 1995 with the goal of facilitating the city's science and technology development. It is now providing email services and plans to provide comprehensive information services. Other networks will likely follow.

3.5 Cooperation among internet players

China's Internet efforts have been uncoordinated and lacking in leadership for top government agencies. This is most likely the result of a lack of funds among the smaller institutions and a lack of interest and manpower by the State Planning Commission which is funding the NCFC (Tan 1996). In an effort to provide some direction, the Chinese Internet Development Policy and Technology Examination Conference was held in Beijing in August of 1995.

The participants to the conference were Chinese bureaucrats from many fields, domestic and foreign specialists, and some industry managers. The impact of the conference will be limited by the fact that it is a temporary organization without solid financial and administrative bases (Tan 1996). The conference covered

- A development vision for the Chinese Internet

- Current government policy
- Experiences and achievements of the Internet in developed countries
- Foreign advise to China
- The exchange of Internet technology and education.

4 POLICY ISSUES

Since Deng Xiaoping's reforms in 1979 China has striven to operate a "socialist market economy." Under such a system greater economic autonomy has been given to local governments, such as the special economic zones, and to business enterprises. However, this autonomy directly conflicts with the government's wish to maintain tight control over China's political, social, and industrial development. A critical component to the success of the Chinese Communist Party system has been strict control of communication within the country. A critical component to the success of a liberalize market economy is access to the means of communication, such as computer networks and international links, and the freedom to use them as, when, and how they are required (Ure 1995).

As in many other countries, the development of communication technologies and of the Internet have outpaced the regulatory processes of the government. But, in China this problem is compounded by the contradiction between the political and economics systems. The result has been a lot of confusion and uncertainty about China's policies with respect to telecommunication and the Internet, and a sever shortage of telecommunication capabilities necessary to support economic growth.

Though the official policy of the central government keeps regulatory control over all telecommunications with the MPT, the MPT has been unable or unwilling to enforce strict control. Faced with rapid economic development, poor telecommunications infrastructure, and the slowness of the MPT to respond, provincial and city governments are taking steps on their own to improve their telecommunications infrastructure. Faced with economic opportunities to capitalized on their existing private networks, ministries other than the MPT are selling services to the public. The PLA is selling satellite services; the city of Shanghai is installing its own data networks to support commerce; Ji Tong and Lian Tong are negotiating with foreign telecommunication companies.

One of the biggest issues dividing the central government and other units relates to the involvement of foreign companies in the delivery of telecommunication services. The expertise of foreign companies in the design, management, and operation of telecommunication networks and services would greatly accelerate China's development. While individual PTBs and other Chinese enterprises are speaking with foreign telecommunication companies, the MPT has reiterated its intent to enforce laws against foreign involvement in the ownership or operations of telecommunication networks.

While the Chinese government's policy toward telecommunications is one of strict central control, its attitude towards electronic bulletin boards and the Internet in general have been surprisingly relaxed, particularly in light of its massive funding of efforts like the NCFC and the CERNET (Johnson 1995). Announcements throughout 1995 from the Minister of State Planning Commission and other official committees have stressed the importance of the information industry in fueling rapid economic development and the need for investment in basic information infrastructure. All of this emphasis on rapid growth and lack of rigid controls should not be mistaken for a long term policy of information openness.

The Chinese government, through the MPT, has begun to show signs of taking over control of the Internet in China. The minister of the MPT, Wu Jichuan, has repeatedly stated that China will certainly need to impose some monitoring and restrictions over the flow of information on the Internet. He has added that China has the capability of imposing restrictions (Lu 1995). On February 4, 1996, the official Xinhua news agency stated that all computer information networks must use international channels provided by the MPT to hook up to networks abroad. All existing interactive networks, after liquidation, will be subject to management by the MPT, the MEI, the State Education Commission, and the Chinese Academy of Sciences (Li 1996). The exact implications of these restrictions remain to be seen.

These new regulations are part of a series of recent high level initiatives to control and censor information entering China from foreign news and information services. In one case, the State Council ordered foreign vendors of economic information to submit to censorship by the Communist Party's Xinhua news agency (Li 1996). Such actions clearly mark a step backward in China's drive for a more market-oriented economy.

We can expect to see a continued move toward centralizing regulatory power over both telecommunication and the Internet in the MPT. Along with this move will come increased isolation of China from the rest of the world. On the other hand, the pressure for reform will also continue to come from sectors of the country interested in economic development. With a large infrastructure and access to the Internet in place, and with the rapid economic growth over the past ten years, the current moves backwards may be temporary. But, firms interested in doing business in China should not underestimate that country's resolve to control information flows and business planning must be adjusted accordingly.

5 ACKNOWLEDGMENT

This research was partially supported by a grant from the Center for International Business Education and Research at the University of Hawaii.

6 REFERENCES

Anonymous (1994), "Business China Supplement: Telecoms," *The Economist Intelligent Unit*, May.

Bien, W. (1994) "The Prospects for Foreign Investment in China's Telecommunication Service Sector," research report, Communications and Journalism Program East-West Center.

Hendry, S. (1994) "Sunset on a monopoly?" *China Trade Report*, p. 2, March.

Johnson, A. and Liu, J. (1995) "China Opens the Internet," CND-Global, April 10.

Li, L. and Macartney, J. (1996) "Chinese Government Issues New Rules to Regulate Internet Access," China News Digest, February 6.

Lu, J. (1995) "Internet Becomes Popular in China," China Time Weekly, No. 200.

Tan, Z. (1996) "Internet in China: Growth, Competition and Policy," *Proceedings of the 18th Annual Pacific Telecommunications Conference,* Pacific Telecommunications Council, Honolulu, January.

Tan, Z. (1994) "Challenges to the MPT's monopoly," *Telecommunications Policy*, 18 (3), 174-181.

Ure, J. (1995) "Telecommunications in China and the Four Dragons," in *Telecommunications in Asia: Policy, Planning and Development,* Ure, J. (Editor), Hong Kong University Press, Hong Kong, 11-48.

7 BIOGRAPHY

William Chismar, an associate professor and chairman of Decision Sciences at the University of Hawaii, received degrees in philosophy, mathematics, and system sciences from Carnegie Mellon University. His research interests include the roles of information technology in international business, the use of information technology in structuring organizations, and the economics of information systems. His studies of international telecommunications have taken him throughout East and Southeast Asia and Australia. He is currently working on a study of telecommunication policy and the internet in China, and a study of the use of information technology for reengineering in the healthcare industry.

Cultural factors in the adoption and use of GSS

R.M. Davison
Lecturer
Department of Information Systems, City University of Hong Kong
Tat Chee Avenue, Kowloon, Hong Kong
Tel: (852) 2788-7534; Fax: (852) 2788-8694;
Email: isrobert@cityu.edu.hk

E. Jordan
Associate Professor in Management
Macquarie Graduate School of Management
Macquarie University, NSW 2109, Australia
Tel: (61) 2 850 9041; Fax: (61) 2 850 9019
Email: Ernest.Jordan@mq.edu.au

Abstract

In this research, we set the agenda for an analysis of organisations that are, or are about to, go through the process of becoming more international by upgrading their interactive communication technologies with products such as Group Support Systems (GSS). The various impacts that national culture can have on an organisation's use and adoption of GSS are identified and illustrated with examples. Two complementary models of organisational structure are also presented and analysed from the GSS perspective. The significant issues which a GSS facilitator/implementer should be aware of in different cultural environments are pointed out.

Keywords

GSS, national culture, organisational structure

1 CULTURE AND INFORMATION

Inside working organisations, as in all areas of human activity, the behaviour of people is affected by the values and attitudes that they hold. The collective patterns of behaviour are important parts of the culture of the work-group or nation, which form a backdrop against which values and attitudes are in turn developed. This cycle is expressed succinctly in Figure 1, taken from Adler (1986).

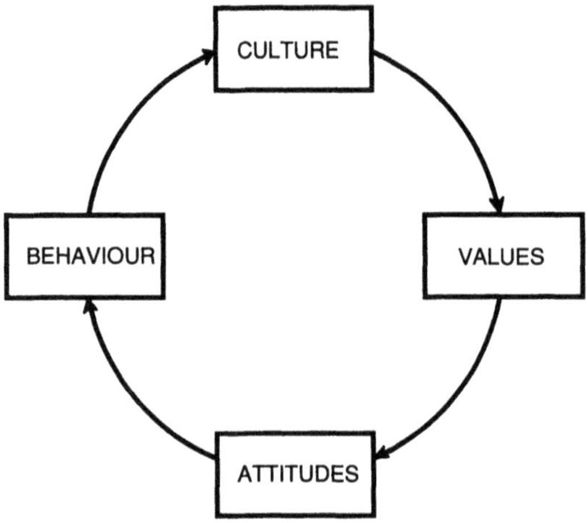

Figure 1 The influence of culture on behaviour.

Data only becomes information when it is interpreted by a person, and this interpretation of necessity takes place against the backdrop of the individual's culture (Tricker, 1988). In decision-making information is a prerequisite (Simon, 1960) and the decision-making process is deeply affected by culture (Adler, 1986). Thus the meaning of information and effectiveness of an information system can vary substantially in different cultures. National cultures have long been associated with differences in the organising and operating of businesses and, more recently, cultures specific to organisations have been studied.

In a wider sense, Ouchi (1981) signalled the importance of national values as they impact upon corporate culture. He established a clear link from Japanese national culture to the corporate cultures of major organisations and then to the outstanding success of Japanese business. His interest was the possibility of transferring or creating Japanese-like corporate values (and hence culture) in American industry in order to generate similar successes. He also reported that some American organisations already had cultures much like Japanese organisations and, he argued, this was significant in their success.

We now examine two alternative theoretical frameworks for culture that can be used to examine information, and specifically the way it is used in a GSS, in an organisational setting. Following this, we discuss how organisational culture and national culture can interact so as to produce a more or less favourable environment for GSS implementation and use. A conclusion follows with a summary of the benefits and dangers of GSS implementation and use in organisations in different cultural settings.

2 THE TRANSACTION COSTS PERSPECTIVE

From the viewpoint of Williamson (1975), organisations come into their very existence because of information. The uncertainty of the marketplace, characterised by information about transactions, drives individuals into forming or joining organisations, while the continuing uncertainty in the environment of the organisation leads it to changes in its strategy and structure. This view reduces all business activity to transactions between individuals and groups, with information as the controlling resource. While such a simple and powerful mechanism is attractive to some information technologists, giving primacy to information and economic activity, it is too simplistic to deal with the real social, psychological and political settings of most organisations. It is an example of what Bolman and Deal (1991) term the 'structural frame' of organisations and does not immediately link to the other frames – the human resource, political and cultural.

Williamson's (1975) ideas were extended by Boisot (1987). Boisot's aim is to incorporate a cultural perspective into the transactional costs approach. He looks at information in organisations through two attributes of the information, its 'codification' and 'diffusion', and the ways that these two dimensions affect information transactions:

- **codification** the degree of formal representation;
- **diffusion** the degree of spread throughout the population.

This builds on Williamson (1975) by realising that the effect of internalising the transaction within the organisation is to reduce its diffusion. Thus the diffused information in the marketplace becomes undiffused in the bureaucracy.

Dichotomising organisational forms based upon the two dimensions of codification and diffusion leads to the categories shown in Figure 2. Codified information is commonplace in formal business settings and so gives rise to the major structural forms. If information is centralised (i.e. undiffused) a bureaucracy is the form, while if it is widely distributed a market is in effect. Bureaucracies correspond closely to Williamson's description of hierarchies. The additional dimension of codification – in particular the absence of codification – produces fiefs and clans. A fief is controlled by an individual in whose mind most of the real ('soft') information resides while a clan has diffused but uncodified information, such as in a group of like-minded professionals.

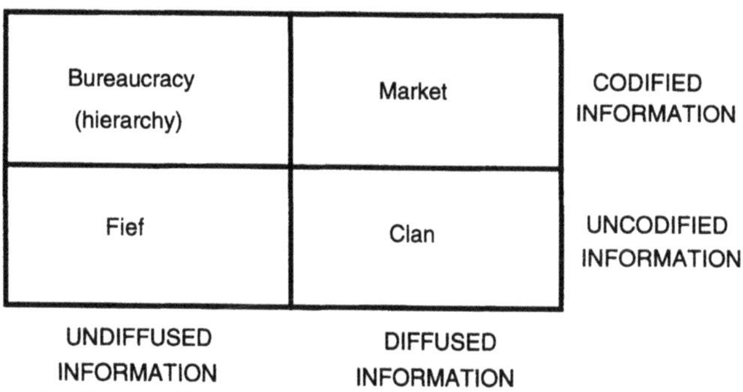

Figure 2 Organisation forms with information codification and diffusion (Boisot, 1987).

It is useful to analyse this model of information codification and diffusion from the perspective of GSS 'forces'. GSS are acknowledged as systems that provide structure to information and to the context in which that information is being used. In this way, the structuration enabled through GSS use parallels the codification of information present in bureaucracies and markets. Such codification is not present in fiefs and clans. Consequently, use of a GSS in a fief or clan context would set in motion forces to structure and codify information - processes that might well be most unwelcome to the fief and clan chiefs. These individuals are able to maintain their control (and power which we will discuss later) over their organisations through a lack of formal structuring. To replace the lack of structure with structure could well be anathema to them as it would have the potential to diminish, even remove, their means of control.

GSS, and other forms of groupware such as email, are also acknowledged as distributors and disseminators of information. The ability of an individual to send a single email message to a list of users greatly enhances the diffusion of information. Similar results are obtainable through the use of a GSS - whatever an individual types into the system will, sooner or later, be seen by all individuals participating (or authorised to participate) in that session. This feature of a GSS parallels the diffusion of information seen in clans and markets. In a perfect market, all information is known to all individuals simultaneously. In a clan, information is shared freely among the clan members - perhaps members of a board or committee where there is little variation in status (which we will also discuss later). On the other hand, bureaucracies and fiefs do not have the same level of diffusion of information. Consequently, use of a GSS in a fief or bureaucracy will set in motion forces that seek to diffuse the existing centralised information. Just as with the issue of information codification, information diffusion may be unacceptable to the chiefs of bureaucracies and fiefs and for similar reasons: when information is (more) freely available, authority that stems from sole (or restricted) possession of information is reduced.

Viewing the codification/diffusion dichotomy from this stance, we can see that, assuming the maintenance of the *status quo* to be paramount, GSS use is practical in markets, has both advantages and disadvantages in bureaucracies and clans, and is contraindicated in fiefs.

3 HOFSTEDE'S DIMENSIONS

Hofstede's (1980) massive study of national culture has since been replicated and used extensively. Its authority is enhanced by its predictive ability and its synthesis of previous partial results. Hofstede collected 117 000 questionnaires from 88 000 respondents in 66 countries, all employees of the same multinational corporation, which enabled employees in different countries to be matched. Four dimensions of national culture were found and index scores developed for each of 40 countries (Hofstede, 1980).

power distance (PDI) – the degree of inequality of power between a person at a higher level and a person at a lower level, (being subservient to the boss),

uncertainty avoidance (UAV) – the extent to which future possibilities are defended against or accepted (not facing the future or trying to organise it),

individualism (IDV) – the relative importance of individual goals compared with group or collective goals (looking after oneself),

masculinity (MAS) – the extent to which the goals of men dominate those of women (assertion - nurturance).

Power distance and individualism are strongly negatively correlated and represented only a single factor in a confirmatory factor analysis, yet Hofstede argues that they are conceptually different and were independently developed as indices with reference to extensive literature bases. Uncertainty avoidance also shows weaker correlations, positive with power distance and negative with individualism. Thus these dimensions are not orthogonal but nevertheless refer to four 'universal problems of mankind' (Hofstede, 1980).

Uncertainty avoidance is the domain of information systems, including group support systems. It is noteworthy, and perhaps paradoxical, that the significant developments in this domain have come from countries that Hofstede found to have low levels of uncertainty avoidance. In these countries, for example the USA, UK, the Netherlands and Denmark, the future is accepted as having much uncertainty with which one must live. In countries with much higher levels of uncertainty avoidance (Greece, Portugal, Mexico, Argentina) unfavourable outcomes must be controlled against. As we have already noted, GSS acts to promote information codification and structuring. These activities are typical of the approach to uncertainty undertaken by organisations in countries with high UAV scores, though organisations in countries with low UAV scores also make considerable use of them.

The second of Hofstede's dimensions that is critical to the GSS facilitator, designer or implementer is power distance, which allows for varying relationships between superiors and subordinates in organisations. The 'spirit' (DeSanctis and Poole, 1994) of GSS is that it promotes the democratic diffusion of information and decentralisation of decision making. If the boss is powerful and cannot be contradicted, then a GSS may be seen as unacceptable, 'insubordinate' and possibly threatening. This issue is best illustrated with reference to a short, and perhaps apocryphal, story:

> In a GSS session organised for the army, a group of soldiers of varying ranks, including at least one General who is the convenor of the meeting, are discussing what is good and bad with current operational practices in the army. At some stage in the meeting, a participant (of unknown identity and rank) makes a comment which evidently displeases the convening general. He gets to his feet and demands to know who made this comment, saying that it is absolutely not true. The answer not forthcoming, the general cancels the meeting and all subsequent meetings.

In this case, the General is unable to accept some (unrevealed) information which he believes is untrue. The system has enabled the dissemination of information which may constitute a threat or just be insubordinate to the general and/or his position. Unable to tolerate this, the General, as convenor, cancels the meeting and thereby eliminates use of the technology responsible for the threat to his position.

A third dimension of importance to the GSS facilitator is Individualism/Collectivism. If a culture is group-oriented, then one might suppose that use of GSS (with its focus on group work) would be more suitable than in an individual-oriented culture. However, this is not necessarily the case. In an individual-oriented culture, GSS will certainly act as a force towards group work inasmuch as the members of the group are required to work together so as to achieve a result that is likely to be acceptable to all group members. The provision of anonymity in the intergroup communications allows members to submit ideas without revealing their identity, but, as the literature has shown, this increases not only the task focus of the meeting (Poole et al., 1991), but also the equality of participation (Sproull and Kiesler, 1986). When, on the other hand, the culture is group-oriented, the use of a GSS that incorporates anonymous communications can have dysfunctional effects, as illustrated by a study undertaken in Singapore and the USA (Watson et al., 1994). In this study, it was found that some features of GSS were not compatible with Singaporean notions of correct group behaviour. These notions include the fact that public dissent is to be avoided, whereas consensus is to be encouraged. Consensus does not necessarily correspond to Senator Fulbright's 'genuine reconciliation of differences' (Tripp, 1976), but more to the notion that members of society have a social obligation to conform to rules that place national interests higher those of individuals. Therefore, when a GSS (designed in accordance with North American cultural norms) was used in a Singaporean setting, certain individuals were able to use anonymous communications - a feature of GSS that is not compatible with Singaporean social norms - to criticise other members of the group (a culturally discouraged behaviour). Watson et al. (1994) suggest that 'anonymity should be a switchable feature' so as to permit the GSS facilitator the opportunity to make communications identified if this is culturally appropriate or necessary. They also hypothesise that GSS might be more suitable in a distributed, asynchronous setting, where identification of individuals is no longer an issue and the critical aspects of communication that might threaten group harmony would be removed.

Further to Boisot's (1987) model, Hofstede specifies an underlying 'implicit model' that describes the nature of interactions taking place between people in (un)codified and (un)diffused situations, that is, the types of transactions. The names for the various elements of the implicit model correspond closely to Boisot's four forms. We can then see some form of association between Hofstede's uncertainty avoidance and power distance and Boisot's codification and diffusion of information. We will discuss the role of Hofstede's individualism dimension later. Incorporating the implicit model in Boisot's model of organisational forms yields a composite framework, shown in Figure 3, that links information and structure to culture.

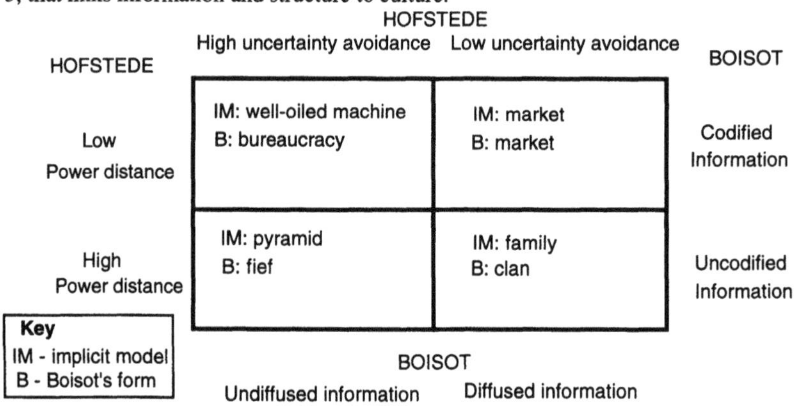

Figure 3 Power distance and uncertainty avoidance impact on organisational types.

The figure has been presented so that it is directly comparable with Boisot's information codification and diffusion model (Figure 2) with Boisot's labels added as well as the 'implicit model' field. This shows power distance and uncertainty avoidance as empirically-established variables that explain more effectively the variation found by Boisot (1987). The information codification and diffusion dimensions augment the power distance and uncertainty avoidance ones, establishing configurations of culture, information and organisation that are self-reinforcing.

Hofstede (1980) goes further, dichotomising national cultures on the basis of uncertainty avoidance and power distance. Thus, for example, English speaking (Anglophone) countries,

Scandinavia and the Netherlands have low uncertainty avoidance and low power distance whereas Mediterranean countries score high on both. These are presented in Figure 4 along with Boisot's categorisation. This is not intended to say that, for example, all Finnish organisations will be bureaucracies; rather, under given circumstances, a Finnish organisation is more likely to be structured as a bureaucracy.

HOFSTEDE	HOFSTEDE High uncertainty avoidance	HOFSTEDE Low uncertainty avoidance
Low Power distance	German-speaking, Finland, Israel B: bureaucracy	English-speaking, Scandinavia, Netherlands B: market
High Power distance	Latin, Mediterranean, Islamic, Japan, some other Asian B: fief	Southeast Asian (esp. HK, Singapore) B: clan

Key
B - Boisot's form

Figure 4 Association of power distance and uncertainty avoidance with national culture.

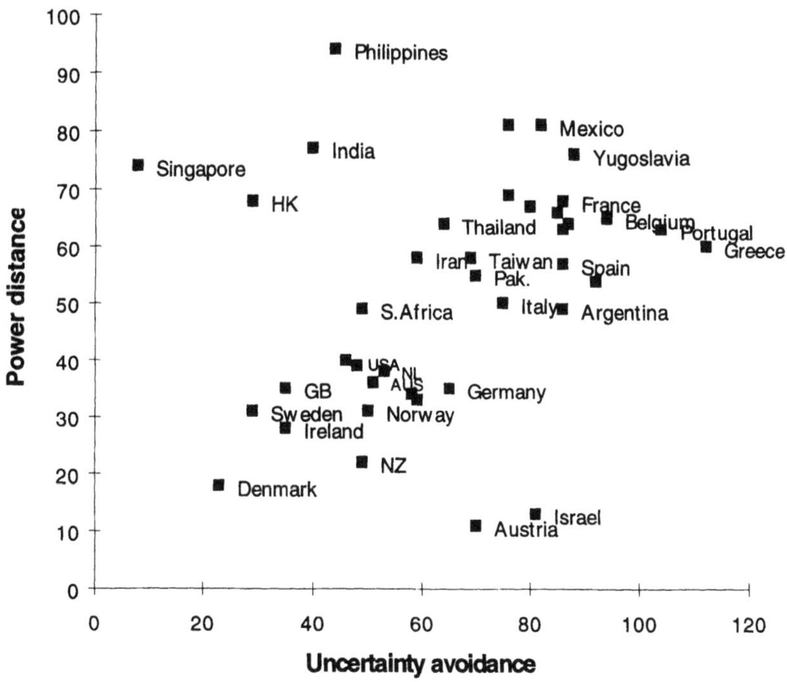

Figure 5 National power distance and uncertainty avoidance values (Hofstede, 1980).

Hofstede (1980) produces a scatter diagram of uncertainty avoidance against power distance, which shows the distribution of the national cultures. This was used in his categorisation of countries that is shown above. This material is widely quoted in the literature and is redrawn in Figure 5 above.

4 DISCUSSION

It is useful to analyse the compound Hofstede and Boisot model presented in Figure 3 from two different but complementary GSS viewpoints: ease of implementation and necessity. These two views are, arguably, of vital importance to the GSS facilitator, designer or implementer, since identification of where a particular group, organisation or culture lies in respect of these factors may determine if and how GSS implementation and use should be approached.

In the idealised market structure of Boisot (1987), with codified and diffused information, low power distance and low uncertainty avoidance, it might seem that a GSS is unnecessary. If information is freely shared around, is structured and there exists a climate where uncertainty needs not to be guarded against, why implement a system that seeks to promote information structuring, sharing of information and coping with uncertainty? Furthermore, given the prevalent low uncertainty avoidance, some managers may be sceptical of the benefits accruing from GSS, thinking that the system will not be able to change anything. This is, of course, a view at the low extreme of the uncertainty avoidance continuum. Nonetheless, it is ironical that it is in the market context that GSS are most widely used. This is supported by Figure 4, which indicates that it is the Anglophone countries, The Netherlands and Scandinavia that belong to this quadrant of the compound model - countries which we know to make considerable use of GSS technologies. While, GSS may not be strictly necessary in the perfect market, it should be easy to implement GSS in a context of low power distance, since there is no boss to threaten. However, those involved in the implementation process should ensure sufficient user participation so as to avoid accusations of authoritarianism - a behaviour disapproved of in a low power difference culture.

In the well-oiled machine or bureaucracy, power distance is low, information is codified, uncertainty avoidance is high and information is undiffused. The low power distance will improve the chances of successful GSS implementation, while the need to avoid uncertainty will be facilitated through a GSS's structuration of the decision making process, aided by the existing codified information. There exists some danger that the output of the GSS will be believed to too great an extent, i.e. too much faith will be placed in its accuracy. This stems from the perceived need to avoid uncertainty, and so the desire to make use of any and every system to help in the achievement of that goal. As described above, the GSS will act as a force in favour of information diffusion. This is perhaps the only warning note, since opposition to such diffusion could hinder the implementation and use of the system.

In the family or clan, information is uncodified but diffused, power distance is high and uncertainty avoidance is low. The high power distance may hinder the implementation of GSS, particularly if the system is seen as a threat to existing norms, for a GSS is recognised as a force for decentralisation of authority and consensual (participatory) decision making. This was illustrated above in the Singapore example. Although information is not codified in the typical clan organisation, the combination of low uncertainty avoidance and high information diffusion suggest that the forces of structuration and information diffusion will not be required in this context.

Hong Kong also lies within this 'clan' quadrant of the compound model (cf. Figure 4). The location of Hong Kong on the scattergram is, like all other countries, dependent on the values obtained for a range of employees at IBM in the late 1970s when Hofstede's (1980) survey was conducted. A unique feature of Hong Kong's management structure is that it is not national culturally homogeneous. Rather, there are many managers who are not Hong Kong Chinese, including those from Europe and North America, as well as elsewhere around the world. This point is made so as to illustrate the limitations associated with relying on a single source of information for clues to the successful implementation of GSS. It will always be essential to conduct a detailed review of an organisation, and its information and organisation needs and norms, before deciding if and how to implement GSS.

Finally, the fief is an organisation which has uncodified and undiffused information, high power distance and high uncertainty avoidance. GSS implementation in such a context will not be easy due to the high power distance. However, there are likely to be other forms of resistance connected with the push factors inherent in the spirit of GSS. As acknowledged already, GSS act as a force towards information dissemination. This is not a feature of fief organisations where the chief holds all information and does not tolerate much criticism. Furthermore, GSS act to decentralise decision making to a group of meeting participants. This too may be anathema to the authoritarian chief who needs to retain his central authority over decision making in order to maintain control. The fact that a GSS would assist in the drive to avoid uncertainty is perhaps the only positive factor to a GSS implementation, when seen from the viewpoint of the *status quo*. Analysed according to the 'spirit' of GSS, a major worry about GSS implementation and use in a fief is the danger that the system would be used for purposes other than those intended by the software's developers. Naturally, users are free to utilise the software in any way they choose, as we have already illustrated. One foreseeable problem in the fief is the pressure that might be placed 'upon the information providers to generate only the information that is acceptable' (Jordan, 1994) to the chief. Subordinates would be unlikely to disagree with this order and as a result, the Group Support System would become an Individual Confirmation System - the GSS could be used most effectively to show that all subordinates thoroughly approved of (or at least complied with) whatever course of action the chief decided upon. To object, even anonymously, could result in the abandoning of the software.

We now turn to Individualism/Collectivism. Individualism is often associated with Western countries and cultures, while Oriental societies and cultures are seen as collectivist. This is not the most helpful of classifications, as much of the world does not easily fit into the West-East bipolar model. Where, for example, should Australia and Papua New Guinea lie? They are geographical neighbours, but at opposite ends of cultural, social and developmental spectra.

Hofstede's (1980) own analysis places the Anglophone and Western European countries at the high end of the Individualism index, while countries at the low end can be found in South America and South East Asia (Hong Kong, Singapore, Taiwan and Thailand among them). We already know that power distance and individualism tend to be inversely correlated and we have shown that it is likely to be more difficult to implement GSS in high power distance contexts. Most of the literature on GSS both originates in the market organisational culture and describes implementations in that culture, where individualism tends to be the norm. This is not to say that those implementations were always successful, and to be sure there are a plethora of other factors influencing the successfulness of GSS implementation. However, while GSS initiate forces to increase information dissemination and to decentralise decision making, they also, and not surprisingly, initiate a push towards group based work. For an individualist culture, this is, perhaps, a new mode of work where individuals have to cooperate with each other as members of a team so as to achieve a common goal. The culture of low power distance associated with high individualism still exists of course. By way of contrast, in a collectivist culture, where high power distance is the norm, group work is already institutionalised. The introduction of a GSS into such a culture 'is a discontinuity in a group's life' (Watson et al.). If a group is forced to accept the new form of information exchange, a form developed in an entirely different cultural environment, it is likely that it will be rejected or else used in ways not intended by the software developers, as was the case in the Singapore example we described above. Individualism, thus, need not be a barrier to GSS use. Paradoxically, collectivism may raise more barriers and groups which are formed in collectivist cultures may need to make more modifications to a GSS in order to use it effectively.

5 CONCLUSIONS

The nature and role of information is central to decision making, and, just as emphatically, culture has a critical impact on the design, selection and use of group support systems. The first step for the GSS facilitator, designer or implementer has to be a study of the organisation's culture, and in the case of transnational and multinational systems, the national cultures involved. Such a study will give warnings of modes of information handling, supervision and control that will be directly related to the introduction of a GSS or any other information system. We suggest that such an investigation could start with the questionnaire of Hofstede (1980) and then use some of the above analyses.

5.1 National culture

Hofstede's dimensions of power distance, uncertainty avoidance and individualism may be of great significance to the GSS facilitator, designer and implementer, especially if the values are extreme, that is, very high or very low. Such extreme values can lead to systematic rejection of information or processes that do not conform to acceptable standards or norms. Other extreme values may lead to over-reliance on the same information or processes to the detriment of the decision making processes in the organisation. By being aware of the cultural and organisational environment, the GSS designer may be able to foresee some of the benefits and dangers that use of a GSS might entail. These benefits and dangers are most critical for a GSS facilitator or implementer who is not a national of the country where implementation or use is taking place. The benefits and dangers can be summarised briefly as:

- If uncertainty avoidance is strong then a GSS will help to structure information and the decision making process. However, there is a risk of overdependence on the output of the GSS.
- If uncertainty avoidance is weak, GSS may be superfluous since it will try to provide structure when none is required. Moreover, fatalism leads to scepticism about GSS usefulness and possible resistance from users.
- If power distance is large then the boss may disagree with the GSS and the boss is right. GSS implementation will be very difficult, though the boss may try to subvert the original spirit of the GSS so as to create support for his own objectives irrespective of reality.
- If power distance is small, it will be easy to implement GSS, but authoritative approaches will be risky as they may alienate the users.
- If individualism is high, GSS use will require the adoption of new work practices - team work - but is likely to result in increased task focus and decreased process losses.
- If individualism is low, GSS may disrupt existing group work practices. Individuals may adapt some features of the GSS so as to indulge in culturally unacceptable behaviour.

5.2 System development and change processes: moving to the IOF

As a consequence of their increasingly widespread use in organisations, GSS are implicitly associated with organisational change. In the future, we can expect to encounter transnational and multinational organisations and meetings with increased frequency. The International Office of the Future may not be recognisable in terms of the cultural values we are familiar with, yet how successful will that office of the future be? We should be deeply concerned about the manner in which national and organisational cultures will influence organisational change - a change that must take place *en route* to the office of the future, if only to accommodate the multifarious new environments - cultural, social and human - that will need to be incorporated into that office. Thus far, there has been precious little research into how multicultural, multilingual offices might function. How successful such transitions - to the IOF - will be depends to a considerable degree on the extent to which organisations face up to and attempt to reconcile the cultural differences between the various component parts of their present and future organisation. The benefits and dangers we have highlighted are just a few of the issues that demand attention. Much more work remains to be done in trying to put all the pieces of this cultural jigsaw together in the right way. However, as Hofstede (1980) has pointed out, we should also realise, aculturally, that there is no one correct solution that can apply to all organisational, cultural or social problems. Each context, each problem has its own jigsaw that has to be solved separately. What we have attempted to do in this paper is to suggest a method for approaching the riddle of how to solve the jigsaw puzzle, not solve the puzzle itself.

6 REFERENCES

Adler, N.J. (1986) *International dimensions of organizational behavior.* Kent Publishing Co., Boston, Mass.

Boisot, M. (1987) *Information and organizations: the manager as anthropologist.* Fontana, London.

Boisot, M. and Child, J. (1988) The iron law of fiefs: bureaucratic failure and the problems of governance in the Chinese economic reforms. *Administrative Science Quarterly*, **33**, 507-527.

Bolman, L.G. and Deal, T.E. (1991) *Reframing organizations: artistry, choice and leadership.* Jossey-Bass, San Francisco, CA.

DeSanctis, G.L. and Poole, M.S. (1994) Capturing the complexity in advanced technology use: adaptative structuration theory, *Organization Science*, **5**, 2, 121-147.

Hofstede, G. (1980) *Culture's consequences: international differences in work-related values.* Sage, Beverly Hills, CA.

Jordan, E. (1994) *National and organisational culture: their use in information systems design*, Working Paper WP94/08, Department of Information Systems, City Polytechnic of Hong Kong.

Ouchi, W.G. (1981) Theory Z: how American business can meet the Japanese challenge. Avon, New York, NY.

Poole, M.S., Holmes, M. and DeSanctis, G.L. (1991) Conflict management in a computer-supported meeting environment, *Management Science*, **37**, 8, 926-953.

Simon, H.A. (1960) *The New Science of Management Decision.* Harper and Row, New York, NY.

Sproull, L. and Kiesler, S. (1986) Reducing social context cues: electronic mail in organisational communication, *Management Science*, **32**, 11, 1492-1512.

Tricker, R.I. (1988) Information resource management – a cross-cultural perspective. *Information and Management*, **15**, 37-46.
Tripp, R.T. (1976) *The international thesaurus of quotations*, Penguin: Harmondsworth.
Watson, R.T., Ho, T.H. and Raman, K.S. (1994) Culture: a fourth dimension of group support systems research, *Communications of the ACM*, **37**, 10, 44-55.
Williamson, O.E. (1975) *Markets and hierarchies: analysis and antitrust implications*. Free Press, New York, NY.

7 BIOGRAPHY

Robert Davison is currently a Lecturer and a PhD student at the Department of Information Systems, City University of Hong Kong where he is investigating how GSS can be applied in the Hong Kong environment and culture. He also maintains research interests in cross-cultural psychology, the ethical use of IT and computational linguistics. His training was as a Slavic linguist before turning to IS in the early 1990s.

Dr Ernest Jordan had some ten years experience in the development of information systems in commerce and industry before entering the academic world. He has just returned to Australia after eight years at City University of Hong Kong, where he helped in the establishment of the information systems department and its bachelor's and master's degree programmes. His research interests include the strategic aspects of information technology, executive information systems, and enhancing teamwork in information systems development. He has published in the International Journal of Information Management, Information Systems Journal, Journal of Strategic Information Systems, and the Australian Computer Journal.

9

Operating systems for the multimedia office of the future

J. Dospisil
Monash University, McMahons Rd. Frankston, Vic. 3199, Australia
Phone: 61 3 9904 4135, Fax: 61 3 9904 4124
e-mail: jdospisi@fcit-f1.fcit.monash.edu.au

E. Kendall
Computer Systems Engineering, Royal Melbourne Institute of Technology, City Campus
GPO Box 2476V, Melbourne, Vic. 3001, Australia
Phone: 61 3 9660 5305, Fax: 61 3 9660 5340
e-mail: kendall@rmit.edu.au

T. Polgar
ISSC Australia, 60 City Rd. Southgate, Vic, 3006, Australia
e-mail: tpolgar@sydvm1.vnet.ibm.com

Abstract

Recent developments in distributed multimedia technology and in the integration of variety of media have the potential to change the nature of dissemination of information. However, it is important to ensure that developers are provided with proper frameworks and system services which help them to develop new applications efficiently. The capability to deliver continuous media to the workstation and meet its real-time processing requirements is now recognised as a central element of future distributed office applications. The objective of this paper is to survey the trends in support for continuous media processing in distributed environments. In particular, we look at the emerging abstractions in operating systems to ensure predictable response times for delivering continuous media at the desktop. In conclusion, we attempt to derive a set of possible directions for future multimedia operating systems.

Keywords

Operating System, Quality of Service, continuous media, reserve

1 INTRODUCTION

It is already recognised that office applications of the future will be heavily reliant on distributed multimedia systems. The user requires uncomplicated access to a great amount of information in real time, in a variety of formats and languages, and in different geographic locations. In addition, the office worker needs to be able to cooperate with other co-workers, sharing documents. From the computational and engineering point of view there are two important aspects of the future office: the availability of multiple media types, and the ability to manipulate them efficiently within a wide information space and with a predetermined **Quality of Service** (*QoS*). In our research, we have identified three interleaving components which have to be considered in order to meet the two requirements of uncomplicated access and maintenance of acceptable *QoS*. These components include 1) an operating system with the capability to process media data with timing constraints (eg. Bollella, (1995) Coulson (1991), Williams (1992), Arbab (1993)) high level powerful constructs for defining a whole range of synchronisation constraints (eg. Staehli (1994), Gibbs (1991)), and Berra (1992)) reliable network transport services for moving time-constrained media data (Hoepner (1991), Williams (1992), Anderson (1990)).

In this paper, we concentrate on advances in operating system (*OS*) design which may lead to improvements in processing time-constrained media data. The paper is organised as follows: Firstly, we discuss the aspects of multimedia applications. In section 2.2 we outline a set of temporal processing requirements. In section three, we overview the emerging abstractions in *OS* to support predictable processing times for continuous media. In section four, we present the summary of technologies for the *OS* of the office of future.

2 MULTIMEDIA AND MULTIMEDIA APPLICATIONS

Throughout recent times there has been development of a variety of media types as well as their integration into complex documents. The office paradigm has moved from a simple voice and paper information representation to complex multimedia presentations. The integration requirements resulted in further requirements for precise synchronisation of multiple media presented as a complex document on the user's workstation. There is a wide range of emerging applications which combine information sources such as high quality digital audio and video, graphics, and images into elaborate precisely scheduled presentations. There are also new classes of applications currently emerging such as collaborative environments and collaborative editors.

The requirement to support multimedia in distributed and collaborative applications has raised a number of issues and discussions. One of the most important issues is that of synchronisation. Multimedia applications need sophisticated support for presentation scheduling (Hoepner (1991)) as well as for maintaining real-time processing of continuous media (Coulson (1992)).

2.1 Continuous media

Video and audio data are compressed and then before the presentation they are processed into their visual presentation. Two common processing paradigms are used: a stream model, and a time-advance model. The processing must take place in any paradigm.

Stream and time advance paradigms

A stream is a time-ordered flow of data from a source to one or more sinks. This paradigm is typically used with large data sets and continuous real-time data. Streams are sometimes likened to a hardware connection of parts. The only difference between hardware and software processing is the speed. The software components are implemented as a set of buffers which cannot process data with anything close to the speed of light. Therefore, the total delay from the source to sink can be substantial. The primary advantage of this paradigm is its ability to *connect* input (commonly known as source) and output (known as sink) streams dynamically. The combination of software and hardware components at the conceptual level is also possible. Typically, it is implemented as a set of buffers (see for example Sync/Stream Subsystem implemented in IBM's MMPM/2 for OS/2).

With the time-advance paradigm, data are computed in presentation order but ahead of real time. This ahead of time processing allows for data to be buffered, timestamped, and then output with low latency. The processor contention or preemption is leveled by the size of buffers; therefore if the source falls behind real-time the sink can still output precomputed data from its buffers, thus minimising jitter. A comparison of the stream and time advance paradigms can be found in Dannenberg (1994).

Distributed multimedia applications

A good survey of distributed multimedia applications and their processing requirements is presented in Berra (1992) and Williams (1992). Distributed multimedia applications typically incorporate digital audio and video which is delivered from a server to a client workstation over a network connection. Processing of continuous media either locally or over a network requires predictable response times throughout the entire end-to-end path. The major components which impose processing delays are the network, communication protocols, Audio/Visual System, and the *operating system (OS)* (Figure 1)

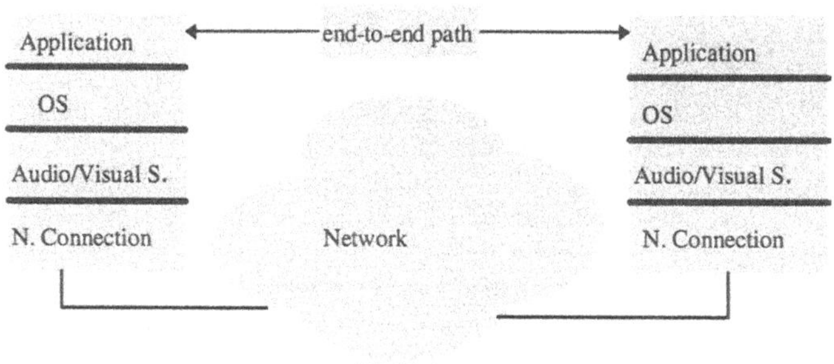

Figure 1 The end-to-end path of distributed multimedia applications.

Current commercially available *OS* (for example UNIX, MS-Windows, Windows NT, OS/2) are unable to support smooth processing of time critical data such as digital audio and video. The reason is the rigid real time processing requirements of so called continuous media. For example, throughput and low latency requirements are to process a frame every 30 or 40 ms (NTSC or PAL) with no delay.

Some conceptual views of multimedia authoring

The ability to combine, modify, and synthesise media data in real-time is a difficult task to support within a conceptual framework. The precise orchestration of multimedia presentations depends on real-time utilities as well as on the authoring tools and their expressive power. The common view is to provide the programming environment first and then build a visual interface over a toolkit (or a set of Application Programmer Interfaces or APIs). The modelling approaches range from providing a full visual environment for design and generation of applications to a simple object oriented (*OO*) model, toolkit and language eg. C++. Although a comprehensive survey of multimedia models is out of the scope of this paper, some examples of object oriented models are in Arbab (1993), Gibbs (1991), and Rossum (1993) to illustrate the current developments. A good survey of complex authoring support tools is in Hardman (1995).

The trend is to create easy to use frameworks which support visual authoring. In our view, the main deficiency of these models is the lack of sufficient expressive power to incorporate temporal constraints of continuous media data and the means to dictate the desired *QoS* expected from the underlying support layers. Furthermore, the coordination between the multiple streams of media data[1] and asynchronous events does not seem to be easy to incorporate into a simple programming model as suggested for example in Gibbs (1991).

Computer-participative multimedia applications

Computer-participative multimedia applications not only process live multimedia sources; they also perform analysis on their audio and video data input and take actions based on the analysis (Christopher (1994)). An example of such a system is a program that is capable of analysing television news and maintain online database of stories organised by subject. The computer here is an active participant in the processing of audio and video data.

2.2 Temporal processing requirements for continuous media

Multimedia such as live digital video and audio processing should coexist with conventional applications. The user expects to watch CNN news in one window while preparing lecture notes in another window. This requires a system which can support conventional and real-time applications without restricting either one. The ultimate goal is to provide a computational model which would support the emerging set of requirements recognised in Jeffay (1995), Mercer (1993),
Anderson (1990):

1. *The application must execute deterministically.* This implies that the system must provide predictable processing times for those active objects which are time constrained.
2. *Adaptive allocation of resources.* Since the amount of resources which could be allocated to a process is limited and the resources must be shared among applications, the application should have a means of dynamically adjusting its requested services. Therefore, the application must have knowledge of the actual system performance and be able to adjust requested resources according to *QoS* parameters.
3. *High level model of QoS. QoS* is a set of parameters which reflects the user's desired quality of presentation. The specification of these parameters as the system concept at the application level is seen as a better conceptual solution since it enables the creation of coherent conceptual development frameworks.

Each part of the end-to-end path (see Fig. 1) may become the processing bottleneck. Our hypothesis is that the improvement in multimedia real-time processing must be in tight cooperation with the application layer (in particular providing high level model and semantics for *QoS*

[1] Our experience is based on the OS/2 MMPM/2 example which seems to represent generic stream model

abstraction) and with the layers below. Yet the cooperation must be built into an abstraction which would not restrict the application's portability over multiple platforms. Furthermore, there is a need to cooperatively handle time-critical multimedia applications with conventional applications.

3 REAL-TIME OPERATING SYSTEMS TO MEET MULTIMEDIA REQUIREMENTS

Conventional operating systems provide a convenient environment for general data processing but they cannot guarantee real-time deadlines for continuous media data. With the perspective of the future multimedia office, the operating system must be designed to accommodate both processing of temporally constrained data as well as conventional tasks while maintaining acceptable *QoS* primarily in terms of predictable response times. We have surveyed five different approaches:

1. Predictable *OS* protocol processing [Mach 3.0] - section 3.1
2. Coexistence of multiple schedulers - section 3.2
3. Real-time producer/consumer paradigm [YARTOS] - section 3.3
4. Coexistence of real-time and conventional *OSs* - section 3.4
5. Reactive objects and the synchrony hypothesis [synchronous language ESTEREL] - section 3.5

Although much research has been devoted to the design of real-time operating systems, the majority of multimedia processing is performed on the commercial desktop systems running conventional *OS*. However, when introducing new concepts into commercial products, it is necessary to consider the cost of the development as well as the current investment of the computer community in the conventional systems such as Windows or OS/2. This implies the need for the implementation of cost efficient changes to the current commercial products.

3.1 Predictable operating system protocol

Models and paradigms have been mostly initiated at the Carnegie Mellon School of Computing with MACH 3.0 *OS*. Multimedia applications require timely service to support time-constrained data types such as digital audio and video. The objectives of such systems include a predictable and reliable distributed real-time environment and a set of tools to allow a system designer to analyse the runtime behaviour at the design stage (Mercer (1994)). Conventional OS's typically employ some time-sharing scheduling algorithms and/ or simple fixed priority scheduling which do not guarantee timely execution of all processes competing for resources. With preemptive kernels an effect known as priority inversion may occur. In summary, scheduling requirements for time-critical threads and conventional threads are incompatible.

The processor capacity reservation mechanism implemented in MACH (Mercer (1993)) takes scheduling of time critical jobs a step further. It allows processes to reserve the capacity they need to run. The principle is based on the separation of the mechanism which controls the resource assumption and delivers resource capacity to programs from an actual policy on how the resources are allocated. Primitives of this protocol use the *reserve abstraction, admission policy,* and *reservation enforcement* mechanism to manage CPU allocation. *Reserve* is a kernel entity which represents access to the processor capacity. A reserve contains information about computation time and a reservation period. The reservation request is subject to the system's acceptance or denial. If the request is denied then the process has to decide how to proceed further. The *enforcement mechanism* measures the usage of each program and uses the associated reservation information to make sure that the usage does not exceed the reservation quantum during any reservation period.

3.2 Coexistence of multiple schedulers

An interesting solution using multiple scheduling policies has been presented in Golub (1994) where the scheduler for the Mach 3.0 microkernel allows multiple scheduling policies to run on the same processor. The conventional *priority* value contains two components: policy and ordering. Within each scheduling policy, a different type of ordering is imposed. Each policy maintains its own *run_queue*. A scheduling policy is modelled as an object with a public interface and private data structures and methods. The selection module scans the highest priority scheduling policy for runable threads to select the thread to run. The preemption is implemented throughout the clock interrupt and associated routines which determine whether the current thread should be preempted.

Two other implementations similar to the above framework are Solaris 2.1 and OS/2. In Solaris 2.1 fixed priority real-time threads may preempt timesharing threads. The real-time threads are also exempt from priority adjustment rules. In OS/2, the threads are assigned to one of four ordered scheduling classes: real-time, fixed priority, timesharing, and background. Each scheduling class contains 32 priority levels, and time critical threads run at the highest priority class. Although this approach improves the predictability of processing it does not guarantee QoS parameters.

3.3 Real-time producer/consumer

The real-time producer/consumer paradigm advocated by Jeffay (1993) models process interaction as a producer/consumer system with a timing constraint on the rate at which the consumer must service the producer. Essentially, the consumer must process data at the rate they are produced. The semantic basis of the system is based on the client/server paradigm and message passing. Each process has a single input port and multiple output ports. Processes exchange messages through communication channels. A process accepts a message on its input port and emits messages via its output ports. The non-blocking emission of messages is achieved through the assumption that messages are produced with a predefined transmission rate function. A process may be blocked on an *accept* statement but never on an *emit* statement.

YARTOS is a micro-kernel application which supports three basic abstractions: tasks, resources, and messages (Jeffay (1991)). In addition, it allows applications to specify the real-time rate of execution of a task (thread of control) that must be completed within a unit of time. The scheduling model is composed of two abstractions: tasks and resources (for more details see Jeffay (1991)). The task is invoked at sporadic intervals and completes its execution at or before its deadline. The task may require access to shared resources in the mutual exclusion fashion. Tasks are reactive in the sense that they execute only in response to events. An experiment with a videoconferencing system which uses YARTOS and a set of IBM-Intel ActionMedia 750 adapters to support live video and audio has shown very promising results.

3.4 Coexistence of real-time and conventional operating systems

The approach taken in Bollella (1995) is based on the notion of two virtual machines which operate over the shared resources (CPU and other system resources). One machine runs unmodified conventional purpose *OS* and the other runs real-time kernel. The access of both virtual machines to the hardware components is multiplexed. From conceptual point of view, this approach provides good processing model. However, it seems that there is still some work to be done to complete the model, in particular in the areas of sharing of pointing devices between two virtual machines and in the maintenance of consistency of data structures for shared devices. The overhead of switching between virtual processors seems to be also too high.

3.5 Class of reactive objects

Reactive systems and synchronous programming languages have been discussed in Harel (1985) and Berry (1988). Reactive systems are repeatedly prompted by the outside world to which they continuously respond in the form of emitted outputs. Reactive objects are effectively real-time controllers which accept events from an outside environment and instantaneously generate new events in response (Papathomas (1995)). Reactive objects communicate with each other and other objects in the system through invocations. This concept offers some useful features to enhance the computational model. For example there is no need to introduce a special representation of time since they may accept an external clock event derived from an external clock.

The computational model is then the integrated coexistence of active objects (Gibbs (1991)) which operate under the control of a set of reactive objects - synchronisation managers. Two concepts are employed to implement the model: the concept of abstract states, and the concept of the state notifications. The state notifications allow the other objects to monitor the state changes and to synchronise accordingly. The claim is that the abstract states may be used in synchronisation conditions together with class inheritance thus avoiding or minimising the effect of the *inheritance anomaly* (Satoshi (1993)) The model is designed to handle multiple media streams in real time, manage compatible *QoS* for related streams, and monitor temporal relationships of multiple streams.

4 TECHNOLOGIES FOR THE FUTURE OFFICE

The office of the future will be characterised by the need for real-time processing of highly distributed cooperative and computer-participative multimedia applications. At present, the commercial multimedia systems like Video for Windows, QuickTime, or Video In from IBM generally support efficient storage, retrieval, and presentation of pre-recorded video clips. However, they do not support adequately the direct processing of live media, live orchestrated multimedia presentations with random user interaction, and computer-participative systems.

The reserve abstraction (section 3.1) has a number of advantages. First, the thread receives feedback and may decide on further processing policy. Second, it is possible to build a *QoS* manager which would maintain expected *QoS* parameters[2]. The paradigm based on real-time producers and consumers (section 3.3) has already proved that it is possible to anticipate processing rates of continuous media by using non-blocking emissions of messages to meet real-time processing deadlines. Both architectures require significant changes to operating system architectures as well as to the designer's 'state of mind' to accept new concepts of management of Inter-Process Communications (IPC).

The abstraction presented in section 3.2 which is based on the cooperation of multiple scheduling policies provides a framework which could be accommodated by the current operating systems with relatively low cost. Some modifications of this framework are already used commercially in OS/2

[2] We have omited the discussion on unbounded priority inversion in micro-kernel systems

and Solaris 2.1. The coexistence of multiple OS'*s* over a single CPU (section 3.4) seems to carry a high processing overhead. The model based on reactive objects (section 3.5) provides a very sound conceptual and programming framework which does not require drastic changes in operating systems. However, a large processing overhead could be incurred for medium and large size applications which exchange many messages.

The management of the allocation of resources to multiple multimedia applications is the crucial point of delivering quality multimedia presentations to a user. In Figure 2, the video conferencing application requesting the processing rate 30 fps will consume a considerable amount of CPU time. While many videoconferencing applications use the frame rate 7-15 fps, the question is whether it is necessary to deliver video data with this precision.

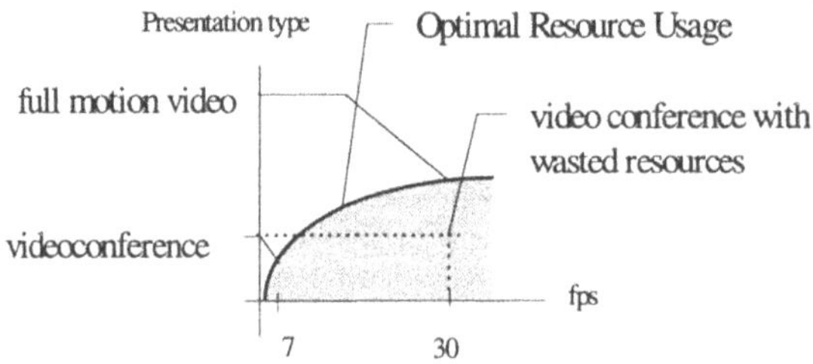

Figure 2 Resource distribution in a multimedia system.

The challenge is to build a system in which multiple resource reservation policies support the management of multimedia presentations according to the user's perception of quality. The following four concepts should be considered in order to lift multimedia processing from its infancy to a mature technology state:

1) Support for temporally sensitive data is controlled via a *QoS* manager which maintains required level of services while optimizing resource allocation. The *QoS* manager's performance observations (events and notifications) are visible to the user and programmer via a high level interface such as an intelligent agent;
2) Real-time processes and threads are isolated from non-real time activities by the new class of schedulers.
3) The distributed system provides predictable response time;
4) Object-Oriented model would interact with the *OS* through a well defined interface (a set of APIs) so that the programmer may easily take advantage of some constructs built into the operating system (eg. synchronisation policies, performance notifications).

5 CONCLUSION

To support predictable end-to-end performance and temporal guarantees for low latency applications is difficult task the success of which depends on many factors. It is out of scope of this paper to provide an exhaustive survey of all approaches which aim at providing the suitable operating environment for multimedia application processing. The research seems to be moving towards providing predictable service to multimedia applications throughout the adaptable resource allocation mechanism. The focus is on isolating real-time activities of multimedia applications from unpredictable interference of other processes, and eliminating unbounded priority inversion.

The movement towards adaptive allocation of resources will promote the development of high level model of Quality of Service. The Quality of Service parameters then will reflect the user's desired quality of presentation. The capability to specify QoS parameters at the application level as the system concept will enable to create coherent conceptual framework for flexible management of shared resources.

6 REFERENCES

Anderson, D.P., Tzou, S., Wahbe, R., Govidan, R., Andrews, M. (1990), "Support for Continuous Media in the DASH System", Proc. of the 10th International Conference on Distributed Computing Systems, pp. 54-61.

Arbab, F., Herman, I., and Reynolds, G.J., (1993), "An Object Oriented Model For Multimedia Programming", *Proc of Eurographics'93*, Blackwell Publishers, Volume 12, No.3, pp. C-101-C-113.

Berra, P.B., Chen, C.Y.R. Ghafoor, A., Little, T.D.C. (1992), "Issues in Networking and Data Management of Distributed Multimedia Systems", Invited paper, *Symposium on High-Performance Distributed Computing*, Syracuse New York, September 1992.

Berry, G., Gonthier, (1988) "The ESTEREL Synchronous Programming Language: Design, Semantics, Implementation", *INRIA report No. 842*, INRIA.

Bollella, G., Jeffay, K., (1995), "Support for Real-Time Computing within General Purpose Operating Systems: Supporting Co-Resident Operating Systems", *Proc. of the IEEE Real-Time Technology and Application Symposium*, Chicago, May, 1995

Christopher J. Lindblad, (1994) "A Programming System for the Dynamic Manipulation of Temporally Sensitive Data", *Technical Report MIT/LCS/TR-637*, August, 1994, MIT Laboratory for Computer Science.

Coulson, G., Blair, G.S., (1992), "Meeting the Real-Time Synchronisation Requirements of Multimedia in Open Distributed Processing", *Technical Report* MPG-92-45, Distributed Multimedia Research Group, University of Lancaster.

Dannenberg, R.B., Rubine, D., (1994), "A Comparison of Streams and Time Advance As Paradigms for Multimedia Systems", *Technical Report CMU-CS-94-124,* School of Computer Science Carnegie Mellon University, Pittsburgh.

Gibbs, S., Dami, L. and Tsichritzis, D. (1991), "An Object Oriented Framework for Multimedia Composition and Synchronisation", *MULTIMEDIA Systems, Interaction and Applications* (ed. Kjelldahl, L.), 1st. Eurographics Workshop, Stokholm, April 18/19.

Golub, D. B. (1994), "Operating System Support for Coexistence of Real-Time and Conventional Scheduling", *Technical Report*, CMU-CS-94-212, School of Computer Science, Carnegie Mellon University, Pittsburg.

Hardman, L., Q., Bulterman, D.C. (1995), "Authoring Support for Durable Interactive Multimedia Presentations", *Technical Report STAR*.ps, CWI, Multimedia Kernel Systems Project.

Harel, D., Pnueli, A. (1985) "On the Development of Reactive Systems", in Logics and Models of Concurrent Systems (ed. K.R. Apt), *NATO ASI Series* F. Vol. 13, pp. 477-498.

Hoepner, P. (1991), "Presentation Scheduling of Multimedia Objects and Its Impact on Network and Operating System Support", *2nd Intl. Workshop on Network and Operating System Support for Digital Audio and Video*, 11, pp. 12-23.

Jeffay, K., Stone, D., F. Donelson Smith (1991), "Kernel Support for Live Digital Audio and Video", *Computer Communications*, Vol. 15, No. 6. (July/August 1992), pp. 388-395

Jeffay, K., Stone, D., Poirier, Daniel, (1991), "YARTOS, Kernel support for efficient, predictable real-time systems", *Real-Time Systems Newsletter*, Vol. 7, No. 4 (Fall), pp. 8-13.

Jeffay, K., (1993), "The Real-Time Producer/Consumer Paradigm: A paradigm for the construction of efficient, predictable real-time systems", Proc. of the 1993 ACM/SIGAPP Symposium on Applied Computing, Indianapolis, pp. 796-804.

Jeffay, K., Bennett, D., (1995), "A Rate-Based Execution Abstraction for Multimedia Computing", *Proc. of the 5th International Workshop on Network and Operating System Support for Digital Audio and Video*, Durham, April 1995, pp. 67-78

Mercer, C.W, Savage, S., Hideyuki Tokuda (1993), "Processor Capacity reserves: An Abstraction for Managing Processor Usage", *Technical Report*, CMU-CS-93-157, School of Computer Science, Carnegie Mellon University, Pittsburg.

Mercer, C.W, Zelenka, J., Ragunathan Rajkumar (1994), "On Predictable Operating System Protocol Porcessing", *Technical Report*, CMU-CS-94-165, School of Computer Science, Carnegie Mellon University, Pittsburg.

Papathomas, M., Blair, G.S., Coulson, G., Philippe Robin (1995), "Addressing the real-time synchronisation requirements of multimedia in an object-oriented framework", in IS&T/SPIE Proceedings Vol 2417, Multimedia Computing and Networking 1995

Rossum, G., Jansen, J., K. Sjoerd Mullender (1993), "CMIFed: A Presentation Environment for Portable Hypermedia Documents", *Tecnical Report* CS-R9304, ISSN 0169-118X, CWI.

Satoshi Matsuoka, and Akinori Yonezawa (1993), *"Analysis on Inheritance Anomaly in Object-Oriented Concurrent Programming Languages", in Research Directions in Concurrent Object-Oriented Programming* (ed. Gull Agha, P. Wegner, and A. Yonezawa), The MIT Press, Cambridge, MA.

Staehli R., Walpole J., and Maier D., (1994), "Quality of Service Specification for MultimediaPresentations", html// /tec-reports/Tech. Report 94-033, Department of Computer Science & Engineering, Oregon Graduate Institute of Science & Technology.

Williams N., Blair, G.S, (1992), "Distributed Multimedia Application Study", *Technical Report* MPG-92-11, Distributed Multimedia Research Group, University of Lancaster.

7 BIOGRAPHY

Jana Dospisil is a Lecturer at Monash University in Melbourne, Australia. She holds MEng from Technical University in Brno , Czech Republic and M(Comp) from Monash University in Melbourne. Prior to moving to Australia, she worked for thirteen years in a number of software development positions in Czech Republic. Her research interests include multimedia and agent based systems.

Dr Elizabeth A. Kendall is a Senior Lecturer in Computer Systems Engineering at the Royal Melbourne Institute of Technology in Melbourne, Australia. She has a MEng from the Massachusetts Institute of Technology and a MEng a PhD from California Institute of Technology. Prior to moving to Australasia, she worked for eleven years in the U.S. aerospace and defence industry. Her research interests are in the agent based systems and advanced applications of object oriented technology.

Tony Polgar is a Project Manager in ISSC Australia in Melbourne. He graduated with MEng degree from the Technical University in Prag, Czech Republic. He has also a M(Comp) from Monash University in Melbourne. Prior to moving to Australia, he worked for twelve years in a number of software development positions in Czech Republic. He is currently involved in research and teaching at Monash University. His research interests are in project management of large complex software applications.

An analysis of IT platform and organizational requirements for multimedia cooperation on the Internet - a case study on the international office of the future

S. Dustdar
Center for Informatics Services, University of Art
Hauptplatz 8, A-4010 Linz, Austria, Tel: 785173, Fax: 783501
e-mail: dustdar@khsa.khs-linz.ac.at

Abstract

Office systems have gained a state of maturity in handling strictly defined business processes. Research on the 'international office of the future' shows that they are inappropriate for handling cooperation in general and are not well suited for the increasing numbers of multi-side/multi-time/multi-culture workgroups. Recent developments on multimedia systems and networking technology show that using desktop multimedia conferencing for group decision making and cooperative work on wide area networks such as the Internet is possible. In this paper the design, hardware and software requirements and organizational issues in a desktop multimedia conferencing system as a fundamental cooperative tool in the 'international office of the future' are reviewed. This article focuses on a case study on urban planning using desktop multimedia conferencing on the Internet. Further some implications for future research on desktop multimedia conferencing tools are discussed.

Keywords

desktop multimedia conferencing, MBone, CSCW, office of the future, Internet

1 INTRODUCTION

Office systems have gained a state of maturity in handling strictly defined business processes. Research on the 'international office of the future' (IOF) shows that they are inappropriate for handling cooperation in general and are not well suited for the increasing numbers of multi-side/multi-time/multi-culture workgroups (Traunmüller, 1995). Recent developments on multimedia systems, networking technology and their integration with cooperative tools on the Internet show that using desktop multimedia conferencing for cooperative work on wide area networks such as the Internet is possible (Macedonia and Brutzman, 1994). Researchers have often discussed the failure of video to support interpersonal communication (Egido, 1990). In this paper some of the conclusions others have reached about computer-supported communication-, coordination-, and cooperation tools are reviewed. Further the design, hardware and software requirements as well as organizational issues in desktop multimedia conferencing systems will be discussed. Prior to the conference discussed in this paper we participated in several desktop multimedia conferences across Europe to learn about the MBone tools as well as the technical and organizational issues. The focus of this paper is on a case study on urban planning using desktop multimedia conferencing on the Internet.

As Johansen (1988) shows, group work and hence group decision making is a natural way of doing business. Early groupware systems and electronic meeting systems lacked the ability of manipulating multiple media types such as audio, video and textual information in one integrated multimedia system. The merging of workstation technology and real-time computer conferencing has had a significant impact on CSCW and group decision making and lead to the term 'desktop conferencing' (Rodden, 1993). Research on early multimedia conferencing systems such as developed at AT&T Bell Laboratories (Ahuja et al., 1990), Bellcore (Root, 1988) or NEC (Watabe et al., 1990) had as their aim the provision of the facilities found at face-to-face meetings with remote groups. It is generally accepted that computer-supported decision making and communication results in many changes in communication patterns (Gaver et al., 1992; Hatcher, 1994), greater task orientation (Niemiec, 1984) and shorter meetings (Harkness and Burke, 1984). Regarding the video component, Ishii et al. (1992) point out the importance of gaze awareness, the ability to monitor the direction of someone's gaze and thus the focus of the attention. Similar results were found by Heatch and Luff (1991) and Mantei et al. (1991).

Short et al. (1976) caution the results found through laboratory settings and propose that they should be validated through case studies with true situational factors, such as real-life relationships and complex tasks. The case study presented in this article is not a laboratory setting of desktop multimedia conferencing. It reviews 'real' problems encountered before, during and after the conference and should be a valueable contribution towards the understanding of desktop multimedia conferencing and decision making processes through computer support.

2 CONFERENCE FRAMEWORK

Preparation and realization of desktop multimedia conferencing for cooperative office work has two aspects, the technical setup procedure and organizational issues which will be discussed in the following sections.

2.1 Technical requirements

The requirements for highly-integrated desktop multimedia conferencing on a packet-switched network, i.e. the IP (Internet Protocol) based Internet, can be divided into three categories:
1. Support for packetized data transport and routing of data packets by the network software.
2. Support of encoding audio and video streams and reassembling of audio and video packets into continuous audiovisual output. This should be accomplished by specialized hardware or software codecs (coder/decoders).
3. The control and application software should be integrated into the graphical user interface, i.e. the widespread X-Window system.

Network and transport protocol requirements

This article concentrates on the usage of packet switched networks. In a packet switched network, transmission lines are not reserved in advance, the data is sent in small portions, called datagrams, from the sender to the receiver or to a group of receivers. On the path from the sender to the receivers, the packets are forwarded by special machines, called routers. The packet switching approach is sometimes called connection-less or state-less delivery service, in contrast to the connection-oriented circuit switching method, where lines are reserved for the connections.

The world-wide Internet is a large packet-switched network, but it is widely believed that real-time traffic requires a connection-oriented network service. Recent research and experiences (Clark et al., 1992; Jacobson, 1994) revealed that packet switching, compared to circuit switching techniques, is not less efficient in meeting real-time scheduling and delivery constraints. The weaknesses of packet-switched networks, namely the variation in the delay of each packet, usually called jitter, and packet loss due to occasionally packet dropping by routers can be diminished by buffering of incoming packets and the usage of loss-tolerant coding methods. The network jitter results in variation of packet interarrival times and out of sequence packet delivery. The audio replay at the receiver without taking into account jitter will at least be hardly understandable. Network jitter is removed by buffering the incoming data packets at the receiver and replaying the signal with some delay. The chosen coding method for audio and video data must be able to reconstruct the data with minimal distortion despite of packet loss.

Due to the nature of video- and audioconferencing events, the need for distributing data to a group of participants, called multicasting, arises. Multicasting of packets differs from unicasting, where datagrams are delivered from one sender to one receiver, and broadcasting, where datagrams travel from one sender to all receivers, in a way that datagrams are only delivered to members in a so called multicast group. To manage dynamically changing multicast groups and individual memberships within these groups, the Internet Group Management Protocol (IGMP), which fits into the existing suite of Internet Protocols, has been suggested and implemented (Deering, 1989). Multicast is not only the native form of delivery in group communication, it also makes efficient use of the network resources as for a number of n receivers it is not necessary to send n copies of each packet, only one copy of each packet is multicasted and only duplicated at branches along the routing path.

The members of one multicast group are allowed to be located anywhere in the Internet. Packets are sent to a multicast group, i.e. audio packets in a conference, are routed to each group member regardless where he is located geographically. The routing of multicast packets is not yet implemented in most of the router boxes, therefore a virtual network connecting multicast-routers was set up. This virtual network is called the Multicast Backbone (MBone) of the Internet and connects more than 10,000 users on 1500 networks in 30 countries. The multicast-routers are connected through tunnels, where multicast packets encapsulated within normal IP packets are being forwarded. A multicast-router can be a production router, e.g. a Cisco router, or a workstation class machine configured for the routing of multicast packets. Figure 1 shows the urban planning conference relevant part of the MBone. The squares represent multicast-routers involved, one at the University of Art at Linz, one at the Austrian Network Operation Center in Vienna and one at the Archlab in Vienna. ACOnet stands for 'Austrian Computer Network'. Multicast packets normally travel along the primary tunnels from Linz to the Archlab Vienna via the ACOnet router and vice versa. If the ACOnet router fails, the connection is established using the backup tunnel.

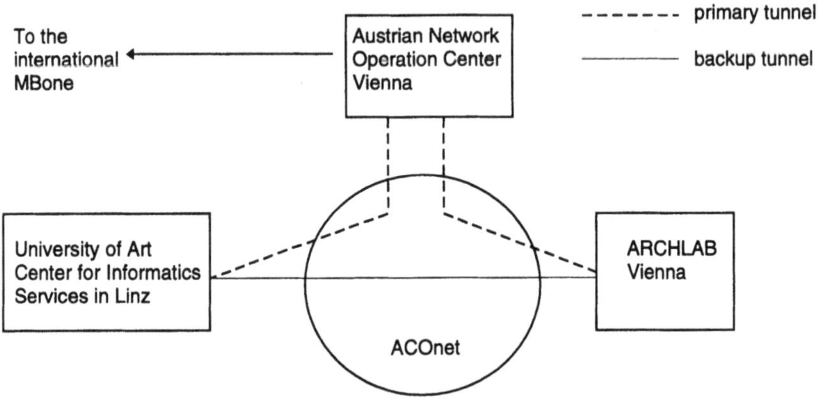

Figure 1 Conference view of the ACOnet MBone.

Each tunnel is associated with a metric and a threshold parameter. The metric counts for routing decisions, a numerical larger values denotes a more expensive path, e.g. a backup tunnel should have a higher metric than the primary path. The threshold is used for scoping of packets, each router compares the packets time to live (TTL) against the tunnels threshold and forwards the packet only if the TTL exceeds the threshold setting. Additionally every multicast router decrements the TTL by one (Casner, 1993).

Desktop machine requirements for cooperative multimedia work

The real-time processing of video and audio data requires adequate processing power, which is offered by workstation class machines. On most workstations Unix derived operating systems are in use, so research activities have focused on these machines. The necessary operating system kernel extensions have been implemented into the most common operating systems by the vendors, like Solaris, Irix and Nextstep. For BSD Unix derived operating systems, kernel modification source code and instruction is freely distributed (Thyagarajan and Deering, 1994).

Most workstations are equipped with audio capabilities, e.g. a build-in speaker or line-out plug, a build-in microphone or line-in plug and device driver software. For video capture a frame grabber board and a video camera is additionally required. The viewing of the video sequence requires a graphics display. Audio encoding and decoding is usually done in software. Video encoding can be done in hard- or software, decoding is usually done in software. Hardware encoding boards are expensive, so encoding on powerful workstations is often done in software. Figure 2 shows a common configuration for a desktop multimedia conferencing system.

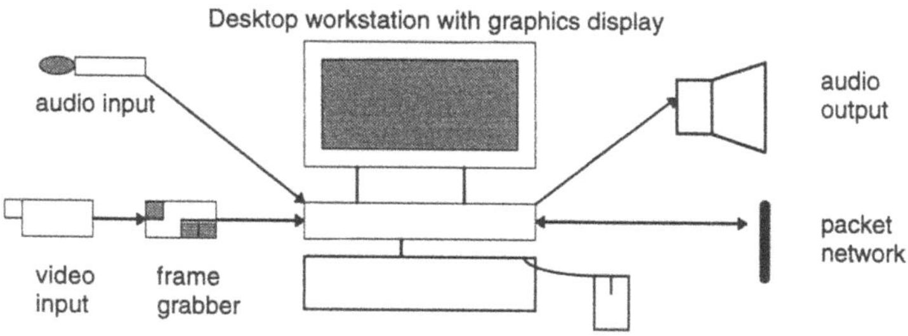

Figure 2 Desktop multimedia conferencing system.

Common coding techniques are Pulse Code Modulation (PCM) for audio, which results in a bit rate of 64 kBit/sec for 8 Bit resolution audio sampled at 8 kHz. The packet overhead, resulting from the address and control information inserted into the packets, raises the bit rate to 75 kBit/sec if the Real-Time Transport Protocol (RTP) is used (Schulzrinne et al., 1994). The RTP adds timing and sequencing information into the packets, which is used to reduce distortion caused by network jitter and packet loss. For the urban planning conference we chose a rate of 64 kBit/sec, although lower audio data rates are possible, due to the reasons discussed in the next section.

For video coding a commonly used value for the data rate is 128 kBit/sec. To reduce the impact on the network one is free to choose a lower rate, i.e. 66 kBit/sec have been used in the described conference. These extremely low rates are achieved through data compression techniques. The methods of video compression implemented in the video tools we used are based on frame prediction, motion estimation and transform coding techniques.

One disadvantage of such a low bandwidth allocation is the low frame rate in the order of magnitude of 2 frames/sec, depending on the motion in the picture. A quick changing image sequence results in unpredictable frames and thus an increased data rate, as frames have to coded without prediction. Fortunately, in a conference session quick scene changes occur seldom, the small movements of the conference participants can be effectively coded using motion estimation. In motion estimation a displacement vector related to a block of pixels in the previous frame is coded rather than the image content itself.

2.2 Organizational context

Conferencing events on the Internet can be divided into two categories, open conferences where everybody can join in, and conferences for closed groups. Open conferences are usually announced a few weeks ahead by sending an electronic mail to the appropriate mailing lists (Casner, 1993), i.e. the MBone-AT mailing list, which has been set up to coordinate the Austrian (AT) MBone activities, in our case. Before the conference actually starts, an announcement in the session directory (sd), an X-Window application program, is made (McCanne and Jacobson, 1994). The sd entry is flooded, according to the conference scope, over the Internet and contains the conference name, a short description, multicast group addresses, coding format, scope and extent of the conference. The conference extend can be any combination of audio-, video and whiteboard-sessions.

The scope of the open urban planning conference, a combined audio-, video and whiteboard-session, was limited to Austria, which was guaranteed by choosing an initial TTL of 40 for all packets. The multicast-router connecting Austria via Paris to other countries has a threshold of 64 on the Vienna-Paris tunnel and therefore refuses to forward packets with TTL lower or equal to 64 along this tunnel.

An alternative to session announcements by sending an e-mail to a list is to use World-Wide-Web (WWW, W3) based forms. The WWW approach provides a better overview on conferences and collision detection, e.g. two conferences at the same time with overlapping scope, could not be registered automatically in a WWW based form. Another feature of the described desktop multimedia conferencing technology is the possibility of ad-hoc conferences, which has been performed for a few times by the system administrators ahead of the actual conference.

Beyond the announcement of the conference training of the conference participants and preparation of the desktop multimedia conferencing facilities is necessary. Specifically the conference participants have to know to use the tools, i.e. how to mute the microphone in the audio tool vat (Jacobson and McCanne, 1994), how to resize windows in one of the video tools like nv (Frederick, 1994) or vic (Jacobson, 1994) or how to load postscript slides into the whiteboard wb (Jacobson and McCanne, 1994). Additionally the surrounding of each participant has to be adjusted, i.e. avoid background noise, locate microphone, speakers and camera close to the human interactor and provide natural lighting conditions. The peculiarity of the urban planning conference was that in Linz a group of people joined the conference, the special setup which was necessary therefore can be seen in Figure 3. Finally one important aspect is to remind the conference participants to take care on discipline, i.e. not to speak concurrently.

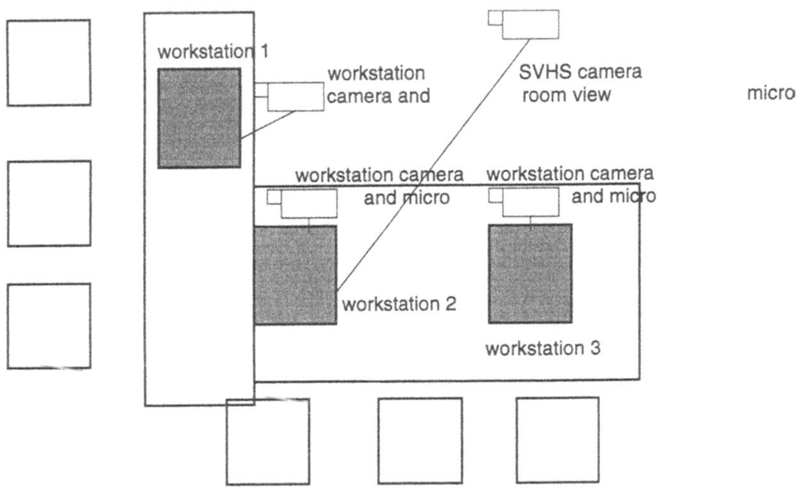

Figure 3 Room layout for group participation.

During the conference one participant should act as moderator responsible for the conference schedule, serving of speak requests and trouble shooting. The trouble shooting in fact is the responsibility of technical staff. If the conference is transmitted to an audience using overhead projection, as it was in our case, additional staff is necessary. Speak requests from the audience has to be coordinated by this person.

After the conference is closed by the moderator a few tasks remain to be carried out by the conference organizers. A very useful information, especially for people planning a conference, might be an electronically recorded conference protocol. We will do that using the WWW infrastructure. Conferences of wide interest should be retransmitted, especially if a conference is held in a different timezone, i.e. conference events originating in North America should be retransmitted at a time suited for Europe. For individual access it is possible to make conference recordings accessible from a Media-On-Demand server (MOD), as the one located in Sweden (Klemets, 1994). Table 1 summarizes actions to be taken before, during and after a desktop multimedia conferencing conference.

Table 1 Actions to be taken in desktop multimedia conferencing

before	*during*	*after*
Announcement	Moderation	Report
Parameter settings	Trouble shooting	Retransmission
User training		Media on demand

3 COLLABORATIVE WORK ON URBAN PLANNING

After discussing the conference framework, this section concentrates on the conference itself. The conference was jointly organized by the Center for Informatics Services at the University of Art and Industrial Design at Linz and the Institute of Urban Planning at the Technical University of Vienna and lasted two hours. The distance between these two sites is 250 kilometres. The purpose of the conference was to discuss issues of urban planning and urban development. Since the conference was announced on the MBone, interested people with Internet-MBone access could participate in the conference as well. At Linz there were five active conference participants, who were members of the municipal authority of Linz, two system administrators, one camera man and several interested students. There were three multimedia workstations each equipped with video- and audio facilities for the active conference participants in Linz. In Vienna there were five active conference participants who presented new projects of urban planning and development in the city of Linz, two system administrators, one camera man, one conference moderator and several interested students. The conference was recorded by Austrian Television and some parts were shown on the same evening, since this was the first national multimedia conference on the Austrian part of the Internet.

The Institute of Urban Planning had prepared digital material on urban planning and wanted to present the plans and digital models to the municipal authority of Linz. These plans and models regarded some buildings and streets of Linz. The purpose of the conference was to present the work done at the Institute of Urban Planning and to initiate a decision making process about the implementation of the presented models in the real world. Following the framework presented in Table 1, we will discuss some problems regarding the desktop multimedia conference.

Before the actual conference we witnessed some technical problems. Several times the tunnel between the two sites went down and so we decided to configure an alternate route (tunnel) between Linz and Vienna in case the main tunnel breaks down during the conference. We prepared a second conference room in which students could participate actively in the conference. The room was equipped with a multimedia workstation connected to the Internet-MBone and to a display unit which projected the workstation screen. Due to the fact that the conference was multicasted in Austria and we did not want to cause too much traffic on the national network, we decided to limit the bandwidth to 66 kBit/sec. Figure 4 shows one conference participant in front of his multimedia workstation.

Figure 4 Conference participant with multimedia workstation.

During the conference we had several problems. The first problem was that the active conference participants had no experience regarding desktop multimedia conferencing. Hence the system administrators had to handle the switching between the used software. After one hour the Austrian part of the Internet, ACOnet, went down and hence no transmission was possible. The time - five minutes - which was needed to fix the problem in Vienna, the conference participants in Linz used to discuss the issues raised during the conference. Since the conference participants had no time to discuss the issues amongst themselves during the conference, they seemed to be quite happy to have the possibility to talk and not being 'broadcasted' all over Austria.

After the conference we interviewed the conference participants. They liked the idea of desktop multimedia conferencing because the municipal authority needed to discuss urban planning issues very often with the researchers in Vienna. In the past they had to travel to Vienna and these journeys slowed down the decision making processes. The second positive point which the conference participants mentioned was the fact that it helped the municipal authority to save travel expenses. Johansen questioned the assumption that conferencing would reduce travel (Johansen, 1984; Johansen and Bullen, 1988). Wc found that it was the subjective feeling of conference participants that they saved a lot of time and hence travel costs and they did not neccessarily calculate the real costs and compare. They did not regard this desktop multimedia conference as a substitute to face-to-face meetings. The participants wanted to use the system for their convenience to be able to hold meetings more often. Except the five minutes breakdown of the network in Austria we had no technical problems. Since the municipal authority used conferencing technology for the first time, we asked them how they experienced the audio and video quality. The system administrators decided to limit the video bandwidth to some 2 frames per second and keep the rest for audio and shared whiteboarding, which they thought would be more important than full motion 25 frames per second 'talking heads'. The reason the system administrators limited the bandwidth for video was that they wanted to keep bandwidth for shared data such as city plans and 3-D computer generated models. Some tests before the conference had shown that if the transmission of the conference was with top video quality, a lot of data packets would get lost. This was a point of critique by the municipal authority. Inspite of the fact that there was no audio packet loss, the conference participants critizised the jitter in the video transmission.

4 RESEARCH AND DESIGN STATEGIES FOR THE IOF

To summarize, it is very important to train the prospective users of desktop multimedia conferencing systems regarding the usage of software and to give guidelines of usage of the conferencing tools. In some situations it was not obvious to the participants that if two participants talked at the same time some audio packets could get lost. The second proposition is that prospective users of desktop multimedia conferencing systems should have a clear idea of what quality they can expect. Particularly we witnessed a high degree in user expectation regarding video quality. The video quality needs to have a minimum frame refresh rate of 15 frames per second to give the impression of real full motion video. This refresh rate can only be achieved in high bandwidth networks.

The conference participants needed some 'private-time' during decision making processes to discuss issues amongst themselves, without the feeling of being 'broadcasted'. Hence we propose the implementation of the functionality to direct video and audio streams to certain users within a decision making group and to implement features in software which shows the remote participant that the local site has switched to mute and therefore is not able to receive audio or video. This would help users to have a feeling of privacy and enhance security. Regarding security and privacy one major problem on the MBone is that it is only possible to configure multimedia conferences reaching the site of the organisation, a region or the world but it is not possible to configure a multimedia conference as a closed conference. Everyone within the scope of the TTL-value is able to receive and send packets. There is no anonymity and the only security measure is that conference participants can see through the e-mail address (or alias), who joins a conference. This restricts the use of multimedia conferencing on the MBone. Interested organizations who have full Internet access can use the MBone for their internal multimedia conferences between distributed sites but they will not be private. Table 2 summarizes the organizational lessons we learned during this desktop multimedia conference on the MBone and contains some proposals for future research regarding the integration of desktop multimedia cooperations tools into standard office tools.

Table 2 Organizational lessons learned in MBone desktop multimedia conferencing

before	*during*	*after*
check user expectations	leave/join mechanisms for participants	integration of results into standard user tools (organizational memory)
software training	private conversations with some conference participants	retrieval of conference results
explain multimedia conferencing 'rules'	integration of conferencing tools with user tools	

Research on desktop multimedia conferencing and its application in decision making processes is interlinked with other information processing, communication and coordination activities (Angehrn and Jelassi, 1994; Chin et al., 1991). Desktop multimedia conferencing is not a substitute to face-to-face meetings, but enables and - as we saw in the case - forces people to change decision making processes and communication patterns. Daft and Lengel's (1984) theory of information richness states that face-to-face meetings have the highest degree of media richness. We argue that desktop multimedia conferencing enables decision making processes and communication processes on a new dimension. The question is not if desktop multimedia is about to substitute face-to-face meetings, but which 'new qualities' or 'opportunity enhancements' (Johansen, 1984) it can offer. For productive use of desktop multimedia cooperation software on the Internet, MBone tools need better integration into standard Internet tools such as WWW browsers. Integration of synchronous communication- and cooperation tools into the WWW infrastructure is a key to widespread use of desktop multimedia cooperation in the Internet.

Further research needs to be undertaken regarding design and implementation issues of desktop multimedia conferencing systems in decision making processes. The author is convinced that this research area needs interdisciplinary efforts since multimedia and CSCW are interdisciplinary fields. We expect new impulses to the emerging field of multimedia systems and propose joint research of the research communities of computer science, communication research, organization design, CSCW and information systems. As Ishii et al. (1994) state, we are interacting not *with* computers, but *through* computers.

5 REFERENCES

Ahuja, S.R., Ensor, J.R. and Lucco, S.E. (1990) A comparison of application-sharing mechanisms in real-time desktop conferencing systems, in *Proceedings of COIS*, 238-248.

Angehrn, A.A. and Jelassi, T. (1994) DSS research and practice in perspective. *Decision Support Systems*, **12**, 267-275.

Casner, S. (1993) Frequently asked questions on the multicast backbone. University of Southern California, Information Sciences Institute, May 1993.

Chin, C., Holsapple, C.W. and Whinston, A.B. (1993) Modelling network organizations:a basis for exploring computer support coordination possibilities. *Journal of Organizational Computing*, **3**, 279-300.

Clark, D.D., Shenker, S. and Zhang, L. (1992) Supporting real-time applications in an integrated services packet network: architecture and mechanism, in *Proceedings of ACM SIGCOMM*, 14-26.

Daft, R.L. and Lengel, R.H. (1984) Information richness: a new aproach to managerial information processing and organization design, in *Research in organizationalbehavior* (eds. L.L. Cummings and B.M. Staw) Vol 6, JAI Press, Greenwhich, CT.

Deering, S. (1989) Request for Comment 1112 - Host Extensions for IP Multicasting, Network Working Group, Stanford University, August 1989.

Egido, C. (1990) Teleconferencing as a technology to support cooperative work: its possibilities and limitations, in *Intellectual teamwork: social and technological foundations of cooperative work* (eds. J Galegher, R.E. Kraut and C. Egido), Erlbaum: Hillsdale.

Frederick, R. (1994) nv - X11 videoconferencing tool, Unix Manual Page, Xerox Palo Alto Research Center, Palo Alto, CA.

Gaver, W., Moran, T., MacLean, A., Lovstrand, L., Dourish, P., Carter, K. and Buxton, W. (1992) Realizing video environment: EuroPARC's RAVE system, in *Proceedings of CHI*, 27-35.

Harkness, R.C. and Burke, P.G. (1984) Estimating teleconferencing travel substitution potential in large business organizations, in *The teleconference resource book: a guide to applications and planning* (eds. L.A. Parker and C.H. Olgren), Elsevier Science Publishers, Amsterdam.

Hatcher, M. (1994) A video conferencing system for the United States Army: Group decision making in a geographically distributed environment. *Decision Support Systems*, **8**, 181-190.

Heath, C. and Luff, P. (1991) Disembodied conduct: communication through video in a multi-media office environment, in *Proceedings of CHI*, 99-103.

Ishii, H., Kobayashi, M. and Arita, K. (1994) Iterative design of seamless collaboration media. *Communications of the ACM*, **37**, 83-97.

Ishii, H., Kobayashi, M. and Grudin, J.(1992) Integration of inter-personal space and shared workspace: clearboard design and experiments, in *Proceedings of CSCW*, 33-42.

Jacobson, V. (1994) Multimedia Conferencing on the Internet, in *Proceedings of ACM SIGCOMM*, Tutorial.

Jacobson, V. (1994) vic, Unix Manual Page, Lawrence Berkeley Laboratory, University of California, Berkeley, CA.

Jacobson, V. and McCanne, S. (1994) vat - X11-based audio teleconferencing tool, Unix Manual Page, Lawrence Berkeley Laboratory, University of California, Berkeley, CA.

Jacobson, V. and McCanne, S. (1994) Using the LBL Network Whiteboard, Lawrence Berkeley Laboratory, University of California, Berkeley, CA.

Johansen, R. (1984) Teleconferencing and beyond: *communications in the office of the future*. McGraw-Hill, New York.

Johansen, R. (1988) Groupware: *computer support for business teams*. The Free Press, New York.

Johansen, R. and Bullen, C. (1988) Thinking ahead: what to expect from teleconferencing, in *Computer-supported cooperative work: a book of readings* (ed. I. Greif), Morgan Kaufmann, San Mateo.

Klemets, A. (1994) The design and implementation of a media on demand system for WWW, in *Proceedings of the First International Conference on the World-Wide Web*.

Macedonia, M.R. and Brutzman, D.P. (1994) MBone provides audio and video across the Internet, *IEEE Computer*, **27**, 30-36.

Mantei, M.M., Baecker, R.M., Sellen, A.J., Buxton, W.A.S. and Milligan, T. (1991) Experiences in the use of media space, in *Proceedings of CHI*, 203-208.

McCanne, S. and Jacobson, V. (1994) sd - Session Directory, Lawrence Berkeley Laboratory, University of California, Berkeley, CA

Niemiec, A. (1984) CMITS: communication and craft, in *The teleconference resource book: a guide to applications and planning* (eds. L.A. Parker and C.H. Olgren), Elsevier Science Publishers, Amsterdam.

Rodden, T. (1993) Technological support for cooperation, in *CSCW in practice: an introduction and case studies* (eds. D. Diaper and C. Sanger), Springer, New York.

Root, R.W. (1988) Design of a multi-media vehicle for social browsing, in *Proceedings of CSCW*, 25-38.

Schulzrinne, H., Casner, S., Frederick, R. and Jacobson, V. (1994) RTP: A Transport Protocol for Real-Time Applications, Internet-Draft, Internet Engineering Task Force, Audio-Video Transport Work Group, July 1994.

Short, J., Williams, E. and Christie, B. (1976) The social psychology of telecommunications. Wiley, London.

Thyagarajan, A. and Deering, S. (1994) IP Multicast Extension for BSD-derived Unix Systems, Release 3.3, Xerox PARC, Palo Alto, CA., August 1994.

Watabe, K., Sakata, S., Maeno, K., Fukuoka, K. and Ohmori, T. (1990) Distributed multi-party desktop conferencing system: MERMAID, in *Proceedings of CSCW*, 27-38.

Traunmüller, R. (1995) Enhancing Office Systems with CSCW-Functions, in *The International Office of the future: A Problem Analysis* (eds. P.W.G. Bots, B.C. Glasson, D.R. Vogel), IFIP Working Group 8.4, Hamburg.

6 BIOGRAPHY

Dr. Schahram Dustdar is head of the Center for Informatics Services at the University of Art at Linz, an associate lecturer for multimedia systems at the IS-Department, University of Regensburg in Germany and a visiting professor at the MIS-Department, University of Tuscon, Arizona during 1996. He heads the Austrian MICE National Support Center (Multimedia Integrated Conferencing for European Researchers), a research project by the European Union. He co-authored the book 'Multimedia Information Systems' (Prentice Hall, 1996). He was a post-doctoral visiting fellow at the IS-Department at the London School of Economics during 1993/94.

11

Meetings bloody meetings: a transition in the concept of meeting as technology reduces dependency on time and geography

W G Hewett

School of MIS (Warrnambool Campus), Faculty of Management, Deakin University, PO Box 423 Warrnambool Victoria 3280, Australia, telephone 61 55 633228, fax 61 55 633320, email billh@deakin.edu.au

Abstract

In geographically spread organisations the cost of meetings can be significantly higher than it is in single location enterprises. The use of technology to support meetings simultaneously held in multiple locations has been promoted as a potential solution. Traditional cost/benefit analysis used in justifying the implementation of this technology shows that success should be assured. The time lost in travel is a visible and easily measured cost of running a meeting, savings in travel (absolute travel and accommodation costs together with notional time lost costs) can be used to justify significant investments in meeting support technology.

There are, however, many problems in successfully changing an organisation's meeting culture so that it freely embraces the use of technology. Many organisations have difficulty in the implementation and use of meeting support technologies. Further, after the initial flush of enthusiasm, facilities are often poorly utilised resulting in significant lost opportunities. There are less tangible costs of corporate meetings which are often more significant than the easily measured savings from travel avoided. The identification of these costs might aid the longer term acceptance of meeting support technology.

Key among the problems to be addressed is the difficulty some meeting chairs have in successfully running a meeting, spread over several locations and supported by technology such as video and audio facilities. These difficulties can be traced to poor pre-meeting preparation and poor understanding of the technologies chosen. They are exacerbated by the failure of participants to understand the true nature of the potential savings available. The result is often failed projects or poorly utilised facilities.

It is with this in mind that this paper has been developed. Only some of the "Pluses and Minuses" in the use of video and audio meeting technology are addressed, along with some of the issues that could be used to develop a "briefing to participants paper" for use in minimising some identified problems in the use of the technology in support of formal meetings. Finally, several unanswered questions are posed. Questions which should be subjected to further study and analysis.

Keywords

Information Technology, Video Conferencing, Meeting Support

1 STRUCTURE OF THE PAPER

Two general case studies have been used to enable the identification of the opportunities, costs and issues involved in meetings held by geographically spread organisations. The first helps support the case that the cost of participants travelling to meetings is significantly higher than a simple calculation of travel time might indicate. The second helps identify a number of issues which emerge when technology is implemented to support multiple location meetings. These cultural and political issues may prove to be the limiting factor in the use of technology to support geographically spread organisations.

The body of the paper addresses proposals to overcome some of the impediments to the successful implementation of meeting support technology. The final section of the paper addresses several issues which emerge as needing further analysis before clear guidelines in justifying and implementing technology to support multiple location meetings.

2 MEETING TYPES AND DESIRED OUTCOMES

It is simplistic in the extreme to imagine there is a single class of meeting. Similarly it is simplistic to imagine that technology can equally support all meeting classes. The following breakdown is offered as a simple, but by no means exhaustive, classification. This is achieved using the frequency of the meeting, its desired outcomes and, to a lesser extent, the type of person attending as a the classification mechanism.

See the bibliography for reference to further reading on meetings and organisations. (Renton, 1994; Shockley-Zalabak, 1991)

2.1 Regular meetings

The following classification of meeting types roughly defines the forms of meetings typically held:

Regular meetings with formal schedule, clear chairperson, and pre-published agenda.
Regular, but, informal meetings with no fixed agenda but clear chairperson.
Regular informal meetings with no fixed agenda and no clear chairperson.
Ad hoc meetings called to address a particular issue with a clear chairperson, and pre-determined agenda.
Ad hoc meetings for general information exchange with no fixed agenda but clear chairperson.

2.2 Spontaneous meetings

Spontaneous meetings, "hallway" meetings or "stand up" meetings are rarely able to be supported by the meeting technology under review here. The expansion of computer mediated communication using groupware[1], however, is having an impact in the area of spontaneous group decision making.

2.3 Inter versus intra organisational meetings

The scope of this paper is limited to observations addressing inter organisational meetings.

However, in both cases reported here, ad hoc meetings were also documented involving members from across organisational boundaries. It is clear from this involvement that simple technology can be used to facilitate intra organisational communication also. One such involved academics from the Faculty of Management, discussing approaches to the introduction of computer mediated

[1] Groupware is defined as a package which may include document management, e-mail, desktop conferencing, scheduling or electronic-forms applications. The groupware market, dominated by Lotus Notes, was evaluated at US$ 1 billion in 1994; it is expected to reach US$ 4 billion by 1998. Computer 28 (9) Sept. 1995.

communication to support the teaching and learning process, with the chief executive of an IT service company. This company decided to involve experienced people from Sydney and Los Angeles in the discussion. This extremely productive meeting was arranged with a minimum of fuss involving facsimile and audio links.

2.4 Expected outcomes

The following classification of desired meeting outcome, or just why meetings are called, could be expected:

To deliver communication.
To deliver communication and seek feedback.
To finalise a decision on a single issue.
To finalise a decision on a number of related issues.
To fulfil a regular meeting schedule commitment of a committee or board.

2.5 People attending meetings

The following classification of people could be expected at meetings.

Committee or board members.
Project team members, eg. people working on a specific problem.
Department members, eg. people involved in the review of department performance against its budgeted goals.
Members from across organisational divisions, eg. people from Marketing and Manufuctiring reviewing plans for streamlined product delivery.

3 CASE ONE

This analysis was of a widely spread manufacturing and retailing organisation. At the time of the analysis it was small to medium in size ($AUS70-80 million in annual sales) and therefore had limited resources to devote to information technology. This organisation differed from most small organisations in a number of ways. For the purpose of this discussion the most significant differences were:

It was a fully vertically integrated manufacturing and retailing organisation.
It was represented throughout Australia.
The company's head office was located in a regional city (some three hours drive from Melbourne) along with its major manufacturing plant.
The company's next most significant corporate presence, its marketing office, was in Melbourne.
The company had significant links with raw material and technology suppliers in both the USA and the UK.

3.1 Technology to support expansion

In 1976 the company was in the middle of a significant expansion. Sales were increasing at a steady rate. Manufacturing capacity needed to expand to meet the demand. Management involvement was required to streamline this expansion. The company had recognised the need to improve its administration and manufacturing systems and had embarked on a radical technology upgrade path. Computer Aided Design and Manufacturing (CAD/CAM) applications were installed. Traditional MIS applications were developed to support management. point of sale (POS) equipment was installed in shops through out Australia to gather sales details. Portable data entry (PDE) equipment and bar code based tracking systems were implemented. Communications networks were implemented to support the POS and PDE data gathering. The company had not recognised, however, the emergence of a significant inter-organisational communication need.

3.2 Internal communications — the limiting factor

This need for heightened inter-organisational communications peaked in the early 1980's and was addressed in a number of ways:

Key executives were included in the monthly board meetings.
Regular meetings involving staff in all of the functional divisions were established.
Annual "management" meetings were formalised
Annual Strategic Planning meetings were held followed by monthly executive meetings examining the company's progress.
Management Information Systems supported by electronic communication networks were introduced.
Electronic mail was introduced, starting at the top and moving down through the organisational layers.
Retail, Manufacturing, and Supply divisions met regularly, supported by electronic decision support and information analysis technology.

3.3 The problem of distance

Inevitably, because of the distances involved, key executives were called upon to travel extensively. This was not seen as a significant imposition since the corporate culture had always involved significant travel. The company grew from an initial travelling salesman's decision to put down roots and build a retail organisation. This organisation grew into a manufacturing/retail organisation when the owner decided a higher level of quality was required. The aim was to supply merchandise at a level of quality and price points not available through the regular suppliers. This approach proved successful in the eyes of the consumers and the company grew into an Australia wide organisation in the 1960's and 1970's.

3.4 The acceptance of travel

The culture of travel was accepted as the norm by all members of the board and the executive group. Travel was seen as good, because it opened opportunities for key personnel to meet customers and employees and to see just what the opposition was doing. What occurred as the need for more and more communications oriented meetings arose, however, was that key executives spent more time travelling without gaining the traditionally accepted benefits of travel. Less and less of their scarce time was spent actually exposed to customers and the marketplace. More importantly, executives spent less time with retail staff, the organisation's interfaces to the market, while at the same time the costs associated with travel increased.

3.5 The acceptance of electronic mail

The electronic mail network, the implementation of which commenced in 1982, was relatively well accepted. In fact the Marketing Director was prompted to comment that the introduction of email had enabled him to "win arguments with the Managing Director he would have lost on the telephone". The reason given was that the asynchronous nature of the email interchange meant that more reasoned and less emotive arguments could be used. The email network was expanded (in a top down fashion) on the back of the communications network installed to deliver traditional manufacturing and retail MIS systems.

3.6 The costs

Increasingly, key executives and managers were participating in meetings held in locations up to three hours from their home base. Many half day and full day strategy and review meetings were held in closed rooms, which could have been anywhere. Because of the time involved in meetings and travel there was little time left for customer and employee interaction.

Thus, the cost of these meetings can be seen as more than travel and accommodation expenses alone. More than the cost of hours lost in executive travel. The indirect cost was a significant loss of market focus. As busy executives attempted to meet more often to address rapid changes in the corporate environment, less and less time was spent involved in the market place.

This loss of market focus is a significant reason for this otherwise technological innovative and outward looking organisation failing to survive the turbulence of the late 1980's and early 1990's. It was found that the company was not well positioned to meet the twin threats of cheap imported goods, as the tariff regime in Australia altered, and a shift in consumer desires towards less durable goods [Hewett & Symons, 1992].

3.7 The important issues from case one

The cost of travel to meetings in an integrated but geographically spread organisation can be significantly higher than the simple addition of the time involved in travel. By only concentrating on travel as a possible cost saving, organisations can overlook the less quantifiable benefits of implementing multi-location meeting technology. The loss of focus and the lost opportunities for wider interaction should not be ignored. Better use of multi-location meeting support technology which was beginning to become available in the late 1980's, when this organisation most needed help, may have enabled the required communication and planning meetings to proceed without the loss of marketplace interaction.

The electronic mail network, while well accepted, is a *one to one* form of communication support and does not address the *one to many* and the *many to many* communication needs which also exist. The introduction of group decision support technology as an extension to the electronic mail network would have been a significant enhancement. Unfortunately GDSS was not readily available at the time.

4 CASE TWO

This analysis was of an integrated but geographically spread University with six campus locations in regional and metropolitan Victoria. Three campuses are located in Melbourne's eastern suburbs (in normal traffic about a half an hour's drive between each), the others are located in regional Victoria (from one to three hours drive from Melbourne). The term *integrated* is chosen here to differentiate this University from similar, geographically spread institutions which have opted for a *federated* model.

This institution emerged in 1990/91 as a result of a series of mergers. The Australian Government facilitated these mergers in an attempt to rationalise the tertiary education sector. As a result of two closely timed mergers the University is now a relatively large institution, 26000 undergraduate and postgraduate students and an additional 20000 students undertaking professional extension courses through out Australia. It also has a significant number of international students both in Australia and studying abroad.

4.1 Technology to support integration

On the administration and academic fronts, the need for change was clear as was the need to involve people from the geographically spread parts of the new entity in new administration and course delivery structures. An early priority was the establishment of electronic communications links between the campuses. One time capital support was used to implement communication links for voice, video and data traffic. Local area networks were put in place and a significant investment was made in desktop technology. A strategic investment was also made in video supported conference rooms. These video rooms were initially thought of, and justified, as multi purpose aimed at both administrative meeting support and academic teaching support. Of a lower priority, but in hindsight possibly just as critical to the success of the merger, was the establishment of informal "voice point" meeting rooms.

During the merging of two, and then three, individual business faculties into a single, integrated, Faculty of Management many meetings were held. Many of these meetings were face to face but a significant number used the video facilities installed in the first days of the merged institution. The technology available in 1990/91 was crude when compared to what is possible today. It did function, however, and this technology enabled many interchanges which otherwise would have been impossible.

4.2 Technology supported ad hoc meetings

As the merger "politics" became consolidated, less and less use of the video facilities was made for ad hoc meetings . This was possibly because fewer of these meetings were taking place, but the emergence of the informal voice point network was more likely the reason. The purchase of voice point equipment was seen as an "expense" issue and therefore able to be justified at a relatively low corporate level. As people came to know each other, the need for voice to be supported by picture became less and less. The ease by which a voice point meeting could be arranged far outweighed the "bureaucratic booking procedures" required for the video facilities. Further the integrated communications network delivered "unlimited" voice lines to all university locations.

4.3 Technology supported regular meetings

Regular meetings persisted over the video facilities. In particular, meetings conducted on a formal schedule, with a clear chairperson, and running to a pre-published agenda are still regularly held using the video facilities. There has been a gradual reduction in the use of video for other formal meetings. This can probably be traced to the consolidation of power in a lesser number of sites. In several instances decisions to call face to face meetings at short notice were seen as deliberate political tactics used to marginalise opponents.

4.4 Reduction in the use of technology supported meetings

The reduced use of the technology can also be traced to the failure of the institution to propagate the video meeting room facilities as campus real estate became scarce during a phase of "geographic" reorganisation and consolidation. The need to move to an unfamiliar building some distance from the regular offices of those attending is often cited as a reason why the meeting could not be scheduled using the technology, but instead must be face to face.

The final reason for the reduced use of the video technology is the difficulty some meeting chairs have in successfully running a video meeting. This last reason is seldom explicitly stated, but often emerges as a resistance by those attending, with the often stated claim that video meetings are just not productive. Informal discussions with both experienced and inexperienced meeting chairs support this contention. Further, discussions with those attending video meetings and with those who fail to attend voluntary video supported meetings also support this conclusion.

4.5 The important issues from case two

The failure to enhance and support the facilities can in itself be seen as an indirect message, from 'corporate management', that the meeting support technology was of only marginal use. Poor meeting outcomes have also been a contributing factor in the reduction of use of the technology. These poor meeting outcomes can be directly linked to the difficulties meeting chairs have in scheduling, running and, controlling multi-location technology supported meetings.

Thus it can be seen that, even after an investment in meeting support technology has been made, a change in corporate culture is still required in order to ensure the full potential of the technology is delivered.

5 THE SOLUTION: PRE-MEETING PREPARATION

Pre-meeting preparation can be broken into two groups, the physical and the logical. On the physical front, such issues as the various locations and the compatibility of the technology available in the locations must be addressed. These problems are best left to the technologists. The logical issues in many ways are no different to the organisation of face to face meetings, however some issues take on new importance.

5.1 Physical issues

Location and time

The simplest and most important physical issue is that those attending the meeting all understand where they are expected to be on the appointed day, at what time and for how long. In the one organisation this can often be a stumbling block. The video facilities may not be well located and many people may never have used them previously. When stretching across organisations, countries, continents, and time zones this issue is likely to be even more critical. The facilities offered will vary across the following:

Meeting room based voice links, eg. voicepoint.
Individual voice links, eg. telephone bridging equipment.
Meeting room based video links using slow scan technology
Meeting room based video links using high speed communication links, ie television quality.
Individual video links using video 'phones or a similar technology.

Convenience of booking

The convenience for booking facilities is also an important issue. When the facilities are readily available, sometimes at short notice, then the organisation will make use of them. On the other hand, when the booking of the facilities becomes too difficult for the normal meeting coordinator, the fall back towards face to face meetings can be quick. Within the second year of availability the booking of the video meeting rooms became a formal and bureaucratic exercise. A significant reduction in use by the Faculty of Management could also be identified as the procedures were entrenched. This was particularly the case for ad hoc meetings.

Cost of usage

A similar, but more subtle, pressure is the visibility of the meeting cost. For example, where the cost of technology supported meetings is debited to a visible budget line while the cost of travel and time lost, associated with face to face meetings, is left unconsolidated the use of the facilities will diminish. Even worse, meetings may be cancelled or put on an extended cycle. This results in the saving of "visible" funds while losing coordination and integration impetus. A particularly unproductive result when typically the provision of the facilities involves a significant fixed cost with only a minor marginal cost for usage.

By late 1994 the University had implemented a user pays booking principle for the video conference facilities. The cost structure set aimed to recover the full (capital and expense) investment in video meeting rooms and technology together with a proportion of the capital investment in communications lines. The costs struck were relatively high when compared to travel costs and when compared to the discretional funds available to faculties and the schools within the faculties. In the Faculty of Management this resulted in the cancellation of pilot exercises using the facilities to support teaching across campus to small student cohorts. It also resulted in a further reduction in the use of the facilities for "lower level" meetings, curriculum reviews, unit team discussions etc. Many of these meetings were just not held with the result that progress towards across campus integration at the grass roots level was inhibited.

Environment issues

A number of environment issues are also relevant, for example:

A soundproof room which is local to the workplace is important. The room should be within easy walking distance of most participants' normal offices, and be sufficiently soundproof for confidential conversations.

The size of room should be appropriate for the group, ie a spacious room with comfortable chairs and an appropriately sized table.

A whiteboard link to other meeting locations is often valuable for meetings when wide ranging discussions and problem solving is involved.

The availability of facsimile transmission equipment can often reduce the problems of distributing late material.

Easy access to technical staff can be critical, particularly when participants are not familiar with the technology being used.

The ability to mute the sound transmitted has both positive and negative aspects. By cutting off the sound transmission, people in a local setting can ask for clarification of points missed due to bad transmission etc. But, if people in one location are able to cut off their discussions from the meeting as a whole sub-meetings can break out without the knowledge of even a well organised chair.

Number of participants

There are also a number of general issues which should be thought about in the context of specific meetings. For most of these there seems to be no clear research to support or guide an answer, for example:

Is there an optimum number of participants?

Is there an optimum number of locations?

Is there a number (participants/locations) above which the technology chosen is not productive?

What other technology can be used to support the meeting?

The question of the number of participants is relevant regardless of the support technology chosen. It does, however, add another dimension to the problem when technology is used to support multi-location meetings.

The question of the number of locations (ie two-way versus multi-way connections) will be answered differently for different meeting types and outcome aims. For example, in the late 1980's many thousands of company employees participated in a world wide hook up for a company announcement from the chairman of Hewlett Packard. A one-way mass communication exercise which swiftly introduced a new corporate structure at the same time to all (or nearly all) employees.

5.2 Logical issues

The meeting chair

To determine just what pre-meeting issues are of importance when planning a remote multi-location meeting the organisers must at the very least:

Establish that a clear meeting chairperson exists

Determine if the meeting chair should lead discussions

Ensure that the meeting chair understands the technology.

Ensure that the chair knows the participants.

It is imperative that a clear meeting chairperson exists and that this chair is recognised by those involved. Without a clear chair a multi-location meeting, even more than a normal face to face meeting, will wander from focal point to focal point and much costly time will be lost.

The selection and briefing of the meeting chair is guided by a decision on whether the chair should lead most discussions or simply coordinate the discussion. Video format unfortunately lends itself to dominance by the chair. In some contexts this may be acceptable but in many meeting types the chair may need to encourage others to participate. This is, again, a more difficult task when the technology imposes constraints on the participants.

Who drives the technology?

Ideally the meeting chair should be comfortable in the use of the technology. This is sometimes difficult. Hence, should the need arise, it is imperative that the chair is supported by a "secretariat" well versed in the technology. By ensuring the chair is confident with the technology, the need for extraneous "helpers" can be avoided and the chair can talk others in different locations through any difficulties which might otherwise be used as a "crutch" for lack of involvement.

Know the participants

The chair should know each of the participants. Again this might seem to be a simplistic observation, but in a technology supported multi-location meeting it is more important for the chair to know the participants, to understand their strengths and weaknesses and, where political negotiations are involved, to be aware of their 'normal' positions on issues to be discussed. Without this knowledge, meetings can be held and decisions reached which are not well accepted by those attending the meeting. Should this occur, the dissenters will often blame the technology for the meeting's outcome when the real culprit is the poorly prepared meeting chair.

Issues impacting those attending

Having established just who should be responsible for running the meeting, the following questions must be tackled:

Have the meeting participants met each other previously?
Do they know each other's strengths and weaknesses?
Are they familiar with the technology being used?
Has a formal agenda been developed and distributed prior to the meeting?
Has all supporting documentation been distributed prior to the meeting?
Are the meeting participants familiar with the meeting format being used?

If the participants have met each other previously then the business can be commenced immediately. If, however, they are unknown to one another the first meeting should be devoted to gaining this understanding and the amount of business should be limited.

Knowing each other's strengths and weaknesses ensures that those attending the meeting can contribute appropriately. It also enables the chair to ensure that discussion flows smoothly between locations and no single location dominates the discussion.

Familiarity with the technology being used ensures comfort and reduces the times that the technology is seen as a distraction to the achievement of goals.

The use of an agenda

The distribution of a formal agenda prior to the meeting ensures that all present can contribute at the appropriate stage. Since technology supported multi-location meetings most often have strict time limits, the use of a formal agenda enables the chair to gauge the meeting's progress, to identify issues which may be omitted if time is short, and to obtain quick agreement for any adjustments needed.

The need to distribute all meeting documentation on time is made more critical when meetings are run in a number of remote locations. Distribution and discipline/planning problems which result in "tabled" papers make meetings difficult to chair. It is true that a properly equipped meeting room will also contain a facsimile machine which can be used for last minute document distribution. This is, however, an extremely poor substitute for prior distribution of material. Inevitably the remote location participants develop a feeling of "last minute inclusion" which tends to breakdown the meeting's solidarity. The need for well planned participation may lead to the rejection of the technology rather than the acknowledgment of poor preparation by meeting participants.

Know the format

When those attending the meeting are familiar with the meeting format, the business at hand is often quickly dealt with. If, on the other hand, the format of the meeting is new to many attending much time will be lost while people determine just how things will be run. Therefore meeting chairs would be advised to allow additional time, or, preferably, reduce the agenda, in early meetings.

6 OTHER KEY ISSUES

6.1 Reaching consensus in technology supported meetings

The counting of votes in remote locations can be difficult. Indeed, the notion of meeting quorums for some organisations may need to be addressed. When a decision making board meets with some members in one location and some in another how is the meeting validated if there are insufficient members at any single location to meet the rules? In these cases it may be necessary to amend formal constitutions to allow for a quorum to be calculated from multiple locations.

Technology exists which can simplify the casting of votes. It is rarely implemented however, in simple video and audio meeting arrangements. The chair needs to determine in advance the method to be used should the counting of votes be necessary. Clearly the nature of the outcome sought will influence the approach taken. But, the issue of voting and decisions taken by acclamation must exercise the mind of a well prepared chair.

Group Think issues take on a new meaning when meetings are supported by technology. Some technologies actively encourage Group Think while other technologies inhibit the development of the herd mentality. The ability of remote members of a meeting to convey visual signals to only a subset of the meeting can be an encouragement to this problem.

The ability of people in different locations to break the 'normal' flow of discussion can lead to disjointed discussions and even the dominance of some people who would normally not be so dominant. At times, however, the masking of traditional hierarchical pressures and non-verbal signals may result in freer discussion. The desired meeting outcome should be reflected upon to determine if this is an opportunity or a problem.

6.2 Security issues

This is a significant issue which cannot be fully covered in this preliminary overview. People should be made aware of the security issues in the use of technology to support multi-location meetings. In many circumstances security is not a necessary consideration. However, the need for other (technical support style) staff to be involved, the nature of the meeting sites, and the communications lines used may make some meetings vulnerable to security breaches.

6.3 People issues

A number of other seemingly minor issues should be given some thought by the meeting organisers and the chair.

The need to start and stop on time becomes more critical with technology supported multi-location meetings. Other groups may have made booking for the technology support rooms. More than a single location is involved in bookings, thus simple time extensions are often difficult. This is a problem for all meeting participants, but one often overlooked by people in organisations with "relaxed" meeting cultures.

Problems will also exist with meetings scheduled over lunch or refreshment breaks. It may be impossible to ensure all meeting members are similarly catered for.

Problems of people wandering in and out can often be tolerated in face to face meetings. In technology supported multi-location meetings, however, this can be much more difficult for a chair to control and very disconcerting for others attending.

The formality of the meeting, eg first name or formal title basis, will play an important part in the ability of the chair to involve many members. Informal signals are often denied the chair when participants are in other locations. Thus a "random" question to members at other locations should be programmed into the chair's meeting procedures. This can be made easier in meetings run on a less formal basis.

Another problem to be avoided, often associated with tight booking schedules, is where there is a temptation for the meeting to continue at one location after the scheduled meeting ends. If this occurs too frequently it will eventually result in the breakdown of communication between participants and may culminate with people travelling to the central locations simply to ensure all of the meeting is attended.

7 SUMMARY

The costs and the benefits of the use of technology to support multi-location meetings are largely in the intangible area. Investments can be justified, however, concentrating on the tangible savings in travel time balancing this with the capital investment and operating costs of technologies to support multi-location meetings. The changes required in corporate culture, to ensure successful integration of the technology into regular decision making, are significant. An understanding of the intangible costs the geographic distribution of an organisation impose is required before this change in corporate culture can be addressed.

8 FURTHER WORK POSSIBLE

It would be of use to examine the familiarity those attending have with the technology being used and the impact this has on the perceived satisfaction with the technology for different classes of attendees. Further analysis could be undertaken into the different methods of running multi-location meetings, linking this with the anticipated outcomes and perceived satisfaction with the technology used.

Enough work has been done on Group Decision Support systems for there to be general agreement that, by specially constructing meeting rooms and providing participants with appropriate technology, anonymity can be introduced and this leads to increased participation [DeSanctis & Gallupe, 1993; Gray & Nunamaker, 1993]. When the environment of meetings is altered by the use of technology to support meeting members in multiple locations it is possible that participation, by those attending, is altered for reasons of perceived anonymity. This leads to the question:

> Under what circumstances does the use of technology increase participation in meetings and where does it limit it?

To establish a set of guidelines for meeting chairs, further analysis into the classification of expected meeting outcomes would be useful. As indicated above, successful technology supported multi-location meetings might well depend upon those attending the meeting as much as the actions of the meeting chair. Some classes of meeting seem to be well translated into multi-location mode, while other classes of meeting seem to fail. This leads to the question:

> Can the benefits of multi-location meetings be used to change the corporate culture towards the more supportable classes of meetings or would this be counter-productive?

The geographical element leading to the choice of Face to Face versus multi-location meetings is but one decision. Equally interesting questions revolve around the time element.

> Do meetings need to be synchronous?

The very nature and reason for calling the meeting can also be called into question.

> Are there some outcome classes that are better arrived at by taking more time?

Indeed the question addressing "what other technology can be used to support the meeting" raised above could be generalised a little. Computer Mediated Communications (CMC) technology involves one or a combination of the following software: e-mail, bulletin boards, list-servers, shared text data bases, etc. The evolution of Groupware or CMC, the most notable product being Lotus Notes, is changing the opportunities open to organisations in the support of group decision making. Group decision making has been previously thought of as the fundamental reason for calling many meetings. Thus the final question to emerge is:

> What form of meetings can be eliminated entirely by using new asynchronous group support technology?

9 REFERENCES

DeSanctis, G., & Gallupe, B. (1993). Group Decision Support Systems: A New Frontier. In S. R. H. & W. H. J. (Eds.), *Decision Support Systems* New Jersey: Prentice-Hall International.

Gray, P., & Nunamaker, J. F. (1993). Group Decision Support Systems. In S. R. H. & W. H. J. (Eds.), *Decision Support Systems* New Jersey: Prentice-Hall International.

Hewett, W. G., & Symons, I. (1992). *A TCF Organisation In a Changing Environment: Some Analysis For The Writing Of An Australian Case Study.* In *The Australian and New Zealand Academy of Management Conference, December 6-9 1992.,* . Sydney:

Renton, N. E. (1994). *Guide for Meetings and Organisations Volume 2 Meetings.* Sydney: The Law Book Company Limited.

Shockley-Zalabak, P. (1991). *Fundamentals of Organizational Communication Second Edition.* White Plains: Longman Publishing Group.

10 BIOGRAPHY

Bill Hewett has been actively working in the IT industry for over 30 years, Bill has worked in both IT consulting/service organisations and companies applying IT. Ten of these years were spent as an executive in a medium sized company responsible to the board for the delivery of IT services.

Since joining Deakin University in 1991 Bill has maintained his involvement with commercial applications of IT by acting as a consultant specialising in the evaluation of IT services. Bill's research interests lie in this area, in particular in attempting to define an appropriate role for IT in organisations, and examining the effectiveness of the IT function.

12

The windmills of our minds: a workshop on culture clash in CSCW

G. J. Hofstede
Wageningen Agricultural University
Department of Computer Science
Dreijenplein 2, 6703 HB Wageningen, The Netherlands
tel: +31 (0)317 484 630, fax: +31 (0)317 483 158
e-mail: gertjan hofstede@users@info.wau.nl

Abstract

This paper introduces a workshop in which teams from a number of "synthetic cultures" have to cooperate in order to design a communication architecture for a multinational company. The communication needed is about the sales and maintenance of windmills manufactured by the company. The synthetic cultures are ideal types of the extreme scale values of five well-established, empirically found dimensions of national culture. Four of them are already being used in workshops for intercultural learning. The case study on windmills is fictive. The workshop is set up with a view to obtain confrontations between the synthetic cultures.

The workshop's aim is twofold. At a methodological level, it is intended as a tool for laboratory research into multi-cultural issues in the introduction of Computer-Supported Cooperative Work technologies. As such the present proposal is only a first attempt, which will no doubt be improved with experience. For the participants, the aim is to convey an experience of culture shock which will make them more aware of the pervasive effects of differences in culture on cooperative design processes, and hence of their importance as an item on the research agenda for the International Office of the Future.

The workshop has been held three times at the time of writing, and has proven to live up to its aims.

Keywords

CSCW, communication architecture, national culture, gaming, training, research methodology.

1 INTRODUCTION

"Different-time / different-place / different-culture workgroups will become the norm."
Pieter W.G. Bots et al. (eds), 1995: *The International Office of the future: A Problem Analysis.* Delft: Technical Univ., Dept. of Systems Engineering, p. v.

"There are barriers to communication that are rooted in culture, and these barriers may keep rational, well-intentioned people from communicating accurately with one another."
Paul B. Pedersen and Allen Ivey (1993): *Culture-centered Counseling and Interviewing Skills.* Westport: Praeger. p. 13-14.

As the global village becomes smaller, neighbours from different cultures cooperate with each other more and more. Information technology makes it possible for colleagues in different parts of the world to communicate in a variety of ways at any time. Competition and globalization make such communication necessary.

Recently, Computer Supported Cooperative Work (CSCW) has become a keyword for a collection of information technologies to enable communication across time and space. CSCW techniques include, for instance, electronic mail and electronic meetings.

People with experience in multi-culture workgroups know how difficult it used to be to get multicultural groups to function before the advent of information technology. People from different cultures tend to misunderstand each other's behaviours and hence come to distrust one another. It would be short-sighted to expect CSCW technology to overcome these problems. Indeed, Bots et al. in their position paper on the International Office of the Future (IOF) remark (pp. 11-12):

> "We expect that within the IOF different cultures will be confronted with one another, creating new cultures. The evolution of cultures will result in changing demands towards the supporting technology. This will make it necessary to gain more in depth knowledge about the relation between organizational cultures and the impact on the possibility and use of supporting technology.
>
> We can illustrate the differences in culture with respect to the inter-personal communication. The "distance" between manager and subordinate may widely differ from culture to culture. When people from different cultures get involved in direct communication, clashes may result. Good examples are the (internal!) consultant who is not expected to speak until he (or she!) is asked a direct question versus the consultant who is expected to take the lead, and the executive who can be approached only through a sequence of intermediaries. Imagine the consequences of these differences when implementing teleconferencing or even e-mail systems!"

This quotation makes it manifest that CSCW technologies cannot just be dumped into multi-culture organizations, in particular multinational organizations. Research is needed on the interplay of technology and multicultural interaction. If possible the technology should facilitate the interaction, whereas in practice the opposite could occur. For instance, the executive in the quotation above might simply refuse to take part in electronic meetings, judging them to be below his dignity.

In the same text, the authors define an agenda for research. As one of the items in this agenda they mention (p. 13:) "a large-scale, international comparative study into the man-labor relationship". I believe that such a study already exists, and that its results can be of great value to address the problem of cooperation across cultures in the IOF. I am referring to the work of Geert Hofstede (Hofstede, 1980, recently described in a more accessible format in Hofstede, 1991). In the seventies, Geert Hofstede got access to data from a large-scale study on work-related values of IBM personnel in many countries. Since then, many have added to his work. His main findings, which have proved to be of value in both research and consultancy, are that the attitude of people towards their jobs and employers can be classified along a number of "dimensions of culture". These were found in a comparison among nationalities. They can be used to study cultural differences between individuals from different nationalities, but they have been found not to be suitable for comparing organizations. The reason for this is that organizations, unlike nationality, are partial in the sense that one is hardly ever a member of an organization to 100%.

Hofstede's dimensions from the IBM study are: (a) power distance, as in the examples from Bots et al. above, (b) individualism versus collectivism, (c) masculinity versus femininity and (d) uncertainty avoidance. A fifth dimension was found with South-East Asian cultures: (e) long-term versus short-time orientation. The first three dimensions represent three fundamental relationships between people: vertical, horizontal, and gender-related. The latter two can be seen as the western and eastern version of a culture's orientation towards time.

Paul B. Pedersen and Allen Ivey (1993) used Hofstede's first four dimensions to create workshops through which they trained intercultural counselors. In these workshops, participants were divided into four groups. The groups then taught themselves a "synthetic culture", i.e. an extreme manifestation of one of Hofstede's dimensions. Then the four groups engaged in various interactions, depending on the context of the workshop.

What I have done is to adapt Pedersen and Ivey's workshops to problem situations that are likely to occur in the International Office of the Future. In the present workshop the participants have to design a communication architecture for an organization (Energy Forever inc.) that is setting up a global structure for sales and maintenance of windmills. Windmills cannot just be sold to customers in remote countries. Some initial training and some assistance in maintenance are necessary. Energy Forever have decided to put in place a proper communication architecture for the Windmill project.

The workshop serves two aims. First, it is a tool for research in intercultural communication in the context of CSCW, and second, it makes the participants aware of the pervasiveness of differences in culture, and hence motivates them to take these differences seriously in their work. As with any tool that is applied for the first time, both the tool and the results will come under scrutiny after the effort.

The paper goes on to describe the hypothetical case and the workshop first. Then, some background is given on CSCW technologies, which it is assumed the reader is reasonably familiar with, and on the "synthetic cultures" used in the workshop. Readers who are not familiar with dimensions of culture may wish to read the section on the synthetic cultures first before reading the rest of the paper. In the discussion which concludes the article, some preliminary results are presented of the three instances of the workshop held to date.

2 THE CASE STUDY: ENERGY FOREVER, INC.

Energy Forever inc. is a large, commercial provider of energy, based in Europe. With a yearly turnover of 3.500 million, bases in over 40 countries, an IS staff of some 500 people, and yearly expenditures on IT of some 10 Million, it is quite an enterprise, and ranks among the Global 100 remarkable IT users worldwide (as given in "Computerworld", June 1995). Energy Forever has been around for some thirty years, and most national branches have led a fairly stable life over the past few years, with typically some tens of employees, including field staff, per country. Its main products are electro-technical installations, ranging from simple gas-powered aggregates to complete power plants. Conventional sources of energy are Energy Forever's stronghold.

The research lab, having worked out the technology in experimental settings, has been advocating for some years that windmills should be added to FE's standard product range. A favourable political mood has now resulted in an advice by the Board and a subsequent decision by the CEO to launch a Windmill project: "the Windmills of Our Minds". The project's aim, apart from delivering sustainable energy at a favourable price, is to alter the company's image as a high-ranking polluter. This is worth a fair investment, so that the WOM project, as it is called, is not short of funds.

Having read Peter Keen's advice (Keen, 1991) that technical architecture and infrastructure should be seen by top corporate management as a long-range capital investment, the CEO wishes to position WOM as a model project in this regard. The project's first deliverable is to be a "communication architecture" for a global network for selling windmills of a variety of types (from modest and easy to maintain, but not very efficient, to extremely leading-edge) in a multitude of countries. The architecture must in particular support a sales and maintenance network for the windmills. Transferring knowledge from experience quickly across the sales and maintenance network is an important objective. As far as the choice of technologies goes, the project team has a free hand, and permission to "go grand".

In short, Energy Forever is a successful company, and the WOM project is a very innovative prestige project. Both the explicit concept of a "Communication Architecture" and the idea of adding windmills to the project range are very new. For the energy installations that Energy Forever currently sells there never has been a conscious design of a communication architecture for sales and maintenance.

Sales information at a company-wide level is only fed back to salespeople through the yearly business report which appears on paper and was also published on the company's WWW site this year. In some national branches there are additional flows of sales information, mostly through face-to-face meetings of personnel at company social events.

Maintenance information is currently not being gathered or kept centrally. There are files of repair jobs and of spare part orders in all national branches, though. From these files, some information about maintenance needs could be derived. Data on why an installation broke down is currently not collected, let alone spread in the organization.

There are some national differences in the way maintenance people are sent to maintenance jobs. Typically, they make fixed tours along a number of installations, and will interrupt these tours for emergency jobs. Most maintain radio contact with country headquarters. In some countries mobile phones have recently been introduced. Anecdotal information about repair jobs and their causes circulates widely and sometimes reaches the company's internal newsletter.

3 THE WORKSHOP

The workshop requires at least eight, but preferably twenty to thirty participants. It takes half a day, e.g. from 12.30 to 16.30. The participants go through the following sequence of events (for each activity, sequence number, starting time in hours / minutes, *title* and contents are shown):

1. 12'30" *Welcome* . The participants fill in a questionnaire in which they give their views on culture-laden questions as well as on IT-related questions so that they will know more or less where they stand themselves with regard to Hofstede's five dimensions.
2. 13'00" *Introduction.* Using the questionnaire, the workshop leader introduces the synthetic cultures. The participants choose one of these as their own. During the rest of the workshop they will playact belonging to that culture.
3. 13'30" *Warming up.* All participants choose a group and do a few warming up-exercises to acculturate. Then each synthetic culture group spends some time

dividing roles: project leader, senior mechanic, junior executive, sales manager, computer specialist, secretary (optional), observant (optional). All read their role briefings.

4. 13'45" *First project meeting*. Each synthetic culture is given the same instructions about its task: to set up a communication architecture for windmill sales and maintenance. The main points of their proposal (including choice of hardware, CSCW software, data sets, organizational procedures, and roles of people), together with the main "dos and don'ts", are collected on flipover sheet or blackboard by the secretaries. Staying in one's role is more important than arriving at a sound proposal!

5. 14'00" *Evaluation of the first project meeting.*

6. 14'25" *Consultant briefing*. Each culture chooses one participant for a consultant. This person is assigned to the task of helping one of the other cultures out with their communication architecture. The group decides which objectives the consultant must absolutely attain with the other group.

7. 14'30" *Coffee Break.*

8. 15'00" *Second project meeting*. The consultants spend the meeting in the host group, then return to their own culture to report briefly. The consultants remain faithful to their own synthetic cultures. The secretaries adapt the flipovers if necessary.

9. 15'15" *Evaluation of the second project meeting*. This evaluation takes place within each culture group. The consultants remain in their original culture, and participants play their role.

10. 15'30" *Plenary de-briefing*. This is a plenary session to compare the various communication architectures and to discuss the confrontations between various cultures during the second project meeting. It includes a brief presentation of each group's communication architecture, as well as the consultants' account of how they fared in the host cultures.

11. 16'15" *Workshop evaluation*. This is a brief plenary reflection on the workshop as a whole.

12. 16'30" *End of the workshop.*

4 CSCW TECHNOLOGIES

The communication architecture for the WOM project is supposed to be leading edge. It is therefore natural for the project team to look to CSCW technology.

For a choice of CSCW technologies, participants can draw on private knowledge and experience if they possess any. It is to be expected that the participants' level of a priori knowledge will vary rather widely. Well in advance of the workshop, participants who are in need of it will be given Roland Traunmüller's paper on CSCW in Bots et al. (1995).

Participants are free to choose conventional technologies such as paper mail, telephone, telefax or face to face contact. As for what is labelled CSCW, Traunmüller gives the following taxonomy (Bots et al. (eds), p. 33):

Table 1 A taxonomy of CSCW technology, from Traunmüller (in Bots et al. (eds), 1995)

	Same time	*Different time (predictable)*	*Different time (not predictable)*
Same place	meeting facilitation	work shifts	team rooms
Different place (predictable)	whiteboarding, desktop or video conferencing	electronic or voice mail	collaborative writing
Different place (not predictable)	broadcast seminars	computer conferences	workflow management

Any of these technologies could be applied.

A critical discussion of experiences with CSCW technologies or, as the author calls it, groupware, is given by Grudin (1994) in an issue on "social computing" of *Communications of the ACM*. Grudin identifies obstacles for success of groupware, some of which are obviously rooted in cultural factors. Table 2 below is taken from his paper. It can be used during the workshop's evaluation to discuss the five communication architectures.

Table 2 Eight challenges for groupware developers (from Grudin, 1994, p. 97)

1. Disparity in work and benefit. Groupware applications often require additional work from individuals who do not perceive a direct benefit from the use of the application.
2. Critical mass and Prisoner's dilemma problems. Groupware may not enlist the "critical mass" of users required to be useful, or can fail because it is never to any one individual's advantage to use it.
3. Disruption of social processes. Groupware can lead to activity that violates social taboos, threatens existing political structures, or otherwise demotivates users crucial to its success.
4. Exception handling. Groupware may not accommodate the wide range of exception handling and improvisation that characterizes much group activity.
5. Unobtrusive accessibility. Features that support group processes are used relatively infrequently, requiring unobtrusive accessibility and integration with more heavily used features.
6. Difficulty of evaluation. The almost insurmountable obstacles to meaningful, generalizable analysis and evaluation of groupware prevent us from learning from experience.
7. Failure of intuition. Intuitions in product developments are especially poor for multiuser applications, resulting in bad management decisions and an error-prone design process.
8. The adoption process. Groupware requires more careful implementation (introduction) in the workplace than product developers have confronted.

Incidentally, it also indicates how many obstacles exist to the introduction of groupware even in the industrialized countries, which seem to be the implicit setting of the article. The first and third obstacles from table 2 in particular are likely to be much higher still in a multi-cultural setting in which "non-industrialized" cultures participate. As for the sixth obstacle, difficulty of evaluation, it may be that workshops similar to the one proposed here can be of use in this area. Furthermore, an obvious, mundane obstacle to the adoption of groupware in developing countries is want of basic enabling technologies such as reliable telephone lines.

5 THE TEN SYNTHETIC CULTURES

The synthetic cultures are based on the work of Geert Hofstede (1980, 1991). Each of the five dimensions of national culture is a scale with two extremes. For each extreme of every dimension there is a synthetic culture, so that there are ten possible one-dimensional synthetic cultures in all.

Four of the synthetic cultures in the workshop are taken from Pedersen and Ivey (1993), who base themselves on Hofstede (1980, 1991). The remaining six are also taken from Hofstede (1991), but without the intermediary of Pedersen and Ivey. The fifth dimension, long-term orientation, did not figure in Hofstede's original data, because the original questionnaires, having been drawn up by a team without South-East Asian members, did not contain questions addressing this dimension. It was discovered later, using a questionnaire designed by South-East Asians. The particulars can be read in Hofstede (1991). Because this fifth dimension was found in a different setting from the first four, and because it has been less extensively researched, its appearance in this workshop is more tentative than that of the first four. All five dimensions are orthogonal, i.e. one's score on power distance has nothing to do with one's score on individualism, masculinity, uncertainty avoidance, or long-time orientation.

The workshop participants are given a presentation about the five dimensions before they make their choice. In some games, participants are not told the "culture bias" of other participants, but Pedersen and Ivey found that usually, telling the participants about all four synthetic cultures worked best in their workshops. Participants can then decide to choose either a synthetic culture that fits them, or one that is unfamiliar to them and about which they wish to learn more.

The **Hipow** culture is characterized by high power distance. Seven key elements of high power distance societies (selected from among many more, given by Hofstede (1991)) are:

1. Might makes right and power is good.
2. Power, status and privileges go together.
3. Less powerful people are dependent on more powerful.
4. Centralization is popular.
5. Subordinates expect direction.
6. The ideal boss is a benevolent autocrat or "good father".
7. Management theories focus on the appropriate roles of managers.

Some words that Hipows will use with a positive connotation are: respect, father (as a title), master, servant, older brother, younger brother, wisdom, favour, protect, obey, orders, pleasing.

Some words with a negative connotation among Hipows are: rights, complain, negotiate, fairness, task, necessity, codetermination, objectives, question, criticize.

The **Lopow** culture is the opposite of the hipow culture. It is characterized by extremely low power distance. Seven key elements:

1. Inequalities among people should be minimized. Privileges and status symbols are frowned upon.
2. There should be, and is, interdependence between less and more powerful people.

3. Hierarchy in organizations means an inequality of roles only, established for convenience.
4. Decentralization is popular.
5. Subordinates expect to be consulted.
6. The ideal boss is a resourceful democrat.
7. Powerful people try to look less powerful than they are.

Words with a positive connotation among Lopows are those that hold a negative connotation among Hipows, and vice versa (see above for a list of such words).

The **Indiv** culture is highly individualistic. Seven key elements:

1. Honest persons speak their mind.
2. Low-context communication (abstract concepts) is preferred.
3. The task prevails over relationships.
4. Laws and rights are the same for all.
5. Trespassing leads to guilt and loss of self-respect.
6. Everyone has a private opinion on any topic.
7. The relationship between employer and employee is a contract based on mutual advantage.

Words with a positive connotation: self, friendship, do your own thing, contract, litigation, self-interest, self-respect, self-actualizing, individual, dignity, I, me, pleasure, adventurous, guilt, privacy.
Words with a negative connotation: harmony, face, we, obligation, sacrifice, family, tradition, decency, honour, duty, loyalty, shame.

The **Collec** culture is the opposite of the Inviv culture. It is extremely collectivist. Seven key elements:

1. Harmony should always be maintained and direct confrontations avoided.
2. Members of one's "in-group" (organization, extended family, ...) are sharply distinct from other, "out-group" people.
3. Relationships are more important than the task at hand.
4. Laws and rights differ by group.
5. Tresspassing leads to shame and loss of face for self and in-group.
6. Opinions are predetermined by group membership.
7. The relationship between employer and employee is perceived in moral terms, like a family link.

Words with a positive connotation are those that carry a negative one among Indivs, and vice versa.

The **Mascu** culture is highly masculine. Seven key elements:

1. Material success and progress are dominant values.
2. Bigger and faster are better.
3. Men are assertive, ambitious and "tough".
4. Women are tender and take care of relationships.
5. Failing is a disaster.
6. Conflicts are resolved by fighting them out.
7. Managers are expected to be decisive and assertive.

Words with a positive connotation: career, competition, fight, aggressive, assertive, success, winner, deserve, merit, balls, excel, force, big, hard, fast, quantity.
Words with a negative connotation: quality, caring, solidarity, modesty, compromise, help, love, grow, small, soft, slow, tender.

The **Femi** culture is highly feminine. It is the opposite of the Mascu culture. Seven key elements:
1. Dominant values in society are caring for others and preservation (e.g. of the environment).
2. Small and slow are beautiful.
3. Everybody is supposed to be modest, men and women alike.
4. Conflicts are resolved by compromise and negotiation.
5. There is stress on equality, solidarity, and quality of work life.
6. Society is permissive.
7. Managers use intuition and strive for consensus.

Words with a positive or negative connotation are the same as for Mascus but with inverted sign.

The **Uncavo** culture is one of strong uncertainty avoidance. Seven key elements:
1. What is different is dangerous.
2. Familiar risks are accepted, but they fear ambiguous situations and unfamiliar risks.
3. There is an emotional need for rules, even if they will never work.
4. An appeal to existing rules is popular.
5. Time is money.
6. There is only one truth and we have it.
7. There is a belief in experts and specialization.

Words with a positive connotation: structure, duty, truth, law, order, certain, clean, clear, secure, safe, predictable, tight.
Words with a negative connotation: maybe, creative, conflict, tolerant, experiment, spontaneous, relativity, insight, unstructured, loose, flexible.

The **Unctol** culture is the opposite of the Uncavo culture. Uncertainty is extremely well tolerated by Unctols. Seven key elements:
1. What is different, is curious.
2. One is comfortable in ambiguous situations and with unfamiliar risks.
3. There should not be more rules than is strictly necessary.
4. Aggression and emotions should not be shown.
5. Being lazy feels good; one works hard when it is needed only.
6. There is tolerance of deviant and innovative ideas and behaviour.
7. There is a belief in generalists and in common sense.

Words with a positive or negative connotation are the same as for Uncavos but with inverse sign.

The **Lotor** culture is extremely long-term oriented. Key elements are:
1. Thrift is good.
2. Never give up, even if results are in want.
3. A sense of shame prevents one from doing what is wrong.
4. Traditions need not be immutable but can be adapted to a modern context.
5. Relations are ordered by status and this order is observed, but
6. There are limits to respect for social and status-related obligations.
7. Achieving one's purpose may be worth losing face.

Words with a positive connotation among Lotors: work, save, moderation, endurance, duty, goal, permanent, future, economy, virtue, invest, afford, effort.
Words with a negative connotation: relation, gift, today, yesterday, truth, quick, spend, receive, grand, tradition, show, image.

The **Shotor** culture is the inverse of the Lotor culture. It is very short-time oriented. Seven key elements:

1. There is a social pressure to "Keep up with the Joneses", even if it means overspending.
2. Quick results are expected.
3. Never lose face.
4. Traditions should be respected.
5. Social demands (e.g. reciprocating gifts) are met regardless of cost.
6. There is a concern with possessing the Truth.
7. Saving is not popular, so that there is little money for investment.

Words with a positive or negative connotation are as for Lotors but with inverse sign.

6 DISCUSSION

CSCW and dimensions of culture

There is ample evidence that introducing technology in other settings than those in which it was invented can be deeply disruptive. In a book on management in developing countries, Kanungo and Jaeger set the scene with the following remark (Jaeger and Kanungo (eds) 1990), p. 1):

> "Most widely dispersed management theories and techniques have their origin in the industrialized countries of the West. Many organizations in these industrialized countries have benefited from their prescriptions. As a result, western management thought and practice have turned into 'sacred cows' for industrial development."

However, it has been acknowledged for much longer that technology transfer across cultures causes the receiving culture to be under pressure. See, for instance, Goulet (1977), who uses a forceful argument as well as numerous case descriptions to make the point that technology from industrialized countries frequently upsets societies in non-industrialized countries if it is introduced there. Such non-industrial societies depend on shared significative values for stability. Stability, in turn, is needed because in non-industrialized societies resources are scarce and usually do not grow over time. Technology has historically taken away the need for stability, due to the manifold growth it entails. Simultaneously, technology enlarges markets, so that the circle of persons every member of society has to communicate with grows. So with the advent of technology, homogeneity in significative values is exchanged for shared normative values. You need to have some shared rules in order to do business, but you do not need to hold the same beliefs. Rather than a global village, we have a global marketplace.

The argument about the different roles of significative and normative values in developed versus developing countries is summed up by Goulet as follows (Goulet 1977, p. 21):

> Whereas in less-developed societies a high level of integration exists between normative and significative values, economic activities are fragmented. A large number of production units - individuals, families, or villages - operate quite independently of others, and little coordination of effort or specialization of tasks is required. The opposite condition prevails in "developed" areas. There the basic symbols which explain history, life and personal destinies have no link to norms for action, but economic activity is so highly integrated that the autarchic subsistence of small units becomes practically impossible. Ultimately, the importance of the nexus between norms and meanings lies in this: In traditional societies work is a cosmic act; in developed societies, a specialized function."

One might object that the IOF is not about technology, but about communication and about the organization of work, so that it need not be disruptive. But the quotation above points out that in less-developed societies, communication and work themselves are subordinate to significative values, embodied in traditions. As a consequence, there is no way to change communication or the organization of work without upturning the significative value system.

In what way can we expect the International Office of the Future, and techniques advocated for use in the IOF, to affect value systems? Consider the visionary article by Roy Jacques in Bots et al (1995). On p. 23 he writes:

> Point: "Workers have to stop doing simply what they are told, increase their job-relevant skills and invest more intelligence and emotional energy in their jobs". Point: " The employment relationship of the future is going to be more contingent; workers are going to have to think of their jobs as temporary. There is considerable tension between these two points".

This quotation, as the rest of Jacques' paper, has nothing to say on "significative values" as Goulet uses the word. It is about shifts that are required in work-related values. This means, perhaps, that to a western mind work-related values *are* significative values. They live in order to work, whereas in traditional societies one works in order to live.

Hofstede's dimensions of culture enable us to articulate just what value shift Jacques is predicting. According to him, a shift is required towards lower power distance, less uncertainty avoidance, and higher individualism. When we look at Hofstede's data, we see that these are the value combinations of Anglo-saxon countries, including the USA in particular. Other parts of the world have value systems that are much different: for instance, power distance is usually high, and individualism is low. So from their point of view, Jacques is foretelling that work in the IOF will require an even greater culture shift than if they had to adapt to current working conditions in industrialized countries.

Using historical data, centuries old in some cases, Hofstede (1991) also shows that value systems are very conservative. Consider once again the quotation from Bots et al. given in the introduction to this paper, which predicts that the IOF will create new cultures: there is a tension there too. So, to sum up, it becomes apparent that designing the multi-cultural IOF is definitely going to be a challenging process.

The workshop as a tool for research

It is very hard to predict the effects of office innovations without actually trying them out in practice. To quote Jacques once more (in Bots et al., 1995, p. 23):

> "It is relatively easy to design an office with future-oriented work flows and technologies. It is relatively more difficult to understand how we will (collectively) create an environment in which workers exhibit the attitudes and behaviors on which these new work systems depend."

Because of the high risks and costs involved, workshops such as the one presented here can be, I believe, of value in directing research efforts in CSCW technologies and architectures that are appropriate for the International Office of the Future. The workshops, if well designed, can link a specific mix of cultures to a specific office design, and see the combination in action. Once an experience base of such "laboratory IOF's" exists, it can be helpful in two directions. If one knows that certain groups will have to cooperate, one can first gather knowledge about their cultural values and then design the office to fit. If, on the other hand, one has some known office design available, one can select personnel of which, given their value system, one can assume they will feel comfortable working within that design. This presumes that one can accurately obtain the candidates' cultural value systems (e.g. with help of Hofstede 1991, pp. 249 ff.).

The key assumptions here are that (a) one's work-related cultural values can be measured, and (b) office systems can be designed to fit workers' value systems. To put it mildly, these assumptions will most certainly not hold fully in all cases. But if only a small measure of improvement in the design of IOF's can be reached, the exercise will have been worthwhile.

CSCW is but one of the many possible subject matters of a culture clash-workshop such as the one presented here. Incidentally, it proved to be quite ambitious to put both culture clash and IOF-related content matter within one half-day workshop. If time permits, a stepwise approach is to be preferred, in which there is a first workshop in which the participants experience the synthetic cultures and the sense of culture clash, followed by a second one in which they attempt to deal with IOF-related subject matter while playacting different synthetic cultures.

The present workshop has a design task as its subject matter, which is itself not supported by advanced technology. Other types of tasks may not be sensitive to their performer's cultures in the same way. To find out about this, one can experiment in workshops with e.g. negotiation, document preparation, or coding tasks, under various conditions of support. This of course necessitates the availability of the supporting technology. At the multi-site IOF Conference planned for September 1997 (see Bots et al. 1995, p. vi) a multi-site culture clash workshop may be held.

The workshop as a vehicle for creating awareness

Pedersen and Ivey distinguish three phases in their work with counselors: awareness, knowledge and skill. First, the would-be intercultural counselors must be aware what differences in culture are, and what their own cultural values are. Then, they can gather knowledge of how meetings between participants from different cultures can go amiss, and what behaviours are appropriate when one communicates with somebody with a particular cultural background. Finally, they can practice skills in effectively communicating across cultures, adapting their behaviour as appropriate.

The workshop proposed here aims at opening the participants' eyes to the first level, that of awareness. This first step is probably the hardest one, and one which is much facilitated through actual experience of culture shock. Such an experience can be a true eye-opener to anyone, and particularly to one who has much schooling in the area of information technology, but little schooling in interpersonal communication and no experience of living in different societies.

Pedersen and Ivey's other phases, knowledge of the effect of differences in culture in workgroups on the design of CSCW technologies, as well as skills in using CSCW technologies in multi-culture groups, are concerns that will have to be addressed in the future. Laboratory situations may be put to good use here. For instance, one can use existing "real-world" technological infrastructures for experiments in which multi-cultural workgroups have to perform IOF-related tasks, as a first step in performing these tasks "for real". The experiments can be used for reflection, and for improving the architecture or the procedures associated with the architecture.

7 EXPERIENCES WITH THE WORKSHOP

The workshop has been held thrice: once in Wageningen in November 1995, once in Amsterdam in December 1995 (as an ICIS '95 pre-conference workshop of the "Cross-cultural research in IS" group) and once in Wageningen in January 1996. Some data on the three workshops are given in Table 3 below.

Table 3 Overview of the three workshops "The Windmills of our Minds" given to date

Workshop	*Number of participants*	*Number of nationalities represented*	*Synthetic cultures played*
Wageningen Nov '95	10	4	Lopow, Mascu
Amsterdam Dec '95	25	13	Hipow, Collec (2 groups), Indiv
Wageningen Jan '96	15	4	Femi, Unctol, Lotor

Overall findings from these three repetitions can be summarized as follows.

a) The workshop fulfills its aim as a vehicle for awareness, according to statements made by the participants about how they *experienced* differences in culture. It is perceived as motivating and enjoyable. A great deal of enthusiasm and many intelligent comments were prompted by the workshop.

b) The workshop serves its aim of investigating the influence of culture on group design activities.

c) The workshop is far too short to allow for reflection. Hence its aim of serving as a tool for research is not realized to the full, simply because there is no time to link the workshop to the participants' real-world experience. A full day would be required at a minimum to allow for discussion about the workshop, and one more day to link the workshop to everyday experience. Despite the lack of time in the current formula, the idea of using conditioned experiments to investigate office environments is definitely reinforced by the workshop.

d) Enacting a synthetic culture truthfully is quite hard to do. Time for reflection about acting performance, and about whether what happened during the meetings was faithful to the synthetic culture being enacted, would be an improvement. Also, having to enact both an individual role and a culture role while at the same time having to perform a design task is really hard to do for many participants. Two remedies apply: first, the personal role briefings can be dropped, and second, the workshop should only be given to people with a background in the content matter of the case study. Having two meetings, so that the first can serve as a starter for the second, proved to be a good idea.

Table 4 gives an impression of how the various culture groups fared with regard to the process and to the result of their first meeting. No claim is being made other than to describe what happened. Repetitions of the playing of identical encounters with different fictive cultures will no doubt show that personal and interpersonal factors play a role which may alter the balance of a meeting completely. I also suspect that players from Europe or the Anglo-saxon countries tend to add femininity when they enact collectivity, and to add low power distance when they enact femininity.

Table 4 Summary of the first meetings

Synthetic culture (date)	*Process*	*Result*
Hipow (Dec. '95)	hostile, subdued	centralized
Lopow (Nov. '95)	time-consuming, nobody decides	egalitarian, internal orientation
Collec (Dec. '95, 2x)	family	various
Indiv (Dec. '95)	noisy. coalitions & fights.	buck passing
Femi (Jan. '96)	warm, outgoing	egalitarian, internal orientation, education
Mascu (Nov. '95)	quick, efficient	external orientation, competitive
Uncavo	-	-
Unctol (Jan. '96)	culture not dominant	enabling communication
Shotor	-	-
Lotor (Jan. '96)	disciplined	strategic

As far as the second meeting is concerned the situation is more complex: 200 combinations of consultant and host culture are possible. One can speculate about what values are in general desirable for a consultant. Femi, Indiv and Unctol are candidates. As far as the host culture is concerned, the experiences so far make me suspect that a Hipow or Collec host culture can induce strong culture shock in most consultants.

In order to obtain results that can be used in practice, it will be useful to experiment with host/consultant culture combinations that one expects to occur in actual practice, and to compare the findings with field data. Also, as stated before, extended time for discussion, e.g. watching video images of the workshop meetings, and including real-world experiences that participants have had with multi-cultural meetings, will help separate incidental results from results that are rooted in culture differences.

The workshop described here will, I hope, be the first in a family. There still are some data to process, i.e. the culture questionnaires filled in by the participants. Also, a number of comments are still awaiting further reflection. Finally, a number of initiatives are under way to extend the formula to other settings: for use in virtual task environments, during courses and trainings, with different subject matter, and with different conditions of conditioning.

8 ACKNOWLEDGEMENTS

Thanks go to Pieter Bots, who encouraged me to pursue the idea which led to this workshop. I am indebted to Geert Hofstede and Paul Pedersen for the comments they made about an earlier version of the paper. I wish to thank Marlies Tjallingii for her advice which helped me improve the workshop's schedule. Thanks are also due to four anonymous reviewers, whose recommendations I have followed as far as time permitted. Finally I am grateful to the participants for "making it happen" on three occasions. Some of them will find I acted upon their suggestions to improve the workshop.

9 REFERENCES

Bots, Pieter W.G. et al. (eds) (1995) *The International Office of the future: A Problem Analysis.* Technical University, Dept. Of Systems Engineering, Delft.

Goulet, Denis (1977) *The Uncertain Promise: Value Conflicts in Technology transfer.* IDOC/North America, New York.

Grudin, Jonathan (1994) Groupware and Social Dynamics: Eight Challenges for Developers. In *Communications of the ACM,* **37**:1, Jan 1994, pp 92-105.

Hofstede, Geert (1980) *Culture's Consequences: International Differences in Work-related Values.* Sage Publications, Beverly Hills, CA.

Hofstede, Geert (1991) *Cultures and Organizations, Software of the Mind: Intercultural Cooperation and its Importance for Survival.* McGraw-Hill, London.

Jaeger, Alfred M. And Rabindra N. Kanungo (eds) (1990) *Management in Developing Countries.* Routledge, London.

Keen, Peter G. (1991) Shaping the Future: Business Design through Information Technology. Harvard Press, Boston, MA.

Pedersen, Paul B. and Allen Ivey (1993) *Culture-centered Counseling and Interviewing Skills.* Praeger, Westport.

10 BIOGRAPHY

Gert Jan Hofstede, a biologist by vocation, has worked as an information systems professional since 1984. He wrote a Ph.D. dissertation, titled "Modesty in Modelling", about the applicability of formal models in decision support systems. He teaches data modelling. His research interests include Soft Systems methodology and the influence of cultural factors on designated tasks carried out by groups.

13

Using the information superhighway to support organizational learning: content, context, and infrastructure

Leonard M. Jessup and Joseph S. Valacich
Department of Accounting and Information Systems
School of Business, Indiana University
Tenth and Fee Lane, Room 560
Bloomington, Indiana 47405-1701
Tel: 812-855-2691/812-855-8966 - Fax 812-855-7332
LJESSUP@INDIANA.EDU and VALACICH@INDIANA.EDU

Abstract

There are a variety of computing and networking technologies available to support organizational learning, including the Internet, World Wide Web, Group Support Systems, Groupware, and Desktop Video Conferencing. These technologies can be used to help organizational members enhance their own knowledge and skills, to enable the organization as a collective to learn and grow, and to support interorganizational learning. In this paper we describe an executive education program that is focused on the content area of the virtual organization and uses technology supported learning as the primary vehicle. In this way the participants would use the technology to learn about the technology and its role in organizational learning. The available technologies described here could be used to radically change the learning infrastructure, which could enable a variety of learning modes and uses. Consequently, it may be more appropriate to think of organizational learning happening across time and space rather than in a particular place and/or at a particular time.

Keywords

Information Superhighway, Internet, World Wide Web, Group Support Systems, Groupware, Desktop Video Conferencing, Organizational Learning, Executive Education

1 INTRODUCTION

Doing more with less, while still remaining competitive, has become a standard operating procedure for managers. To cope, managers have traditionally used information systems to automate old business processes. Times have changed. Managers are currently employing business process reengineering, organizational downsizing or rightsizing, total quality management, and a host of other management techniques which utilize information technology as the engine of productivity, the vehicle for organizational memory and learning, and the enabler of organizational change and competitive advantage. Now more than ever, the strategic management of information technology is key.

Among the new information technologies that show the greatest promise are a suite of telecommunication and computer-based systems that include desktop video conferencing, Groupware, and the Internet World Wide Web. These technologies can be used to transform a traditional, rigid organization into a virtual organization, which we define for this paper as an organization that uses a variety of information technologies to cross, extend, or do away with boundaries, to overcome limits and barriers, and to enable real time collaboration across space and time. This paper describes how these technologies can and should be used to support organizational learning in the form of a "high tech, high touch" executive education program. We first briefly review what is meant by organizational learning. Next, we describe the relevant content, context, and infrastructure for an executive education program that enables such learning to take place as part of, and as a result of, the education program. Finally, we conclude with a brief summary of the benefits and implications of technology supported organizational learning.

2 ORGANIZATIONAL LEARNING

An organization learns if, through its processing of information, the range of its potential behaviors is changed (Huber, 1991; Hoffer and Valacich, 1993). Organizational learning is based in four related constructs:

1. knowledge acquisition - obtaining knowledge,
2. information distribution - sharing information which leads to new information or understanding,
3. information interpretation - information is given one or more commonly understood meanings, and
4. organizational memory - means by which knowledge is stored for future use (Huber, 1991).

In other words, organizations learn by encoding inferences from history (memory) into routines that guide behavior (Levitt & March, 1988). Behavior is an evoked, repeatable response and is an adaptation of stored routines, much as the muscles of an athlete learn certain moves without the overt direction of the brain. Behavior is purposeful, and is viewed as picking an appropriate action from matching the current situation (pattern) with past situations (patterns), rather than consciously choosing among alternatives. Actions are extensions of history, more than the result of anticipating the future.

Organizational learning deals with either cognitive changes or behavioral changes by the organization (Fiol & Lyles, 1985). Cognitive change results in new shared understandings and conceptual schemes by organization members; behavioral changes are a change in the range of potential behaviors of organizational members (Huber, 1991). The literature on organizational learning has been summarized as reflecting two basic perspectives: the systems-structural perspective and the interpretive perspective (Daft & Huber, 1987).

The **systems-structural perspective** emphasizes the acquisition and distribution of information as a resource that is necessary for learning. The systems-structural perspective focuses on the process of learning. Message routing (the distribution of messages) and message summarizing (compression of ideas without loss of meaning) are important processes. The **interpretive perspective** focuses on a deeper reason for information exchange. In the interpretive perspective, information has utility, as it can reduce uncertainty and equivocality, and can therefore change one's understanding about the external world (Daft & Macintosh, 1981). Uncertainty can be simply defined as the absence of information. This is distinct from equivocality, which can be defined as the existence of multiple and conflicting interpretations about a situation. Uncertainty and equivocality are reduced, in part, by collecting and organizing information into shared repositories.

Many factors influence the ability of technology-based aids to support the information gathering, equivocality reduction, and subsequent understanding processes. Factors such as the capacity of the communication channels available (media richness), the flexibility of the representation schemes, and the ease of sharing information among group members all influence information gathering and understanding.

Organizational learning, thus, can be viewed as the acquisition and sharing of assumptions and cognitive maps among organizational (group) members (Shrivastava, 1983). Learning can occur when individuals compare their own assumptions and maps to what actually occurs. This comparison may result in two types of learning, single- and double-loop learning (Argyris & Schon, 1978). In single-loop learning, misconceptions are corrected (facts changed) within a fixed infrastructure. In double-loop learning, organization norms, strategies, assumptions, and structures are fundamentally changed. Double-loop learning requires greater flexibility that supports dynamic changes to both the structure and content of the repository. The constraints of using technology-based aids as a foundation for organizational learning may cause learning to be systematic and restricted. Yet, as technology evolves, the ability of technology-based aids to effectively support organizational learning processes will be enhanced.

Double-loop learning is more fundamentally action-oriented and, thus, may be more desirable for an organization anxious to improve. Indeed, Garvin (1995) argued that a learning organization is one that "is skilled at creating, acquiring, and transferring knowledge, and at modifying its behavior to reflect new knowledge and insights...without accompanying changes in the way that work gets done, only the potential for improvement exists." (p. 80) For example, Garvin describes Boeing's Project Homework, for which employees collected in a notebook the "lessons learned" from previous development projects and subsequently used this knowledge to build the 757 and 767, the most successful, error-free launches in Boeing's history.

Information technology plays a critical, enabling role in this action-oriented, double-loop learning. As Zuboff has shown (1984), to use information technology this way means that we move beyond mere automating - using Information Technology to do faster and cheaper what we did before. We must use the technology for informating - to improve what we did before AND also to learn about and change how we do things. For example, a new computer-based loan application data base enables us to process loans faster and with fewer errors. In addition to this automating, the new system also creates information about the process, which enables us to better understand the patterns of the data, decisions, and the entire process so that we can better monitor, control, and change the process. Similarly, many organizations are using the Internet (e.g., e-mail, on-line discussion groups, Web-based feedback forms) to conduct a real-time dialogue with customers so that they can continually improve products and services and improve brand image, recognition, and loyalty (Bessen, 1993; McKenna, 1995). Indeed, McKenna (1995) argued that, "The dialogue is the brand..." (p. 92).

Before a firm can become a learning organization, its members must fundamentally learn how to learn and, second, learn how technology can help. One effective form of instruction for organizations is the use of intensive, tailored executive education programs. Below we describe the content, context, and infrastructure for one such proposed program. This design of this approach is guided by our teaching of these topics in undergraduate and graduate courses and in teaching related topics in existing executive education programs. This is necessarily exploratory; the proposed program would have to operationalized and refined as needed.

3 CONTENT

There are several ways to define content in this instance, so some explanation is necessary. We are proposing an executive education program for which instructors and participants will use a variety of technologies throughout. The content of study for this program is the virtual organization, including the relevant technologies and issues. Given this content and the process that the participants will go through, the participants will have learned a lot about how to transform their own organizations into learning organizations.

Focusing on the virtual organization as the content of the education program seemed to be a reasonable place to begin. The content of a technology supported educational program could involve literally anything in or about the organization. For example, organizational members could use technology as a vehicle for learning about continuous quality improvement, strategic planning and competitive advantage, interpersonal communication and team building, and a myriad of other content areas. One particularly interesting and important set of content issues, and a reasonable place to begin with such learning, involves learning about the technologies that make organizational learning possible. Thus, below we outline the sample content goals for an educational program that is focused on the virtual organization and is based technologies that enable this type of organization. Programs to support organizational learning in this area would be designed to help managers to:

- adopt, implement, use and manage information technologies that are key to the virtual organization
- use these advanced decision and communication technologies to improve organizational productivity, memory, and learning, to shorten cycle times, to enable organizational change, to support the organization's strategic plan, and to achieve competitive advantage
- manage continual technology-driven change
- develop a vision of the future for how these technologies will influence managers, organizations, the economy, and society

4 CONTEXT AND INFRASTRUCTURE

Below we describe several relevant technologies and how they can be used to support real-time, interactive organizational learning. For the proposed program, the content of the learning is the virtual organization. The participants are literally using the technology to learn about technology (i.e., they learn with, through, and about the technology in this case). Keep in mind that the technological infrastructure could also be used to learn about other content areas, but the virtual organization as a content area is chosen here as a reasonable place to begin.

The technologies used to deliver this infrastructure would include Group Support Systems, Groupware, Desktop Video Conferencing, and the Internet World Wide Web. These technologies are being used in business to compress time, to enable collaboration across time and space, and, in some cases, to improve collaboration. For these same reasons, these technologies are used to support the proposed educational program. Each of these different technologies is described below. Sample tools for each technology category are also discussed. We use as a foundation the distance learning infrastructures already used by many institutions, including the Open University. The infrastructure builds on these by making extensive use of the Internet, World Wide Web, and multi-point interaction among instructors and participants.

Information Superhighway

The electronic information superhighway is a developing collection of interconnected, high speed digital networks around the world. It is a highway in that it will be a way to ship large amounts of various kinds of data from one place to another. In reality, it is more like a system of highways, which is typically comprised of a lot of individual roads, streets, byways, highways, and freeways, each with different characteristics and each "locally" developed and maintained. The information superhighway is being developed primarily by corporations in the digital communications and related industries. Thus, it is envisioned as a vehicle for broadcasting interactive entertainment and shopping into the home, and for seamless, international, interactive video conferencing. The information superhighway now includes, and is being constructed on top of (or along side of), the Internet.

Internet

The Internet is a global network of computer networks that is currently being used to move packets of information (text, graphics, audio, video) back and forth. Among the many features of the Internet are electronic mail, listserves (e-mail distribution lists used for discussions of particular topics), file transfers, telnet (a user logs on one computer by accessing it from another), newsgroups (bulletin boards containing discussions on a variety of topics), information searches, and information retrieval. There are an estimated 30 million users accessing the Internet from well over 20,000 unique networks, with a near doubling in subscribers reported each year. The Internet, as a whole, is not a commercial enterprise and is not sponsored by any government, although the Internet is now being used for electronic commerce and pieces of the Internet are subsidized by public universities. In addition, the Internet is not administered or regulated by any one organization or association; rather, the Internet functions and evolves based on consensus, tradition, natural selection, and the generosity of various sites and people.

World Wide Web

The World Wide Web, thought by many as the Internet's "killer application," provides easy, fast, graphical access to an ever expanding cornucopia of information sources (text, graphics, audio, video) located throughout the world, each having a unique address and each with the capability of being linked (using hyper text) with any other piece of information anywhere else on the net. Some of the related tools that could be used in the program described below include Web server software (e.g., Netscape Communication Server), Web browsers (e.g., Netscape Navigator), Web document editors (e.g., HotJava and HotMetal), Web programming tools (e.g., Java), file transfer applications (e.g., WSFTP), and search tools (e.g., InfoSeek and Lycos). Like the Internet and the Web, the technologies described below also support collaboration.

Group Support Systems

Group Support Systems are computer-based information systems which are used with group decision making and facilitation methodologies to support intellectual, goal-directed, collaborative work (for discussion see Jessup & Valacich, 1993). A GSS typically consists of personal computers interconnected via a local area network with software that supports work group processes such as the interactive generation, evaluation, and organization of ideas, several methods for ranking or voting on alternatives, interactively composing and editing text together, or interactively creating and modifying graphic images. GSS are typically housed in a facility which includes audio/visual presentation support and printing capabilities and is dedicated for same time, same place computer-supported group work. GSS for distributed group work, where the group members interact with each other using the system from different places and/or at different times, have recently become available. Some GSS products which could be used for the program below include Ventana's GroupSystems and Option Technologies' OptionFinder. In addition, there are now test versions of GSS-like tools for collaboration over the Internet's World Wide Web.

Groupware

Groupware software tools also support group member collaboration, but these tools are designed to provide more general, less goal-directed support to work groups. Groupware tools typically provide one or more of the following three types of support: communication, group management, or resource sharing. Communication includes features such as computer conferencing and electronic mail. Group management includes features such as scheduling and project management. Resource sharing can include the sharing of hardware, software, documents, data, and so on. Lotus Notes, considered by many to be the Groupware standard, would be an ideal form of Groupware for the program described below

Notes is designed to run across an organization's wide area network (a collection of local area networks), and also enables remote group members to dial in via modem and PC and continue to collaborate electronically with the rest of the group. In addition, Lotus is now beta testing InterNotes, an application which will allow users to use Notes applications over the Internet's World Wide Web.

Desktop video conferencing

Desktop video conferencing systems with fully integrated interactive collaborative software have recently emerged as a viable technology. These systems represent a merging of several technologies that have existed independently, but not in a fully integrated fashion. Desktop video conferencing systems represent a convergence of video conferencing, collaboration support software, and audio, all packaged in a familiar personal computer. The most unique feature of these systems is the collaboration-support software that allows remote parties to jointly (and synchronously) work on documents, spreadsheets, and graphics (i.e., any Microsoft Windows-compatible software) via an increasingly common ISDN (Integrated Services Digital Network) telephone call. Through the collaboration support software, either party can control the application program and any changes are immediately reflected on both screens. Sample systems include Intel ProShare and AT&T Vistium.

With the use of these technologies to deliver the infrastructure for learning, the organizational members are no longer restricted to traditional contexts for learning. Traditionally, learning within the organization took place either within formal education and training settings (e.g., corporate classrooms and executive education programs at universities) or happened informally via mentoring, stories, legend, and so on. For the learning program, proposed here, the context is not restricted to a "classroom" in the organization or a university. Indeed, the classroom is now virtual. In addition to changing the context of learning, the technologies used also enable a variety of modes of learning, from traditional lecture format, to real time distributed collaboration, to individual deliberation supported by on-line research. Each participant will have a high-end personal computer at their place of work, with Internet connection, multi-media equipment, and desktop video conferencing equipment. These computers will be configured so that each participant can quickly and easily use their computer to interact with instructors and other participants located at other sites.

This program will be delivered in three phases (see Figure 1). In the first phase, delivered via distance learning technologies, each participant works from their own office. Each participant masters a foundation knowledge base on the virtual organization. This knowledge base will consist of a physical readings packet, some on-line readings, and links to various sites on the Web. In addition, each participant will complete an on-line self and organizational assessment with regard to their readiness for the shift to a virtual organization. Throughout this phase each participant will also interact with the instructors and other participants to better understand the course and get to know each other. They will each do so using desktop video and computer conferencing, Groupware, and the Internet World Wide Web from their own computer in their own location.

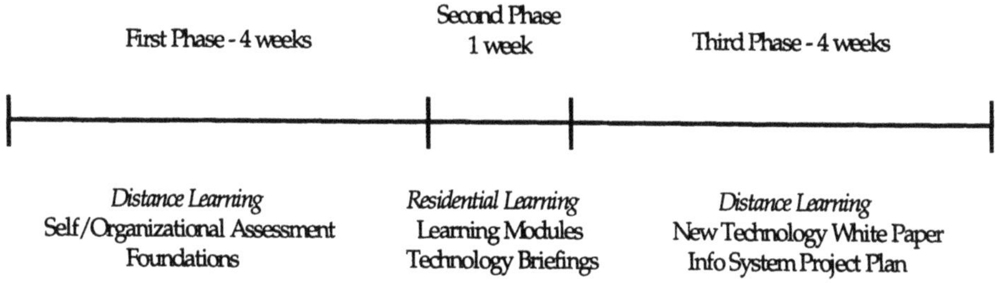

Figure 1 Three phases of proposed executive education program.

Because it is still useful and necessary for face-to-face interaction, the second phase of the program is a one-week, residential seminar series on the virtual organization. Participants will attend same time, same place seminars covering four modules: The Virtual Organization, The Virtual Office, The Virtual Team, and The Virtual Marketplace. In each module participants will consider, "what are the relevant technologies and issues," "why are they important and useful," and "how can they best be adopted, implemented, used, and managed." Participants will share ideas and information with others and gain content area knowledge which builds on their foundation knowledge. This phase will include short lectures, discussions, exercises, case studies, group projects, presentations, and technology briefings. Figure 2 presents descriptions of the primary modules of the second phase.

Module	Description	Disciplines
The Virtual Organization	How technology is enabling organizations to reshape and eliminate boundaries, both within and across the organization. Topics include: using technology for business process reengineering, rightsizing, change management, organizational memory and learning, and strategic management	Info Systems Operations Management HR
The Virtual Office	How technology can enable the virtual office. Topics include: Using computing and telecommunications technologies to move the office into the home or into the field, telecommuting, human resource (HR) issues (e.g., motivation, monitoring, evaluation).	Info Systems HR
The Virtual Team	How technology enables any time, any where team member computing. Topics include: using distributed Group Support Systems, Groupware, workflow automation, scheduling, desktop video and computer conferencing.	Info Systems Management HR
The Virtual Marketplace	How to conduct and the ramifications of electronic commerce. Topics include: Information Superhighway, Internet, World Wide Web, Electronic Data Interchange, electronic commerce, network security.	Info Systems Marketing Accounting HR Finance

Figure 2 Descriptions of the primary modules of the second phase.

For the third phase participants go back to their own locations and, again, collaborate via the distance learning technologies. Participants complete a New Technology White Paper and a Project Plan on a technology of their choice. For example, a participant might write a white paper on a new Groupware technology, such as Lotus Notes, and then develop a plan of how and why that technology should be implemented in his/her own organization. To accomplish this the participant will likely use their newly acquired Web skills to surf the Web for, for example, information on Notes products, case studies, and related technologies. Throughout this phase participants will continue to work with and learn from the instructors and other participants, but they are able to do so from their own organizations. For example, each participant would periodically meet via desktop video conferencing with their instructor for general project guidance and to address difficult or complex issues and questions. In addition, participants could interact in this way with other participants to "compare notes" on their final projects. E-mail could also be used for "leaner" messages passed among instructors and participants.

After the program is completed, all content materials (e.g., readings, student papers, and so on) are kept on-line for reference by future learners and instructors. In addition, the former learners and instructors are also on-line and available to current learners and instructors. By archiving content and linking former and current participants, the organization further supports learning.

5 SUMMARY AND CONCLUSIONS

There are a variety of computing and networking technologies available to support learning in organizations. These technologies can be used to help organizational members enhance their own knowledge and skills, to enable the organization as a collective to learn and grow, and to support interorganizational learning. The content of such technology supported learning can vary, but it makes sense to begin with the technologies themselves. In this proposal we described technology supported learning which focused on the virtual organization as content. In this way the participants would use the technology to learn about the technology. The available technologies described here could be used to radically change the learning infrastructure, which could enable interactive, real-time learning in a number of modes. For example, there could be individual, self-paced learning, supported efficiently through a variety of electronic modes. Alternatively, interaction among learners and instructors could be supported in a variety of modes, creating a virtual classroom. Consequently, the context for learning will change too. It may be more appropriate to think of organizational learning happening across time and space rather than in a particular place and/or at a particular time.

There are a variety of benefits that can accrue to an organization with enhanced capabilities for technology supported learning. Essentially, individuals within the organization can learn faster and better from each other and from individuals in other organizations. More important, perhaps, the benefits can go beyond organizational learning. Because learning is the foundation for other things, technology supported organizational learning can also help organizations to operate more effectively and efficiently. For example, imagine having a sales representative, his/her manager, an engineer, and a customer, linked together via desktop video conferencing running on their PCs. Because they can interact face-to-face while being separated geographically, and because they can also simultaneously collaborate using their PC software tools or any data, they could solve a mutual problem quickly and, perhaps, better than they might have if they had to play telephone tag and explain and re-explain the problem to each others' voice mail message boxes. Technology supported learning could help here to solve problems faster and could directly improve service quality. Such real time learning has become essential to firms trying to gain or sustain competitive advantage.

One important implication of technology supported organizational learning is that it provides a new way to learn and change. Indeed, the emphasis would be on continually learning and changing, which may be difficult for some individuals. Further, such technology would also provide a new way to work, manage, and organize. Managers would need to change their expectations of how, where, and on what time frame work gets done. With technology supported organizational learning an employee could be incredibly productive by, literally, sitting in their office glued to their PC. While s/he interacts electronically with a variety of people and draws on a myriad of information sources, others in the organization might mistakenly assume that this person is closed off from the world, wasting time performing computer-based analysis, or, worse, playing Solitaire. To the extent that individuals are working more electronically and/or remotely, managers will need to learn to trust employees more.

Another interesting implication of technology supported organizational learning is that it presents a potentially difficult new entrant into the organization's technology mix. These are not traditional technologies (e.g., mainframe data base management systems) to support traditional business processes (e.g., transaction processing or inventory management). Thus, managers and technologists may not readily see the value of these new technologies and technology uses. Managers willingness to embrace these new technologies is critical. They must believe that these technologies are worth investing in. They also must see that they are building the technological infrastructure to take advantage of new technological opportunities for organizational learning that are sure to come.

The sophistication and power of the enabling technologies for organizational learning are continually improving. The information superhighway comes closer and closer to reality every day. The Internet and World Wide Web continue to grow and improve, with an incredible outpouring of new tools for Web-based collaboration and commerce. In addition, PC-based alternatives for collaboration, such as GSS, Groupware, and desktop video conferencing continue to improve. Technologically, the capabilities and opportunities for supporting organizational learning abound. Similarly, the needs for improved organizational learning become stronger and stronger every day. Given the demands on organizations today and the speed with which competitive forces bring about change, it appears that technology supported organizational learning will very quickly become the rule and not the exception.

6 REFERENCES

Argyris, C. and D. A. Schon (1978) *Organizational Learning: A Theory of Action Perspective*, Reading, MA: Addison-Wesley.

Bessen, J. (1993) Riding the marketing information wave. *Harvard Business Review*, September-October. Pages 150-160.

Daft, Richard L. and George P. Huber (1987) How Organizations Learn: A Communication Framework, *Research in the Sociology of Organizations*, (5), pp. 1-36.

Daft, Richard L. and N. B. Macintosh (1981) A Tentative Exploration into the Amount and Equivocality of Information Processing in Organizational Work Units, *Administrative Science Quarterly* (26), pp. 207-224.

Fiol, C. M. and M. A. Lyles (1985) Organizational Learning, *Academy of Management Review* (10), pp. 803-813.

Garvin, D. A. (1993) Building a learning organization. Garvin. *Harvard Business Review*, July-August, Pages 78-91.

Hoffer, J., and J.S. Valacich (1993) Group Memory in Group Support Systems: A foundation for Design. In *Group Support Systems: New Perspectives*, L.M. Jessup & J.S. Valacich (Eds), New York: Macmillan, pp. 214-229.

Huber, George P. (1991) Organizational Learning: The Contributing Processes and the Literatures, *Organization Science*, (2:1), pp. 1-28.

Jessup, L. M., & Valacich, J. S. (1993) *Group Support Systems: New Perspectives.* Macmillan Publishing Company, New York, New York.

Levitt, Barbara and James G. March (1988) Organizational Learning, *Annual Review of Sociology*. (14), pp. 319-340.

McKenna, R. (1995) Real-time marketing. McKenna. *Harvard Business Review*, July-August. Pages 87-95.

Shrivastava, P. (1983) A typology of organizational learning systems, *Journal of Management Studies*. (20), 1-28.

Zuboff, S. (1984) *In the age of the smart machine: The future of work and power.* New York, NY: Basic Books, Inc. Publishers.

7 SELECTED READINGS

IT & Organizational Change
A framework for managing IT-Enabled change. Benjamin and Levinson. *Sloan Management Review*, Summer 1993. Pages 23-33.
Hurdle the cross-functional barriers to strategic change. Hutt, Walker, and Frankwick. *Sloan Management Review*, Spring 1995. Pages 22-30.

Virtual Organizations
Managing by wire. Haeckel and Nolan. *Harvard Business Review*, September-October 1993. Pages 122-132.
Trust and the virtual organization. Handy. *Harvard Business Review*, May-June 1995. Pages 42-50.

Technology for Teams
Technology for teams. Bock and Applegate. Harvard Business School, 1995, #9-196-008.
Electronic Meeting Systems to support group work: Theory and practice at Arizona. Nunamaker, Dennis, Valacich, Vogel, and George. *Communications of the ACM*, 1991, 34:7:40-61.
Learning through experience: How companies are really using Groupware, Turrell, *Proceedings of Groupware* '95 Europe. Pages 149-163.
Chemical Bank: Technology support for cooperative work. Applegate and Stoddard. Harvard Business School, #9-193-131.

Electronic Commerce & Internet
Electronic markets and virtual value chains on the information superhighway. Benjamin and Wigand. *Sloan Management Review*, Winter 1995. Pages 62-72.
Paving the Information Super highway: Introduction to the Internet. Applegate and Gogan. Harvard Business School, 1995, #9-195-202.
Electronic Commerce on the World Wide Web: A Case Study. Ives and Jarvenpaa. Southern Methodist University. Case write-up is available on the World Wide Web; URL is http://www.cox.smu.edu/mis/cases/webcase/home.html
Open Market, Inc. Gogan and Applegate. Harvard Business School, 1995, #9-195-205.

Learning Organization
The coming of the knowledge-based business, Davis and Botkin. *Harvard Business Review*, September-October 1994. Pages 165-170.

8 BIOGRAPHY

Leonard M. Jessup is an Associate Professor of Accounting and Information Systems in the School of Business at Indiana University. He teaches in various areas of Management and Management Information Systems and has published and presented widely on using computer-based tools to support collaborative work, electronic commerce, and on related topics. With Joseph S. Valacich he co-edited the book, Group Support Systems: New Perspectives, and, with his wife, won Zenith Data System's annual Masters of Innovation award.

Joseph S. Valacich is an Associate Professor of Accounting and Information Systems in the School of Business at Indiana University. His current research interests include group decision behavior and the design and investigation of communication and decision technologies to support collaborative group work, including distance learning. His past research has appeared in publications such as MIS Quarterly, Information Systems Research, Management Science, Academy of Management Journal, Communications of the ACM, Decision Science, Organizational Behavior and Human Decision Processes, Journal of Applied Psychology, and Small Group Research.

14

Dual information systems for organizational working and learning: the business and breakdown layers*

Timo K. Käkölä
Department of Computer Science and Information Systems
University of Turku, DataCity, FIN-20520 Turku, Finland
Tel.: +358 40 5519645, Fax: +358 21 6338600
E-Mail: timo.kakola@utu.fi

Kalle I. Koota
Orion Corporation, Orion-Farmos, R&D
P.O. Box 425, FIN-20101 Turku, Finland
Tel.: +358 21 2727665, Fax: +358 21 2727546
E-Mail: kalle.koota@orion.mailnet.fi

Abstract

The conceptual structure of most computer-based information systems reflects a dualism of technology. During the development phase, part of the work-domain related knowledge is formalized and encoded in the software, making it difficult for users to reflect upon and use this knowledge. This dualism deters the interpretive flexibility of information systems. Dual Information Systems (DIS) are needed that enable and reinforce both effective, institutionalized enactment and questioning and (re)construction of computer-supported work routines. DIS have a three-layered conceptual structure: (1) people draw on the business layer to work and learn; (2) people use the breakdown layer to handle unexpected breakdowns; (3) self-organizing project teams use the project layer to create innovative work and IS (re)designs. We outline the theoretical background, conceptual structure and generic services of DIS. We elaborate on the services and the conceptual design of the business and breakdown layers of DIS (bDIS). The services help people work effectively and develop competence needed to handle breakdowns and participate in the redesign

---

* Timo Käkölä is responsible for the theoretical development of this paper. Both authors contributed equally to Section 4. Kalle Koota programmed the ReDIS prototype.

project teams. The conceptual design extends Chang's hyperknowledge framework. Finally, we demonstrate the conceptual design and services in a financial services organization with the help of the ReDIS prototype.

Keywords
Act Orientation, Dual Information Systems, Hyperknowledge Framework, Hyperknowledge Organization, Interpretive Flexibility, Knowledge-Creation Nets, Organizational Interfaces, Organizational Creation of Knowledge

1 INTRODUCTION

Information systems researchers have paid considerable attention to developing systems to enhance managerial decision making and learning (e.g., group and executive support systems) and to automate office routines (e.g., workflow systems) (Swanson and Ramiller, 1993). While this research remains relevant, it undermines the need for new knowledge about the development of systems that enable *organizational* creation and sharing of knowledge, not only the learning and decision making of middle managers and executives. Organizations' existing office systems remain at least as important sources of new knowledge as the new coordination technologies. It becomes crucial for researchers to determine how to redesign these systems to facilitate organizational creation and sharing of knowledge.

Redesign presumes changes in the conceptual structure of office systems. But first, one must understand the role of computer-based information systems (CBIS) in organizations and why many systems are inadequate. We draw upon the work of Orlikowski (1992), Nurminen (1988), and Nonaka (1994) in this paper to reach a conceptual understanding. Orlikowski (1992) recognizes that information technology can be seen as enacted by human agency and as institutionalized in structure. She calls this "the duality of technology." Duality implies that organizations can employ information technology as a source of working and learning, if agents* can use and modify the technology whenever it is necessary to redesign computer-supported work practices, and if the technology can be institutionalized as a legitimate component of the organizational working and learning environment.

Unfortunately, too many organizations today suffer from *dualistic, institutionalized* CBIS that hide the constructed nature of CBIS from agents (Käkölä, 1995a). They (1) limit lateral communication, coordination and knowledge sharing; (2) provide little feedback to agents (especially in the lower echelons of an organization) on work arrangements and on the coordination and communication patterns that emerge from their use; (3) limit agents' ability to reflect and inquire within the social and technical contexts in which the agents are embedded, restraining them from creating, questioning, and modifying practical knowledge when problems emerge; and consequently (4) endanger the process of reinvention that any complex technological artifact should undergo when put to use (Ciborra and Lanzara, 1994). For instance, changing the computer-supported work processes through user-driven work and IS design is almost impossible unless agents thoroughly understand the content and organization of work (Hellman, 1989).

* We use the word "agent" to refer to people whose work is computer supported. We want to avoid the term "user" since that term connotes that information systems can be used and studied independently of other types of work.

Dual Information Systems (DIS) are needed that enable both effective, institutionalized working and the questioning and (re)design of computer-supported work. Orlikowski (1992) provides neither a conceptual model nor practical guidelines to help organizations design DIS. This paper continues the efforts of Käkölä (1995a) to do so. Käkölä (1995a) complemented Orlikowski's work by drawing on the act-oriented perspective (Eriksson and Nurminen, 1991). This perspective narrows the dualistic gap by interpreting the functions of computer software as an inseparable component of the work of knowledgeable people (Nurminen, 1988). It helps agents even on the shop floor gain a comprehensive understanding of their work, its computer-supported parts, and its relationship to the business as a whole. In light of the perspective, a necessary but insufficient condition for a CBIS to qualify as a DIS is that it helps agents develop such an understanding.

In Section 2, we outline the theoretical background of DIS. In Section 3, we outline the conceptual structure of DIS and elaborate on the services of the business and breakdown layers of DIS (bDIS). The services help people work effectively and develop competence needed to handle breakdowns and redesign work. Next, we present and extend the hyperknowledge framework (Chang, Holsapple, and Whinston, 1994) to develop the conceptual design of bDIS. We conclude Section 3 by discussing the use of work and software process modeling in Dual Information Systems. In Section 4, we demonstrate the conceptual design and services in a financial services organization, describe their potential organizational benefits, and encourage commercial implementations with the help of the ReDIS prototype. We state our conclusions and discuss issues for future research in the last section.

2 DUALITY OF TECHNOLOGY, ACT ORIENTATION, AND HYPERTEXT ORGANIZATION

To design Dual Information Systems, a comprehensive theoretical understanding of the role of CBIS in organizational working, the creation of knowledge, and learning is necessary. We recapitulate the work of Orlikowski (1992), Nurminen (1988), and Nonaka (1994) in this section to provide the requisite background.

2.1 Duality of technology, interpretive flexibility, and time-space disjuncture

Orlikowski (1992) introduces three constructs that are central to this paper: the duality of technology, its interpretive flexibility, and time-space disjuncture. The duality construct sees information technology as enacted by human agency and as institutionalized in structure. Designers produce a technology to provide resources and rules by creating and encoding work-domain related knowledge into it. Agents socially construct a technology by assigning it different meanings and using it flexibly in their work. But technologies usually become reified and institutionalized over time because agents cannot continuously reinterpret or physically modify them, if the agents are to accomplish their work efficiently.

The duality of technology recognizes that "technologies are products of their time and institutional context, and will reflect the knowledge, materials, interests, and conditions at a given locus in history" (Orlikowski, 1992, p. 421). However, the dual nature of CBIS is masked by the time-space disjuncture arising from the various phases (e.g., design, implementation, and employment) of interaction between a technology and organizations. Within and between these phases, the actions constituting the technology are separated temporally and spatially from the actions constituted by the technology.

The interpretive flexibility construct aims to collapse the time-space disjuncture. It emphasizes that "there is flexibility in how people design, interpret, and use technology, but that this flexibility is a function of the material components comprising the artifact, the institutional context in which a technology is developed and used, and the power, knowledge, and interests of human actors . . ." as well as time (Orlikowski, 1992, p. 421). Orlikowski (1992, p. 421) summarizes the causality between the time-space disjuncture and the interpretive flexibility of technology as follows: "The greater the temporal and spatial distance between the construction of a technology and its application, the greater the likelihood that the technology will be interpreted and used with little flexibility."

2.2 The dualism of information technology: implications and alleviations

The interpretive flexibility of information technology is often poor (Bødker and Grønbæk, 1991; Eriksson, Hellman, and Nurminen, 1988; Gasser, 1986; Tyre and Orlikowski, 1994; Zuboff, 1988). This inflexibility results in part from agents with insufficient shared knowledge of the nature of social practices as a whole; of the articulation of these practices in time and space by the structural properties of organizations; of their own roles in the organization; and of the role of information systems as a structural property mediating work processes.

One important reason for agents' lack of awareness is that the conceptual and material structures of computer software reflect a *dualism* of technology; the constructed nature of CBIS is masked by the software. Information systems separate symbolic information from the material and social systems the symbols represent, hide the processing rules and retention structures in the software and database schemas, and blur the role of people as the producers and consumers of information (Boland, 1991; Nurminen, 1988).

The prevalent dualistic structure and poor interpretive flexibility of information technology have costly implications. Agents are restricted to using functions expressed in the software (Kogut and Zander, 1992, p. 390). They also face considerable difficulties monitoring their actions since they cannot fully interpret and validate the meaning of information produced by the systems, and they cannot see and feel the outcomes of their computer-supported actions (Zuboff, 1988, pp. 79-96). Because of their limited ability to control all aspects of work, including computerized tasks, the agents cannot necessarily be responsible for their work as a whole. Finally, the agents' ability to intervene in and transform existing social practices is limited because the agents cannot easily criticize and challenge the interpretative schemes, resources and norms embedded in the algorithms and databases of the CBIS (Lyytinen and Ngwenyama, 1991; Orlikowski, 1992).

Agents can regain control of their jobs in computer-supported work environments. Orlikowski (1992, p. 418) states: ". . . knowledgeable and reflexive human agents are capable of altering the controlling influence of the technology. The extent to which individuals modify their use of technology, however, depends on whether they acknowledge its constructed nature. This is determined by the degree to which individuals can recognize the mediating role of technology, can conceive of an alternative beyond it, and are motivated to action." Thus, agents' ability to control their work depends on their domain and technology-related skills and knowledge as well as the shared stocks of knowledge that inform them about their own and other agents' roles and normatively regulated and sanctioned behaviours (Lyytinen and Ngwenyama, 1991; Zuboff, 1988).

The conceptual structure and services of DIS must help agents control and redesign their work as a whole, including its computerized aspects. For this purpose, DIS need to help bridge the time-space disjuncture both vertically (between users and designers) and horizontally (between agents coordinated through the systems).

2.3 Act-oriented perspective: toward DIS on the level of human agency

The time-space disjuncture between the design and use of CBIS and the dualistic nature of computer software imply that agents often cannot see the link between their work as a whole and its computerized parts. Orlikowski (1992) provides no conceptual solution to uncover this missing link.

Käkölä (1995a) used the act-oriented perspective (Eriksson and Nurminen, 1991; Nurminen, 1988) to provide a solution. According to this perspective, a CBIS cannot be separated from agents' work because no CBIS can serve as a conscious actor. Therefore, every computerized task must have a responsible human agent. Conceptually, each agent has his or her own information system receiving, memorizing, processing, and transmitting the information necessary for his or her work.

The act-oriented perspective bridges the time-space disjuncture *vertically* by seeing the knowledge encoded in software by designers in time-space context A as the acts of the responsible agents in time-space context B and *horizontally* by making explicit the coordinating role of information systems, even when the computer-supported acts of agents are inter-connected through shared objects of work in integrated databases. Once this bridge has been built, agents can better exploit the interpretive flexibility of Dual Information Systems to work and share knowledge.

2.4 Hypertext organization: toward DIS on the organizational level

Knowledge-creating organizations are required to institutionalize reflection-in-action in their processes and structures so that their members need not depend on the established wisdom (Nonaka, 1994). Analogously, they require Dual Information Systems that support institutionalized reflection-in-action. Nonaka (1994) proposes 'hypertext organization' as an organizational design prototype for institutionalized reflection-in-action. Hypertext organization is a *dual* organizational structure: it "coordinates the allocation of time, space, and resource within the organization" (Nonaka, 1994, p. 33) so that an organization can achieve high performance in routines and simultaneously ensure long-term survival by creating and applying new knowledge. Therefore, the conceptual structure of Dual Information Systems must reflect the hypertext organization structure.

Hypertext organization is formed by the dynamic combination of hierarchically organized business units and self-organizing project teams that pursue the equivocal visions of the top management by drawing upon and accruing organizational knowledge base. Nonaka (1994, pp. 32-33) states: "The core feature of the hypertext organization is the ability to switch between the various 'contexts' of knowledge creation to accommodate changing requirements from situations both inside and outside the organization. . . . Each context has a distinctive way of organizing its knowledge creation activities. . . . Hypertext organization design first distinguishes the normal routine operation conducted by a hierarchical formal organization from the knowledge creating activities carried out by self-organizing teams. . . . By establishing the most appropriate organizational setting for the two activities, an organization can maximize the efficiency of its routine operation, which is determined by bureaucratic principles of division of labor and specialization, and also the effectiveness of its knowledge creation activities."

Hypertext organizations are comprised of three layers; knowledge-base, business-system, and project-system (Figure 1). The 'knowledge-base' layer "embraces tacit knowledge, associated with organizational culture and procedures, as well as explicit knowledge in the form of documents, . . . computerized databases, etc" (Nonaka, 1994, p. 33). Normal work routines are enacted by a formal, bureaucratic organization in the 'business-system' layer (hereafter "business layer"). The 'project-system' layer (hereafter "project layer") provides a field of interaction where loosely linked project teams create knowledge.

In a hypertext organization, knowledge is created through the circular movement of agents among the three layers. Members of project teams are selected from different functions and business units across the business layer. They interact with the knowledge-base layer at the bottom and make an 'inventory' of the knowledge acquired and created in the project layer. "After categorizing, documenting, and indexing the new knowledge, they come back to . . . business-system layer and engage in routine operation until they are called again for another project" (Nonaka, 1994, p. 33).

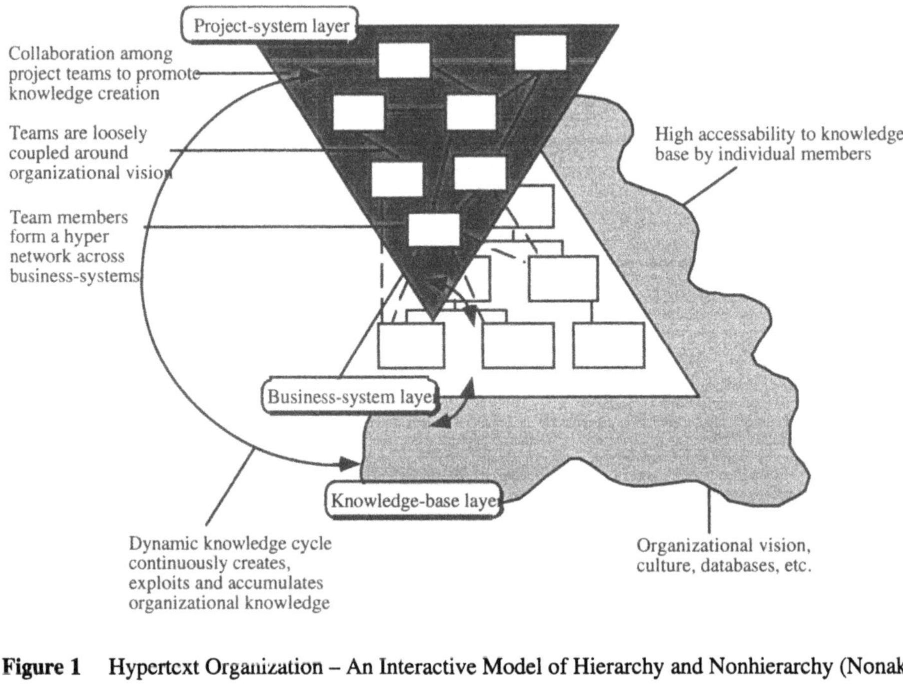

Figure 1 Hypertext Organization – An Interactive Model of Hierarchy and Nonhierarchy (Nonaka, 1994, p. 34).

3 DUAL INFORMATION SYSTEMS AND COMPUTER SUPPORTED WORK

3.1 The conceptual structure of DIS

Dual Information Systems (DIS) enable and reinforce both effective, institutionalized enactment and questioning and (re)construction of computer-supported work routines. In accordance with our theoretical framework, they have a three-layered conceptual structure (Figure 2): (1) agents continuously draw on the business layer of DIS to work, learn, and coordinate routines in the business units; (2) agents use the breakdown layer of DIS to zoom in on the details of their work to handle unexpected (coordination) breakdowns; (3) self-organizing project teams use the project layer of DIS to create innovative work and IS (re)designs that can be enacted on the business layer. DIS are implemented by combining a coordination technology platform (Rein, 1992) with hyperknowledge systems (Chang, Holsapple, and Whinston, 1994). Consequently, we call hypertext organizations that enable and are enabled by DIS hyperknowledge organizations.

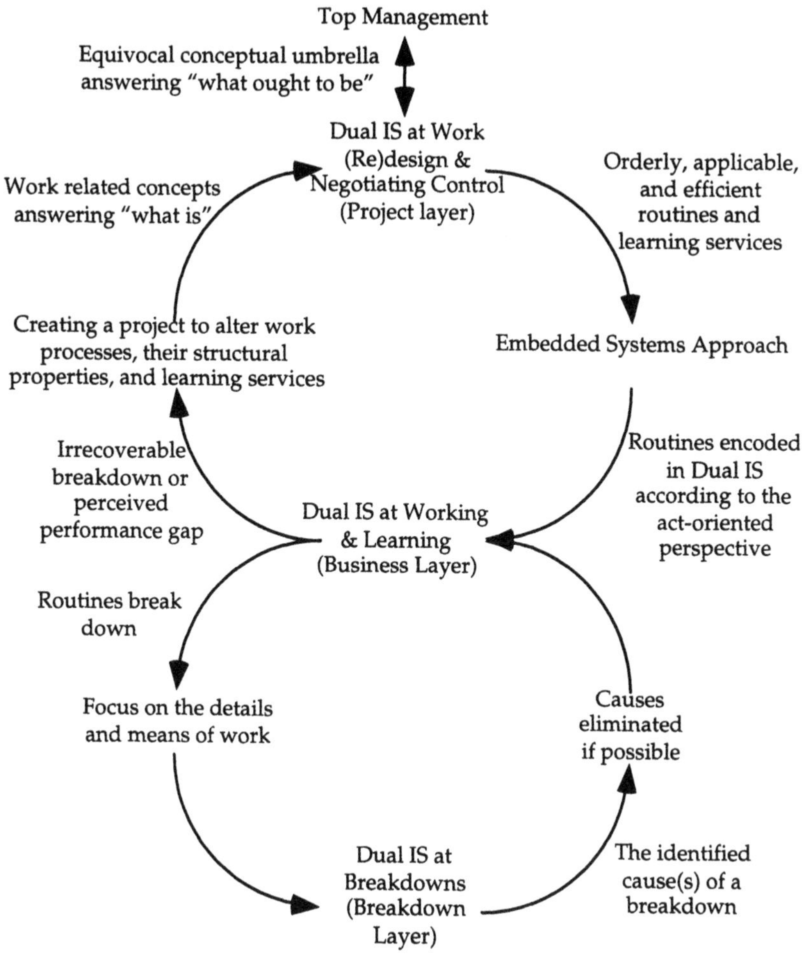

Figure 2 The conceptual structure of Dual Information Systems.

From the point of view of institutionalized reflection-in-action, the importance of routine use of information systems cannot be over-stated. Information systems as a structural property of organizations remain constitutive of organizational realities that can be known, understood, and acted upon (Lyytinen and Ngwenyama, 1991; Orlikowski, 1992; Orlikowski and Robey, 1991; Tyre and Orlikowski, 1994). For example, Tyre and Orlikowski presented and analyzed three case studies and found (1994, p. 111) that ". . . routine use was . . . necessary for on-going adaptation; it provided the raw data that, if utilized, could lead to improvements in the technology or the way it was applied in the local context." Furthermore, the creation of new knowledge to improve work in ambiguous circumstances is rarely possible without the objective information obtained by monitoring and measuring organizational routines, because this information can be used to refute or support and legitimate more subjective interpretations (Daft, Lengel, and Trevino, 1987). For these reasons, we focus on the business and breakdown layers of DIS (bDIS). Käkölä and Koota (1996) discuss the project layer.

3.2 Business and breakdown layers of DIS

Käkölä (1995a) presented the Embedded Systems Approach (ESA) to instantiate the business and breakdown layers of DIS into Embedded Application Systems (Eriksson and Nurminen, 1991). Embedded Application Systems follow the act-oriented structure (Eriksson and Nurminen, 1991). They enable the effective enactment of routines in the business units and allow agents to reflect and inquire into their work practices as a whole, including computerized tasks. In a continuous knowledge-creating spiral, ESA relies on and enables the project teams of the hyperknowledge organization. The teams develop new concepts of computer-supported work and share them among the business units. Work processes are externalized, visualized, and memorized by using organizational and software process modeling formalisms. Process models (subsection 3.5) serve as the building block of the organizational interface (Malone, 1985) through which the computerized tasks and knowledge become inseparable components of the agents' working and learning environment. Breakdown management services let agents zoom in on the details of their work practices, check shared databases for mistakes, and fix many breakdowns locally. Additional learning services can easily be provided. We will elaborate in subsection 3.4 and section 4.

3.3 Hyperknowledge as a basis of Dual Information Systems

Dualistic technologies embed work-related knowledge in the form of linearly organized, fairly immutable concepts and procedures. These concepts and procedures are hidden in the software and tend to promote the institutionalization of work practices to those envisioned by designers in earlier time-space contexts. Consequently, DIS must transcend these linear structures and let agents organize computerized information, concepts, and work procedures as flexibly as they organize their manual work practices and materials. In this way, agents can work effectively and construct multiple interpretations of work in a hyperknowledge organization.

Hyperknowledge (Chang, Holsapple and Whinston, 1994) is a promising way to design DIS with high interpretive flexibility. It is strongly related to the concepts of hypertext and hypermedia (Bush, 1945; Engelbart, 1963), and to the architecture of hypertext systems (Nelson, 1987; Nielsen, 1990). However, the idea of hyperknowledge is wider than those of hypertext or hypermedia. Hyperknowledge is an ideal working and learning environment that holds work-related knowledge and, at the same time, defines the nature of hypertext or hypermedia. Such an environment partly eliminates the reifying effects of the time-space disjuncture: the designers still encode a part of work-related knowledge into the environment, but now this knowledge is transparent and partly nonlinear. Agents can navigate flexibly in the environment, widen their knowledge, and actively externalize their tacit knowledge and combine new knowledge into the environment.

Chang, Holsapple, and Whinston (1989; 1993; 1994) originated the framework of the hyperknowledge environment. It recognizes that an agent "cognitively possesses many diverse and interrelated pieces of knowledge (i.e., concepts). Some are descriptive, others are procedural in nature, yet others are concerned with reasoning, and so forth. The mind is able to deal with these concepts in a fluid and inclusive manner via controlled focusing of attention. In effect, the decision maker actively acquires (i.e., recalls, focuses on) desired pieces of knowledge by cognitively navigating among the universe of available concepts" (Chang, Holsapple, and Whinston, 1993, p. 30). Dual Information Systems should be designed in the same manner so that they become natural extensions of people's working and learning environments.

According to the hyperknowledge framework (Figure 3), the configuration of a hyperknowledge environment consists of three components: the Language and the Presentation System, the Problem Processing System, and the Knowledge System. The Language and the Presentation System mediate messages to and from the hyperknowledge environment. The Problem Processing System contains the dynamic part of the system and may possess inferential abilities. The system consists of three different parts – the data manager, model manager and dialogue manager – with which it can handle all the user requests or responses to and from the various knowledge sources in the system. The Problem Processing System is capable of presenting the knowledge in different ways, as chosen by the user through the user interface. The Knowledge System contains all the encoded, explicit knowledge, which can be descriptive, procedural, linguistic, reasoning, etc. It stores, in groups, concepts that are related to each other by definition and/or by association.

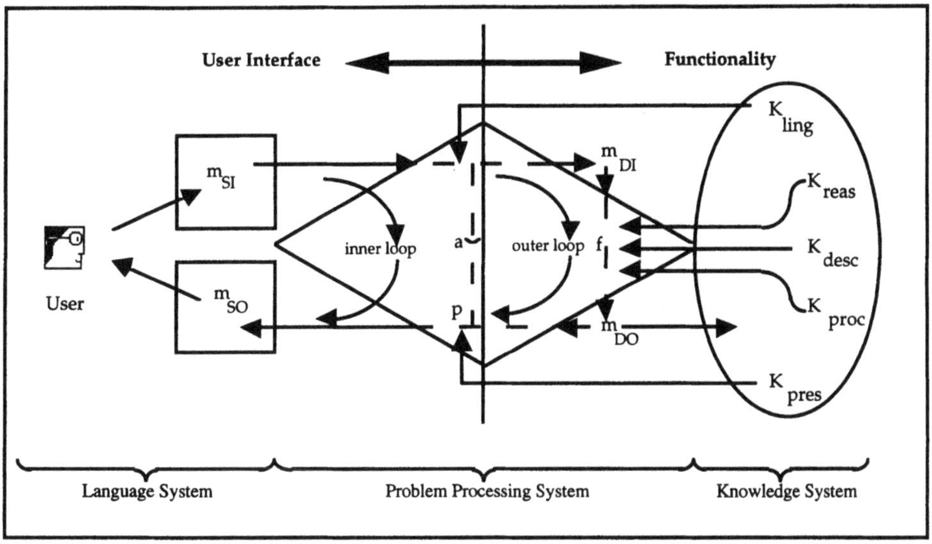

Figure 3 The hyperknowledge framework (Chang, Holsapple, and Whinston, 1994, p. 482).

Figure 3 depicts the hyperknowledge framework. The symbols in Figure 3 signify the following:

m_{SI} = surface input message; key strokes, mouse movement, touching the screen, etc.

m_{DI} = deep input message; specifies what the Problem Processing System must do in order to satisfy the request expressed in m_{SI}
a = an assistance function; a request for further elaboration, a correction or error message
f = a function which combines new knowledge from the available explicit knowledge
p = a presentation function
K_{ling} = linguistic knowledge available to the Problem Processing System in the Knowledge System
K_{reas} = reasoning knowledge available in the Knowledge System
K_{desc} = descriptive knowledge available in the Knowledge System
K_{proc} = procedural knowledge available in the Knowledge System
K_{pres} = presentation knowledge available in the Knowledge System
m_{DO} = deep output message; derived knowledge produced by the Problem Processing System
m_{SO} = surface output message to the user.

In an ideal hyperknowledge environment, the agent first receives an impression, possibly several impressions, of the same underlying concept. Each impression presents an image or images (visualization) on the user interface screen. The negative is an internal characterization of the image created by the problem processor. The agent sees the concept through several windows and can thus internalize a holistic view of the concept. To avoid the problems presented by Conklin (1987), the "lost in space" and "cognitive overhead" feelings, the hyperknowledge environment needs concept maps to guide both the designers and the agents (Chang, Holsapple, and Whinston, 1994).

Hyperknowledge framework is somewhat limited to the working, learning, and decision-making of individuals, yielding systems that primarily augment the intellect of individuals. Organizations may not become significantly more efficient or effective simply by giving everybody a definitive and associative access to organizational knowledge. Uncontrolled, unguided exploration and extension of available knowledge are unlikely to converge into meaningful concepts (Nonaka, 1994).

3.4 The conceptual design of the business and breakdown layers of DIS

To remedy the individualistic orientation of the hyperknowledge framework, we develop the conceptual design of the business and breakdown layers of DIS in this section. The Embedded Systems Approach uses the *organizational role* concept (Roos and Starke, 1981; Stryker and Statham, 1985) to divide each business unit in the business layer of a hyperknowledge organization into a set of functional work groups. Each group is responsible for a clearly defined part of the work process(es) of a business unit. Each agent in a functional group enacts the same work role.

The efficiency and effectiveness of the approach depend on two factors. First, agents must be able and motivated to internalize specialized role-centric language and norms and to exploit the role-centric information resources to a maximum degree. Second, agents must be offered redundant information to help them construct shared stocks of knowledge about the interconnections between their computer-supported work routines and the organizational work and performance. Redundant information helps agents recognize their location in an organization, interact, develop a common direction, create new concepts, enter each others' spheres of operation, provide advice, fix coordination breakdowns, and even do each other's jobs if necessary (Nonaka, 1994).

The factors promote both efficiency and effectiveness. When clear role-specific knowledge and resource requirements have been established, organizations can offer learning services and agents can use them to internalize quickly the skills necessary for role enactment. A shared language helps agents share tacit knowledge and use contradictions in their perspectives as a source of new knowledge to improve work practices (Nonaka, 1994; Zuboff, 1988).

Clear boundaries between shared and role-centric stocks of knowledge are often difficult to determine. Moreover, the organizational creation and sharing of knowledge changes these boundaries over time: roles are merged or the job content and knowledge requirements are upgraded in other ways. The distinction is made for analytical and design purposes only.

The organizational interface of bDIS must offer agents a Language System with a balanced mix of shared and role-centric technology-enabled and constrained languages (Figure 4). To comply with the act-oriented perspective, the role-centric language defines institutionalized, prenegotiated responsibility for and control of the means and objects of work. For this purpose, bDIS must provide at least the following role-centric services: (1) *Work enactment and coordination* services help agents allocate resources and take care of their routines. (2) *Learning* services help agents develop a theoretical understanding of work, including its computerized aspects, needed to enact roles effectively. (3) Performance monitoring services help agents monitor both their work activity and its results. They also help agents benchmark their performance with agents within functional group(s) (Spendolini, 1992). They promote internal competition and motivate agents to use the other services of bDIS effectively and to figure out ways how to exceed performance expectations; all these are of great importance to accelerate the creation of knowledge (Nonaka, 1994).

No matter how well people do their work, routines may break down unexpectedly. Agents face two challenges in often chaotic breakdown situations. First, they must get their routines back on track as quickly as possible. Second, they must develop and test multiple hypotheses about what went wrong to ensure a lasting solution (Zuboff, 1988). In this respect, breakdowns play a fundamental role in stimulating the creation of knowledge (Heidegger, 1977; Nonaka, 1994; Winograd and Flores, 1986).

Breakdown management services help agents meet both challenges. When routines break down, they let agents shift their focus of attention from normal objects of work to the routinized patterns of interaction and the means of work, including the rules and resources afforded by software (Käkölä, 1995a). Hyperknowledge is especially useful here because the definitive and associative relationships between different chunks of knowledge in the Knowledge System help agents shift focus rapidly. For example, agents can perform audit trails to trace what happened earlier to artifacts (e.g., documents) for which they are responsible and use the learning services to understand what should have happened. If they hypothesize that the problem stems from mistakes of agents in other roles, they can use the redundant information services to better understand how and why such mistakes are possible.

If the analysis reveals that the breakdown stems from coordination or other organizational problems spanning multiple functional work groups, agents can discuss the problems with middle managers. A project team can then be assembled to reconstruct computer-supported work practices and learning services to help eliminate in advance similar breakdowns. The project layer of DIS supports work redesign (Käkölä and Koota, 1996).

A shared language is developed by sharing redundant information according to the norms and rules negotiated and agreed upon in the project layer of a hyperknowledge organization. For this purpose, the business layer of DIS offers agents in functional work groups at least the following redundant information services: browsing, simulated enactment, and benchmarking of inter-connected roles (i.e., the roles interacting with an agent directly or indirectly through Embedded Application Systems). In this way, agents can experiment with the jobs of their colleagues in inter-connected functional work groups and understand bottlenecks in work performance. The norms and rules preserve the autonomy and privacy of agents by defining what information is shared and what is private. They can be reinforced by encoding some of them in the services of bDIS (e.g., through role-centric access rights to the Knowledge System of bDIS).

We divide the Knowledge System of bDIS into role-centric and shared components (Figure 4). The role-centric component is further divided into two subcomponents: tasks that people do and computerized tasks that Embedded Application Systems do for the people. Role-Connected Task Knowledge externalizes how people should do their routines (enactment knowledge), what are the objects of work (retention knowledge such as paper documents), what are the performance and skill requirements of successful enactment, and where work is physically done (ecological knowledge). These concepts are intertwined and enable the role-centric services of bDIS. For example, performance requirements must be tied explicitly with enactment knowledge so that people can use benchmarking to find and eliminate weaknesses in work performance. Role-Connected Computerized Task Knowledge presents a role-centric view of Embedded Application Systems. In accordance with the act-oriented perspective, the view defines the computerized aspects of work and relates them explicitly to the work of individuals in functional groups.

The shared Knowledge System is also divided into two parts: (1) Inter-Connected Role Knowledge views the work process of a business unit as a set of temporally and spatially distributed interacting roles. It also includes generic knowledge of the objects of the process (e.g., products and services), external stakeholders (e.g., suppliers and customers), and the goals that connect these concepts to a whole. The staff knowledge component stores knowledge of performance, skill profiles, and availability of agents. It supports resource allocation and coordination of work. (2) Inter-Connected Computerized Role Knowledge presents an inter-connected role view of Embedded Application Systems. The view defines how the work of agents in different functional groups is coordinated and mediated by the systems.

The Problem Processing System dovetails with the Language System on the organizational interface side, and with the Knowledge System on the functionality side. The term "Problem Processing System" in the conceptual design of bDIS emphasizes that 'routine work' involves significant problem-solving and articulation work and must be supported by information systems to the same extent as 'decision-making work' (Gasser, 1986; Gerson and Star, 1986; Wynn, 1991).

3.5 Process modeling and dual information systems

How can organizational interfaces be developed to enable effective working, the creation of knowledge, and learning through smooth navigation in DIS? Most traditional structured systems analysis and design approaches are ill-suited to the development of organizational interfaces because (1) they focus almost exclusively on modeling data flows, data structures and other components of *technical* systems and (2) the models are difficult for agents to understand and use (Curtis, Kellner, and Over, 1992). These modeling languages reinforce the development of dualistic, reified in ormation systems (Käkölä, 1995a; El Sawy and Khorshid, 1994, p. 12).

Fortunately, process modeling languages (Curtis, Kellner, and Over, 1992) remedy many of the weaknesses of the technically oriented modeling languages. Curtis, Kellner, and Over state (1992, p. 75): "Process modeling is distinguished from other types of modeling in computer science because many of the phenomena being modeled must be enacted by a human rather than a machine." Käkölä (1995a; 1996) found the Role Interaction Net process modeling language (Rein, 1992) is reasonably effective in alerting people to the dual nature of information systems. Drawing on this research, we have developed the Knowledge Creation Net (KCN) language (Koota, 1995; Koota and Käkölä, 1996).

The KCN language is based on organizational role (Roos and Starke, 1981; Stryker and Statham, 1985) and knowledge creation theories (Nonaka, 1994), Petri nets (Peterson, 1981), and Role Interaction Nets (Rein, 1992). In accordance with role theory, the language provides two primitives: roles and interactions. A KCN is composed of a set of concurrent roles. The behaviour of a role is described by its solitary actions and its interactions with other roles. Unlike the RIN language, the KCN language also describes how knowledge is created, shared, and converted in interactions between agents. This helps clarify the dual nature of information systems. People create and share tacit and explicit knowledge through the processes of socialization, externalization, combination, and internalization (Nonaka, 1994). Computerized systems enable and constrain these processes by combining existing knowledge according to the rules and procedures encoded into these systems by people in earlier time-space contexts. This distinction between what people do and what computers 'do' can be made explicit when the Knowledge Creation Nets are employed in DIS. Figure 5 clarifies a few notations of the KCN language.

Techniques from Petri nets are used to give the language process description and enactment capability. Enactment capability means that the KCN models can be directly executed on a proper coordination technology platform (Rein, 1992). This is vital for DIS. First, contrary to static models, executable models provide organizations with clear incentives to maintain them. Second, executable models can be used both to measure the performance of work processes and to capture deviations between the specifications and the way work is really done. Consequently, the variances in performance and the underlying reasons for these variances can be quickly identified and fixed, and specifications can be updated to reflect improved work practices.

We illustrate the use of Knowledge Creation Nets in DIS with the help of the ReDIS prototype.

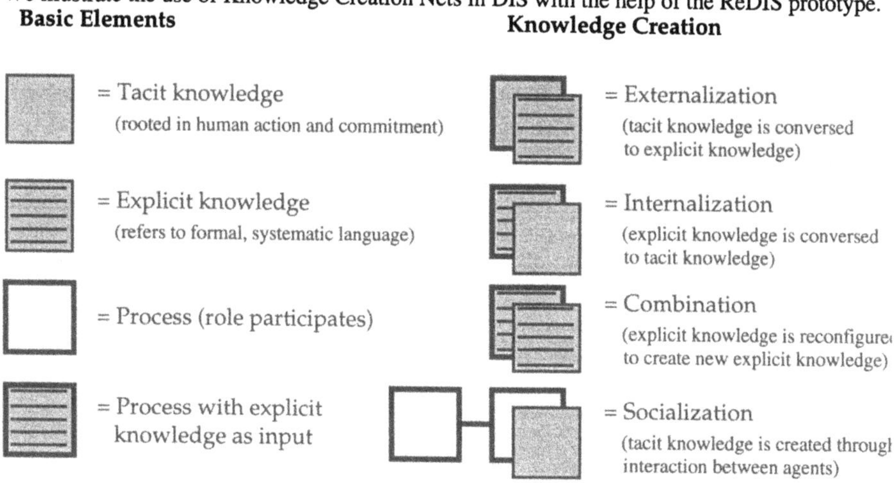

Figure 5 Notations of the KCN language (Koota, 1995; Koota and Käkölä, 1996).

4 WORKING AND LEARNING WITH THE ReDIS PROTOTYPE

In this section, we present the ReDIS* prototype to illustrate the business and breakdown layers of Dual Information Systems. Käkölä and Koota (1996) describe the project layer of ReDIS. The case organization and the work processes described in subsection 4.1 are fictitious, but the ideas stem partly from the IBM Credit Corporation case (Hammer and Champy, 1993). The case study gives ample opportunity to research the development and use of hyperknowledge-based DIS to support organizational coordination and the creation and sharing of knowledge. The ReDIS prototype helps business units process credit requests and issue credit. The ReDIS project was conducted in a laboratory environment. Personal computers and the Microsoft Access™ system (Jennings, 1993) were selected as the development platform.

4.1 The case organization and its credit issuance process

We make the following assumptions about the case organization and the role of ReDIS in the organization. (1) The Credit Corporation is a subsidiary of a much larger organization. (2) Issuing credit effectively is important for the organization as a whole because financing customers' purchases can be extremely profitable. (3) The Credit Corporation is organized as a hyperknowledge organization. The business units that issue credit within their regions form its business layer. (4) ReDIS systems support each business unit locally.

We focus on one business unit. Its credit issuance procedure goes as follows (Figure 6). After negotiating a sale, a sales agent in the Sales unit writes a standardised credit request and sends it electronically to the Credit unit for his region. The creditworthiness of the customer is checked. Rejected requests are sent back to the sales agent. Approved, standard loan contracts are modified to meet customer requirements. An interest rate is determined. A quote is developed and sent back to the Sales unit.

Workers in different functional roles are responsible for their own work. If they cannot accomplish their tasks, they can seek help from "specialists," who are typically employees with more experience and expertise. Relying on a specialist slows down the procedure but is sometimes unavoidable. If workers face a breakdown (e.g., an error in a credit request), they can enter into others' spheres of operation and perform audit trails to see what has gone wrong. Spontaneous quality assurance in every step of the process is an integral part of the organizational culture of the Credit Corporation.

Different characteristics of a work process such as time, quality, and expense are measurable by analyzing various key figures. Each process step is measured by analyzing:

- Number of people involved in the step.
- Average processing time of credit requests.
- Average queuing time for the step.
- Percentage of requests that require a specialist's help.

Agents use these measurements to benchmark their performance with agents in the same and inter-connected roles. Work redesign project teams use them and many other measurements to continuously improve the credit process and to periodically redesign it (Käkölä and Koota, 1996).

---

* The ReDIS project (1994-1996) is led by Timo Käkölä at University of Turku.

4.2 The main components of the business and breakdown layers of ReDIS

Organizational interface

The organizational process models constructed using the Knowledge Creation Net (KCN) language serve as the organizational interfaces of the business units in ReDIS. The organizational interface of each unit has four basic functions. First, it provides agents with role-centric views of the Embedded Credit Application System (ECAS). These views let agents see both the manual and computerized parts of their work as a whole, and thus carry out their responsibilities. Second, agents can use the organizational interface to enact the role-centric functionality of ECAS. Third, it provides a full-fledged hyperknowledge environment with the services envisioned in the conceptual design of the business and breakdown layers (section 3.4); agents can navigate, run different types of queries, and internalize redundant, real-time information about the business unit, its work processes and performance, and ECAS. Fourth, it provides access to the project layer of ReDIS (Käkölä and Koota, 1996).

The performance monitoring services of ReDIS collect performance data from each process enactment and store them in the Knowledge System.

The knowledge system

The procedural and descriptive chunks of knowledge visualized by the KCN model are stored in the Knowledge System of ReDIS. The system is implemented as a relational data base that holds all relevant information about the business unit, the cast (agents associated with certain roles), the process, and process enactment (the number and characteristics of agents in different roles, and the interactions that occur during the process). Naturally, all the relational tables accessed by ECAS are part of this larger knowledge system.

The problem processing system

An interactive working and learning environment is generated by the Problem Processing System that is driven by the Knowledge System's procedural knowledge in the form of Access™ scripts and KCN models.

4.3 Using the business and breakdown layers of ReDIS

We use working scenarios to illustrate how ReDIS fosters the enactment, coordination, and learning of computer-supported work processes. We assume that our imaginary persons, a credit checker and a clerk, have been trained for their jobs, but that they have not yet internalized the process of issuing credits. They do not work in other roles.

The credit checker begins to work by entering ReDIS with his user id and password. The system now knows that he is working at the workstation, registers him as "present" in the Persons table of the staff knowledge system, and determines his role-connected rights and responsibilities. The KCN model of the credit issuance process appears on the screen. It serves as a concept map of the organizational interface to help agents construct a shared understanding of the process (Figure 6). The credit checker can see the different roles and tasks involved, and realize that he is an integral part of the unit with an important organizational function, not just another part of a mechanistic system.

The process fragments within the rounded rectangle visualize the inter-connected role view of the Embedded Credit Application System. In the earlier research of the first author, each computerized task performed by an Embedded Inventory Application System was visually represented in the role column of the agents responsible for the task. This design reflected the act-oriented perspective: the inseparability of agents' manual and computerized tasks. However, when this design was tested in a laboratory environment, users sometimes mixed up manual and computerized tasks (Käkölä, 1996). Therefore, we have visualized the computerized tasks under the role ECAS. The database column facilitates the bridging of time-space disjuncture horizontally by visualizing the objects of work (here credit request documents) that mediate interactions between agents in different roles. Consequently, the structuring of work in time and space by ECAS is made explicit: agents can see when, where, how, and by whom these objects are stored and retrieved.

The number of requests in different stages of the work process is shown by the organizational interface in real time. This up-to-date reflection of work brings the KCN model to life and gives agents a sense of control over their work. Twenty-two requests are now waiting for the credit check.

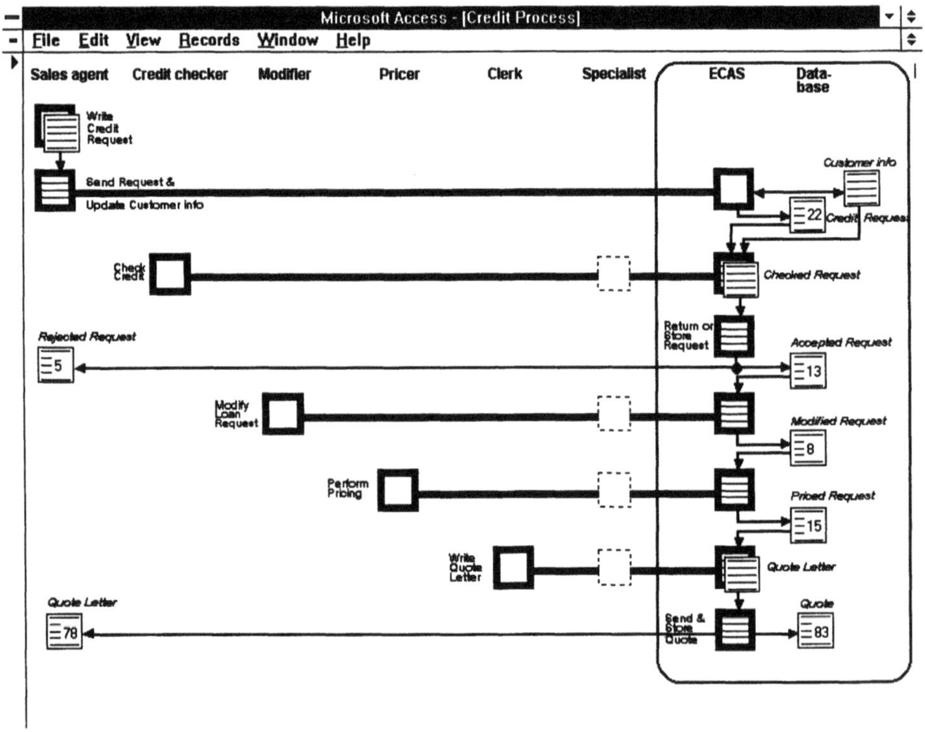

Figure 6 The organizational interface of the business unit.

The organizational interface provides agents with more detailed knowledge of the business unit and its processes to help coordinate and control work effectively and to handle breakdowns. The credit checker can use the KCN-based interface to zoom in on the details of the work processes. In Figure 7, he has opened the Process Description form to view the interactions and ECAS-modules of the Check Credit task. The KCN model shows that credit checkers use ECAS to retrieve queuing credit requests from the data base, and then approve or reject the requests, possibly with the help of specialists. ECAS automatically provides customer information, stores approved requests in the data base and sends rejected requests back to sales agents.

Learning services related to each interaction are available by clicking the ÒInstructionsÓ button. The credit checker can click the KCN-icons of the ECAS modules to see the role-centric computerized tasks and the resources and rules designers or colleagues have encoded in these tasks. He can tailor these rules according to the norms the work redesign project teams have negotiated using the project layer of DIS. These services help bridge the time-space disjuncture vertically between designers and workers.

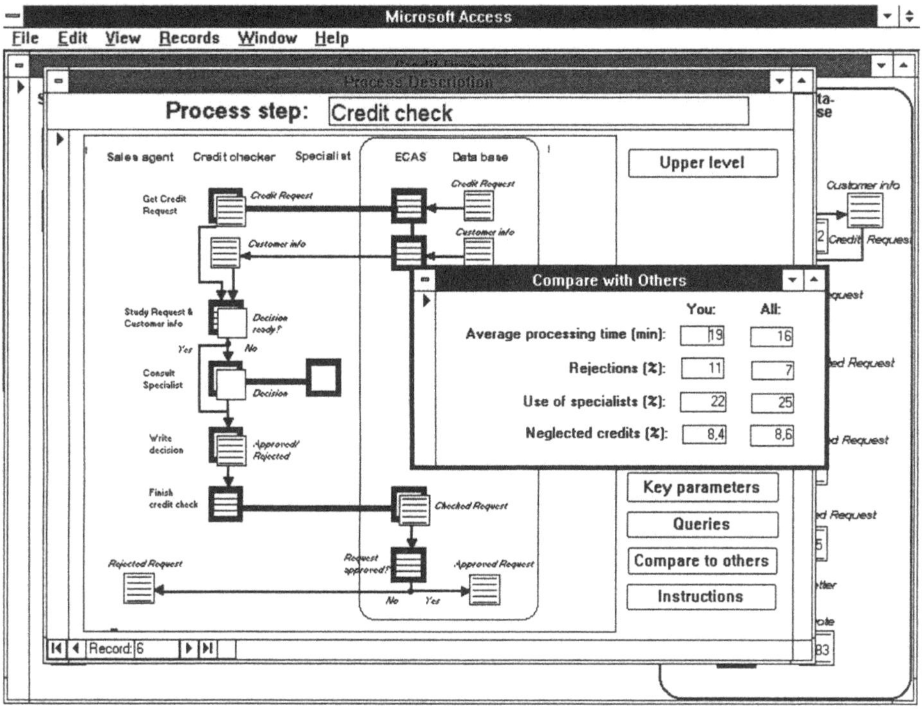

Figure 7 The organizational interface of the credit checkers. The role-centric benchmarking service has been activated.

The worker can run predefined queries, make own queries, and associatively navigate in the Knowledge System to retrieve information about different roles, interactions, and people. It is also possible to do role-centric benchmarking. The credit checker clicks the ÒCompare with othersÓ button of the Process Description form (Figure 7) and enters the three-month time frame as a parameter to compare his performance over the last three months to the average of the credit checkers in his business unit. ReDIS automatically executes all the predefined queries of the "credit check" process step. It selects from the Interaction table, which stores process enactment and resource use information for performance monitoring and breakdown management services, the credit-check interactions of the business unit during the last three months and uses their starting and finishing times to calculate the average cycle time of the process step. The same process is repeated for the interactions performed by the querying credit checker. He can then compare these two benchmarks to evaluate his personal performance.

"Compare with Others" form (Figure 7) shows the results of the queries. The credit checker sees that he has been stricter than the average: he has rejected 11 per cent of the requests during the last three months, whereas the average is 7 per cent. The average cycle time (19 minutes) of his credit checks is also higher than the 16 minutes of the average worker. His personal record, however, does not differ from the average in the use of specialists or in the percentage of requests that have led to credit losses or other problems. Stricter policy and lengthier inspection of requests have not increased the quality of his credit checking process. He decides to aim to reduce the processing time and accept more requests in the future.

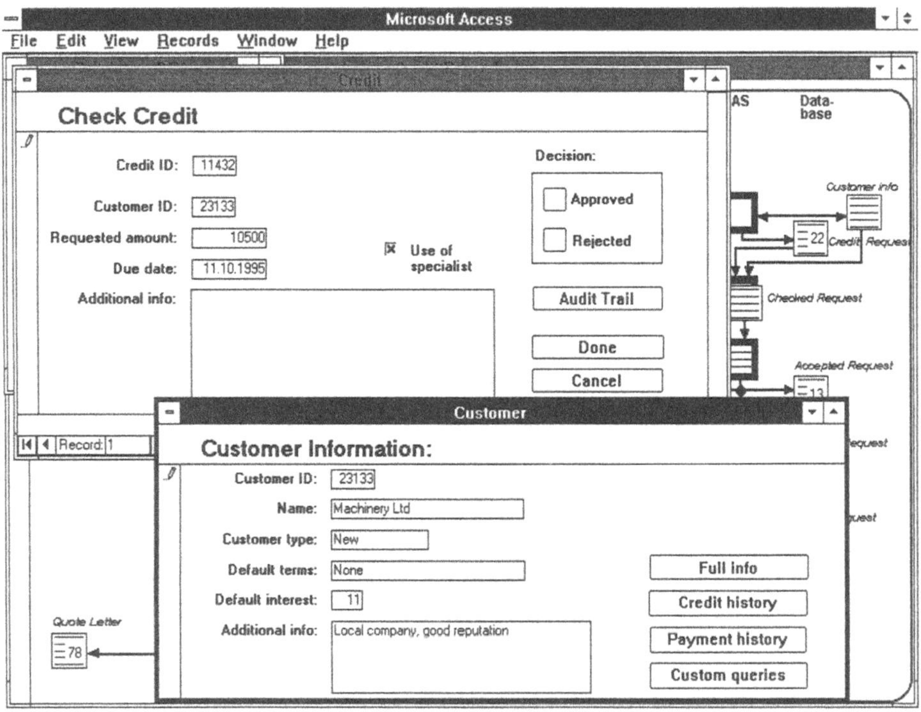

Figure 8 Credit check using the Embedded Credit Application System.

To start checking new credit requests, the agent clicks with a mouse the ÒCheck CreditÓ process element of the organizational interface (Figure 6). The respective module of ECAS is executed. It opens the Credit form of ECAS and retrieves from the Credit table the next request in the queue (Figure 8). It also opens the Customer form to provide detailed customer information. A new instance is added to the Interaction table that relates the worker, the process step, and the credit request, and also tells when the interaction started and ended. Finally, the credit checker is registered as ÒengagedÓ in the Persons table.

In the following scenario, we assume that the agent faces a tricky request and needs to consult a "specialist." He clicks the concept "specialist" in the organizational interface to open the Cast form (Figure 9). Information about specialists is automatically filtered from the staff knowledge system. He can then check out which workers are specialists, which are present, and, if possible, not busy, and where the suitable workers are located. He can contact the most suitable person, possibly using e-mail (the Contact button).

The credit checker records the outcome of the check using the Credit form (Figure 8). He also fills the check box to indicate that a specialist took part in the interaction. ECAS updates the Credit table and, in the case of approval, forwards the request to wait for modification. Finally, the performance monitoring service of ReDIS stores the use of specialist, the finishing time, and the outcome of the process in the Interaction table.

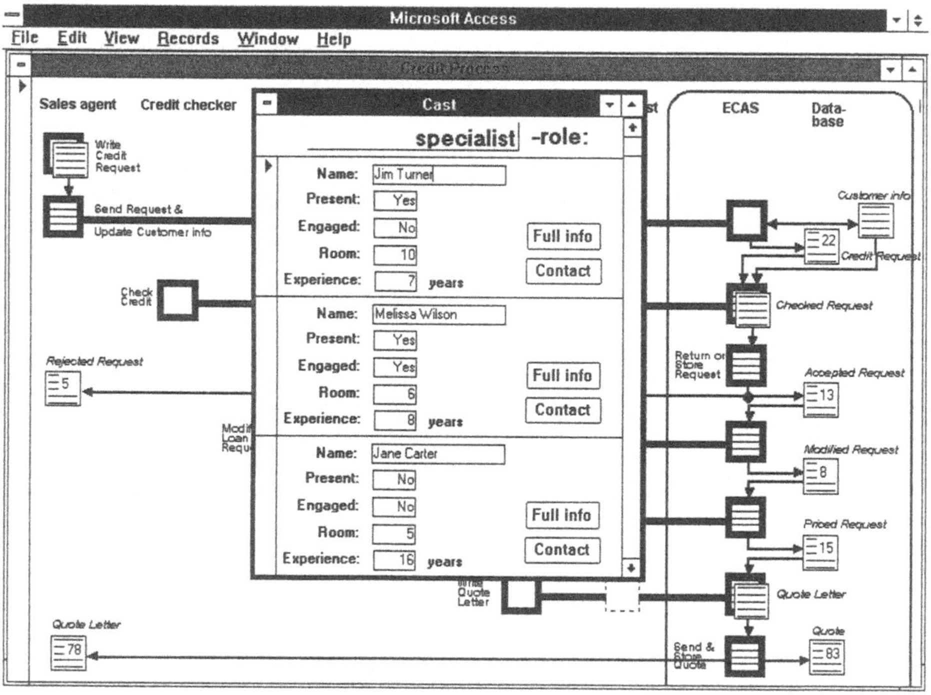

Figure 9 The cast form of the organizational interface.

The breakdown management services form the breakdown layer of ReDIS. They help agents during breakdowns quickly shift focus from routines to various details, including ECAS and the databases in which part of the work-related knowledge of agents has been encoded. The audit trail and other breakdown management services offer support during breakdowns that may emerge during the credit issuance process. After all, all situations cannot be solved simply by consulting a specialist. The audit trail service helps agents track down the life cycles of credit requests. The hyperknowledge characteristics of ReDIS play an important role when more knowledge is needed about previously unimportant aspects of work.

We illustrate the use of breakdown management services in the following scenario: A clerk is writing a quote letter for a significant sum of money. He knows that the customer has a poor credit history and begins to wonder whether the credit request should have been accepted in the first place. Maybe an error has taken place earlier in the process. He decides to investigate before completing the letter. But how to tackle the problem? First, he needs to understand how credit requests are checked in the credit issuance process. Second, and more importantly, he needs to know who is responsible for checking this particular credit request.

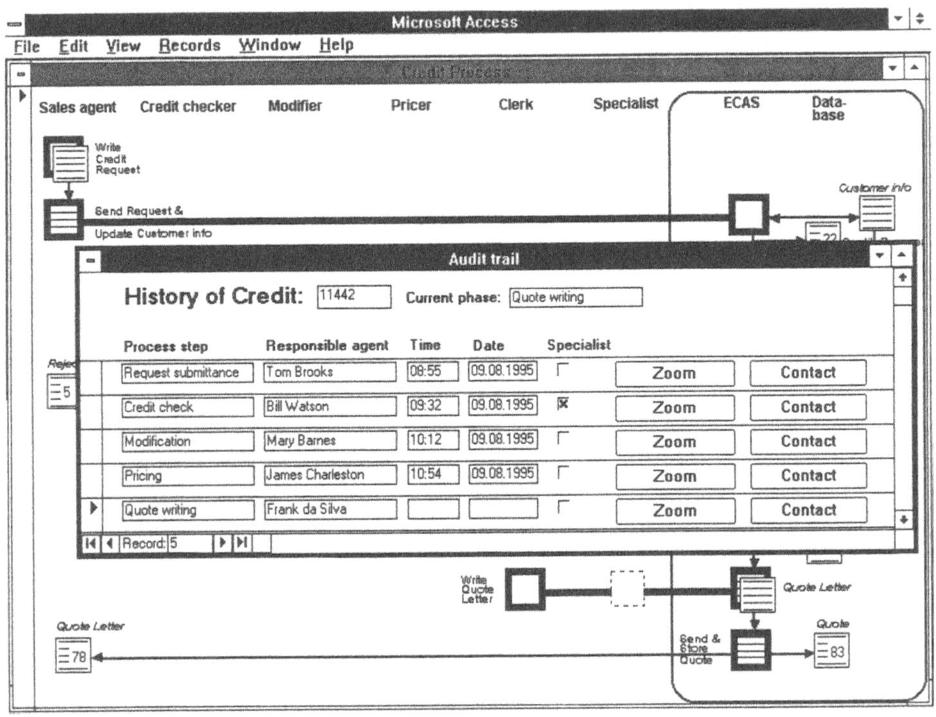

Figure 10 The audit trail form.

The clerk has internalized from the organizational interface (Figure 6) that credit checkers are responsible for checking incoming credit requests. He activates the audit trail service (Figure 8) to trace the life cycle of the credit, and zooms in on the details of the credit-check process (Figure 10). He stepwise executes the KCN model of the credit-check process (Figure 7) using the simulated enactment services of ReDIS. The original credit request and customer information are available during the simulation. The customer information confirms his doubts about the creditworthiness of the company. He sees from the KCN model how ECAS automatically forwards requests according to the decisions of credit checkers. He realizes that the request would have automatically gone to a modifier rather than being returned to the sales agent, if the credit checker had *accidentally checked* the request approved. Convinced that the case is worthy of more effort, he contacts the responsible agent to discuss it. The KCN models of ReDIS help agents in different roles create a shared explicit language of their work routines, making the sharing of tacit knowledge easier. Fixing breakdowns is facilitated.

In summary, the services of the business and breakdown layers of ReDIS help people (1) develop a theoretical understanding of their office work, including its computerized aspects; (2) work effectively; (3) maximally exploit knowledge gained from the routine use of ReDIS to monitor and continuously improve their performance; (4) develop and test multiple hypotheses of possible causes of breakdowns to get office routines back on track fast; and (5) participate in and contribute to work redesign projects on the project layer of the Credit Corporation.

5 CONCLUSIONS AND FUTURE RESEARCH

Insufficient knowledge of work practices and the role of CBIS in enabling and conditioning these practices, especially in the lower echelons of organizations, reduces the interpretive flexibility of CBIS. CBIS with high interpretive flexibility help people master their computer-supported work as a whole, share knowledge of their work practices, and maintain constructive, internal competition that motivates the creation of knowledge. We offered Dual Information Systems, a reconceptualization of CBIS that reduces the time-space disjuncture between the development and use of information systems *vertically* by interpreting all the computerized tasks and chunks of knowledge as the work and knowledge of agents, and *horizontally* by offering agents redundant information about their inter-connected work processes.

In Section 2, we provided a theoretical backing of DIS. In Section 3, we presented the conceptual basis of DIS, augmented it with the hyperknowledge framework to develop the conceptual design of the business and breakdown layers of DIS, and proposed the use of the KCN language as a generic work, knowledge conversion, and software process modeling language to construct organizational interfaces of DIS. In Section 4, we described a part of the ReDIS prototype to crystallize the conceptual design and encourage commercial implementations.

This paper has identified several design principles for the next generation of information systems in office environments. First, to reach and maintain high interpretive flexibility of information systems, it is fruitful to focus design on three conceptual layers of DIS: the project, business and breakdown layers. Second, the design of DIS must ensure that agents in the business layer of a hyperknowledge organization can easily enact routines according to partly prescribed work flow procedures, develop a theoretical understanding of their computer-supported work, and monitor their work performance using quantitative and qualitative benchmarks. Third, the design must offer breakdown management services to help agents deepen their theoretical knowledge during breakdowns, find out what is wrong, and recover. Fourth, the design must help agents quickly return to their routines or, if recovery is not possible due to the severity of breakdowns, enter the project layer to redesign work.

Process modeling languages and hyperknowledge environments are the cornerstones of the business and breakdown layers of DIS. Work routines, including their computerized parts, can be designed using process models, encoded in hyperknowledge environments, and visualized for enactment and reflection through organizational interfaces. Agents can flexibly navigate in the hyperknowledge environment, deepen their knowledge of the specific details of work, and understand the interconnections between their work and the business process as a whole.

We have drawn on Nonaka's hypertext organization model because a dual organizational design and a dual information system design mutually reinforce each other, increasing the interpretive flexibility of information systems. In traditional bureaucracies, (1) the creation of knowledge is fairly limited to the upper echelons of organizations (Nonaka, 1994); (2) rigid, narrowly defined jobs make it difficult for nonmanagement workers to exploit the knowledge-creating potential of hyperknowledge-based DIS (Zuboff, 1988); and (3) the performance monitoring services of DIS are likely to subject workers to unilateral managerial control. Managerial performance monitoring in hyperknowledge organizations should focus on results rather than on precise measurement of work steps to ensure the autonomy of functional work groups in the business layer (Hammer, 1990, pp. 108-112). Moreover, the extent of managerial control should be negotiated *constructively* by managers and functional work groups in the project layer, and subjected to renegotiation if managers or work groups cannot carry out their responsibilities or meet performance objectives. Käkölä (1995b) presents a more detailed analysis of the implications of interactions between managerial control patterns and coordination technologies for organizational working and learning.

Future research must establish more elaborate guidelines for the design of hyperknowledge organizations in which *all* agents can exploit the interpretive flexibility of DIS to work efficiently in the business layer, to create knowledge effectively in self-organizing project teams, and to accumulate knowledge in the knowledge-base layer. The conceptual design of bDIS must also be extended so that it covers the project layer of hyperknowledge organizations.

The next step is to assess and validate the utility of the services of business and breakdown layers of DIS by testing ReDIS first in the laboratory and later in the field. Although this research is still in progress, earlier research of the first author indicates that a system like ReDIS can be useful for working and learning. First, process model-based organizational interfaces help agents work and understand their work as a whole (Käkölä, 1996). Second, useful hyperknowledge-based working and learning environments can be built (Vanharanta, Käkölä and Back, 1995; Vanharanta, Käkölä and Kangas, 1995). Consequently, we are confident that Dual Information Systems in general, and their business and breakdown layers in particular, offer substantial benefits to organizations that implement them to increase the interpretive flexibility of information systems in office work.

6 ACKNOWLEDGEMENT

We are grateful to Inger Eriksson and Markku Nurminen, whose innovative visions about Embedded Application Systems inspired our research, and Tomas Isakowitz and the four anonymous reviewers for their constructive comments on earlier versions of this paper.

7 REFERENCES

Bush, V. (1945). As We May Think. The Atlantic Monthly, 176(1), pp. 101-108.

Bødker, S. and Grønbæk, K. (1991). Design in Action: From Prototyping by Demonstration to Cooperative Prototyping, in *Design at Work* (eds. J. Greenbaum and M. Kyng), Lawrence Erlbaum Associates, pp. 197-218.

Boland, R.J. Jr. (1991). Information Systems Use as a Hermeneutic Process, in *Information Systems Research: Contemporary Approaches and Emergent Traditions* (eds. H.-E. Nissen, H.K. Klein and R. Hirschheim), Elsevier Science, pp. 439-458.

Chang, A-M., Holsapple, C. W., and Whinston, A. B. (1989). A Decision Support System Theory. Working paper. University of Arizona, Tucson, USA.

Chang, A-M., Holsapple, C. W., and Whinston, A. B. (1993). Model Management Issues and Directions. Decision Support Systems, 9(1), pp. 19 - 37.

Chang, A-M., Holsapple, C. W., and Whinston, A. B. (1994). The Hyperknowledge Framework for Decision Support Systems. Information Processing and Management, 30(4), pp. 473-498.

Conklin, J. (1987). Hypertext: An Introduction and Survey. IEEE Computer, 20(9), pp. 17 - 41.

Ciborra, C.U. and Lanzara G.F. (1994). Formative Contexts and Information Technology. Accounting, Management & Information Technologies, 4(2), pp. 61-86.

Curtis, B., Kellner, M., and Over, J. (1992). Process Modeling. Communications of the ACM, 35(9), pp. 75-90.

Daft, R.L., Lengel, R.H., and Trevino, L.K. (1987). Message Equivocality, Media Selection, and Manager Performance: Implications for Information Systems. MIS Quarterly, 11(3).

El Sawy, O.A. and Khorshid, H.S. (1994). A Design Theory of Virtual Workflows. Research Paper IOM 94-13, School of Business Administration, University of Southern California.

Engelbart, D. (1963). A Conceptual Framework for The Augmentation of Man's Intellect, in *Vistas in Information Handling* (eds. P. W. Howerton and D. C. Weeks), Cleaver-Hume Press, London, 1, pp. 1-29.

Eriksson, I., Hellman, R., and Nurminen, M. I. (1988). A Method for Supporting Users' Comprehensive Learning. Education & Computing, 4(4), pp. 251-264.

Eriksson, I. and Nurminen, M. I. (1991). Doing by Learning: Embedded Application Systems. Journal of Organizational Computing, 1(4), pp. 323-339.

Gasser, L. (1986). The Integration of Computing and Routine Work. ACM Transactions of Office Information Systems, 4(3), pp. 205-225.

Gerson, E.H. and Star, S.L. (1986). Analyzing Due Process in the Workplace. ACM Transactions of Office Information Systems, 4(3), pp. 257-270.

Hammer, M. (1990). Reengineer Work: Don't Automate, Obliterate. Harvard Business Review, 68, pp. 104-112.

Hammer, M. and Champy, J. (1993). Reengineering the Corporation: A Manifesto for Business Revolution. HarperCollins Publishers, New York.

Heidegger, M. (1977). The Question Concerning Technology. Harper & Row, New York.

Hellman, R. (1989). User Support: Revealing Structure Instead of Surface. Behaviour & Information Technology, 8(6), pp. 417-435.

Jennings, R. (1993). Using Access™ for Windows™. Que Corporation, Carmel, IN.

Kogut, B. and Zander, U. (1992). Knowledge of the Firm, Combinative Capabilities, and the Replication of Technology. Organization Science, 3(3), August, pp. 383-397.

Koota, K. (1995). Tietojärjestelmien käyttäminen CSCW-prosesseissa organisaation oppimisen ja tiedon luonnin tukena. Pro Gradu-tutkielma. Turun Yliopisto, Tietojenkäsittelyoppi.

Koota, K.I. and Käkölä, T. (1996). The Knowledge Creation Net-process modeling language. Manuscript.

Käkölä, T. (1995a). Increasing the Interpretive Flexibility of Information Systems through Embedded Application Systems. Accounting, Management, & Information Technologies, 5(1), pp. 79-102.

Käkölä, T. (1995b). Designing and Deploying Coordination Technologies for Fostering Organizational Working and Learning: From Vision to Reality? Forthcoming in Scandinavian Journal of Information Systems, 7(2).

Käkölä, T. (1996). Evaluation of an Embedded Application System for Supporting Organizational Working and Learning. Manuscript submitted for publication.

Käkölä, T. and Koota, K.I. (1996). Redesigning Work with Dual Information Systems: the Work Process Benchmarking Service. Proceedings of the 29th Annual Hawaii International Conference on System Sciences, Vol. 3, pp. 461-471. IEEE.

Lyytinen, K.J. and Ngwenyama, O. K. (1991). What Does Computer Support for Cooperative Work Mean? A Structurational Analysis of Computer Supported Cooperative Work. Accounting, Management & Information Technologies, 2(1), pp. 19-37.

Malone, T.W. (1985). Designing Organizational Interfaces. Proceedings of CHI '85 Human Factors in Computing Systems, pp. 66-71. ACM, New York.

Nelson, T. (1987). Literary Machines. The Distributors, Indiana.

Nielsen, J. (1990). Hypertext and Hypermedia. Academic Press Inc, San Diego.

Nonaka, I. (1994). A Dynamic Theory of Organizational Knowledge Creation. Organization Science, 5(1), pp. 14-37.

Nurminen, M. I. (1988). People or Computers: Three Ways of Looking at Information Systems. Studentlitteratur, Lund, Sweden & Chartwell-Bratt.

Orlikowski, W. (1992). The Duality of Technology: Rethinking the Concept of Technology in Organizations. Organization Science, 3(3), pp. 398-427.

Orlikowski, W. and Robey, D. (1991). Information Technology and the Structuring of Organizations. Information Systems Research, 2(2), pp. 143-169.

Peterson, J.L. (1981). Petri Net Theory and the Modeling of Systems. Prentice Hall, Englewood Cliffs, NJ.

Rein, G. (1992). Organization Design Viewed as a Group Process Using Coordination Technology. Ph.D. dissertation. MCC Technical Report CT-039-92, Austin, Texas.

Roos, L. L. Jr. and Starke, F. A. (1981). Organizational Roles, in Handbook of Organizational Design, 1: Adapting organizations to their environments (eds. P. C. Nyström and W.H. Starbuck), pp. 290-308. Oxford University Press, Oxford.

Spendolini, M.J. (1992). The Benchmarking Book. American Management Association, New York.

Stryker, S. and Statham, A. (1985). Symbolic Interaction and Role Theory, in Handbook of Social Psychology, 1 (eds. G. Lindsey and E. Aronson), Random House, New York.

Swanson, E. B. and Ramiller, N.C. (1993). Information Systems Research Thematics: Submissions to a New Journal, 1987-1992. Information Systems Research, 4(4), pp. 299-330.

Tyre, M.J. and Orlikowski, W.J. (1994). Windows of Opportunity: Temporal Patterns of Technological Adaptation in Organizations. Organization Science, 5(1), pp. 98-118.

Vanharanta, H., Käkölä, T., and Back, B. (1995). Validity and Utility of a Hyperknowledge-Based Financial Benchmarking System. Proceedings of the 28th Annual Hawaii International Conference on System Sciences, Vol. 3, pp. 221-230. IEEE.

Vanharanta, H., Käkölä, T., and Kangas, K. (1995). Usability of a Hyperknowledge-Based Executive Support System for Financial Benchmarking. Proceedings of the 28th Annual Hawaii International Conference on System Sciences, Vol. 3, pp. 130-139. IEEE.

Winograd, T. and Flores, F. (1986). Understanding Computers and Cognition: A New Foundation for Design. Ablex Publishing Corporation, Norwood, NJ.

Wynn, E. (1991). Taking Practice Seriously, in *Design at Work* (eds. J. Greenbaum and M. Kyng), Lawrence Erlbaum Associates, pp. 45-64.

Zuboff, S. (1988). In the Age of the Smart Machine - The Future of Work and Power. Oxford: Heinemann Professional Publishing Ltd.

8 BIOGRAPHY

Timo Käkölä is a research scientist at the Department of Computer Science and Information Systems, University of Turku, Finland. His research interests include IT-enabled organizational designs for effective organizational creation and sharing of knowledge, and the integration of collaborative technologies such as workflow, hyperknowledge, and group support systems into Dual Information Systems that support work and work redesign. He has published a number of articles in leading scientific journals and conferences.

Kalle Koota is a systems analyst in the R&D department of Orion Corporation, Finland. His research interests include computer supported cooperative work, process simulation, and process modeling. His practical interests include document management and IT support for shared knowledge creation.

15

Towards a common architecture paradigm for the global application of information technology

Hans Lehmann
Department of Management Science and Information Systems
University of Auckland, New Zealand
Private Bag 92019
Auckland, New Zealand
Tel 64 9 373 7599 x 8659
Fax 64 9 373 7430
Email h.lehmann@auckland.ac.nz

Abstract:

The serious difficulties facing the developer of international systems (ie supporting business functions in different countries) are widely acknowledged. Despite their often pivotal importance, however, scholarly research in this field has been sparse and global information technology applications are still largely unstudied and under-explored. This investigative paper attempts to establish whether there is some commonality to the structure and nature (ie. the 'architecture') of international systems. The investigative method selected is based on a grounded theory approach, attempting to establish a set of preliminary theoretical 'concepts' and 'categories'. Three case vignettes from the author's own experience are used to establish a conceptual base.

A two-dimensional topology emerged as a candidate for an architecture paradigm. The implications of this concept are discussed in terms of its impact on the development of international information systems. A correlation between the shape of the systems topology and the underlying global business strategy was found. Directions for further research are outlined.

Keywords

International information systems, architecture of information systems, qualitative research in information systems, theory building methodology, systems architecture modelling

1 INTRODUCTION

Information systems technology is often critical to the international operations of the globally oriented firm, either as the key to its expansion, or even as the main profit driver. Despite their obvious importance, however, transnational information systems technology is still "largely unreported [and] unstudied" (Cash, McFarlan and McKenney, 1992) and "..generally ignored." (King and Sethi, 1993). While scholarly research into this field is sparse, there is an increasing amount of anecdotal evidence and technical reports indicating a strengthening interest by practitioners in this field.

1.1 Definition of 'International Information Systems'

The literature does not clearly identify a generally accepted term for the application of information systems technology across borders. Often "global" is used (eg by Ives and Jarvenpaa, 1991), but "transnational" is also in general use (eg by King and Sethi, 1993) for such systems. The first inevitably invites associations of vast enterprises covering the planet, whereas "transnational" is open to possible confusion with the precise use of the term coined by Bartlett and Goshal (1989) for describing one specific style of a firm's operation in more than one country. In this paper, therefore, the term "international"[1] is used.

Another definition is needed to distinguish international system from other distributed systems. Information systems which support different business *activities*, eg in multi-divisional companies, are different by definition, whether theses divisions are in a single or multiple locations, national or international. Similarly, systems supporting different business *functions* (such as Sales, Manufacturing, etc) are different for each function, again independent of their location, be they all in one place or spread over several continents[2].

'International Information Systems' are defined as distributed information systems which support similar *business activities* in highly diverse environments commonly found *across country boundaries.*

A classification of firm's international operations along the dimensions of 'business focus' and 'environmental diversity' (of their operating locations) may help to sharpen the definition. *'Business Focus'* is high in operators who concentrate on a single business activity. Examples are car rental firms, international banks and international franchises. Low business focus is present in diversified conglomerates with many activities. Examples are the large Japanese and American multinationals. Low *Environmental Diversity*[3] would typically be encountered within one country and high diversity across different countries with divergent business cultures.

This paper deals thus with the information systems for the 'International Operator', ie where a single business activity is carried out in different countries[4].

---

1 This too has been used by Bartlett and Goshal, but in a more general sense.

2 However, where these disparate sites have a common information need, such as common management and financial information across divisions and/or functional sites, the (sub)systems serving this need are 'international' in the sense of our definition.

3 This includes differences such as business practices, cultural influences, political regimes;

4 However, this is not a limiting restriction as each of the divisions or functional entities of an international conglomerate is often an 'international' operator itself.

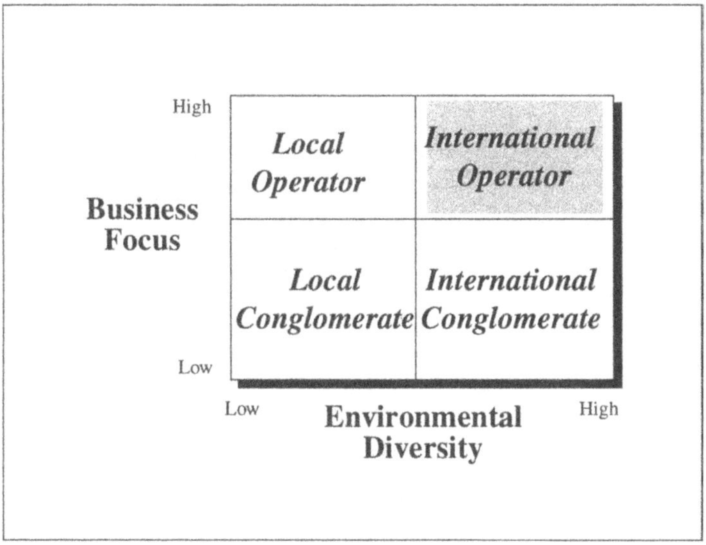

Figure 1. Classification of firms by business focus and diversity of their operating environment

1.2. Structure of the Paper

The paper is structured as follows:

- First, the literature on international systems is reviewed;
- Second, research approaches for international systems are discussed and a method is suggested to develop a base concept for initial research;
- Next, three case vignettes are used to test the base concept;
- Finally, the resultant concept is critically evaluated and directions for further research are outlined.

2 INTERNATIONAL INFORMATION SYSTEMS IN THE LITERATURE

Past research into international information systems is sporadic and spread over a wide array of topics. In the 1970s a main focus was on the issues of trans-border data flows (summarised by Hamelink ,1984). Since 1985 the issues have widened to also include planning, decision support and management contingencies.(summarised by King and Sethi, 1993 b). A number of attempts have been made to set out a taxonomy of issues and to classify the research areas related to international information systems: Sethi and Olson (1993) and King and Sethi (1993 b) both attempted to establish a framework for international information systems, the former addressing the firm-internal environment and the latter also encompassing the external influences on the international firm. Other work concentrated on the 'drivers', ie the factors exerting pressure on firms to operate information technology globally. Applegate and Mason (1991) and Ehrlich (1989) link the business reasons for global expansion to the nature of information technology employed. Ives and Jarvenpaa (1991) defined a set of ten 'business drivers for global information technology'. Whereas most of those are operations oriented, Butler Cox (1991) and Neo (1991) also found a significant marketing dimension as a factor in shaping global information technology.

2.1 Difficulties with international information systems

Whilst scholarly research concentrated on the wider issues, within the practitioner community there seems to be a widespread consensus emerging that international systems are a not only a major element of any global strategy but also a major, potential, stumbling block for global operators. The fact that only 8% of a large sample of European multinational companies have managed to implement international systems satisfactorily (KPMG, 1993) indicates the difficulties encountered. The issues are technology related problems and those of cultural diversity. A selection of - sometimes anecdotal - evidence for this is presented below.

Technology related difficulties

In a comprehensive review Huff (1991) identified critical, constraining issues as extending practically across all functional areas of the traditional systems management and development framework:

- Failure to link information technology and business strategy (Popper, 1990, LaPlante, 1991)
- Unsuitable development methods (Passino, 1990, Popper, 1990 and Laplante, 1991);
- Technical complexities and adverse legal aspects of telecommunications (LaPlante 1991 and Kobielus,1992);
- Hardware incompatibility and failure to establish interconnectivity (LaPlante, 1991);
- Lack of and/or incompatible technology standards (Palframan,1991);

Issues of cultural diversity

The assumption that international business is just a replication of domestic business, has been refuted for general business a long time ago (eg. Doz, 1980, Buss, 1982). Several researchers have more recently established that this assumption is also wrong for information systems.

Robey and Rodriguez-Diaz (1989) found that cultural differences proved a significant impediment to the implementation of an accounting system in one of two Latin American countries. Heitzman (1990), in a study on the acceptance and the influence of information technology in South East Asia sees the regionalisation/localisation of system development and implementation efforts as a way to ameliorate the difficulties experienced across cultural and developmental divides.

These findings were confirmed in a wide ranging analysis of multinational issues in information technology in less developed countries (Saraswat and Gorgone, 1991).

Whereas these studies concentrate mainly on the effect of different development levels there are also differences in value systems, business philosophies (especially ethics) and general living habits between different locations of an international system. Goodman and Green, (1992) demonstrate this with an analysis of the information technology environment in the Middle East. A recent comparative study of management styles, perceptions and expectations across western Europe (Barsoux, 1992) revealed a variety of differences in the role of management, which can be of major significance for systems design and implementation.

In conclusion, the past research on international information systems is wide spread and not always sharply focussed. There is as yet no coherent theory of the specific nature of international information systems (or even consensus on whether such specificity indeed exists) which could be of sufficient practical value to address the difficulties experienced with international information systems. However, some research has been done about the architecture of international information systems - an area which may have a bearing on the difficulties experienced.

The literature is not conclusive on the link between the 'goodness' of systems architecture and the effectiveness of systems development approaches. However, the value of an ‘infrastructure‘ (Weill, 1992) of sufficient 'reach and range' (Keen, 1991) is accepted as essential for providing the flexibility to deal with future systems demands. Earl (1989) suggests that a typical information technology architecture (which he also defines as the prerequisite for such an infrastructure in Weill's sense) contains 'blueprints' for the development of application systems. It is thus safe to assume that establishing an appropriately specific architecture for international systems would have a beneficial impact on their development.

Systems architecture is defined in many ways. For the purpose of this exploration a working definition of architecture is borrowed from Earl (1989): "[Information technology architecture is] the technology framework which guides the organisation in satisfying business and management information systems needs". This also encompasses functional applications in the sense of Weill's (1992) "enabling foundation [for the application of the technology]".

2.2 The structure of international systems in the literature

A number of researchers have found that the architecture of international systems seems directly influenced by the strategy and structure of the international firms which use them (King and Sethi, 1993; Sankar, Apte and Palvia, 1993; Kosynski and Karimi, 1993; Butler Cox, 1991; Ives and Jarvenpaa, 1991). Therefore the strategic management of global firms is briefly discussed first, before systems architectures are investigated.

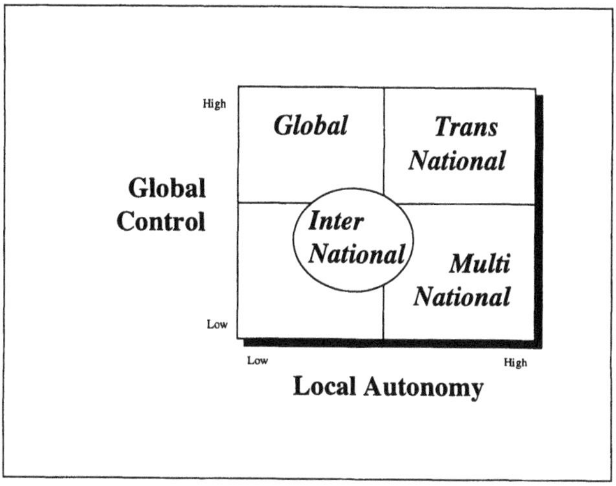

Figure 2. Global business strategies

The major factors shaping an international firm's operations and management structure seem to be the level and intensity of global control versus local autonomy. The model developed by Bartlett and Goshal (1989), illustrated in Figure 2, seem best to integrate business strategy with the organisational forces acting upon the international firm:

- The 'global' business strategy shows a high degree of global control at the expense of local autonomy;
- Juxtaposed to this is the 'multinational' strategy with loose global and high local control;
- 'Transnational' organisations balance tight global control in certain aspects with a policy of vigorously fostering local autonomy, particularly for the diffusion of innovation. These firms "think global and act

local" (Bartlett and Goshal, 1989). This strategy is considered optimal for many multinational corporations;

- Defined as an interim stage, the 'international' firm strikes a balance between global and local control, often with neither control modus dominant.

In the context of international systems, there is very little evidence of research towards an architecture model specifically derived for this class of system. There is evidence of the importance of having an 'architecture strategy' for global systems (IS Analyzer, 1991). The architecture of the 'global village' (Targowski, 1990), with its backbone of electronic highways connected to information utilities could provide a starting point for an architecture model. The need for an 'infrastructure' to allow connection between individual parts in the form of a central network (IS Analyzer, 1991) - points in the same direction. Bingham and Pezzini, (1990), researching logistics systems, set out the requirement for a 'common carrier information system' into which generic, packaged application systems can interface.

Butler Cox (1991) classify information systems structures according to systems management style. In their model (in which 'systems' is defined as technology and applications) there is a direct, one-to-one relationship between the global business strategies and these systems architectures. They distinguish between

- 'Centralised' systems, with local terminals connected to a centrally developed and operated system;
- 'Replicated', ie. copies of one (centrally developed and maintained) system are operated in all local sites;
- 'Autonomous', ie. locally developed and operated systems which have little in common with each other; and finally
- 'Integrated' systems, locally operated and assembled from compatible components developed at different local and /or central sites.

Kosynski and Karimi (1993) develop a very similar relationship between information systems structure and business structure, which (in the same sequence as above) they name 'centralisation', 'inter-organisational' (to emphasise the link-up between local databases and processes), 'decentralisation' and 'integrated architecture'. The key elements in their architecture model are network and data management strategy.

Sankar, Apte and Palvia (1993) define global information architecture mainly in terms of the configurations of two architectural elements, one mainly hardware and the other mainly operating software of the 'middleware' type. Their architecture model thus explicitly excludes application systems. These elements can then be structured in three configurations:

- Integrated (elements are physically separate, but logically connected);
- Centralised (together and connected);
- Decentralised (separate and disconnected).

The three configurations of the two elements result in nine possible architectures of which four, however, are either not feasible or inappropriate. Three are the 'pure' versions (with both elements in the same configuration) and two are mixed.

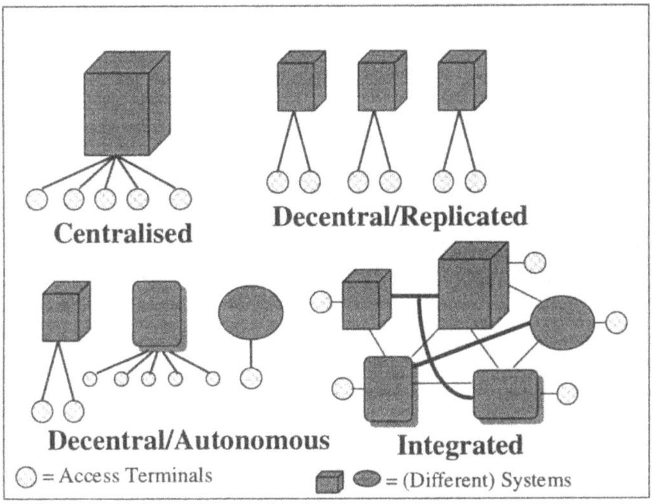

Figure 3. Architectures and configurations of international information systems

Figure 3 summarises the architectures and systems configuration structures discussed above. If the replicated/decentralised structure is disregarded as a physically distributed incarnation of the centralised architecture, there are thus three generic architectures outlined, namely **centralised, autonomous/decentralised** and **integrated**.

Whilst these studies are a first approach towards increasing our understanding of international information systems, they are well short of providing a research agenda which can address the issues in a methodical way.

3 SELECTION OF A RESEARCH METHODOLOGY FOR INTERNATIONAL INFORMATION SYSTEMS

Given the rudimentary state of the body of research into international information systems, it seems that theory building methods are an appropriate choice of methodology. These tend to be qualitative and inductive in nature.

Such methods are now well accepted for organisational research and are also becoming more widespread in information systems research (Turner, 1983, Benbasat et al, 1987, Galliers et al, 1987, Yin, 1989, Lee, 1989, Orlikowski et al, 1991, Zinatelli et al 1994). In particular, Eisenhardt (1989) describes the process of building theory, especially the central inductive process and the role of literature, ie the incorporation of previous research. Glaser and Strauss (1967) had set out - for sociological research initially - how to develop theory that is actually grounded in data and how this empirical connection permits the development of a testable, relevant and valid theory. Orlikowski (1993, 1995) in particular has pioneered the use of grounded theory in Information System Research.

There is no clear guidance in the Information System Research literature for what the nature of the 'starting point' in a theory building exercise should be. Whilst Eisenhardt (1989) acknowledges the importance of a 'well focused research question' she also puts a strong emphasis on '[beginning the research] as close as possible to the ideal of no theory under consideration and no hypotheses to test'. Similarly, Galliers and Land (1987) show a theory development progression which begins straight off with 'case study/action research', from which is developed a research question which in turn aids theory development.

Glaser and Strauss (1967), on the other hand, actively encourage the use of what they call 'anecdotal comparisons':

> *"Through his own experiences, general knowledge, or reading, and the stories of others, the sociologist can gain data .,.that offer useful comparison. This kind of data can be trusted if it has been 'lived'. Anecdotal comparisons are especially useful in starting research and developing core categories"*

Their theory development progression therefore starts with such a conceptual construct with which to start the research. During the research, the empirical facts unearthed then harden these into 'categories and their properties'. A linked set of such categories then forms the first 'substantive' theory, which in further research may be widened into a 'formal' theory.

Glaser and Strauss' progression of theory development seems to tie in closest with the prevailing thought on knowledge acquisition within the philosophy of science. Although there does not seem to a common terminology, the underlying ideas seem related among researchers. In a classic work, Wolf (1922) sees 'working ideas', formulated as 'principles' or 'postulates' (Glaser and Strauss' 'concepts') turning into hypotheses by the application of a method. Kuhn (1970), often referred to as the doyen in this field, defines a 'paradigm' as the igniting force for the forming of new theory. This is a set of propositions

> *"sufficiently unprecedented [and] ..simultaneously, sufficiently open-ended to leave all sorts of problems...to resolve"*

Merton (1968) refers to 'seminal ideas', often developed with the aid of a 'serendipity factor' as the starting point of a process to formulate what he terms 'theories of the middle range'. These are at the bottom of a hierarchy of knowledge and are roughly congruent with Glaser and Strauss' 'substantive' theories. Wartofsky (1968) sees such constructs as the end product of a process of stepwise abstraction, beginning with abstractions of (sensory) perception and ending with 'conceptual abstraction, ie the codification of such singular abstractions into 'concepts'. These are then the first building blocks for

> *"..further reflection on the concepts themselves which marks.. the beginnings of theoretical scientific inquiry.""*

Ziman (1984) refers to this class of seminiferous thought as 'patterns of fact' in need of 'simplifying generalisation' and 'definite association'. Donovan et al (1988) refer to the need for 'guiding assumptions' as the prerequisite for any research undertaking. Gergen (1978) and Pfeffer (1982) argue even further that the very selection of research objects is conditioned by pre-established concepts and values and that the notion of 'pure' theory is a mirage. Selye (1964) also subscribes to a more deductive view: new 'idea-units' are classified into existing categories and new research questions are developed from reviewing where current research has left gaps - ie, the process of 'normal science' in Kuhn's (1970) terms. However, Selye's model also leaves space for the 'intuitive flash (hunch)', the inductive element, without which no really new ground can be explored.

In conclusion, it seems therefore appropriate to adopt the Glaser and Strauss theory building model, as the basis for grounded theory research using their method of comparative analysis.

The starting point of such a course of investigation is thus the establishment of a suitable concept as the 'seed' for the theory. Having selected the architecture of international information systems as an appropriate topic of research to address the difficulties experienced by practitioners, such a concept should have an architecture model as its subject.

3.1 An architecture model for international information system

International information systems are defined as supporting a common function across a number of local sites. The first and most fundamental common sense deduction from this is the obvious requirement that such systems would have parts that are common to all sites and other parts which are specific to individual localities.

Not surprisingly then, the need for variation in international systems to accommodate differing local circumstances has been established early on by Buss (1982), when he found that using 'common' systems across different countries can be fraught with difficulty. In the same year Keen, Bronsema and Auboff, (1982) first articulate a paradigm of a 'common core' of information systems applications with 'local' alterations. There has been little further development of this model as far as the functionality of application systems is concerned, and Ives and Jarvenpaa, (1991) conclude that "the literature offers little guidance for...local versus common applications". The notion of a common structure, linking together divergent (local) elements of a global system, however, has been further developed by Keen (1991) who states that a 'transnational platform' is required to carry the 'transnational information technology capability' required for global operations.

Both Kosynski et al (1993) and Sankar et al (1993) mainly include hardware and 'middleware' elements in their interpretation of information technology architecture. However, Butler Cox (1991) include application systems in their definition of systems architecture. Also, information technology infrastructure, in the sense Weill (1992) and Weill et al (1994) define and interpret it, does include (common parts of) application systems. This is in line with Earl (1989) who argues that if the architecture in question should have relevance to the development of business systems, then all the elements which make up such business systems need to be included in it.

An architecture for international systems could therefore be postulated, which has two dimensions to it, namely the system's 'topology' and the characteristics of its 'elements'. The topology of the system is what designates the parts and defines their relation to each other[5]. The parts of the topology would thus consist of a 'common core' and 'local variations' of the system, linked together by a 'core/local interface'. Figure 4. illustrates such a architecture model. Using Kroenke and Hatch's (1994) practical definition of the components of an information system, these parts consist of five elements, namely people, procedures, data, software and hardware. The sum of the characteristics of each element (such as the typical technology platform, typical application programs, etc.) together shape the characteristics of the overall system.

In line with Glaser and Strauss' (1967) requirement that such a basic conceptual mode should be grounded in the researcher's experience and should be based on 'lived' anecdotal evidence, it seems appropriate to contrast this concept with some live experiences with international information systems.

---

[5] The term 'topology' is chosen (rather than 'structure') because what is being described is likely to appear in many disguises; a structure always needs to be recognisable as such, whereas a topology, by definition, is "the [set of] properties..which remain unchanged even if [the shape] is bent, stretched, etc." (Chambers Twentieth Century Dictionary, 1972 Ed)

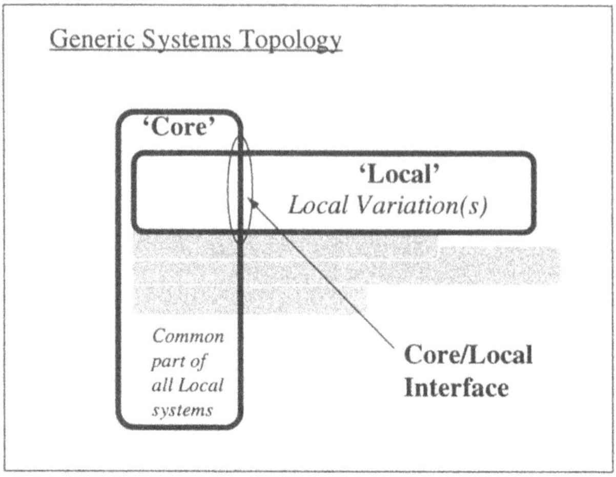

Figure 4. The conceptual 'Core/Local' topology

4 THE ARCHITECTURE MODEL AND EMPIRICAL OBSERVATIONS

Three case vignettes from the author's own experience are used to explore whether the architecture model postulated *eo ipso* is useful in the practical explanation and interpretation of the cases as well as a candidate for a 'paradigmatic' theory of the structure of international information systems.

4.1 The leasing subsidiary of an international bank

The firm was acquired by an Asian international bank to give them a base in the leasing business with branches in the USA, the UK and three European countries. The central computer into which all offices were linked was in New York. It soon transpired that systems were inadequate for expansion and the hardware was obsolete. A complete re-design of their information systems technology was therefore needed.

The business in the various countries was firmly limited to instalment credit transactions and differed mainly in magnitude. This premise of business being the same did, however, not translate into systems terms. While the lease set-up process was similar, the lease administration part, which makes up more than two thirds of the system, differed significantly from country to country.

To cope with this diversity the new international system had two main components:

- A common leasing module dealt with credit and exposure management; it would set up the lease deals and the receivables stream;
- Local country modules would receive the basic data for input into the country-specific receivables and marketing modules, to cope with local languages as well as differing business practices.

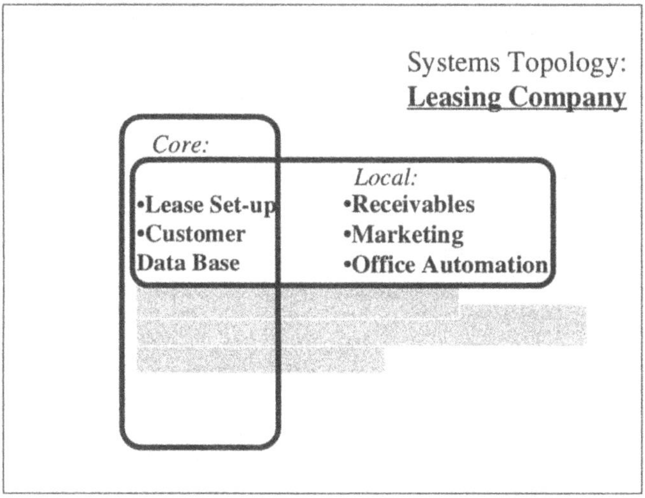

Figure 5. The balanced topology of the Leasing Company

The topology of the new systems was thus characterised by

- A 'core of central application software for those key functions which need to be globally controlled,
- Freedom for 'local' information technology applications, apart from stringent data interface standards;
- Technical people at the centre and business-oriented applications managers at the 'local' sites.

In terms of global business strategy, the leasing company balances strong global control over with wide local autonomy to use the local environment to best advantage. This classifies them as Global Co-ordinator/*Transnational*.

4.2 An Australasian merchant bank

This New Zealand based merchant bank with substantial branches in Australia and London had expanded rapidly. The business of the bank consists mainly of money market dealing, investment banking and stock broking. Information systems technology at the head office was fragmented and the branches ran odd assortments of software and equipment, loosely linked by public networks. A newly appointed central Treasurer set out to install systems and controls.

There were two levels of information and systems needs:

- A comprehensive management control system to monitor exposure and risk internationally as well as for each local firm;
- Operations, specifically in the money market and stock broking activities required more systems support.

The resultant international system consisted thus of a narrow 'core' which only contained detailed and stringent data interface and communication standards for input into the Treasurer's own monitoring system. As an incentive to comply with the standards, an electronic mail and bulletin board service was offered on the 'core'. The 'local' systems were seen as entirely composed of the best suited local software, adapting to the diverse environments for money market and stock broking operations, provided they could comply with the data and information interface requirements. The branches would rely entirely on local, external technical and applications support.

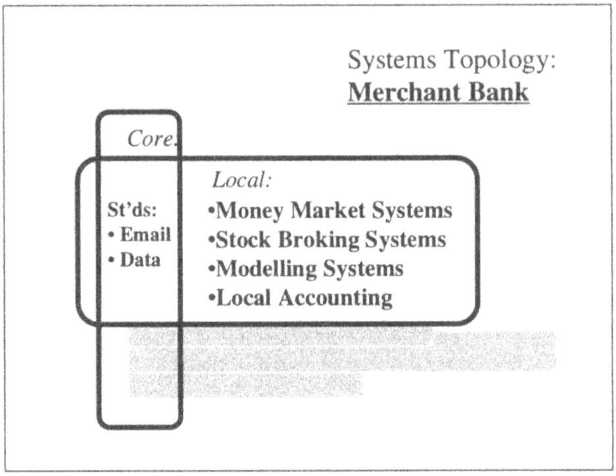

Figure 6. Dominance of local systems in the Merchant Bank's topology

The main characteristic of this system's topology is thus a thin 'core', consisting entirely of standards and recommendations. The 'locals' enjoy freedom of choice of information systems technology as long as they comply with the laid down interface standards. Only some of the system elements are well defined:

- Data and information standards for the group management information system are non-negotiable;
- Hardware standards rely on incentives;
- Operating procedures are largely locally defined and local systems are all supported by external agents;

The merchant bank gives thus high autonomy to its local offices and imposes only a reporting regime from the centre. It is low on global control and classified as a National Adaptor/*Multinational*;

4.3 A New Zealand commodity exporting board

The Board has a virtual monopoly in the purchase of fruit from producers. It owns packing houses and cool stores in New Zealand, operates its own charter fleet and runs a number of European sales offices, while North American sales are controlled through an agency. Asia is an important target for development in the near future.

The Board's systems strategy centres around strong production systems with some marketing modules integrated into them. The international part is, however, the smallest part of the system and consist mainly of common messaging formats. The shipping system is designed to send shipment details and forecasts to the branches who can send sales statistics back to the centre. Some of the overseas sales offices use sales order entry systems specific to their environment.

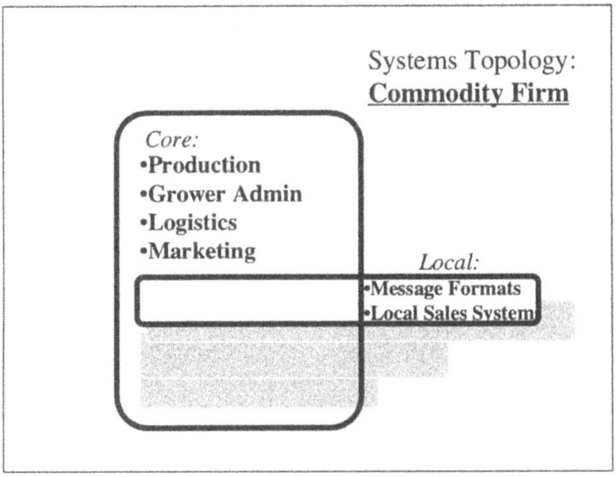

Figure 7. Systems Topology of the Commodity Firm

The architecture consists of:

- A - large - 'core' of extensive and sophisticated systems in the production, logistics and marketing (forecasting and decision-support/modelling) areas;
- The messages and the independent sales and administration support systems at the branch offices are thus the only 'local' parts in the topology of this international system.

The commodity firm is strong on global control, leaving relatively little autonomy to the local sales offices. This classifies them as Exporter/*Global*.

4.4 Summary of the Case Vignettes

Table 1 overleaf summarises the topology and systems element characteristics of the three cases.

The degree of balance between local autonomy and global control in these three cases seems to be closely correlated to the topology of international systems. This confirms the literature on the influence of strategy on information systems structure mentioned above (see 2.2). A topology of large 'local' technology, compared to thinner 'core' components seems to correlate to the higher degree of local autonomy and low level of global control as reflected in the Merchant Bank's organisational strategy. The balance in global vs. local control in the structure of the leasing company is reflected in a medium-to-large 'core' and equally sized 'local' systems. High global control and little autonomy for the branch sites in the commodity firm has lead to an architecture characterised by a large 'core' of systems at the centre and only a thin smattering of 'local' systems.

Table 1. Summary of the case histories

Architecture Elements	LEASING FIRM	MERCHANT BANK	COMMODITY BOARD
'Core'	'Medium core'; Selective Customer Data Base; Central Leasing Application	'Thin core'; Data and Information standards and communication standards; Electronic mail and Bulletin Boards (the 'incentives') for free-format communication;	'Large core"; Large central system at the production sites and head office
'Locals'	Local variations of the Leasing Receivables and Marketing systems	Locally selected packaged technology;	Message formats and protocols for communication to smaller, independent local systems;
Hardware	Indirect standard, based on data interface requirement	Hardware and technology guidelines with incentives for compliance;	Different for each location;
Software	Local software has to accommodate the standard data formats output by the central applications;	Locally selected packages; guidelines for common accounting modules; Electronic mail and Bulletin Boards (the 'incentives') for free-format communication;	Customised, large system at the centre; at the local offices discretion, some customised, some packaged;
Data	Stringent data and communications standards;	Stringent data and information standards; detailed data communication standards (protocols and time schedules);	Message formats mainly;
Procedures	Stringent procedures for credit control and lease deal set-up;	Stringent reporting schedules (ie. the effect of the data standards);	Reporting requirements for the local offices;
People	Applications managers and external technical support at the local centres; Technical management at the centre;	External applications and technical support; technician employed by head office to install and support 'recommended' technology;	Large staff at the central system; no systems staff at the local offices;

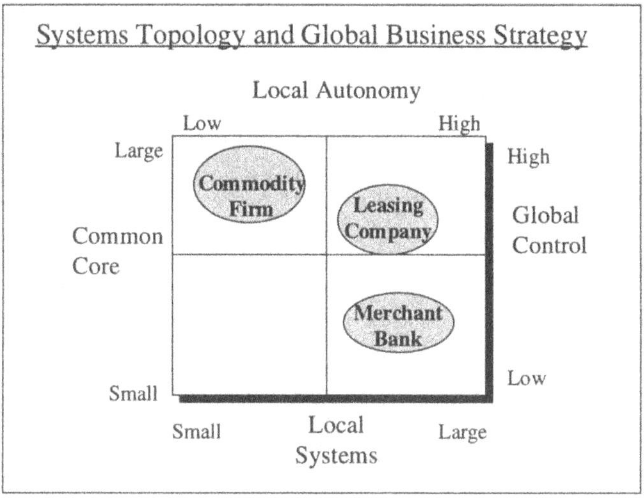

Figure 8. Link between architecture and global business strategy

Figure 8 above shows the position of the three cases with respect to their topology and global business strategy

This relationship is also indirectly confirmed by King and Sethi (1993), who in their case study also point to the "overriding role of business strategy". The optimal strategy depended to a large extent on the affinity (or otherwise) in terms of business culture and developmental level between the centre and the local sites. This flexibility to local demands and issues they identify as the key success factor for the development and implementation of an international information system.

5 SUITABILITY OF THE ARCHITECTURE MODEL

The model could be used with considerable ease to demonstrate and explain the nature of the systems in the cases. Furthermore it allows the demonstration of a significant property of the architecture of international information systems, ie a perceived dependency on the prevailing business strategy, in much grater clarity than the previous literature. It can thus be concluded that the architecture model is useful for practical purposes.

To ascertain whether the model is also appropriate for developing a theory from it, a set of criteria for the goodness of a theory may be applied. Mayhew (1981) and Pfeffer (1982) suggest three criteria for a good theory:

- Clarity
- Parsimony; and
- Logical coherence

Glaser and Strauss (1967) add to this a number of criteria specific for the social sciences:

- Density
- Scope
- Integration (into a larger set of theories)
- Fit (with the data)
- Ability to work

We will now assess the model against each criteria in turn:

- **Clarity**; the model has only three simple terms, readily understood by any intelligent non-expert;
- **Parsimony**; the model can explain and implement the more elaborate architecture exemplifications contained in the literature and cited above (in *italics)*:

    * *Centralised* architectures have a 'local' content of (near) zero;
    * *Decentralised* architectures have a 'core' of (near) zero;
    * *Integrated* architectures have a varying 'core' to 'local' ratio for each element and/or for each location.

- **Logical coherence**; the model is derived directly from the definition of its underlying subject (ie the international information systems);
- **Density**; there is very little redundancy in the model:; to determine a unique manifestation of the model, each element in use would only need to be defined twofold:

    * In terms of its own functionality to define the core/local split;
    * In terms of its interface with its correspondent part in the core/local dimension;

- **Scope**; the model is defined without any restrictions in terms of application class or type; There is also no structural hurdle in the 'core/local' topology for the firm to migrate between global business strategies:

    * The large 'core' of an *Global*[6] firm would
    * shrink as the autonomy of the parts of an *Multinational* increases;
    * re-establishing global control for the *International* would increase the size of the 'core' again and decrease 'local' parts until they reach
    * equilibrium in the *Transnational* with specific 'core/local' ratios for each business unit.

- **Integration**; the model seems to correlate well to the underlying business strategy; whether it also integrates well into other theoretical constructs within the - sparse - research into international information systems still needs to be investigated;
- **Fit**; Fitting the model to the case vignettes was possible without any 'forcing' of the data;
- **Ability to work**; by this is meant whether the application of the model will actually be relevant and beneficial to the problem in question, ie the difficulties with e development and implementation of international information systems. This needs more discussion.

---

[6] *Bartlett & Goshal* nomenclature

5.1 Potential benefits of the 'core/local' architecture

Two main areas of benefit could conceivably arise from the adoption of the proposed architecture model:

- It would provide a coherent and separate framework aimed specifically at the use and exploitation of information technology in applications of high environmental diversity (ie. international systems);
- It would point to a different, more economical and less risky way of building international systems.

Each is now discussed in turn.

A framework for using information technology globally

King and Sethi (1993) point out that "Past literature has generally ignored the international aspect of IS.." and they therefore expected that international systems developments "would fail to show any coherent strategy..".

A framework such as the two-dimensional topology, which can cater for all constellations of business strategy and the resulting systems and technology architectures, could be useful

- In the first instance as a formal, structured depository for case experience in order to build up a body of knowledge;
- Subsequently as a vehicle for developing codes of good practice for the creation and implementation of international systems; eventually this could lead to the development of a specific systems development life cycle for international systems.

Impact on systems development

Designing and developing an international system, following the two-dimensional topology architecture, would involve three systems parts:

- The 'core' of common systems (infrastructure and applications);
- The 'local' systems;
- The 'core'/'local' interfaces.

These systems parts would be developed in three distinct steps:

1. First, the global business strategy would guide the definition of the 'core' parts. Deciding the nature of the infrastructure elements and delineating which functional applications are to be rigid across local sites would be the major design parameters.
2. The definition of the core parts would then allow a detailed specification of the core/local interfaces, in terms of technical standards for the infrastructure elements and in terms of data and information standards and formats for the functional and application systems parts. The technical specifications, taking into account any processing requirements and constraints as implied by the data/information interfaces, would then define a common technology platform.
3. 'Local' systems would be defined to complement 'core' applications requirements where these exist, or follow, within the framework of the technology platform, entirely their own specifications.

Furthermore, the design modules can be tackled by independent teams within overlapping, or, in the case of 'local' systems acquisition projects, parallel time frames. This would spread, and thereby reduce, the development risk and would undoubtedly bring tangible time savings[7].

6 CONCLUSION AND DIRECTIONS FOR FUTURE RESEARCH

The proposed architecture model has proved to be a practical and flexible tool to describe and understand data from a set of case vignettes. It also seems to fulfil some main criteria for a candidate for valid information systems theory. It may therefore be concluded that it may well be of use as a paradigm for future research into the structure of international information systems.

The architecture model could also have significant implications for the modus of development of international systems. Using it as a framework for the building and implementation of international information systems would allow in the first instance a systematic accumulation of a body of knowledge about this process and in the second instance enable a modular and parallel systems building approach.. This could make the development process more predictable, shorter and less risky. The two dimensional structure could also provides in-built flexibility for gradual future enhancement.

To be of practical use, however, this architecture model now needs to be validated on a much larger, diversified and altogether more representative scale. More empirical research into analysing the structure and architecture of international information systems is needed. The use of a grounded theory approach seem appropriate.

7 REFERENCES

Anonymous, (1991). Building a Global IT Infrastructure. *I/S Analyzer,* 29, 6, 1-12, 13-14.

Applegate, L.M., Mason, R.O. (1991). *Information Technology and Globalization.* New York. Proceedings of the 12th International Conference on Information Systems.

Barsoux, J.-L. (1992). Following the Leaders. *International Management,* 47, 7, 40-41.

Bartlett, C. A. and Ghoshal, S. (1992). What is a Global Manager? *Harvard Business Review,* 203.

Benbasat, I., Goldstein, D.K. and Mead., 1987. The Case Research Strategy in Studies of Information systems, *MIS Quarterly*, September, 369-386

Bingham, J. E. and Pezzini, P. S. (1990). Systems Design for International Logistics. *International Journal of Technology Management (Switzerland),* 5, 4, 472-479.

Buss, M. D. J. (1982). Managing International Information Systems. *Harvard Business Review,* 153-162.

Butler Cox plc. (1991). Globalisation: The Information Technology Challenge. *Amdahl Executive Institute Research Report.* London.

Cash, J.I. Jr., McFarlan, W.F. and McKenney, J.L. (1992). *Corporate Information Systems - The Issues Facing Senior Executives.* Homewood. Irwin.

Donovan, A., Laudan, L. and Laudan, R., 1988 Testing Theories of Scientific Change. In: *Scrutinising Science - Empirical Studies of Scientific Change.* Kluwer Academic Publishers, Dordrecht.

Doz, Y.L. (1980). Management in Multinational Companies. *Sloan Management Review.* 21, 2.

[7] This development methodology is not new and is, for example, very similar to good practice in the creation of operating systems software where often a standard 'kernel' (the *core*) of functionality is to be applied in a number of (*local*) environments, some of them unknown and unpredictable at the time of writing.

Earl, M. J. (1989). Management Strategies for Information Technology. Prentice-Hall, London.
Ehrlich, E. M. (1989). Information Technology, Global Linkage, and U.S. Competitiveness. *Vital Speeches,* 55, 24, 755-759.
Eisenhardt, K.M., 1989. Building Theories from Case Study Research. *Academy of Management Review*, 14,4, pp532-550
Galliers, R., (1993). IT Strategies: Beyond Competitive Advantage. *Proceedings of the XII Conference of the South East Asia Computer Confederation,* 1993, Vol.2, 105-109
Galliers, R.D. and Land, F.F., 1987. Choosing Appropriate Information Systems Research Methodologies. *Communications of the ACM*, 30,11,pp.900-902
Gergen, K.J. 1978. Toward Generative Theory. *Journal of Personality and Social Psychology,* Vol 36, p1344-1360
Glaser, B.G., and Strauss, A.L., (1967). *The discovery of grounded theory.* Aldine Publishing Company, Hawthorne, New York.
Goodman, S. E. and Green, J. D., (1992). Computing in the Middle East. *Communications of the ACM,* 35, 8, 21-25.
Hamelink, C.J. (1984).Transnational data flows in the information age. Lund, Sweden: Student-litteratur AB
Heitzman, J. (1990). Information Systems and Development in the Third World. *Information Processing and Management (UK),* 26, 4, 489-502.
Huff, S. L. (1991). Managing Global Information Technology. *Business Quarterly,* 56, 2, 71-75.
Ives, B., Jarvenpaa, S.L. (1991). Applications of Global Information Technology : Key Issues for Management. *MIS Quarterly.*
Keen, P. G. W. (1991). Shaping the Future: Business Design Through Information Technology. *Harvard Business School Press.* Boston, 1991
Keen, P. G. W., Bronsema, G. S. and Auboff, S. (1982). Implementing Common Systems: One Organisation's Experience. *Systems, Objectives and Solutions.* 2.
King, W. R. and Sethi, V. (1993). Developing Transnational Information Systems: A Case Study. *OMEGA International Journal of Management Science,* 21, 1, 53-59.
King, W.R. & Sethi, V. (1993 b) A framework for transnational systems. In *Global Issues in Information Technology,* Idea Publishers, Harrisburg
Kobielus, J. (1992). Privacy Issues Loom as Global Net Hurdle: Part I. *Network World,* 9, 3, 27-51.
Konsynski, B. R. and Karimi, J. (1993). On the Design of Global Information Systems. *Globalization, Technology and Competition.* Bradley, S.P., Hausman, J.A. and Nolan, R.L. (Ed's). Boston. Harvard Business Press.
KPMG Peat Marwick. (1993). Pan-European Business Systems. London. *KPMG Management Consulting Private Research Report.* Brussels.
Kroenke, D. and Hatch, R. (1994). *Management Information Systems.* New York. McGraw-Hill.
Kuhn, T.S. , 1970. *The Structure of Scientific Revolutions.* University of Chicago Press, Chicago.
LaPlante, A. (1991). Global Information Officers Entering IS Picture. *Computerworld,* 25, 33, 70.
Lee, A., 1989. A Scientific Methodology for MIS Case Studies, *MIS Quarterly*, 13,1,pp32-50
Mayhew, B. H.,1981. Structuralism versus Individualism: Part II, Ideological and other Obfuscations. *Social Forces.* Vol 59. P627-648.
Merton, R.K., 1968. *Social Theory and Social Structure.* The Free Press, New York.
Neo, B. S. (1991). Information Technology and Global Competition: A Framework for Analysis. *Information and Management (Netherlands),* 20, 3, 151-160.
Orlikowski, W.J., 1993. CASE tools as organisational change: Investigating incremental and radical changes in systems development. *MIS Quarterly,* Sept 1993, p309-337

Orlikowski, W.J., and Baroudi, J.J., 1991. Studying information technology in organisations. *Information Systems Research* (2:1), March 1991, p 1-28
Orlikowski, W.J.,(1995). *Organisational change around Groupware.* Working Paper CCS 186, Massachusetts Institute of Technology.
Palframan, D. (1991). The Great Software Sort-Out. *Management Today,* 86.
Passino, J. H. Jr. (1990). Harnessing the Potential of Information Technology for Support of the New Global Organization. *Human Resource Management,* 29, 1, 69-76.
Pfeffer, J. 1982. *Organisations and Organisational Theory.* Ballinger Publishing Company, Cambridge, Massachusetts.
Popper, W. J. (1990). In Pursuit of Foreign Affairs. *Computerworld,* 24, 19, 96.
Robey, D. and Rodriquez-Diaz, A. (1989). The Organizational and Cultural Context of Systems Implementation: Case Experience from Latin America. *Information and Management (Netherlands),* 17, 4, 229-239.
Sankar, C., Apte, U. and Palvia, P.(1993). Global Information Architectures: Alternatives and Trade-offs. *International Journal of Information Management,* (1993), 13, 84-93.
Saraswat, S. P. and Gorgone, J. T. (1991). Multinational Issues in Information Technology: A Perspective from Less Developed Countries. *Information and Management,* 21, 2, 111-121.
Selye, H. 1964. *From Dream to Discovery - On Being a Scientist.* McGraw-Hill, New York.
Sethi, V. and Olson, J.E. (1993) An integrating framework for information technology issues in a transnational environment. In *Global Issues in Information Technology,* Idea Publishers, Harrisburg
Targowski, A. S. (1990). Strategies and Architecture of the Electronic Global Village. *Information Society,* 7, 3, 187-202.
Turner, B.A., 1983. The use of grounded theory for the qualitative analysis of organisational behaviour. *Journal of Management Studies* (20:3) July 1983, p333-348
Wartofsky, M.W., 1968. *Conceptual Foundations of Scientific Thought.* Macmillan, New York.
Weill, P. (1992). The Role and Value of information Technology Infrastructure: Some Empirical Observations. *Working Paper No. 8, University of Melbourne.* Melbourne, July 1992.
Weill, P., Broadbent, M. and St.Clair, D., 1994. Information technology value and the role of information technology infrastructure investments. In: *Strategic Alignment,* Luftman, J. (Ed), Oxford University Press, Oxford.
Wolf, A. 1922. *Essentials of Scientific Method.* George Allen & Unwin Ltd, London.
Yin, R.K. 1989. *Case Study Research: Design and Methods.* Sage Publications, Newbury Park, Ca.
Ziman, J., 1984. *An Introduction to Science Studies.* Cambridge University Press, Cambridge, United Kingdom.
Zinatelli, N. and Cavaye, A., 1994: Case Study Research in Information Systems: Strategies for Success and Pitfalls to avoid. *New Zealand Journal of Computing*, Vol 5, Nr 1, June 1994, pp17-22

8 BIOGRAPHY

Hans Lehmann is a management professional with some twenty five years of international experience in information technology. After a successful career in data processing management on two continents, Hans has been a management consultant with Deloittes (a large international firm of auditors and management consultants) since 1980 where he specialised in the development and implementation of international information systems for a number of blue chip companies. Austrian by birth, Hans has worked in continental Europe, the UK, Africa, North America and Australasia. In 1991 he joined the University of Auckland where his research focuses on the global application of information technology.

16

The conference/classroom of the future: an interdisciplinary approach

M. Mühlhäuser, J. Borchers, C. Falkowski, K. Manske
Telecooperation Research Group, Dpt. of Computer Science, Linz University
Altenberger Str. 69, 4040 Linz, Austria
Phone: ++43-732-2468-9239, Fax: ++43-732-2468-10
E-mail: {max,jan,chris,knut}@tk.uni-linz.ac.at
WWW: http://www.tk.uni-linz.ac.at/

Abstract

A vital step towards the vision of an 'international office' is to create actual environments in which different design options and solution strategies can be evaluated in practice. This paper describes the Conference/Classroom of the Future (CCF) project which aims at setting up a learning and working environment that uses advanced information technology to support cooperative activities. The CCF project takes an integrated approach to address aspects ranging from interior design and information technology to software support and work organization.

From a characterization of learning and working in the next century, we develop usage scenarios, and explain our design decisions concerning furniture, hardware, operating systems, and especially the necessary software infrastructure to support cooperation. Our initial 'visions' are described as well as what we found was achievable under real-world financial and technological constraints. We also outline what software support is still missing for such an environment, and our plans to provide this support in the course of the project. We conclude with a realistic 'shopping list' for people who have to manage similar projects.

Keywords

Classroom, learning environments, conference room, design, CSCW, telecommunications, telemedia, teleteaching, cooperative systems, IT platform requirements, IS infrastructure

1 INTRODUCTION

1.1 Motivation

The rather ambitious idea of an 'international office of the future' requires that different strategies and approaches are not just being discussed, but implemented and evaluated under real-world conditions. In the Conference/Classroom of the Future (CCF) project, our research group is currently creating such a sample environment. While the CCF project is still under development, the design phase has been completed.

The authors are responsible for the definition of concepts ('visions') for this area, and for the delivery of suitable exhibits that put those concepts into practice ('reality'). Due to these two different tasks, we have tried where possible to compare our 'visions' for certain aspects with the 'reality' we have been able to achieve with given current state-of-the-art tools and our budget constraints. We hope that this form of presentation will be helpful to those who are planning or designing similar environments.

1.2 Overview

The remainder of this paper is organized as follows:

Section 2 introduces the **project environment** in which the CCF is embedded, the Ars Electronica Center (AEC) and its Telemedia/Teleteaching floor. We briefly sketch the overall goals, components, and project status of this organizational framework, as far as they are relevant to the CCF.

Given that background information, we turn to design: Section 3 presents how we expect learning and working processes to change in the future, and how this is reflected in our usage assumptions and **conceptual design** strategies. The 'overall message' that we will try to convey to visitors and users of the CCF is presented here.

Starting with section 4, we describe our design decisions in a bottom-up fashion: First, we summarize our ideas regarding CCF **furniture**, i.e., which desk configurations are required, and how this effects the design of individual computer desks.

Section 5 then addresses **base technology** questions like the choice of workstations, displays, portable devices, network technology, and periphery.

Our decision for a certain **operating system** with its advantages and disadvantages is explained in section 6.

Section 7 deals with the **software infrastructure** required for meaningful cooperation across application and computer boundaries. Since this is still a research-intensive area, we have focused our own development efforts on this problem, and describe them in more detail in this section. Problems addressed here include cooperation control applications, mobility and workflow support, hypermedia access beyond WWW, telepresence, electronic books, low-bandwidth multimedia collaboration, and semantic meeting assistance.

On top of this infrastructure, **applications and curricular contents** have to be added to the CCF scenario. Section 8 addresses this issue.

Section 9, the **conclusion**, summarizes what we think can be learned from this project already, and, for the practitioner, gives a list of hardware and software components we recommend as equipment when designing similar environments.

2 BACKGROUND

This section outlines the background of the CCF project, the AEC and its Telemedia/Teleteaching floor.

2.1 The Ars Electronica Center (AEC)

The AEC is an exhibition and activity venue centered around the question how new information technology will influence the way we will live, work, communicate, and relax in the next century. The AEC project developed out of the annual Ars Electronica festival, one of the most influential computer arts festivals in the world since 1979. The AEC is currently being designed and built in the very heart of the city of Linz, the capital of Upper Austria. This part of Austria belongs to the 'motors of Europe', a number of regions selected by the EU as pace-makers on the way to the common european market due to their economic strength and innovative potential. The AEC will open in September 1996, and will consist of five floors addressing different aspects of innovative information technology, its applications and implications, like virtual realities, the Internet, etc.

2.2 Telemedia/Teleteaching floor

A major part of the AEC is the **Telemedia/Teleteaching floor** where special emphasis is laid on the future of learning and working. It will consist of the following areas which are described below:

- the Conference/Classroom of the Future (CCF);
- an 'extended living-room';
- an exhibition area.

The **CCF** is a thoroughly designed environment for cooperative learning and working. The remaining paper will focus on this area because it is the most important project for an 'international office of the future'. Although the remaining two areas are no less interesting, they can only be presented briefly here.

The **'extended living-room'** is a leisurely equipped area contrasting the 'ergonomically correct' office equipment of the CCF. It puts Mark Weiser's vision of such an area (Weiser, 1991) to a test, offering a group of comfortable armchairs and sofas where people can relax in a comfortable environment and still use mobile computing devices to access network resources. We hope that this relaxed atmosphere will help overcome hierarchical, social, and cultural barriers, in the same way as the most fruitful discussions at work often take place informally, during a break or at similar occasions where the standard office environment is left.

The **exhibition area** will consist of a number of individual interactive exhibits, or 'actibits', which are intended to give insight into new ways of learning and working, as affected by upcoming networked multimedia and computing technology. The planned installations comprise

- **New Media:** demonstrating the pitfalls and potential of interactive TV (ITV), and the role of the Internet among the publication media (includes Internet guided tours);
- **New Learning:** e.g., presenting novel approaches to understanding musical concepts and composing and playing music, optionally together with remote players over the net (the **WorldBeat** project);

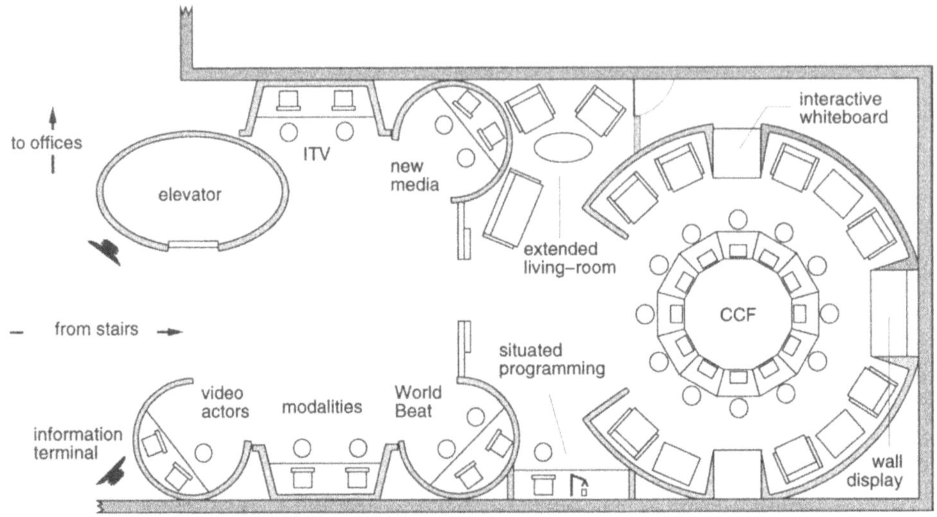

Figure 1 Overview of the Telemedia/Teleteaching floor.

- **New Interfaces:** investigating the use of new input methods like hand-gesture recognition, and new user interface metaphors like video actors ('avatars');
- **Situated Programming:** gaining programming experience with immediate feedback, based on robot programming with a simple language.

Figure 1 gives an overview of the Telemedia/Teleteaching floor. Note that for administrative and security reasons, the 'Situated Programming' installation is co-located with the CCF.

3 CONCEPTUAL DESIGN

This section presents the 'messages' we had in mind when we started to think about CCF design, and our usage concept for the environment.

3.1 Integration of learning and working

As the term 'Conference/Classroom' indicates, we envision that the classical boundaries between scholarship and worklife, between classroom and cooperative office space, may and should become blurred in the future. Cooperative learning and cooperative work tend to resemble each other more and more, so that future classrooms will have to look more like conference or meeting rooms. We will give two main reasons for this assumption here:

1. Traditional one-to-many teaching scenarios are outdated in a world in which facts and even concepts become outdated too fast for any teacher to keep pace with. Moreover, cooperation and information acquisition skills, rather than individual facts or concepts, become the very subject of

learning. As a result of these trends, future classrooms should support teacher-mediated cooperative information acquisition in which learners play an active role and mutually teach each other.
2. At the same time, it is well-known that learning is becoming a life-long task. Proper information acquisition and processing becomes a major productivity and success factor in organizations worldwide. Organizations are becoming regionally dispersed, i.e., physically distributed, even on a world-wide scale. Cooperative work in locally and remotely distributed systems becomes crucial in such an environment, as does networked access to worldwide information resources.

After all, the idea of a conference is to have a meeting, usually moderated by one person, where people learn from each other, develop new ideas together, and finish with a new status and new tasks for their project – and doesn't that sound just like the ideal form of a school lesson as well?

Finally, information propagation becomes as important for an organization as information acquisition. Thus, the Class/Conference Room of the Future has to facilitate proper generation of networked, multimedia information as well as its retrieval and consumption.

As a consequence, we label this combination of learning and working in the future as **'cooperative information processing'**, or simply **'learning'**. In the remainder of this paper, we ask the reader to understand the term 'learning' in this broader sense.

3.2 Work focus objects

The fact that learning and working scenarios converge had to be accomodated by our design. Conference and classroom environments as they are known today, however, show very divergent design and setup characteristics. Looking for common ground between the two environments, we isolated a concept which we labelled 'work focus object':

At both sorts of activities, whether conference- or tutorial-like, attention is usually focused on a central object. This can be a report to be discussed in a meeting, a paper to be written in a joint editing session, or a tutor and the material he presents in a seminar. Thus, a **work focus object** in the general case is the object which the cooperative information processing activity uses to represent its current state and history. As everybody knows from meetings, such an object is essential, even if it is just to ensure that everybody is talking about the same thing.

Our idea of a work focus object influenced subsequent design decisions. For example, it needed a medium to represent it, which we provided through interactive collaborative whiteboards for group work, and through a large wall-mounted display for tutorials.

3.3 Three major aspects of future learning/working

With learning and working scenarios merged and centered around work focus objects, we continued our design of a CCF concept by investigating which major changes new technology will be able to bring to this way of information processing. We identified three major attributes that we think will characterize 'learning' in its broader sense in the next century, and that can be improved through the use of cooperative hypermedia concepts and technology:

1. **situated:** There will be a tendency to embed learning into a real situation ('learning by doing'). This may be achieved in three different ways:

   - **simulated:** The computer simulates technical processes; by controlling or programming these 'digital worlds' (e.g., virtual realities), the learner understands their underlying concepts.

- **analog:** The computer serves merely as a tool to organize work in a 'real-world' project; it serves as an amplifier of, not as a barrier from, the actual project contents (Kay, 1991).
- **digital:** The things to be learned are actually taking place inside the computer, or the network; by joining this process the learner understands its nature (example: internet commerce).

2. **associative:** Structure, contents, and participants of a working or learning process are considered part of a network:

- **interdisciplinary:** Material is presented as 'seamless' hypermedia instead of being limited by classical subject/faculty borders and linear structure.
- **cooperative:** It is understood that in the future people and organizations will only be able to work together in a cooperative environment, emphasizing team work aspects.
- **networked:** The technical infrastructure of world-wide (mobile) communication networks will grow to support this style of learning and working.

3. **motivating:** Making learning fun remains the biggest challenge. Computer support can make learning more:

- **individual:** Personal preferences (way of presentation, specific interests, etc.) can be taken into account.
- **didactic:** New so-called instructional strategies can draw from the unique advantages of computer use for making cooperative information processing more interesting (example: group adventure framework to convey a certain subject).
- **attractive:** Presentation of learning material that makes reasonable use of hypertext concepts and multimedia technology can make teaching come alive.

3.4 Usage scenarios

Having defined which aspects of future learning we wished to emphasize, we needed to understand how the room was to be used before we could make decisions about its interior design and equipment. After all, we wanted this room to be much more than just an exhibition area where casual visitors pass by, read some of our 'visions' on cardboard posters (or on-screen presentations, for that matter), play with some neat innovative input device, and walk on – we wanted the infrastructure to be usable by actual meetings, industrial seminars, classroom lessons, or any other kind of cooperative activity that could take advantage of the technology available. Of course, the casual visitor would still represent a major part of the people visiting the CCF, so we could not neglect this target group.

At this stage the decision to merge conference and classroom concepts – as elegant as it may be – posed a number of complex design problems. As Shneiderman (1995) points out, workplaces have to be flexible to accomodate different configurations that cater for a variety of usage scenarios.

Therefore, we decided on the following assumptions regarding CCF usage:

1. 'Cooperative work' comprises both learning scenarios ('Tutorials' with 1 teacher/tutor and n learners) and conferencing scenarios (with n participants and possibly 1 moderator).
2. Target groups of the CCF are

- individual, casual visitors;
- school classes;

- adult education courses;
- internal seminars carried out by the AEC;
- external, industrial seminars.

3. The room is always in one of two states: **used** (e.g., for tutorials, conferences, etc.), or **unused** (when only individuals are accessing the workstations).
4. Cooperative work is always centered around 'work focus objects' that constitute the focus of attention. They may be a person (e.g., a teacher, tutor, or moderator), and/or a document (blackboard, overhead presentation slides, lecture notes, handout, etc.)
5. Cooperative projects are usually carried out in a sequence of two alternating phases:

   - individual contribution by means of personal computer access;
   - cooperative verification, using a common medium (like a blackboard) to represent the work focus object.

6. According to their size, events taking place in the CCF can be classified into five scenarios:

   (a) **individual use** by single interested visitors who wish to try out the technology available (the only configuration where the room is considered **unused**);
   (b) one or two **small groups** of up to four people each, working in a cooperative, meeting-like manner, and using CCF technology to talk about a common subject;
   (c) **Seminar** of up to twelve people, where the focus of attention is a tutor/teacher presenting some information on a large display;
   (d) **Conference** of four to twelve people, using a U-shaped desk configuration that is **virtually extendable** via a large, wall-mounted display (see section 7);
   (e) **Class** of 12 to 24 people, using a large U-shaped, or a circular configuration of workplaces which are usually shared by two learners.

4 FURNITURE CONSIDERATIONS

The above descriptions showed clearly that a very versatile furniture concept was needed. We met the requirements by choosing a collection of twelve separate desks. These desks were designed with a trapezium-shaped desktop at an angle that allows a circle configuration. They are accompanied by optional triangular connecting pieces (at 30°) to create linear configurations like the ends of a U-shaped conference desk.

While Figures 1 and 2 show setups with one seat per workstation, the desks are large enough for two people to work in front of each computer. This setup is recommended by many experts in the field of computer-aided learning – see, for example, Shneiderman (1995) –, especially since it encourages discussion.

By replacing half of the desks with standard tables, a more spacious setup can be created which is essential for some curricular activities where a lot of additional learning material (e.g., robotics construction kits), has to be accessible at the workplaces. For very large groups, four additional tables can be added, resulting in 16 tables altogether, for example in an oval instead of the circular arrangement.

The interior design of the CCF was subcontracted to an architect with experience in exposition design, and is not within the scope of this paper.

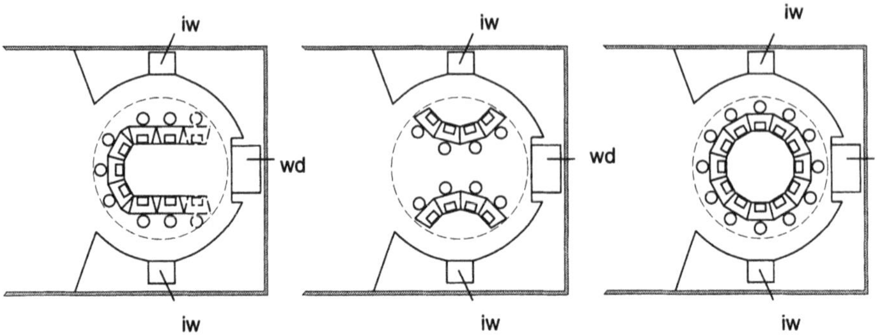

Figure 2 The three alternative desk configurations within the CCF: conference, small groups, and circular setup (iw: interactive whiteboard, wd: wall-mounted display).

5 BASE TECHNOLOGY

5.1 Workstations

For individually oriented subtasks, we decided to equip the CCF with twelve networked workstations, usable by one to two people each. This number was chosen not only due to available space, but also has didactic reasons: Twelve workstations divide nicely into a number of smaller groups, and groups larger than 24 persons make cooperative work increasingly complex and hard to manage. (Four additional desks workstations are available for extraordinarily large groups.)

Our vision was to put into reality the idea of **ubiquitous computing** (Hayter, 1993): The computer becomes 'invisible' and unobtrusive, getting 'out of the way of work'. The specific device becomes exchangeable because the network allows for automatic migration of personal data and applications to whatever device the user picks up.

This was where a basic conflict first became visible: while ambitious projects such as 'ubiquitous computing' are intriguing from a theoretical point of view, the hardware and software for such projects is usually not available for general use yet. Furthermore, most commercial application development takes place for industry-standard machines and operating systems, which means that a variety of software is available at a much lower price for those environments. This is a serious issue when budget constraints are to be considered.

In addition, a learning environment such as the CCF has to take into account that it is supposed to be usable by companies, schools, etc. Teachers, for example, will want to use their Powerpoint slides without having to create them from scratch or go through complicated conversion routines. This shows that projects like the CCF are always a compromise between innovation and compatibility with existing standards.

Unix workstations, for example, would have been advantageous for a number of reasons: their operating and file system architecture inherently supports multiple users and preemptive multitasking, which makes them much more robust, secure, and less prone to complete system crashes. Also, their widespread use in the research domain makes them attractive since it means that many prototype implementations first become available on these machines.

We also considered Macintosh machines, which would have been preferable due to their more homogeneous system architecture, more intuitive user interface, and clean support of extensions like multiple monitors for a single desktop, audio/video applications (through QuickTime), etc.

In our case, however, software availability, price levels, and our cooperative talks with hardware producers showed that a PC-based solution would be the best choice. We finally agreed with Siemens-Nixdorf Information Systems (SNI) to install their Scenic Multimedia PCs in the CCF. These machines are from SNI's latest series of personal computers, based on a 100 MHz Pentium board with PCI bus technology, and come with 16 MB RAM, a 1 GB hard disk, a quad-speed CD-ROM drive, sound card, fax modem, and a Windows '95 licence. We will add MPEG compliant video hardware to all machines. We aim at keeping the configuration of those machines as homogeneous as possible to minimize maintenance problems.

Nevertheless, we decided to incorporate at least one Unix machine (as file server to reduce data redundancy), and one Macintosh computer (for the music installation and as a multimedia production station) into the Telemedia/Teleteaching area, to ensure that we could also run future software for those systems, in case it is of interest to us as demonstration or educational content.

5.2 Displays

LCD panels would be preferable as display technology because they have a flat, non-distorting surface, are flicker-free, and non-emmissive, putting less strain on the eyes. Nevertheless, we equipped each workplace with a colour CRT monitor, as it is not only substantially less expensive, but also still offers higher resolution and faster response (moving objects do not leave shadows behind). Those aspects are especially important for animation and live video transmission.

To move the rather large monitors 'out of the way' we chose to lower them into the desktop so that people can look across them to see each other. Since our goal was to support social interaction through the computer instead of preventing it, this design detail was important to avoid blocking human-human communication.

5.3 Interactive group devices

To support cooperative activity, we found that interactive whiteboards (touch-sensitive boards with computer-generated rear projection, in our case those from Smart Technologies, Inc.) were most suitable.

In the 'small groups' scenario described above, they serve as work focus objects by displaying and representing the status of a discussion, brainstorming, or other cooperative activity. In the circular and conference scenarios, the two interactive whiteboards are used in a new kind of setup. They are fully synchronized, so that participants can easily look at the display of the work focus object at the opposite wall without having to turn their head. For active contribution, users can either access the computers on their desks, or use the whiteboard closest to their seat (which will usually be different from the one they look at).

We also included a large, modular, LCD back-projection based electronic projection wall for presentations and the virtual conference desk extension. Its initial size will be 2x2 modules, i.e., approx. 1.8×1.5m. It is scalable, so that it can be extended later as budget allows. This device can be accessed as a single screen, and will be particularly useful in the 'Telepresence' context discussed in section 7.

5.4 Portable devices

We wanted to add portable computing devices to part of the workplaces, for note-taking as well as to take to the extended living-room. Our options were to choose a PDA, notebook, or mobile i/o device. Most PDAs do not offer sufficient display resolution yet. This is less of a problem with notebooks, but they are often too heavy to be used comfortably, especially in the extended living-room. Moreover, they mean another computer per workplace, which results in additional maintenance load and possible system compatibility problems.

Because of this, we also considered installing **Zenith Cruisepads** in the CCF. These portable LCD panels are touch-sensitive and work as combined screen and input device for the computer to which they are connected wirelessly. This design results in less weight and battery usage, important points for everyday use in a public space. However, while our vision had been to use such devices with high-resolution, color displays, reality showed that Cruisepads and similar devices are not available yet in higher than standard VGA resolutions, mostly black and white, and also seem too slow for graphical aplications. Our final decision for a certain technology therefore still has to be made.

5.5 Network and periphery

With telecooperation as a central aspect of our visions, state-of-the-art network infrastructure was compulsory. In this case, we managed to make reality come up to our expectations. The whole AEC will be equipped with three types of network connections, Ethernet, FDDI, and ATM. Since, at least today, the applicability of ATM technology is still very limited, and the Ethernet connections will offer a capacity of 100Mbit/s switched, we decided to postpone ATM boards unitl they become necessary for future applications. Within the CCF, combined power/network outlets will be integrated into the floor at a number of places so that desks can always be easily connected to an outlet nearby, for all configurations mentioned above.

An important issue, especially with occasional visitors who do not have adequate hardware at home, is that the interface to and from printed media is of high quality and easy to use. To accomplish this, we added a colour scanner and two laser printers (one colour, one black-and-white) to our equipment list.

We also had to address the question of peripheral devices. Should camera, disk drive, or CD-ROM drive be made available at each of the workplaces? Due to public access, we decided not to make any local drives available to the user, also because of the danger of copyright infringement. Floppy disks and CD-ROMs will be directly accessible on a dedicated and supervised machine instead, or they may be inserted there and accessed simultaneously by several people in the CCF (useful for CD-ROMs). CD sharing software can help overcoming problems of concurrent access by multiple users.

A camera, however, is something we believe belongs in every workplace, especially as it is required for video-conferencing scenarios.

6 OPERATING SYSTEMS

Our vision for the CCF was to use a single operating system that supported migrating windows and applications, that included system-level support for collaborative applications (like document sharing, joint editing, etc.), and that was widely available together with standard applications.

Reality was different, however: Magic Cap, for example, would be an interesting choice due to its extensions beyond the desktop metaphor, but most specialized hardware (like the interactive whiteboards, for example) comes with drivers and dedicated applications for some MS Windows variant only. Moreover, since all computers are to be supervised by a central control station, each additional operating system meant that an interface to this control system would have to be implemented. To keep a minimum of multi-user, security, and multitasking capabilities, we decided to use Windows NT as predominant operating system. We created a boot-time option to run Windows 3.11 or 95 in case an application does not work under NT's compatibility modes as expected. Some Mac and Unix systems will be available as well, as indicated in our machine decisions in section 5, which, of course, cannot really be separated from an OS decision.

7 SOFTWARE INFRASTRUCTURE AND APPLICATIONS

For the reasons described in the last section, we focused on developing a suitable software infrastructure for Windows NT platforms.

Our primary task in the AEC Telemedia/Teleteaching project was to coordinate its design and equipment. This meant that we had three choices for the various subtasks:

- find appropriate third-party applications, academic or commercial, and agree with their authors upon terms for incorporation into the CCF environment;
- find external developers who create certain software on our behalf;
- develop software ourselves within our research areas.

Depending on the nature and size of the different projects we chose one of the above options for each of the subprojects we agreed upon. These projects, which are being worked on at the time of writing (February '96), are described in the following sections.

7.1 Process control and remote operation

To keep the maintenance of CCF workstations manageable, a system is being developed that will provide access to the processes running on all systems, allowing easy surveillance of tasks, and error recovery support.

While this system will be used to do local maintenance, we are also planning to include a remote control option for CCF workstations so that we can access the machines from our research facilities for testing purposes. In a limited form, this functionality will also be useful for curricular use: A teacher, for example, will be able to directly access a student's computer to help him with problems he has with an application. A number of software packages already exists for this task, including Symantec's 'Norton pcANYWHERE for Windows', Ocean Isle's 'ReachOut Remote Control', and 'Remote Teach/ Remote Desktop' developed at Linz University.

7.2 Integrated cooperation services

On of the most important features of the CCF from a user perspective will be cooperation-awareness, i.e., the possibility to use CCF facilities for group activites. Our goal is to provide services for joint editing, shared whiteboard access, and other forms of application sharing that can be used even with standard applications that are not cooperation-aware themselves.

To resolve concurrent access conflicts, we decided that two models of joint control should be supplied:

1. alternating input device control – only one user controls the input activities on a device at any time, and device control is managed through a 'token' mechanism and/or assigning different 'roles' (e.g., teacher/student) to the users;
2. cooperative input device control – several users concurrently use the input device; e.g., movement of the mouse pointer is determined by summing up the movement vectors of all participating physical pointing devices.

The SmartBoard designers have developed quite useful tools for application sharing and joint hypertext authoring. However, just providing cooperative services is not enough. A set of intuitive graphical user interface metaphors also has to be designed so that users of standard applications can easily take advantage of the added functionality. For example, to broadcast a window from his screen to another machine, a user could select the window with a rubber-band metaphor, and then drag it onto a target host which he chooses from a graphical representation of the room.

Because of this, we are working on a representation that will show the CCF in a simplified $2\frac{1}{2}$-D form. It will serve as an easily understandable interface that represents the complete CCF as a single 'object', offering cooperative functionality as well as access to the extended periphery (SmartBoards, etc.). It will also be a simple entry point to the virtual learning environment, VLE (see below).

7.3 VLE – Virtual Learning Environment

While the above cooperation control application still places the CCF as an object 'in front of the user', the 'Virtual Learning Enviroment', VLE, aims at bridging the gap between existing teleteaching technology and recent advancements in audio-visual representation. With VLE, users will be placed into a 3-dimensional world where every participant has his own workplace, following either an office- or a classroom/desk metaphor. Different kinds and levels of conversation and collaboration can be used by 'picking up' a virtual tool, or by moving into someone else's virtual office, into a lecture room, a marketplace, etc. To this end, different metaphors will be composed and offered alternatively, such as a book, library, classroom, blackboard, cinema, marketplace, auditorium, and office.

Together with these metaphors, authors of didactic material receive a toolbox to integrate their knowledge (e.g., as video or text) into the learning enviroment. The design of this collection of metaphors will leverage off recent developments in the areas of game consoles, virtual realities, PDA/PIC user interfaces (e.g., Magic Cap), etc. One important aspect is to make use of state-of-the-art telecommunications technology, e.g., teleconferencing, within these metaphors.

Those metaphors make up a consistent tool to navigate through (video) data, and to browse and retrieve information. They make cooperation and video-conferencing **transparent** to the users. Currently, the most promising technological basis for this project is VRML (Bell, 1995).

7.4 Telecooperation

As the six-year project Nestor (Mühlhäuser, 1995) on cooperative multimedia authoring and learning has proven, the cooperative use of 'cooperation-unaware' software is often insufficient for effective cooperation. Today's CSCW efforts are too much devoted to providing special-purpose cooperative tools, whereas component-based programming for usage-specific, individualized, 'cooperation-aware' software is not sufficiently addressed. In Nestor, we developed such a supporting environment and used it, e.g., to develop custom cooperative courseware. Further development of such tools is planned in the context of a European-Union funded project to be carried out in the CCF.

7.5 Mobility and workflow support

In our research on mobile computing – a crucial technology for flexible cooperative work – we realized that mobility support can be augmented considerably in the context of workflow management in its broadest sense. In the context of a long-lived workflow, mobility support can draw from a lot of semantic knowledge. The path of a mobile user, for example, can be automatically determined in the context of his future work items, the data reconciliation of 'home' and 'mobile' data can be achieved depending on the data semantics (known from workflow descriptions), etc.

As part of the MCW (Mobile Community and Workflow) initiative headed by Digital Equipment Corp., the Telecooperation research group currently co-develops a mobility-augmented ODBC service, enabling truly mobile use of many common PC tools which adhere to the ODBC standard.

This 'mobile OBDC' service is to become part of a 'mobile workflow' tools suite which is intended to draw from the synergy of the two domains as described.

7.6 AHA – Advanced Hypermedia Access

One central aspect of learning as we see it will be that information is not kept locally like the traditional library, but accessed via a network, overcoming the manifold problems of up-to-dateness, storage capacity, and abolishing the need to carry around a certain device containing your data, to name just a few.

To convey this message, CCF users need to be supplied with instant, high-speed, and effortless access to Internet resources, which are currently available through the World-Wide Web.

However, to show that the Web in its current form is far from being the perfect networked electronic medium, we wish to make users aware of its shortcomings as well as of its advantages.

One design option to address and overcome those problems is to use a **Hyper-G** server and/or clients. Hyper-G servers offer a number of conceptual advantages (Andrews, 1995):

- the concept of document **collections:** directory-like structures of documents and other collections which can be arranged hierarchically;
- document **clusters:** possibly mixed-media sets of documents to be presented in parallel, or to contain different language versions of a single document (this structure is orthogonal to the collections hierarchy);
- **guided tours:** a third independent way to specify relations between, or paths through, a number of documents;
- **separation of contents and link information:** this allows users to create links even in remote documents they do not have write access to;
- **bidirectional links:** links are stored in both directions, enabling administrators of a site to automatically inform all other sites with pointers to a certain page when it has moved elsewhere;
- **automatic indexing of all documents:** this makes full-text search in all documents a standard feature of any Hyper-G site;
- **automatic caching:** each Hyper-G server automatically works as a Proxy, using an object ID system that prevents old versions from being accessed;
- **downward compatibility to standard WWW servers:** a package exists that automatically converts an existing WWW server into a Hyper-G server.

Even though Hyper-G currently still has its own markup language (HTF), it understands HTML as well, and a beta version already supports the HTML 3.0 standard. Hyper-G servers are available for

Unix platforms only; however, this would not pose problems for us since we have included a Unix fileserver in our equipment.

Clients for Hyper-G systems are available for Unix, PC, and Macintosh platforms. Their primary advantage is that they can display multiple views of the relation between the current document and its neighbours in the hypertext net, minimizing the risk of getting lost in hyperspace. Moreover, they allow the user to create new links interactively. Nevertheless, Hyper-G servers can be accessed with standard Web browsers like Netscape as well, and the loss of functionality is marginal, while at the same time many other features (like convenient hotlist management) become available.

While we will possibly run a Hyper-G server in the CCF, our WWW browser will probably be a standard system like Netscape, since the Hyper-G consortium also focuses its development efforts on the server side.

Another currently emerging standard, **Java** (Arnold, 1996), also represents a promising extension of WWW functionality. In our AHA installation, we will explain its advantages in terms of distributed component software (which may well change radically the way software is being distributed in the near future), but we are also currently using it as a platform-independent development tool, e.g., for the CCF control application.

7.7 Telepresence

Computers should primarily be used to augment the real (office) world where necessary and beneficial. One of those areas is bringing people together for a meeting, regardless of physical distance. While video-conferencing packages are readily available today, we want to go further. Participants should not sit in front of their PCs, staring at their monitors, but sit together at a desk which is partly real, and partly virtually extended. The wall-mounted display shows an extension of the conference desk, around which the external participants are arranged by the telepresence system.

This environment may be able to fulfil the need of a more personal and natural environment for telepresence activities, as recommended by similar efforts like, for example, the GreenSpace project (Mandeville, 1995).

The electronic wall described above will play a central role in the Telepresense setup, with its unique support for close-up, narrow-angle views. It will allow us to provide the illusion of a mirrored conference table in which the 'virtual' mirrored part is in reality a remote conference room.

7.8 The electronic book

Both conventional, paper-based, and modern, electronic media have a number of clear advantages (Wellner, 1993): Electronic documents are quick to edit, copy, transmit, share, file and retrieve. They allow for keyword searching, spell-checking, instant calculations, etc. Paper documents, on the other hand, are still cheaper, universally accepted, portable, familiar, and easier to read because of higher resolutions. They allow tactile handling and can easily be annotated with a pencil (and you can wrap them around your breakfast).

Up to now, research has not succeeded in combining those two sets of characteristics. Nevertheless, this will be a necessary precondition for electronic books to become a serious replacement for traditional paper in all its fields of application. Our group is doing research in that direction, and we hope to establish some cooperation with hardware vendors, using the AEC as a testbed for innovative devices.

7.9 MMC/EI: Multimedia Collaboration over EuroISDN

Featuring ATM broadband networks, the German BERKOM multimedia teleservices (MMTS) demonstrated the feasibility of multimedia mail (MMM) and multimedia collaboration (MMC – audio/video conferencing, application sharing, and sophisticated conference management) on highly heterogeneous platforms. MMC/EI will extend the usability of MMC via specific adaptions to the EuroISDN narrowband standard. We hope to be able to showcase those developments in the Telemedia/Teleteaching floor.

7.10 SEAM – Semantic and Electronic Assistance for Meetings

Most electronic meeting assistance projects are still limited to telecooperation features like application sharing and telepointing, remote liveboard control, audio/video conferencing, and joint editing. The SEAM project at the Telecooperation group aims beyond this level of support: It is intended to 'know' about semantic elements of meetings, such as topics, schedules, presenters, experts, moderators and other roles, presentations and discussions, action items, etc. That way, it can support more useful ways of querying multimedia meeting recordings, e.g., answer the question, 'What did John talk about while he used the interactive board to comment Anne's report on last year's sales?' by accessing the respective audio recordings and video indices directly.

8 DEMONSTRATIONAL AND CURRICULAR CONTENTS

As a computer science research group, we cannot create all the necessary end-user applications and curricular contents ourselves. Finding those components, however, is a task on its own that is not to be underestimated. The AEC is member of a number of EU projects (DEMOS, Employ, and others) that address those issues.

This, as well as cooperations with schools, adult education institutions, companies, and researchers all over the world, offers valuable contact to application and content providing partners who are in turn interested in the technical possibilities the infrastructure the AEC and esp. the Telemedia/Teleteaching floor have to offer. Describing that various sub-projects we are currently managing in this direction would, however, be outside the scope of this paper.

9 CONCLUSION

This paper presented our Class/Conference of the Future (CCF) project, an interdisciplinary effort to create an environment for cooperative working and learning, two activities which we identified as becoming more and more similar. After a summary of our conceptual goals for the project – to convey that learning will become a more situated, associative, and motivating experience – we described our solution strategies in bottom-up order.

Furniture considerations showed the necessity of reconfigurable desk setups, while hardware and operating system choices emphasized the importance of having different platforms available, with a focus on industry standards. Software infrastructure proved to be the major gap in cooperative systems today, and we described our own research projects in this area, while providing curricular content turned out to be a task that should be accomplished in close cooperation with external providers and institutions.

In all, the conflicts between our CCF visions and practical considerations often forced us to accept compromises in our design, which is nevertheless an important experience for anybody who wishes to bridge the gap that still exists on our way to a real-world, usable international office of the future.

9.1 Inventory recommendations

For those who are confronted with the same problem as we were, to equip a learning and/or conference room using innovative concepts and technology, the following list may be helpful. It is divided into furniture, hardware, operating system, software infrastructure, and application requirements.

This list is by no means complete or compulsory, but rather a suggestion. Actual equipment decisions depend not only on what you plan to do with your room, but also on alliances with hardware providers and other companies: Your mileage may vary.

Table 1 Recommended equipment list for CCF-like projects

Pcs.	Item
16	configurable computer desks for 2 persons each
1	Unix / Windows NT server
16	Pentium Multimedia PCs
6	Portable notebooks or similar devices
16	cameras
16	video boards
1	wall-mounted display
2	SMART Boards
2	active ISDN boards for video-conferencing
1	color laser printer
1	b/w laser printer
1	color scanner
	power and Ethernet/FDDI/(ATM) network connections
1	Unix or Windows NT server licence
16	Microsoft Windows 3.11, '95, and NT client licences
1	process control application (running on server)
1	Hyper-G or WWW server licence
16	Intel ProShare licences + Smartboard driver
16	application sharing software licences
16	Microsoft Office licences
16	Netscape licences
	additional 'contents' and demonstration applications and data

10 REFERENCES

Andrews, K., Kappe, F. and Maurer, H. (1995) Serving information to the Web with Hyper-G. *Computer Networks and ISDN Systems*, **27**, 919–926.

Arnold, K. and Gosling, J. (1996) *The Java Programming Language*. Addison-Wesley, Reading.

Bell, G., Parisi, A. and Pesce, M. (1995) *The Virtual Reality Modeling Language – Version 1.0 Specification (clarified)*, November 1995 (http://www.oki.com/vrml/vrml10c.html)

Hayter, M. (1993) Some computer science issues in Ubiquitous Computing. *Commun. ACM*, **36**, 7, 75–84.

Kay, A. (1991) Computers, networks, and education. *Scientific American*, Sept. 1991, 138–148.

Mandeville, J., Furness, T., Kawahata, M., Campbell, D., Danset, P., Dahl, A., Dauner, J., Davidson, J., Kandie, K. and Schwartz, P. (1995) GreenSpace: Creating a Distributed Virtual Environment for Global Applications. *Proc. IEEE Networked Virtual Reality Workshop*, Boston.

Mühlhäuser, M. (Ed.) (1995) *Cooperative Computer-Aided Authoring and Learning*. Kluwer Academic Publishers, Boston.

Shneiderman, B. (1995) Windows of Opportunity in Electronic Classrooms. *Commun. ACM*, **38**, 11, 19–24.

Weiser, M. (1991) The Computer for the 21st Century. *Scientific American*, Sept. 1991, 66–75.

Wellner, P. (1993) Interacting with paper on the Digital Desk. *Commun. ACM*, **36**, 7, 87–96.

11 BIOGRAPHY

Max Mühlhäuser is a Full Professor of Computer Science at Linz University, Austria, and head of the Telecooperation Research Group. After receiving his Doctorate in computer science from the University of Karlsruhe, Germany, in 1986, he worked as researcher there and at the Digital Equipment CASE Engineering Group in France, and set up and managed the CEC, a Digital Equipment research facility in Karlsruhe. After several years as professor in computer science at the Universities of Kaiserslautern and Karlsruhe, he visited the Eurecom Institute in Sophia Antipolis, France, in 1994, and has since accepted his new position at Linz University.

His research domain is software engineering for multimedia and multimodal interfaces, mobile and ubiquitous computing, human-human and human-computer cooperation. Applications include telelearning and telepresence, using distributed object-oriented and distributed hypermedia models as engineering approaches. He has published more than 70 articles, co-authored and edited books about distributed software engineering and computer-aided authoring/learning, and is a member of ACM, GI, and IEEE.

Jan Borchers studied computer science in Karlsruhe and London, and received his Master's Degree from the University of Karlsruhe in 1995. He now works on his Ph.D. at the Telecooperation Research Group, and is interested in user interfaces for new media and computer-aided learning, esp. in music education. He is the author of several papers about layout rules for electronic media, has written an interactive book about OSF/Motif, and is a member of ACM.

Chris Falkowski studied computer science and communications engineering in Aachen, and received his Master's Degree in 1989. After working as a software engineer for a large German software company for six years, he now works on his Ph.D. at the Telecooperation Research Group. His research interests focus on designing cooperative user environments.

Knut Manske studied computer science in Karlsruhe, where he received his Master's Degree in 1994. He now works on his Ph.D. at the Telecooperation Research Group, and is interested in video integration into multimedia systems, and multimodal user interfaces.

17

An example of the use of the WWW as a tool and environment for research and collaboration

Freddie Quek, Information Systems Manager & Ph.D. Candidate
Electronic Press and London School of Economics
34-42 Cleveland Street, Middlesex House, London W1P 6LB, Tel:+44 (0171) 323 0323, Fax:+44 (0171) 636 6911,
Email: freddie@cursci.co.uk, or f.k.quek@lse.ac.uk

Ian Tarr, Managing Director
Electronic Press Ltd
34-42 Cleveland Street, Middlesex House, London W1P 6LB, Tel:+44 (0171) 323 0323, Fax:+44 (0171) 580 1938, Email: ian@cursci.co.uk

Abstract

This paper, being a practice paper, addresses the conference theme directly by reporting on and demonstrating how one idea, in the biomedical field, has been implemented and works in practice. It presents BioMedNet as an example of a new work environment akin to the definition of IOF, as a means to illustrate: one design option (that is actually implemented); one solution strategy (that is currently used and evaluated) and one environment which researchers and practitioners can interact (that can be used as a model).

BioMedNet is a virtual club or cyberclub built on the Internet to provide professional and focused services of interest to its members anywhere in the world. In essence, it is more than just a club. It is a laboratory or office-based working tool giving users powerful resource on their desktop. If all goes according to plan, BioMedNet hopes to become a model workplace of at least the biomedical research community if not the world research community, not only in changing the way researchers work, but also in the way information and service providers such as publishers and online service providers communicate with their customers.

In conclusion, the authors point out the two-fold mission of this paper - to get researchers onto the Information Superhighway, and to show an example of the use of BioMedNet as the way biomedical scientists will work in the future.

Keywords

BioMedNet, cyberclub, model workplace, research collaboration

1 INTRODUCTION

This paper, being a practice paper, addresses the conference theme directly by reporting on and demonstrating how one idea, in the biomedical field, has been implemented and works in practice. It has been said that the key problem for technology providers will be with integration, not in the integration of the various technologies, but the integration of technology into the social and organisational dimensions of work. Despite technological advances in information and communication technologies, and their wide-spread proliferation in organisations, there is a danger that as office systems and their tools get more sophisticated, they may end up as solutions looking for problems.

The challenge is therefore in the design and implementation of office systems that really *'work'* (Bots, Uijlenbroek and van den Herik, 1995). Hence, this paper presents a real example of a new work environment akin to the definition of the International Office of the Future (IOF) by Bots et al, as a means to illustrate:

- one design option (that is actually implemented);
- one solution strategy (that is currently used and evaluated);
- one environment which researchers and practitioners can interact (that can be used as a model).

This paper merely attempts to provide a model already implemented, so that there is a basis to start answering the questions and issues raised so far, in the hope that we will have some indication whether IOF is a flawed concept or an inevitable future, what other (new) questions that will be raised, as well as potential research directions for both academia and industry.

2 WHAT IOF MEANS

In this age of rapid technological advances, the term IOF may be seen as one of the many coinages that pops up regularly in the computing world. To the ordinary office worker, what does it mean? Questions like what an office is, what the characteristics of an office environment are and what office work entails are no longer trivial questions to answer or easy to understand.

2.1 Definitions

From examining the literature on this topic, there are many competing terms that mean about the same thing, or at least overlap considerably with office and its association with 'computer-supported work' (Greif and Cashman, 1984; Englebart and Lehtman, 1988; Kraemer and King, 1988; Ellis et al, 1991): office automation, technological support for work group collaboration, computer-supported cooperative work (CSCW), collaborative systems, workgroup computing, group decision support systems (GDSS), augmented knowledge workshops, computer-assisted communications (CAC), group process support system, teamware, decision conferences, coordination technology, flexible interactive technologies for multi-person tasks, computer conferencing, electronic meeting systems (EMS) and groupware.

Adding to this confusion, there is also the reality of office workers who work from home or other remote locations (terms like telecommuting, teleworking and teleconferencing), the globalisation of businesses and communications, and the resulting interorganisational information exchange both nationally and internationally.

IOF can be seen to encompass a number of concepts: Office Automation in the 1970s (Englebart), the CSCW movement in the 1980s (Greif and Cashman, 1984), Groupware (Johnson-Lentz et al, 1992) and 'Groupware technologies' in the late 1980s. Driven by technological advances in telecommunications, networking, groupware etc., significant changes have taken place in the support of the office, the office work and the office workers, as can be seen from Hollingsworth's (1993) account of four generations of office systems and related technologies that found their way into the office.

In an attempt to explore the IOF concept, Bots, Glasson and Vogel organised a series of activities, the first of which began with four position papers presented at the IFIP WG 8.4 workshop held in conjunction with the IFIP World Congress in Hamburg, Germany, August 1994, and two brainstorming workshops, one at the same conference and the other at the IFIP WG 8.3 working conference in San Sebastian, Spain, September 1994.

In the first workshop, the participants were asked to consider the question *'What are the issues that come to mind when you think of the International Office of the Future?'* (Bots and Uijlenbroek, 1995). From an analysis of 45 unique responses recorded, many issues were raised about the 'I' in IOF, and it is not difficult to understand why this is so. With the advances in technologies, there is now a major challenge for organisations to respond to the new world order of working on a global scale unprecendented in history. Practically organisations of all shapes and sizes will no doubt have to find a way to deal with interorganisational information exchange, and combining with the issues raised (see table 1), will have more questions than answers. Nevertheless, it is important that these issues are out in the open so that they can be taken into consideration in future research.

Table 1 Internationalization issues of IOF

we must think about asynchronous work (time zoning)
impact of national policies
different cultures
awareness of participants' background
different languages/translation
interpersonal communication requires more than just vocabular translation
mechanisms for cross-cultural creativity (remove inhibiting differences)
facilities to deal with ambiguities between cultures (slang, cultural terms, etc)
managerial awareness of cultural differences
is foreign experience prerequisite for functioning in an IOF?

In the second workshop, the participants were asked to consider the question *'What do you visualize (or think of or imagine) when we speak of the International Office of the Future?'* (Glasson and Quek, 1995). From an analysis of the 39 unique responses recorded, most of them (about 54%) were clearly technology-related visualisations, and it is not difficult to see that some aspects of IOF is already happening today. Table 2 represents the authors' attempt at clustering some of the responses under the heading of Office work, Office and its environment, and Office systems:

Table 2 Clustered responses to visualisation of IOF

Office work	Office and its environment	Office systems
eliminate dead (i.e. waste) time in decision making (e.g. travel etc.)	transparent remote portability	simultaneous translation
access to flows of telecommuting information		more enriched communications (i.e. multi-media)
asynchronous work	portable office (e.g. satellite connection)	routine inter-organization document and image transfer

There may not be any consensus about what a definition of IOF is, but it is obvious that we are all aware of the kinds of technologies that will shape the IOF, as well as the questions that will continue to be asked. The work place of tomorrow is pointing to one where place and time do not matter, as the technology can bridge the gap of instant communication and face-to-face interaction. The key is to 'get connected' and 'get online', via modems, ISDN, satellite links, etc., and that the office paradigm of a work place will give way to a work space; portable offices such as home offices, cars, airports, airplanes and the subways.

2.2 New work environment

The availability of computers and computing, once strictly in the domain of government agencies, researchers and scientists, has been a major factor in changing the way we work today and in the future. Their pervasiveness in homes and offices, across all age groups and occupational levels, began with the advent of personal computers and other equally inexpensive products in the mid 1970s. Many of the office applications of computers lie in non specialist uses, and the nature of these applications influences the development of interactive systems (Newman, 1987).

Not surprisingly, organisations are increasingly moving toward more flexible working, flatter structures and project-based teams. Living in an age of widespread global communication, office workers are no longer static (geographically), immobile groups working in a single unit. Telecommuting, the technology of bringing the work to the workers than the other way round (Kelly and Gordon, 1986) is already widespread, especially with doctors, lawyers, sales people and researchers. In America, it has been projected that by the end of 1995, about 9.2 million teleworkers will work from home or from remote sites (Wired, Oct 1995).

Another emerging trend and market which impacts upon the office and office work is Groupware, a class of office applications that provide 'electronic, computer-based support for any group of individuals working towards a common goal' (Data Sciences and Novell 1994). Groupware technologies provide integrated email, calendaring, scheduling, desktop conferencing, document management and task management, examples of which are the likes of GroupWise from Novell and Lotus Notes from IBM.

So what will this new environment of the future be like? One prediction for the year 2000 is that it will be about ubiquitous mobile computing (Byte, 1995), of "portable technology for portable work". We can already see a number of examples today. Schools and colleges are embracing the technologies of tomorrow by training a new generation of students experienced with virtual lectures, virtual libraries and virtual collaboration.

2.3 Challenges ahead

Having defined what IOF means, and what the new work environment will be thus sets the background for the remainder of this paper. The promise of a 'paperless office' offered by office automation never came about. office systems as surveyed by Traünmuller (1995), still need improvements in i) providing basic CSCW mechanisms, ii) introducing additional features, iii) models and theories governing interaction, and iv) interdisciplinary approach to design. And the current fad of groupware technologies and proprietary groupware applications may not face up to the more open Internet, which can possibly replace the need for groupware packages (Computer, 1995).

The challenges facing IOF are therefore similar to the challenges faced by those mentioned above. According to Bots et al (1995), "a decade of office systems literature shows that the real problem lies in determining the office functionality for a specific organisation". Hence, developing more modelling tools for office analysis or creating more generic functionalities is not the solution. As Traünmuller (1995) puts it, "most of the easy things have been done".

Existing office computer systems do not always offer the flexibility required to meet the needs of today's user, and the problem is that people need to have access to organisational information in a relatively unstructured manner, access from any location. The answer may lie in the statement expressed by Columbia University professor Eli Noam (1995) about a reversal in the historic direction of information flow: "In the past, people came to the information, which was stored at the university. In the future, the information will come to the people, wherever they are". And this is where the authors believe that the Information Superhighway can hold the key in revolutionalising the way businesses are conducted, offices communicate and workers interact.

3 AGENDA FOR RESEARCH

One of the key topics which this conference is keen to explore, is on the "effective use of the Internet and the Information Superhighway". The Internet is threatening to invade our homes just as the personal computers have done. While the personal computers offer computing power, the Internet offers access to information on a scale unimaginable even a few years before.

There is no doubt that the Internet, and in particular, the World Wide Web, has become an important form of communication. The growth in the Internet's interest and usage has been phenomenal, evidenced from the amount of commercial investment and the number of people who are already connected to it. It will come to be as important a development in communications as the telephone over 50 years ago.

3.1 Information superhighway

The Internet, more popularly known as the Information Highway, is not new. It came into existence in 1969 as ARPANet, a US Defense Department network supporting military research (Krol, 1992). It was developed to satisfy the need for researchers at different geographical locations to be able to communicate with each other on a more rapid basis than they had been communicating (Uhlig, Farber and Bair, 1979). With the development of Ethernet local area networks (LANs) and workstations in the 1980's, it was eventually expanded to include academic research establishments. However, connection only became more easily available in 1982. In the late 1980's, it was superseded by NSFNet which finally allowed everyone access to the network.

Today, the Internet is a technology that is extremely mature and practical. Internet access could not be simpler, as practically anyone, from educational institutions to private individuals can get access by using a personal computer, an Internet Access Provider (IAP), a phone link and some type of access software (PC User, 1995).

With the explosion of popular interest in networked computer systems and the Internet, this conference is expected to play an important role in framing and extending the discussion about the role of the Internet in the future of work and its work place.

3.2 Research collaboration

Ironically, despite the fact that researchers have always been the first to benefit from Internet access, it did not exactly take off until 1992 with the introduction of the World Wide Web (WWW), a collection of servers working together to form a graphically-based hypertext network which can incorporate many different text styles, pictures, sound and video (PCM, 1994). Today, the Internet is often quoted as being made up of 50,000 networks, four million computers and 30 million users (though no one knows exactly what the real size is).

Revisiting the original purpose of ARPANet, and examining the purpose of this conference, it seems coincidental that they both have similar aims, that of satisfying the needs of researchers. In the words of this conference, it is to "provide a forum and prototype environment in which researchers and practitioners can interact". In this light, the authors have deemed appropriate to explore IOF in the context of using the Internet towards future research collaboration.

One of the main facets of research collaboration is the need for access to information relevant to the research topic at hand. Traditionally, libraries and online information and services providers have catered to the researchers' needs. Information search and document delivery are areas that are affected by the way the information is held in the first place, and as more and more information are being made available on the Internet, researchers will need to use the 'virtual library' more effectively by learning to use the cognitive gateway with which to approach an access source and the concept of a search strategy and its formulation (Loomis and Fink, 1993).

Another facet of research collaboration is the need to work and interact with other fellow collaborators which involve discussions and meetings. Undeniably, the most effective way of holding a conference is to *"actually gather the people together in a room, for face to face discussions. In such a discussion, the full richness of non-verbal expressions, facial expressions, inflections of the voice, and what is called 'body language' contribute significantly to the ability of an individual to convey to the audience the meaning underlying his words"* (Uhlig, Farber and Bair, 1979). However, given the demands on the researchers today and the technologies that are available, there are feasible alternatives to meetings and conferences which can be just as effective, e.g. two-way video conference, telephone conference and computer conference.

One other facet of research collaboration is the culminating in the production of a research document, such as a research paper to be submitted for publication in an academic journal. The point here is that the publication of research papers in traditional academic paper-based journals are painfully slow as the publication cycle is still time consuming. Even the fastest of scholarly publications would normally take between 4-8 weeks. However, the Internet has already shown that electronic publishing can cut this cycle time. To quote the chairman of McGraw-Hill Joseph Dionne, *"If you take this (Internet) technology, you have someone submit his research, have it reviewed by knowledgeable people, the process could be done in a week or two weeks"* (Financial Times, 1995).

As can be seen, the Internet is changing all the above facets of research collaboration. It is not a case of the Internet needing the researchers, but the researchers needing the Internet. This paper aims to provide one design option (that is actually implemented) of an Internet application that focuses on this topic of collaboration for researchers.

3.3 BioMedNet as an example

In line with the thinking of the IOF series of events, an Internet application which the authors are involved with seems to lend itself very well to "present a real working environment in which researchers and practitioners can interact".

BioMedNet is a new club built in cyberspace, offering a new work (virtual) environment for its members. It offers i) meeting rooms for real-time discussions that can incorporate the simultaneous sharing of documents and images, ii) searchable noticeboards that are set up by societies, journals or conference organisers, iii) a full-text electronic library featuring an extensive collection of journals and databases in biomedicine, and iv) a shopping mall which provides information, catalogues and ordering mechanisms for relevant products and services. Using a variety of search strategies, including searches on chemical sub-structures, members can purchase and retrieve individual items/articles from the library or take out on-line subscriptions.

BioMedNet can be seen as falling under the CSCW banner, where *"the need of people to co-operate in groups when doing their work, with the distinctive feature being identified that people liked to move to the workstation style usage"* (i.e. usage of their personal computer to work individually and with others).

BioMedNet, already a researcher's tool on the Internet, thus seems very relevant to the agenda set for this conference. The authors aim to illustrate BioMedNet by way of a live demonstration of researchers collaborating together on a specific task, so that everyone in the audience will be able to experience first hand how it can work and cannot work, thereby to start answering the questions raised so far, and to raise new questions.

4 WHAT BIOMEDNET IS

BioMedNet is the world's first working environment built in Cyberspace for researchers, scientists and clinicians in all areas of biology and medicine (The BookSeller, 1995, Electronic Press 1994). It is based upon the simple concept of a club, which allows people of similar interests to get together to share ideas, resources, and services. Members may be separated by geography and time-zones, but the resources they share, from the library to the real-time discussion groups, are central to their working lives, and being a club will help to provide a professional and focus service to its members.

The club concept is a very powerful metaphor (as is explained in the next section), especially with the way the Internet is today. Despite the Internet's big advantage in providing instantaneous and all-hour accessibility to the huge amount of information on offer, its biggest downfall to date is its lack of 'organisation', where its growth has been almost organic, without a clear set of rules as to how it should be developed. As the Internet's potential continue to excite many quarters as a medium of global communication, there will certainly be a push towards making the Internet more 'organised' and secure. One such example is the OCLC Office of Research project, which started the categorisation of textual information on the Internet, and this could lay the groundwork for classifying traditional reference sources to enable better searching of information on the Internet (OCLC, 1992).

In this light, BioMedNet can thus be seen to be taking a step towards not only belonging to a new generation of Internet-enabled systems, but also to help with some of the 'sign-postings' on the Information Superhighway.

4.1 Concept of a club

"Although scientists can already discuss issues with like-minded scientists, join user groups with specific interests, gain limited access to journals and order books on the Internet, these activities have not yet been brought together in a single space designed for researchers."

The above statement can be seen as the design goal of BioMedNet. BioMedNet is not about merely having an online presence on the Internet. It is about building an environment on the Internet where researchers can work either individually or with others. It addresses the issue of the needs of researchers on the one hand, and the opportunities or problems (depending on your personal point of view) of the Internet on the other.

At this point, it is important to also briefly discuss about the role of online services today like online databases such as Dialog, online services such as Compuserve etc in light of the Internet. There is a number of differences between online services and the Internet, and understanding these differences would reveal why the former will continue to prosper along side the Internet instead of being swallowed by it. For example, unlike the Internet, forums provided by online services are moderated, and any information uploaded are checked to prevent from infringement of copyright. The information and services provided are focused and targeted at specific groups of users of the services. The Internet however, is a 'free-for-all' situation, and there is little or no control over what is said and what is done. Already, despite the relatively young age of the Internet, the Information Highway is filled with masses of information, and in a way, is already the Information Junkyard since all kinds of information are being dumped on it.

Online services such as Compuserve has been described as 'a kind of club of clubs' (PCM, 1994). It is a club which not only can offer its own proprietary services, but also services of others. This concept is also adopted by BioMedNet as a means to achieve a positive and responsible answer towards imposing some form of control over content, use and membership on the Internet. The idea of BioMedNet is therefore to create a virtual club or cyberclub to provide professional and focused services of interest to its members anywhere in the world. It is like an imaginary space around which BioMedNet provides the walls for researchers in the field of biology and medicine. The use of the club metaphor is not unlike the real scientific world, where clubs and societies emerged to cater to the specific interest of their members, and like-minded people form a closed circle to share similar interests and work together for their own professional interests or towards the general well-being of the club as a whole. A club will therefore be the natural place for like-minded professionals to conduct their professional work and further their interest, with the traditions of reward for recognised contribution. It will be the place where they will feel comfortable, and to know that they can expect certain services provided by the club as privileges enjoyed as members.

Recognising the tradition in the scientific community to work in societies with like-minded professionals, there is also further evidence drawn from the Theory of Clubs* (Buchanan, 1965; Ng, 1973; Berglas, 1976; Helpman and Hillman, 1977) to suggest that the club concept is not merely a use of a metaphor for understanding and designing work systems on the Internet, but also recognising a very important aspect of the social, political, economic and professional arrangement in the scientific community, which lends itself very well to provide a natural way of organisation for

---

* Many characteristics of collaboration are similar to that of a club.

researchers using the Internet. A club will therefore be able to offer both services as well as rules and regulations that all members must obey and observe for the interest of everyone. There is also the implicit and explicit respect for order and professionalism within the scientific community. Unlike the Internet where unmoderated forums and data conferences can degenerate into 'slanging' matches, the club will be able to facilitate the respect for intellectual and professional discussion.

The club concept in the electronic world, is also an active conduit among the members, the societies and the publishers. As a club of clubs, it brings together the three parties much closer than ever before as evidenced by comments made below:

"On the outside people are running around like crazy: there is disorder and confusion. Inside it is beautiful. There are guides to explain where to go and what to do. There are places where you can go to chat with friends, and in this space we go to all the buyers and say come and buy, we go to all the sellers and say come and sell. If we can get them to interact within the space, we will have created another sort of business." - a publisher

"Most people will go to a site if their friends go there. The scientific community is organised into groups (and as such), should be recruited as groups. For example, if you get the members of the editorial board to join all at the same time, then everyone else will follow." - an immunologist

4.2 Club membership

As a professional club, BioMedNet is similar to any scientific and professional clubs in the biomedical field. Researchers can apply for individual memberships. Alternatively, if they are already members of societies that have applied for society memberships, then their members can become members too. Members will pay a fee to use the club services and facilities for a period of time which is renewable.

BioMedNet also brings the societies, the publishers, information and services providers, and the members more closely together. In order for BioMedNet to achieve its fullest potential, it is imperative that the three groups must work together to make this new club workable and sustainable. At the time of writing, BioMedNet already has about 4,000 members, 10 societies and and 20 publishers working together. By the end of 1995, the projected figures are 12,000 members, 25 societies and 40 publishers, growing to over 100,000 members during 1996. We shall look at what the club can offer to each of the group in turn:

For the societies

Any society's role is to serve the interest of its members. Many societies have already recognised the importance of the Internet and the information sources that are relevant to their members. Participating in BioMedNet thus give their members an instantaneous 24-hour club service. Societies' journals and publications are the obvious candidates to provide an electronic version. Not only will their publications be searchable, but other societies' publications will be available too for cross-searches.

University College London, part of University of London, UK, became a member of BioMedNet in 15 November 1995, and in effect, all its 15,000 students become members of BioMedNet too.

For the publishers, information and services providers

It has become necessary for publishers, information and services providers to have a presence on the Internet, and this means making available an electronic version of current services and products. Increasingly, information becomes available on the Internet even before the printed version, and there is also 3-D Molecular models and scientific text that are available only online with no print equivalent.

Being a club of clubs, BioMedNet allows other publishers, information and services providers, whether big or small, to participate in setting up an environment providing relevant services and products to a target group without having to resort to a go-alone approach. For example, publishers do not have to put their titles into the BioMedNet database in order to sell articles through the system. They can hold all their journals on their own server, and if a BioMedNet member wants to access a journal held by a publisher, the BioMedNet software will forward the request to the publisher who can then sell the copy of the article for whatever price it chooses. For others who do not have the capability to go into electronic publishing, BioMedNet, from its range of services, can offer a service to other publishers, or societies to provide the administration, database design, maintenance, software development, customer service, and technical support.

For the members

It is obvious that with the tradition of scientific research, researchers become members of professional societies to collaborate with others in a professional environment. BioMedNet offers a similar arrangement which is an extension of the current practices. It offers tailored services to suit the interest of its members.

Each member will have a profile. Part of the profile will be information other members can see. They will be able to search for members according to the information in this part of their profile. This is particularly useful for searching for members who share similar interests to collaborate together. Another part of the profile will be for controlling access and manage charges which is confidential to the club. Each member will be obliged to have a personal account, usually based on credit card or bank credit arrangement. It will allow the club to charge all purchases approved with the personal password to be charged by the club against the members personal account.

Each member will be able to have a number of additional accounts, such as an institutional account where the member's institution will agree to pay for member purchases. The profile will also contain information on any discounts or access privileges a member may have, e.g. discount given by publisher for members subscribed to paper version of the publication, or member of a society.

4.3 Electronic library

The BioMedNet library provides members with the full content of an extensive collection of journals, monographs, dictionaries and databases, which is one of the largest online collections in biomedicine. Via the Internet, it increases the accessibility and speed up the delivery of information by sending it directly to the member's computer. Members will be able to search the entire body of research literature in the field of biology and medicine for articles and references. They will then buy the material they want at the price of a copyright fee to the publisher. This will enable them to cut and paste the material, keep it in their files, or print it out. It moves away from a single concept of the 'research article' as the sole and exclusive way of disseminating research information. It enables detailed and related literature to be searched in a well-stocked but focused electronic library, together with other products put up by other publishers, information and services providers.

Another feature of the library is the creation of a citation web, which is the creation of bi-directional links between any citation (reference) and

- bibliographic database e.g. Medline entry for the citation;
- a full text document of the citation (if available);
- any other document containing the citation as a reference.

This will allow browsing by following a citation trail and maximise the number of pointers at any item in the library, increasing the opportunity for a hit (for the member) and a sale (for the supplier).

To help with the searches, the library operates a sophisticated search engine, using helpful lists (authors, sources, etc.), user-definable relevancy, intelligent numeric ranges (dates, measurements etc.), and a thesaurus. Also, searching is not limited to text; tables, captions, mathematical symbols, and chemical structures are searchable as well. For example, chemical substructures are stored and retrieved via MD Molfile format, the industry standard for chemical substructure data. This is the beauty of the electronic medium where graphics and images are seen in their full glory; can be displayed in full colour, and can be rotated or sized in a variety of ways.

There is also a choice of output. Abstracts, to full text of an article can be accessed and printed in PDF format (optimised for printing), or as web pages from whichever browser that the members uses.

By far, the main distinction between the BioMedNet library and other electronic libraries that exist on the Internet already (in a sense they are all electronic libraries), is that the web pages retrieved will be highly interlinked. The simple retrieval of a web page will be given value added from the cross-linking achieved as a result of publishers and other information providers working together to service a community. Such interlinking is very useful and important. For example, it enhances the opportunity to come across interrelated things on the off-chance, such as finding a citation with an offer to purchase the full text there and then. For the researcher, it is very useful as it allows the following of a train of thought more easily and more likely to navigate to other relevant links.

Librarian service

Like in a real library or society, the club has a librarian that members can go to for assistance, a free service as part of the membership.

4.4 Discussion groups/conferences/lecture theatres

In the scientific world, the format of conferences and meetings is a guide for structuring the social dynamics on the Internet because it already works that way and people are familiar with. One definition of a conference is *"a special meeting called to bring a group of qualified individuals together for the purpose of discussing (and hopefully solving) problems or sharing information on a specific subject or related group of subjects"* (Uhlig, Farber and Bair, 1979).

Hence in BioMedNet, it offers a number of rooms to provide facilities for discussion rooms, conferences, lectures and seminars, thereby providing a collaborative work environment enabling members to reserve meeting rooms for real-time discussion while at the same time sharing documents and images. This facility can be used for virtual lectures and discussions, and could even be used by journal publishers to carry out their peer review process.

Discussion rooms

A discussion room is a private room where participants must be on the invitation list. A number of meetings can be held in it over time, and a record of dates, times and notes on the meetings should be maintained. The main purpose of these discussion rooms is to provide a way for a group of collaborators to meet, discuss, work on documents of various types together, and keep a record of their meetings.

In this room, all participants have an equal right to speak. However the initiator of the meeting has a control of certain functions, such as changing a document (word processing, graphics or other one) while all can see the changes and can save both the conversation and the changes on their local machines for future reference. The initiator can also pass the control to others in the room. The room can stay open until the initiator closes it.

Public rooms

Members will also be able to open a public discussion room. It will have the same facilities as the private room but every member will be able to enter it freely, and the room will be listed in a list of currently open public rooms, with their title and other information available.

The rooms have the facility of opening and closing at specified times and dates, and rooms open beyond a reasonable time will be closed by the club after suitable checks.

Lecture rooms

The lecture rooms are rooms where the speaker has control over presentation, while other members present in the room can pose question or comments, but the speaker has an option on when to ask for them and when he wants to reply. There is an interrupt option, allowing a 'listener' to interrupt the speaker to pose a question. Because it is a club and the identity of the member is known, it will be less proned to abuse such as interrupting by dissent.

The lecture rooms can be private or public, just as the discussion rooms can

Noticeboards

Notice boards and news groups are also part of the BioMedNet system. Societies, journals, conference organisers and groups of members can also set up their individual noticeboards, and for cross-purposes, are fully searchable.

Conferencing tools

BioMedNet is currently working on customising Netscape Chat, an IRC real-time chat client application for use within its meeting rooms. The current major conferencing tool used within BioMedNet will be for data only so that it provides the lowest common denominator to all its members. As the bandwidth improves and members have higher specification machines, BioMedNet will certainly introduce voice and video conferencing tools when the time comes.

Also, as a business partner with Netscape, BioMedNet will gain from working with others, for example, the acquisition of Collabra by Netscape incorporate Collabra Share groupware capabilities into Netscape Navigator browser and Netscape servers in early 1996 (Information Week, 1995).

4.5 Shopping mall

BioMedNet offers a shopping mall which provides information, catalogues and ordering mechanisms for relevant products and services, and all information is fully indexed and searchable. Through a sophisticated, state-of-the-art billing mechanism to ensure a secure method of buying online, members can order products and services from the supplier directly conveniently and hassle free.

4.6 Billing system

Pricing and developing billing systems on the Internet are new areas for businesses. BioMedNet is working with Netscape and Oracle to develop a Billing System for its use.

Pricing options is left to the publishers to decide the price of accessing the full text of publications, databases, whether individual articles/records, or by online subscription. Publishers can change the price of access (at reasonable intervals) and set different prices for different types of articles (e.g. review article vs book review). They can also set different prices for the same title, based on member profile criteria (e.g. society affiliations, print subscribers, personal or institutional subscribers etc.).

4.7 Job exchange

Another service offered to members of BioMedNet is a Job Exchange service which provides related and relevant job posting, such as positions wanted and available.

4.8 More than just a club

BioMedNet exploits the potential of the Internet and the advantages of a club concept to open up the opportunities for other related activities, services and resources to be made available to its members. In essence, BioMedNet is not exactly publishing, bookselling or document delivery. It is also not just a club, but a laboratory or office-based working tool giving users powerful resource on their desktop. If all goes according to plan, BioMedNet will eventually become a model workplace of the world research community, not only changing the way researchers work, but also the way information and service providers such as publishers, online providers etc. communicate with their customers (The BookSeller, 1995).

5 BIOMEDNET IN ACTION

"I imagine that the easiest, most natural way for a biomedical scientists to work, should be inside BioMedNet."

The vision statement above, to some, may seem like a bold claim. It is not easy for researchers who have worked individually or collaborated with others to be told that the way they have worked in the past thirty years may not be that natural in the future, and to give way to a new way of working on the Internet. On the surface, it may sound daunting, but in actual fact, researchers have been gradually exposed to whatever technology that come their way, from online services, CD-ROM databases to the more common telephone and fax correspondences. The Internet looks like the next most popular mode of information gathering and communication channel right from the researcher's own desktop computer.

The purpose of this paper is not to prove or disprove the vision statement, but rather, in the context of IOF, to provide a model already implemented, so that there is a basis to start answering the questions and issues raised so far, in the hope that we will have some indication whether IOF is a flawed concept or an inevitable future, what other (new) questions that will be raised, as well as potential research directions for both academia and industry.

Hence, it is useful to examine how BioMedNet works, and what experiences we can draw from the field of biology and medicine in their effort to herald in the work environment of the future. As this is a practice paper and the medium of presentation is a live demonstration of BioMedNet, it will not be possible to capture its essence on paper. Instead, the authors will present two scenarios in this paper, one on how researchers work individually, and another on how they collaborate with others, and then describe how using BioMedNet will provide a change of tools, interaction and environment in the way that they work in the future.

5.1 Working alone

In Table 3, the authors present a scenario, albeit a simplistic one, to highlight the way a researcher works individually via non-Internet means, the Internet and as a BioMedNet member.

Other possible scenarios are listed below, and due to space constraint, will not be expanded.

Finding research literature:
- usage of search facilities available;
- finding information from a specific resource;
- searching for full-text of cited reference in an article in a journal;
- browsing for information.

Preparing and producing research document:
- typing materials gathered in a word processor;
- copying any information (text, pictures, tables) into the document;
- usage of personal bibliographic manager and electronic documents;
- usage of spelling checkers, thesauri, special characters or symbols;
- usage of measurement tables and conversions, chemistry and mathematical writing aids;
- performing statistical analysis of data.

In the Functional Analysis of Office Requirements (FAOR) Project (Shafer, 1988), the project developed the concept of 'office technology potential', which is "the potential of the office system to change the support of office work". This concept is useful, not only in the case of an office system but also BioMedNet, as an analysis of its potential (categorised as possible quality improvements in the form or the handling of the information objects due to support by office technology) will help to identify possible improvements or deteriorations in the support of office activities. In BioMedNet, the Internet technology plays a very important part in defining and changing the way researchers work in the future. Therefore, we must look at the situation before and the situation after its introduction. To date, BioMedNet is an example of having merely identified the potential, so there will be room for further research.

Table 3 Scenario of a search for the full-text of an article in a journal

Activities	Non-Internet Researcher	Internet surfer	BioMedNet member
Library Search Collection of information in various media. Library provides resources acquired as well as from information services and products by commercial providers	Visits the library, or use online library system from library's or researcher's desktop computer to check whether library subscribes to journal, and that copies are available for browsing or loan. Also uses various online services and databases	From researcher's computer, uses Internet search tools to locate journal or journal publisher. Visits publisher's web site	From researcher's computer, uses web browser bookmark to go straight to BioMedNet Club home page. Log onto BioMedNet using membership name and password. Searches BioMedNet library for journal article
Requires assistance with search Cannot find journal article. Needs further assistance to determine other means of acquiring it	Seeks librarian for help with further search, perhaps available via interlibrary loan	Virtual library, but no librarian support. Perhaps post email	Goes to electronic librarian page and posts message for guidance. Electronic librarian responds immediately with relevant information
Contacts Publisher direct As a last resort, contacts the publisher of journal for assistance	Finds out contact telephone, calls customer service department of publisher for journal article availability	Checks publisher web site for reprint service online. If not, jots down telephone and calls customer service department	Found bibliographic reference with full-text available
Document delivery Publisher has reprint service. For a fee, full-text reprint of article from the journal arranged to be delivered to researcher	Researcher agrees to pay a fee for reprint and to be delivered via post within x time	Publisher has full-text document online. Makes credit card payment and gets authorisation to download document in PDF or HTML format	Makes use of membership payment account to pay for document conveniently. Downloads document in PDF, HTML or SGML format

5.2 Research collaboration

In the scientific community, it is often common for researchers and scientists to collaborate with others with similar interests. They may be from the same or different organisations. In fact, most often a number of individuals representing their organisations will work on something together without getting together physically to collaborate. It is a virtual organisation of people void of geographical distinction, physical space or physical place. When they do meet up face-to-face, it is often at conferences or society meetings, on a social level rather than actual work basis. Collaborations range from writing papers together, sharing data collected to continuing research and investigation of someone else's work.

For the scenario to depict research collaboration, perhaps the best visualisation of BioMedNet is from the following interview with Vitek Tracz, the visionary behind BioMedNet (BookSeller, 1995):

"Say I am writing a paper (in London) and my collaborators are in New York and Tokyo. We can all three of us meet here, and we can start talking to each other across the world. We can go to the library and look up articles and we can send pieces of text to each other. In the end we have a record of everything that we have been working on. We have effectively had a meeting.

At present, if three scientists want to work on a paper together, it can be very hard for them. They can use the fax, they can talk on the telephone. It is however (difficult and cumbersome), when you want to find something from the library. As things are, the speed at which you can search and see the real thing is very slow."

When a number of members are working on a document together, everyone will all see the same document, able to make changes and additions to it using tools, aids, macros etc. available to them from the club, their desktop, or downloadeble plug-ins from external suppliers. Scripts typed by one member can be seen by others in real time. The changes made can be saved and a record made of the discussion and the changes.

The multimedia capabilities of the Internet will also provide the means to work on illustrations together, or on tables, calculations and chemical problems. There are already examples of researchers working on the same chemical structure via VRML modelling.

5.3 Change of tools, interaction, environment

BioMedNet, as a collaborative tool, allows members to exchange ideas and information, to circulate and annotate documents, to communicate in real-time, and even to attend virtual conferences and lectures complete with colour illustrations and real-time question and answer sessions. As a work tool, it is a powerful desktop resource, providing access to an extensive library of journals, monographs and databases. As an environment, it brings together publishers and information services providers, societies and researchers so that relevant resources, products and services can also be researched and ordered directly through the system.

The BioMedNet experience has shown that the changes that are taking place are not exactly new, or for that matter, considered as real changes in some quarters. This is because the above description of BioMedNet is actually an ideal and natural environment that researchers have always dreamt of, and it may actually be a much closer reality that we think.

There will still be a certain amount of resistance to change that has to be overcome. On one hand people may not be Internet-aware or familiar with BioMedNet, and on the other hand, people who are sceptical that this vision of the future is possible.

Nevertheless, BioMedNet, despite its early days, can be seen as the first of a new generation of Internet-enabled systems that will help bring this reality to the fore. However, though the paper has shown how BioMedNet was designed and the choice of its solution strategy, it must be noted that it still has a lot to learn and implement to allow it to achieve its full potential.

It will be officially launched in mid February 1996, and come April 1996, the authors will hope that they will be able to report back more experiences and lessons learnt in their contribution towards this IOF conference.

6 CONCLUSION

This practice paper has a two-fold mission: i). to get researchers onto the Information Superhighway, and ii). to show the example of the use of BioMedNet as the way biomedical scientists work in the future. Having said that, it does not mean that they are mutually exclusive or that one must happen before the other can. In fact, they are so closely intertwined that you cannot have one without the other.

To get researchers onto the Internet, it is no longer a question of why, but how. BioMedNet has taken the initiative to encourage publishers, societies and researchers to help build this new environment. It is a big challenge as anyone can imagine. It would be unheard of today if a researcher would to claim that he does not use the telephone as a means of communication. The same can be said about the Internet in the near future. As one Immunologist commented, the real challenge is not the group that is already on the Information Superhighway, *"but those who would sooner pick up the phone than e-mail are the ones you want to reach"*.

To show the example of the use of BioMedNet, it is providing the investigation of the IOF concept with an example of a design option and a solution strategy that works in practice. This must not be misconstrued to say that BioMedNet is the 'total solution', or that it has implemented all the features available within its design. Office systems of today still have 'big deficiencies' that should be improved by adding specific CSCW functions (Traünmuller 1995), and BioMedNet is no different. With the emergence of CSCW as a body of research concerned with the social organisation of human conduct in technologically mediated cooperative work environments, it will help prevent the problems of earlier attempts at introducing technology to the work place taking a technocratic approach in the design and implementation of office systems.

And in order for BioMedNet to work as a model workplace for at least the biomedical research community, it is vital that support is forthcoming from the publishers, the societies and the researchers. Only time will tell whether BioMedNet's model can really become the model work place for the world research community for other fields and disciplines as well. And the involvement with this conference will allow BioMedNet and the authors to help speed up this learning process.

7 REFERENCES

Berglas, E. (1976) On the theory of clubs. *American Economic Review,* **68** May, 116-121

BioMedNet- The World Wide Club for Biomedical Scientists. (1994) *Electronic Press Ltd.*

Bots, P.W.G., Uijlenbroek, J.J.M. and van den Herik, K.W. (1995) The International Office of the Future: A search for issues and challenges, in *The International Office of the Future: A Problem Analysis* (ed. P.W.G. Bots, B.C. Glasson and D.R. Vogel), Technische Bestuurskunde, Delft.

Bots, P.W.G. and Uiijlenbroek, J.J.M. (1995) Developing an International Office of the Future Vision Statement: Workshop I, in *The International Office of the Future: A Problem Analysis*, (ed. P.W.G Bots, B.C. Glasson and D.R. Vogel), Technische Bestuurskunde, Delft.
BioMedNet at The Electronic Press (1995) in *OutLook on Scholarly Publishing* (ed. L.T. Meer, D. Brown & A. Pearce, **1** (8), August, 6.
Buchanan, J.M. (1965) An economic theory of clubs. *Ecnomica,* **32** February, 1-14.
Computer Supported Cooperative Work (1992) Kluwer Academic Publishers, **1** (1-2).
Curran, S. and Mitchell, H. (1984) *Office Automation.* Macmillan Press, London.
Ellis, C.A., Gibbs, S.J. and Rein, G.L. (1991) *Groupware: Some Issues and Experiences.* CACM, **34** (1), January, 38-58.
Engelbart, D. and Lehtman (1988) H. *Working Together.* Byte, 245-207.
Get Ahead, Get Online. (1994) *Personal Computer Magazine*, October, 281.
Glasson, B.C. and Quek, F. (1995) Developing an International Office of the Future Vision Statement: Workshop II, in *The International Office of the Future: A Problem Analysis*, (ed. P.W.G, Bots, B.C. Glasson and D.R. Vogel), Technische Bestuurskunde, Delft.
Groupware makes it market move. (1995) *Computer* **28** (9) September, 11.
Helpman, E. and Hillman, A.L. (1977) Two remarks on optimal club size. *Economica*, August, 293-295.
Hirscheim, R.A. (1985) *Office Automation: A Social and Organizational Perspective.* John Wiley, Chichester.
Hollingsworth, D. (1994), Toward the 4th Generation Office: A Study, in *Office Systems Evolution*, ICL Technical Journal, November.
Humphreys, P.C., Berkeley, D. and Quek, F. (1992) Dynamic process modelling for organisational systems supported by SASOS, in *Dynamic modelling of information systems*, North Holland, Amsterdam.
Johnson-Lentz, P. and Johnson-Lentz, T. (1992) The process and impacts of design choices, in *Computer-Mediated Communications Systems: Status and Evaluation* (ed. E.B. Kerr and Hiltz, S.R.), Academic Press, New York.
Kelly, M.M. and Gordon, G.E. (1986) *Telecommuting: How to make it work for you and your Company.* Prentice-Hall, New Jersey.
Kraemer, K.L. and King, J.L. (1988) Computer-Based Systems for Cooperative Work and Group Decision Making. *ACM*, **20** (2), June, 115-146.
Krol, E. (1992) *The Whole Internet User's Guide and Catalog.* O'Reilly and Associates, CA.
Kupperman, R. and Wilcox, R. (1972) *Proceedings of the First International Conference on Computer Communication*, Washington DC, October, 117.
Lab Test: Internet Access Packages. (1995) *PC User*, 18-31 October, 119.
Loomis, A. and Fink, D. (1993) Instruction: Gateway to the Virtual Library, in *The Virtual Library: Visions and Realities* (ed. L.M., Saunders), Meckler, London, 47-69.
McGraw-Hill Plans Electronic Academic Publishing. (1995), *Financial Times*, 16 October, 19.
Millard, G. and Williamson, H. (1976) How people react to computer conferencing. *Telesis*, August, 218.
Newman, W.M. (1987) Designing Integrated Systems for the Office Environment. McGraw-Hill, New York.
Ng, K.Y. (1973) The economic theory of clubs: Pareto optimality conditions. Economica, 40 August, 291-298
Noam, E. (1995) What then is the role of the university? *Science* **13**, October, 247.
OCLC Office of Research project. (1992) *OCLC Newsletter*, March/April, 13-15.

Predictions for the year 2000 (insert). *Byte* **20** (9), September, 110.
Saffady, W. (1981) *The Automated Office - An Introduction to the Technology.* National Micrographics Association.
Schlosberg, J. (1995) Is groupware for you? *OPEN COMPUTING,* **12** (9) September, 30-36.
Schafer, G. (1988), *Functional Analysis of Office Requirements: A Multiperspective Approach.* John Wiley, Chichester.
Strassman, P.A. (1985) *Information Payoff. The Transformation of Work in the Electronic Age.* Free Press, New York.
Telecommuting - high tolls, light usage. (1995) *Business Communications Review,* **25** (7) July, 8.
Traünmuller (1995) in *The International Office of the Future: A Problem Analysis,* (ed. P.W.G, Bots, B.C. Glasson and D.R. Vogel), Technische Bestuurskunde, Delft.
Uhlig, R.P., Farber, D.J. and Bair, J.H. (1979) The Office of the Future, *Communication and Computers.* North Holland, Amsterdam.
Vitek Tracz's £20m scientific experiment. (1995) *The Bookseller,* September.
Weiser, M. (1991) The Computer for the 21st Century. *Scientific American,* September.
Wired Magazine (1995), October.

8 BIOGRAPHY

Freddie Quek is an Information Systems Manager at Electronic Press Ltd (UK), which is the electronic publishing arm of the Current Science Group of medical publishing company. He received a Masters of Science from the London School of Economics, and is currently pursuing his Ph.D. in Information Systems at the same institution. He is also the Professional Activities Division Editor of ISWorld Net. His current research interests include decision support systems, electronic publishing, databases and the use of web-based technologies to support collaborative work.

Ian Tarr is the Managing Director of Electronic Press Ltd (UK). His current professional interests is in electronic publishing and in developing commercial applications for the pharmaceutical industry.

18

An electronic social space for consultation and collaboration.

S. Qureshi
EURIDIS, Erasmus University Rotterdam
Burg. Oudlaan 50, P.O. Box 1738
3000 DR Rotterdam, The Netherlands
Tel: +3110 408 2287, Fax: +3110 452 6134
Email: squreshi@fac.fbk.eur.nl, or qureshi@clus1.ulcc.ac.uk

Abstract

This paper describes the use of a distributed group communication system to support consultation and collaboration among people in different international agencies who cannot meet face to face. Following a description of the network of international agencies and the technology that they use, two types of interaction are presented. The study culminates with an analysis which provides practical insights into the type of support required for a globally networked way of working.

Keywords

Social space, electronic social space, appropriation, adaptation

1 INTRODUCTION

Group processes have been identified as being one of the main factors contributing to the development of networks in the work place. Kanter (1983) refers to group processes as integrating devices that enable the organisation to maintain a degree of cohesion among its many dispersed departments. Electronic support for facilitating group processes has arisen as a response to the need to support problem solving processes not only in face to face meetings but also among a group of geographically dispersed individuals who cannot meet physically. This latter form of communication is seen to support a network form and is the subject of this paper.

Group Support Systems (GSS) are more frequently applied to structure face to face meetings. Ideas and comments generated by the participants in the electronic group meetings appear together on one screen without the identity or the source of the comments ever being disclosed (as in the case of

GroupSystems V). GSS have been useful in providing anonymity to the members' comments in a face to face discussion, and facilitating the problem solving process. Proponents of GSS argue that the outcome of these meetings result in better quality decisions (Dennis et al 1988, Nunamaker et al 1988). Although there has been much research into the areas in which GSS may be effectively used, authors such as DeSanctis and Gallupe (1987) and Perin (1991), state that there are situations in which GSS technology, especially in its current state, may not help. For example, simple tasks requiring two or three people may be accomplished more effectively in a regular setting. This suggests that the technology alone cannot ensure that distributed group meetings are effective and efficient.

There is a sense that the support of work processes in which people do not physically meet or see each other may be provided within `virtual structures' through Computer Mediated Communications Systems (CMCS). As defined by Hiltz and Turoff (1992), *these systems use computers and telecommunications networks to store, deliver, regulate and process communication among the group members and between the computer and the group*. Although the most common form of CMCS is electronic mail, other computerised conferencing and bulletin board software is classified under this heading. This medium of communication has been supporting very large scientific and professional communities. In the context of a network form in which there is a need to coordinate geographically dispersed activities on a regular basis, the existence of networking is increasingly being seen as a necessity (Charan 1991, Drucker 1988, Keisler et al 1987).

This paper describes the use of an electronic communication system to support communication between a group of people from different international agencies. A brief description is provided of an international agency network which is seen to evolve a network way of working and requires electronic support for consultation and collaboration. An electronic communication system that provides this support is introduced and two ways in which it is used to support the meetings are described. Insights from this description are distilled using an interpretivist research strategy into practical conclusions on how the technology may best support consultation and collaboration between a geographically distributed group of people in different organisations.

2 RESEARCH APPROACH

The approach of this research follows an interpretivist strategy using a single case study. An interpretivist research strategy enables communication relations to be considered in their natural setting. As research into human networking is still in its formative stages, the use of a case study is valuable in that a real world situation is described in great depth. The case study is not used in this research to validate a theory or hypothesis but it is used to generate conceptual insights which may apply to other situations. In remaining consistent with an interpretivist research strategy, an international agency network is examined in its natural setting (the electronic notice board) as a case study and the researcher is part of the phenomena being investigated. A justification of this approach is provided in greater detail in Qureshi (1995).

When investigating electronic meetings it is useful to consider social structures. The structuration perspective proposes an emergent view, in that there are deep structures of power, and influence which constrain human action and the patterns of relations that emerge. At the same time human action helps to shape and define social structure (Giddens 1984). The analysis of this paper employs a structuration perspective and builds upon Linda Harasim's term, *social space* to describe the way in which human communication has transformed computer networks into what she calls `places' where people `connect' with each other. This research takes the notion of the social space as described by Harasim (1993) a step further by considering the social processes that affect interaction on the electronic medium of communication. It recognises that the technology may have an affect on the social processes and thus the patterns of relations and behaviours that emerge. Hence the term, *electronic social space,* is used to describe the environment in which the network phenomena are investigated. This notion of the creation of social structure on the electronic medium of communication provides us with a basis upon which to tackle the vaguer more complex aspects of human interaction which are nonetheless significant components of a network way of working.

3 A NETWORK OF INTERNATIONAL AGENCIES

The Informal Consultative Group of Information Technology for Development (ICGITD) was proposed at a collaborative meeting called "Information Technology for Development: Informal Consultation for Mobilising Resources" co-hosted by the Commonwealth Secretariat and the International Development Research Centre (IDRC) in London from the 26th to the 28th of January 1993. It comprised representatives from all the major and key agencies active in the field of IT for development. At the time, the ICGITD included the following international and donor agencies: the Canadian International Development Agency (CIDA), Commission of the European Communities (CEC DGXII), Danish International Development Agency (DANIDA), International Development Research Centre (IDRC), International Conference for Computer Communication (ICCC), United Nations University (UNU), United Nations Development Programme (UNDP), United Nations Educational, Social and Cultural Organisation (UNESCO), USAID Centre for Development, World Bank, and the African (ADB) and Caribbean Development (CDB) Banks. The ICGITD consisted of people representing a set of donor agencies who wanted to be able to exchange ideas and experiences on information technology projects in developing countries.

The purpose as set out in the agenda of the Conference, was to "allow informal dialogue to be extended in order to facilitate collaboration". It was agreed that "identified officials from a diverse range of agencies, including many of those represented at the meeting, could share concerns, opportunities, and outline project proposals on a strictly "off-the-record" basis. The issues raised could be confidential and sensitive, and yet required a degree of open discussion and debate. Project information, ideas and experiences, joint funding initiatives, and publications were the main areas requiring consultation among members of the group. The intention was to encourage brainstorming and an active exchange of ideas to ensure informed and thus effective collaboration in projects.

3.1 The mechanism

A mechanism for consultation and collaboration was put in place to enable the members of the ICGITD to communicate on a regular basis with respect to their initiatives in the developing world. The primary objectives of this mechanism as proposed at the collaborative meeting in January 1993, were:

> *"Methods and criteria for identifying appropriate officials within key agencies.*
>
> *Electronic mechanisms for rapid sharing of proposals and developments.*
>
> *Suggestions regarding procedural mechanisms for sharing information without implications of formal agency commitment - through the Journal of IT for Development."*

An electronic mechanism for meeting and consultation was agreed upon in which the members of this group were able to communicate electronically. The intention was to:

"Facilitate the operation of the software and enabling the registration of ICGITD members.

Provide training support and documentation for those using this facility.

Moderate the discussions to ensure that members are able to share their views and at the same time allow other members to do so. Ideas and views generated by these sessions are then compiled and distributed to those involved."

In response to the above, an electronic communication system was made available to all the ICGITD members and was used to encourage confidential electronic discussion. It was enhanced to accommodate the needs of the ICGITD members. The result of this development work was an asynchronous capability for structuring discussions, and a synchronous talk facility allowing electronic meetings to take place at the same time among people situated in different parts of the world. Technical considerations such as confidentiality and privacy meant that other users were not given access to information generated by ICGITD users.

4 THE DISTRIBUTED GROUP COMMUNICATION TECHNOLOGY

The technology used to support the ICGITD is a bulletin board facility known as The Notice Board which runs on an internet machine at the University of London Computer Centre and has been developed at the City University Computer Support Centre. The Notice Board has been designed to suit the requirements of the ICGITD. It is a closed system, operating on a high security machine, which provides confidentiality and at the same time accessibility to a wide range of participants who connect to it from different parts of the world. In order to be able to access the Notice Board, ICGITD members must have an account on the ULCC machine. This entails a process of registration afterwhich members receive documentation and support for using the facility.

The Notice Board enables essentially two types of communication to take place. Using the classification of DeSanctis and Gallupe (1987), it enables *different time different place* communication through the *discussion board* facility. While its functionality is similar to that provided by Vax Notes, the discussion board is more user friendly in that it enables participants to air their views relating to certain topics of discussion by automatically creating *menus and files. On the ICGITD discussion board, participants may enter comments on a particular topic within a file in which the different contributions are marked with the names of their respective authors. Within this discussion board facility, comments may be grouped into a tree structure in which different topics may be pointers to a set of topics or they may include files containing comments. This facility is intended to enable participants to structure and organise their contributions.

The second type of communication enabled by the Notice Board is *same time different place* communication which is available through the *talker*. The talk facility on the notice board, similar in functionality to the internet IRC, allows participants from different parts of the world to communicate with each other synchronously (at the same time). The communication is not anonymous, and comments typed by each participant are displayed next to their name on the virtual space. Communicating on the talker enables meetings to be held without having to move the participants away from their offices or their countries. In the course of these synchronous meetings, the talker also enables private conversations to take place in virtual rooms. Participants may go into one of these virtual rooms, invite other selected participants and once the invited participants enter the private room, the room can be locked to restrict others from joining in the private conversation.

4.1 Supporting consultation and collaboration

The technology alone cannot be seen to support the network. Preparation well in advance of the meetings is essential to ensure that the time people spend in the electronic meetings is fruitful. The purpose of the meetings has to be clear in the minds of the participants. For the purpose of the ICGITD, the discussion board facility is used to make announcements of forthcoming projects and workshops, and the talker is used to follow up issues with interactive meetings.

Selection of target group

At the first instance, it is important to be clear about who is going to attend these sessions and for what purpose. The nature and importance of a particular consultation exercise has to be established properly. In the case of the ICGITD this process is carried out outside of the electronic communication system as much of this is based on the institutional pressures that govern the nature and function of the network. It has been the experience of the authors that it takes a few weeks for people to coordinate their agendas and sort out any technical or connectivity problems that may arise.

Definition of items to be discussed

Once a group of participants have confirmed intent to have a meeting, it is necessary to proceed with defining an agenda. This agenda is then sent to all the participants for feedback and further modification if necessary. This establishes the nature and importance of meetings to participants. Agenda items do not have to be volumes of text, but well thought out simple easy to understand points that participants can identify with. These are posted on the discussion board facility and emailed to the participants well in advance of when the meeting is scheduled to take place especially where a group may have a low level of cohesion.

Conducting electronic discussions

The role of the chairperson is important when conducting an electronic discussion. For professional meetings conducted electronically in real time (same time, different place), it is customary to appoint a *facilitator* who is conversant in the topics being discussed and is familiar with the technology. The role of the facilitator is to guide the participants through the discussions drawing upon the capabilities of the technology. Electronic meetings that are conducted asynchronously (different place, different time), need to be *moderated* so that key issues are highlighted and superfluous comments are removed from the system. The role of the *chairperson* in the distributed electronic meetings appears to be a dominant one, where there is pressure to ensure effective discussion and participation, and to focus on key issues.

4.2 Structuring discussions

The ability to structure information is a notable feature of the discussion board facility. The generation and evaluation of ideas takes place on the discussion board facility as it enables topics of discussion to be organised and potentially evaluated. These discussions are asynchronous and require moderation in that superfluous or repetitive comments need to be removed and important comments placed within appropriate headings. This means that users have to make a choice early on in the presentation of their points on how to structure their ideas on the discussion board. The first level of the ICGITD discussions as illustrated in Figure 1, are composed of four main topics: The topic *Impacts* is a file and the other three are menu items. The first topic, *Impacts,* is entered as a file (there is an *Add* written next to it) and can be accessed by pressing **I** on the keyboard. A portion of the discussion file containing comments from different participants is illustrated in Figure 2.

IVI ICGITD Discussion Board <D> IVI
| |~~~~~~~~~~~~~~~~~~~~~| |

Add [I] - Impacts
Menu [P] = IT Policy
Menu [R] = Projects
Menu [G] = Regional Issues

Select, or **[RET]**:Back **[SPACE]** [/]:Find **[E]**:Edit Menu
[?]:Help.

Figure 1 The ICGITD Discussion Board.

- Is the effect of the existing It policy manifest in the organisation's IT
planning strategies? If so, to what extent is the stipulated change
measurable?
----------[Thu Nov 17 11:25:03 1994]------
From: Okot-Uma Rogers (rogers)
Subject: Impacts/Country Aspects of IT Policy
The following aspects of IT policy in developing countries may be worth
considering:
- Operational problems
- Problems of Context
- Strategy Problems

[Q]/[RET]:Exit [S]:Send Reply [A]:Add [E]:Edit
[?]:Help (100%)

Figure 2 The ICGITD Discussion Board: A Portion of the Impacts File.

In this file, participants add their comments for discussion or respond to existing comments on the file by either sending private messages to the author of a comment or by adding additional comments to this file. The *Impacts* file provides the capability for idea generation on a particular topic. Although a certain amount of brainstorming may have occurred in the file, it is not possible to evaluate the topic as the nature of the discussion on a file is more fluid and less structured than a discussion that may have been taking place under menu items.

An illustration of the way in which structured discussions take place using menu items is provided by the topic, *IT Policy*; this is a menu item comprising two topics created as files. As illustrated in Figure 3, the two topics being discussed are: *IT Policy in Africa*, and *Is there is a need ?* In this way a particular topic may be broken down to into separate menu items of discussion files. The **R** option in the ICGITD discussion board reveals a deeper menu structure. This aspect of the discussion board is concerned with posting material on the various `Projects' with an underlying purpose of seeking collaboration on projects. As is illustrated in Figure 4, it displays a structure that reflects the need for more concrete outcomes. We find that all three areas being discussed under `Projects', are menu items and hence give rise to deeper levels of topics. If we consider `Pipeline Projects' (the **P** option) we find that there are two topics upon which the discussion has focused: `Equipment' and `Training' (both of which are files) and are illustrated in Figure 5.

```
     |M|              IT Policy <DP>              |M|
| |~~~~~~~~~~~~~~~~~~~~~| |

                  [I] - IT Policy in Africa
                  [T] - Is there a need ?

Select, or [RET]:Back [SPACE] [/]:Find [E]:Edit Menu
[?]:Help.
```

Figure 3 The ICGITD Discussion Board: IT Policy.

There are no voting tools available on the discussion board. As the discussion board is not used take decisions yet, the need for voting tools has not been expressed. However, voting does take place in the face to face meetings which suggests that this technology is more suitable for exchanging information and ideas for consultation rather than for decision making. At the same time, the discussion board does enable certain areas for collaboration to be identified as a large amount of information may be posted on it for participants to scrutinise at their own leisure.

```
     |M|              Projects <DR>               |M|
| |~~~~~~~~~~~~~~~~~~~~~| |

           Menu  [A] = Areas for collaboration
           Menu  [E] = Existing Projects
           Menu  [P] = Pipeline Projects

Select, or [RET]:Back [SPACE] [/]:Find [E]:Edit Menu
[?]:Help.
```

Figure 4 The ICGITD Discussion Board: Projects.

The value of this form of communication to the ICGITD appears to be in the ability to raise issues, exchange information and ideas in order to achieve some sort of understanding of the situation. The final purpose is to be able to identify certain areas for collaboration and build working relations based on this joint understanding. In comparison, Dennis *et al* 1988 and Nunamaker et al 1988 have demonstrated that the use of group support systems have supported problem solving processes and have brought about better quality of decisions.

```
|M|          Pipeline Projects <DRP>          |M|
           | |~~~~~~~~~~~~~~~~~~~~~| |

     ( 6 Wks 2 Days) Add  [E] - Equipment
     ( 6 Wks 2 Days) Add  [T] * Training

Select, or [RET]:Back [SPACE] [/]:Find [E]:Edit Menu
[?]:Help.
```

Figure 5 Projects: Pipeline Projects.

In summary, the discussion board provides a means of exchanging information and ideas while at the same focusing on certain topics. It is not conducive however, to enabling participants to take certain topics further into meetings, brainstorming sessions and/or debates. This requirement is addressed by the synchronous talker described in the following section.

4.3 Conducting meetings

The synchronous talker provides a different mode of interaction than the discussion board. Electronic meetings held using a talk facility can support up to 450 people at any one time, but a productive meeting has between 5 and 7 people. The talker enables participants to communicate within their own rooms in which they may invite people from the default common room to engage in private conversation. While these rooms are used in trial sessions, the main ICGITD meetings take place in the virtual *common room* on the talker. In this, the talker facilitates brainstorming on specific issues and enables focus to be achieved on specific areas requiring decisions to be made or further discussion to be carried out. This form of synchronous computer conferencing is seen by the consultative group to be useful as long as there are some clearly defined objectives. As stated by a participant of an electronic ICGITD meeting:

> *"Our experience with computer conferencing ..... is that the more clearly defined the objectives of the exercise and the topic of the problem being discussed, the more likely something concrete can come out of it."*

The synchronous talker is useful in enabling greater focus on the more general topics posted on the discussion board. The synchronous discussion begins on a very broad topic and focuses on a particular practical, workable aspect of the topic. At the same time, some differences of opinion do emerge while ideas are being generated. This is illustrated in transcript 1, of an electronic ICGITD meeting.

L *'We have found in our INDIX meetings with other donor organizations at the bilateral level that government policy still severely limits information sharing and access between countries'*

R *'I am sure governments are able to isolate information that can be put into the public domain as opposed to sensitive information. Transparency in the age of open governance should facilitate this.'*

Transcript 1: Opinions and Open Discussion

In their study of computer conferencing, Hiltz and Turoff (1993) observe that there are always one or two individuals that dominate distributed synchronous meetings. The experience of the international agency network confirms this and suggests that the role of an `effective chairperson in such an environment is not democratic but draws upon the more traditional functions of maintaining structure and focus through authority based upon position. This is illustrated in transcript 2. The role of the chairperson is very explicit. There is no question about his command over the discussion, selection and time given for debate of the items on the agenda. Although all members do get a chance to air their views, experience suggests that it is the members with projects that are making clear progress that have the most to say. In addition, those members who just want to air their ideas without making any significant contribution to the discussion find themselves at the fringes of the discussion while the influential members get on with their own agenda. Influence in an electronic group meeting is not only associated with the activities that the participants are involved in but also the status of members in their own organisation; this bears considerable weight on their influence in the group discussions. In addition, the information that members have access to gives them an element of credibility in the general discussion.

Chairman *'We were planning begin with a pilot database at the Commonwealth Secretariat and then transfer it to an institution in a user country such as Malta as its is a small country and it provides a window to developing and developed countries. But do you have other suggestions ?'*

I *'If you have developed the data base it is absolutely essential to use it , to connect to it otherwise it is dead, useless and soon becomes inefficient'*

N *'with the database, it seems to me that we need to think about 1 willingness to use it; 2 ability to use it; and 3 need to use it'*

R *'a most practical mechanism would be to incorporate such information in a database that is widely or easily globally accessible by interested parties such as on the WWW'*

Transcript 2: Chairing

It is worth noting that while the talker facilitates and enables a mechanism for consultation and collaboration, it could also be seen to bring out the views of people of the different institutions to each other. This is illustrated in transcript 3. This mechanism for consultation and collaboration involves a politically sensitive form of communication among a group of donor agencies who have until recently been unaccustomed to this use of the technology. This points towards certain implications for group support and how it may be made conducive to the network way of working.

R *'something like good government is very relevant and well defined and finds an audience easily.*

V *'OK. If one is to discuss IT in government, how about a specific issue like "Access to Government Information"?'*

Chairperson *'Could you please suggest a more focused topic V, as you already have a DSS workshop.'*

R *'we can get a few different groups in different cities of the world listen to a panel discussion and send in their own comments in real time'*

O *'or government information systems (gis).'*

R *'access to govt information sounds very attractive we have lots of govt information, but not the access!'*

:

V *'slightly different group than "government officials" although the government folk are the ultimate beneficiaries of all this technical work (plus of course the people THEY in turn service).'*

Transcript 3: Different Views

5 IMPLICATIONS FOR SUPPORTING A NETWORK WAY OF WORKING

When supporting a group working as a network using electronic group communication technology, it is worth considering certain functionalities that may be built into the technology. At the same time, the social processes that govern interaction on the electronic media need to be considered in the light of communication etiquette, institutional and political sensitivities, and cultural considerations. In other words, the electronic social space must be sustained and strengthened in order to provide appropriate and effective support for a network way of working. In the following sections, results from the project are distilled into practical insights drawing upon structuration theory to guide the inquiry.

5.1 Appropriation

Structuration theory (Giddens 1984) provides valuable insight into such social processes. A particular application of structuration theory to computer mediated communication is offered by DeSanctis and Poole (1994). They propose a `Theory of Adaptive Structuration' which states that as group members use GDSS to complete a task, they are developing and applying rules and resources for the conduct of behaviour. The rules and resources of the group direct members as to which features of the technology they should appropriate. They found that when individuals in a group interact using GDSS, each group produces and reproduces its own *structures-in-use*. This process, they claim, accounts for the continual changing nature of social structures involved in the use of group decision support systems. The Notice Board provided the ICGITD with very simple tools that participants could use to support their own ways of communicating.

At the same time, members of the network bring with them their own perceptions and cultural backgrounds when interacting on the electronic media. The result, is a curious amalgamation of these norms and perceptions. These manifest themselves on the communication media and can be seen to add to the ordeal of moderating a meeting. In effect, these social interactions that take place on the electronic media can be seen to create an electronic social space in which a set of norms and perspectives develop and become accepted within that group of people. The electronic social space creates within it a totally different way of communicating and brings forth sets of interactions that as yet have been non existent (Qureshi 1995b). This suggests that the technology has to be flexible enough to support changing work patterns and at the same time requires a design that is stable enough to merit use over a long period of time.

5.2 Adaptation

In view of supporting the fluid nature of interactions on the electronic social space, while at the same time providing the necessary tools to structure meetings, three types of adaptation need to be considered. The technology has to be appropriate with a sufficient set of tools from which users may choose to support their communication. The experience of this study suggests that the technology also has to be simple, and easy to use. Extensive windowing facilities intended to yield user-friendliness tend to hinder rather than facilitate use. The results of a related study, in which the same technology was used by a different group (Qureshi 1995b), suggest that groups go through processes of adapting to the electronic social space. These processes of adaptation to the technology, the work environment, and the emergent social processes are also identified in the study reported in this paper. These processes are considered in greater detail in Qureshi (1995a, 1995b) but for the purpose of this paper, the following sections focus on a consideration of adaptation among participants of the international agency network.

Technological adaptation

In this study, technological adaptation entails learning how to use the technology and more importantly how to get around the numerous difficulties that it presents. The participants had to get accustomed to the environment of the software; in particular, how to use the basic commands, entertain themselves with the more amusing commands and then communicate with each other using these commands. An examination of the meeting transcripts suggests that this particular group of participants were relatively familiar with the technology and were comfortable enough with it to be able to discuss important and somewhat sensitive issues on the electronic social space. They did not use the additional `rooms' available on the talker. However, the technology did have the potential of influencing the meetings as contributions were very much dependant upon the typing skills of the participants. In effect, the lack of turn yielding cues available in face to face communication meant that chairing the meetings was not straightforward. Tool support for chairing the meetings could enhance the electronic social space considerably.

Work adaptation

The electronic social space presented the ICGITD members with a work environment that was different from what they were accustomed to. These participants brought into the social space ways of working that are familiar to them in their own organisations (as would be the case in face to face meetings). When these varying perceptions and norms of behaviour come together on the electronic environment, new ways of working emerge. The study reported in this paper reveals a set of working relations that are inherently political. The lack of visual cues and subtle intonations on the electronic social space meant that the political meandering, common in the face to face meetings among these civil servants, was impeded. Thus the participants adapted to this new work environment by having more formal and, compared to the face to face meetings, more focused interaction. Supporting work adaptation, the process of getting accustomed to a work environment that takes place electronically, entails a dual relation between the behaviours of the participants and the ways of working that they are accustomed to. It is thus necessary to consider the rules and regulations, responsibilities of the users, their positions with respect to their colleagues and the importance (immediacy) of the tasks (Dawson 1986, Child 1988).

Social adaptation

The social process is perhaps the most important and least understood of the factors that influence interaction on the electronic social space. Values, norms and perceptions created over time in the minds of human actors are manifest in the way in which human actors behave on the electronic social space. Interaction among human actors also contributes to changing these values, norms and perceptions and thus behaviour. In view of this, supporting social adaptation is not quite as straightforward as one might expect, especially as it is most effective when social adaptation emerges when people learn more about their environment and are thus able to shape the social space to suit their own habits. In the study reported here, the technology tempered the ability of the participants to express their perceptions, norms and values, and the very subtle cultural nuances were brought to bear in different ways. Communication etiquette developed gradually and benefited from the participants who were more familiar with communicating electronically.

6 CONCLUSIONS AND SUGGESTED FURTHER RESEARCH

This paper describes the use of an electronic communication system supporting a network of international agencies. It follows an interpretive research strategy to obtain a rich in-depth description of how the network way of working, the network of international agencies (ICGITD), operates using the technology in a real life situation. From this description, issues arise relating to group support for structuring decisions and conducting meetings. It appears that structured discussions may be more appropriate for topics that require an exchange of information and ideas whereas synchronous communication has a more definite purpose as it allows a degree of social interaction. The paper suggests that the technology enables a network way of working, and in so doing must provide users with the tools to allow them to use the technology to suit their own ways of communicating. Further research investigating the leadership function, in particular the role of the chairperson, considering carefully the nature of the electronic social space may potentially provide further insight into appropriate and effective support for a network way of working.

7 REFERENCES

Argyris, C., R. Putnam and McLain Smith, D. (1982) *Action Science - Concepts, Methods and Skills for Research and Intervention.* Josey-Bass, San Francisco.

Charan, R. (1991) How Networks Reshape Organisations for Results . *Harvard Business Review.* 91503, 104-115.

Child, J. (1988) *Organisation: A Guide To Practice and Problems.* Harper and Row, London.

Dawson, S. (1986) *Analyzing Organisations.* Macmillan, London.

Dennis, A.R.J.F., L.M. George, L.M. Jessup, J.F. Nunamaker and Vogel, D.R. (1988) Information Technology to Support Electronic Meetings . *MIS Quarterly.* 12(4), 591-624.

DeSanctis, G. and Gallupe, R.B. (1987) A Foundation for the Study of Group Decision Support Systems . *Management Science.* 33(5), 589-609.

DeSanctis, G. and Poole, M.S. (1994) Capturing the Complexity in Advanced Technology Use: Adaptive Structuration Theory . *Organization Science.* 5(2), 121-147.

Drucker, P. (1988) The Coming of the New Organisation. *Harvard Business Review.* January-February.

Giddens, A. (1984) *The Constitution of Society.* Polity, Cambridge.

Hiltz, S.R. and Turoff, M. (1992) Virtual Meetings: Computer Conferencing and Distributed Group Support. in *Computer Augmented Teamwork* (ed. R.P. Bostrom, R.T. Watson and S. Kinney), Van Nostrand Reinhold, New York.

Hiltz, R.S. and M. Turoff. (1993) *The Network Nation, Human Communication via Computer.* Addison-Wesley, London.

Kanter, R.M. (1983) *The Change Masters.* Unwin, New York.

Keisler, S., J. Seigal and McGuire, T. (1987) *Information Technology Social Issues: A Reader.* Hodder & Stoughton, London.

McCall, G.J. and Simmons, J.L. (1969) Issues in Participant Observation: A Text and a Reader. Random House, New York.

Nunamaker, J.F., L.M. Applegate and Konsysnski, B.R. (1988) Computer-aided Deliberation: Model management and Group Decision Support. *Operations Research, Special Issue on Decision Support Systems.* 36(6), 826-848.

Perin, C. (1991) Electronic Social Fields in Bureaucracies. *Communications of the ACM.* 34(12), 75-82.

Qureshi, S., (1995a) Supporting Electronic Group Processes: a social perspective. in *Supporting Teams, Groups, and Learning Inside and Outside the IS Function* (ed. L. Olfman), SIGCPR/ACM, Nashville.

Qureshi, S., (1995b) *Organisations and Networks: Theoretical Considerations and a Case Study*, PhD Thesis, London School of Economics.
Sproull, L. and S. Kiesler. (1991) Computers, Networks and Work. *Scientific American*. 265(3), 84-91.

8 BIOGRAPHY

Dr Sajda Qureshi is a research fellow at the Erasmus University Research Institute for Decision and Information Systems (EURIDIS) and a visiting assistant professor at the Rotterdam School of Management at Erasmus University Rotterdam, in the Netherlands. She has been Coordinator of the Commonwealth Network of Information Technology for Development (COMNET-IT) at the Commonwealth Secretariat in London, the UK. She has also been employed at the London School of Economics as a research assistant developing an organisational modelling system as part of an EEC project. She has research and consultancy experience in developing information systems in Italy and the UK.

19

The office tyrant: abuse of power through e-mail

C. T. Romm
University of Wollongong
Wollongong, NSW 2500
Australia
Tel: (042)214043, Fax: (042)27278 , E-Mail: c.romm@uow.edu.au

Nava Pliskin
Ben Gurion University
Beer-Sheva
Israel

Abstract

The changing role of technology in the modern office has been accompanied by a proliferation of research activity focusing initially on the technical aspects and more recently on the social and political aspects of the diffusion process, including power and politics. This paper builds on the work of Markus on power and politics in IT, extending it to e-mail and more specifically, to the use of e-mail for petty tyranny. We start with a review of the literature on petty tyranny and its implications to Information Technologies and e-mail. The review is concluded with a series of assertions about the use of e-mail for petty tyranny. To demonstrate how these assertions can operate within an organisational context, a case study is presented. In the case, e-mail was used by a department head to manipulate, control, and coerce employees. The discussion synthesises the analysis by demonstrating that e-mail features made it amenable to political abusive tyrannical uses. The paper is concluded with a discussion of the implications from this case to e-mail research and practice.

Keywords

E-mail, Power and Politics, abuse of technology in organisational settings

1 INTRODUCTION

The last decades have witnessed an exponential increase in the diffusion of office technologies. The new technologies, particularly e-mail, have redefined the nature of office work, making different-time/different-place/different-culture teams the norm in many organisations. The changing role of technology in the modern office has been accompanied by a proliferation of research activity focusing initially on the technical aspects (Culnan, and Markus, 1987; Eveland and Bikson, 1988; Pliskin, Ball, and Curley, 1989; Pliskin, 1989; Pliskin and Romm, 1990) and more recently on the social and political aspects of the diffusion process (Pliskin, Romm, Lee, and Weber, 1993; Romm, Pliskin, Weber, and Lee, 1991; Markus, 1994).

One of the more intriguing lines of research on diffusion and implementation of Information Technologies has been the study of the power and politics of these processes. In this context, the work of Kling (1978, 1980) and Markus (1981, 1983) has been particularly important. Their pioneering research has not only provided us with a definition of power and politics in the Information Technology context, but also with a theoretical framework that can be applied to new and emerging technologies, such as e-mail.

The major objective of this paper is to build on the work of Kling (1978, 1980) and Markus (1983) by extending their power and politics perspective to e-mail. In particular, our research is intended to address the issue of petty tyranny through e-mail. In this context, the major objectives of this paper are:

1. To demonstrate how e-mail features can facilitate mis-use of power by petty tyrants.
2. To describe the effects that petty tyranny through e-mail can have in a work environment.
3. To discuss the theoretical, practical, and ethical implications that the use of e-mail for petty tyranny has for the Information Systems profession.

To frame the discussion, we start with a review of the literature on petty tyranny and its implications to Information Technologies and e-mail (section 1). The review is concluded with a series of assertions (based on Markus, 1983 and Ashforth, 1994) about the use of e-mail for petty tyranny. To demonstrate how these assertions can operate within an organisational context, a case study is presented in section 2. The case study describes a series of events which took place in a university department. In the case, e-mail was used by the department head to manipulate, control, and coerce employees. The discussion (in section 3) synthesises the analysis by demonstrating that e-mail features made it amenable to political abusive tyrannical uses. In fact, the analysis suggests that it was the abuse of e-mail by the Department Chair that motivated employees to eventually turn against him. The paper concludes with a discussion of the implications from this case to further e-mail research and practice.

2 THEORETICAL BACKGROUND

As indicated before, the pioneering work on power and politics in Information Systems was undertaken more than a decade ago. Kling (1980) provided a starting point to this research by identifying six theoretical approaches that can explain resistance to diffusion of Information Technologies: Rational, Structural, Human Relations, Interactionist, Organisational Politics, and Class Politics. Kling indicated that these theoretical approaches differed on a variety of dimensions, such as their view of technology, the social setting into which technology is introduced, and the implications for the dynamics of the diffusion process.

Building on Kling's work, Markus (1983) defined three major categories for theories of resistance to diffusion: people-determined, system-determined, and interactionist. The main focus of her paper, however, was on one of the variants of the interactionist theory, i.e., the political. According to this variant of the Interactionist theory, resistance is explained as a product of the "interaction of system design features with the intra-organisational distribution of power, defined either objectively, in terms of horizontal or vertical power dimensions, or subjectively, in terms of symbolism" (p. 432). In other words, this theory predicts that information systems would be resisted by potential users if they cause a re-distribution of power that either conflicts with the organisational structure (objective definition) or with the interests of individuals who are likely to lose power as a result of the implementation (subjective definition). This view of power and politics as determinants of implementation outcome has been elaborated on in further work by the author, including, Markus and Robey, (1983), and Markus and Robey, (1988).

It should be acknowledged that even though Markus has never explicitly applied her political theory of resistance to e-mail, she has recently suggested this direction for future research by concluding her paper on e-mail use (Markus, 1994, p. 523) with the following assertion :

> "The adoption, use, and consequences of media use in organisations can be powerfully shaped by social processes such as sponsorship, socialisation, and social control, which require social perspectives to understand them."

The next sections follow the direction proposed by Markus by exploring the ways in which e-mail can be used for manipulation of power within organisations. In particular, the ways in which e-mail can facilitate petty tyranny in the office are explored.

What is a petty tyrant? According to a definition recently proposed by Ashforth (1994, p. 1), a petty tyrant is a person who "lords his or her power over others". Based on his own survey research, Ashforth (1994) has identified six characteristics that are typical of petty tyrants: (1) arbitrariness and self aggrandisement, (2) belittling subordinates, (3) lack of consideration, (4) a forcing style of conflict resolution, (5) discouraging initiative, and (6) non-contingent punishment.

As indicated by Ashforth (1994), while the concept of petty tyranny is well understood at the intuitive level, there has been surprisingly little research on the nature of petty tyranny in organisations. The limited research that is available suggests that petty tyranny is determined by individual predispositions and situational facilitators.

The pioneering work on **individual predispositions** associated with petty tyranny has been conducted by Adorno, Frenkel-Brunswik, Levinson, and Sanford (1950) who described the "authoritarian personality" as one which has the tendency to be dominant toward one's inferiors and submissive toward one's superiors. Thompson (1960), building on Adorno et al's work, described the "bureaucratic individual" who is domineering, impersonal, inflexible and insists on the rights of authority and status. McGregor (1960) has attributed similar characteristics to managers who hold theory X beliefs, namely, the beliefs that employees are inherently lazy and lacking in motivation and, therefore, need discipline, direction, and control from their superiors. Kipnis (1976) has identified low self confidence as an important antecedent of tyrannical behaviour, while Ray (1981) has singled out "directness" as the tendency to impose one's will on others. Finally, Feather (1971) and Norton (1975) have listed lack of tolerance for ambiguity as a personality trait that would lead superiors to over-control subordinates.

Topping the list of situational factors that have been associated with petty tyranny are **organisational values**. Thus, Goffman (1961) and Haney, Banks and Zimbardo (1973) discussed the phenomenon of "institutionalised tyranny", typical of total institutions such as prisons, mental hospitals, and army barracks, where inmates are subjected to extreme forms of authoritarian supervision. Mintsberg (1989) and Hofstede (1978) stressed the effects of mass production on formalised, standardised, and, consequently, often dictatorial management procedures. On the other extreme, Mintsberg (1989) and Kets de Vries (1989) found that "entrepreneurial organisations" were often controlled by individuals who had: (1) strong need for independence and control, (2) distrust of others, and (3) a desire for applause.

Another line of research on situational aspects of petty tyranny considered its **micro level antecedents**. Within this level two conflicting phenomenal were identified. On one hand, House (1988) and Kipnis (1976) mentioned lack of power as cause of tyrannical behaviour. Individuals who perceive that they are relatively powerless often lord what power they do have. On the other hand, Kipnis (1976) argued that the acquisition and successful use of power tends to corrupt the power holder in several aspects: (1) power becomes an end in itself, (2) the power holder develops and exalted sense of self-worth, (3) power is used increasingly for personal rather than organisational purposes, and (4) the power holder devalues the worth of others.

Finally, **stressors** may also contribute to petty tyranny. Managers tend to respond to stressors by becoming more directive (Mulder, De Jong, Koppelaar and Verhage, 1986). Under pressure, managers' decision making tends to become more centralised, hasty and arbitrary (Janis, 1982) and as a result they tend to withdraw psychologically from others, treating them more like objects than people (Maslach, 1982). Furthermore, one may justify this stance by blaming others. Thus, Lee and Ashforth (1993) found that managers experiencing emotional exhaustion tended to depersonalise their subordinates and in extreme cases even take perverse pleasure from abusing them.

The purpose of this study is to explore the ways in which e-mail can be used to facilitate petty tyranny in organisations. Based on a case study that is presented in the next section, and along the lines suggested by Markus' (1994) and Ashforth (1994), we make the following assertions:

Assertion 1. - E-mail's features can lend themselves to different types of political mis-use by petty tyrants.
Assertion 2. - Petty tyranny through e-mail can have devastating effects on subordinates.
Assertion 3. - The use of e-mail for petty tyranny has far reaching implications for Information Systems research and practice.

These assertions and their implications to office technology research and practice are explored in the discussion sections of the paper.

3 CASE STUDY

3.1 Data collection

Data for this study were collected by the authors at a small suburban university (see more details about the university in the following sections). Emphasis during data collection was put on reconstruction of all stages of the implementation process as well as on relevant organisational issues. Textual analysis, interviews, and observations were employed in the study. These were comprehensive and mutually supportive. For example, observations were a source of interview questions while the interviews enabled cross-checking of historical details, exploring discrepancies, and probing into personal perceptions. To maximise reliability, both authors were involved in all data analysis activities and were able to reach agreement whenever findings or their interpretation were in dispute.

Textual analysis: A variety of documents were collected, including e-mail promotion materials, training transparencies, and minutes of relevant meetings. Textual analysis also included in-depth study of the organisational chart, hard copy and soft copy of intra-departmental correspondence. A major source of data for this study were about 50 e-mail messages that had been collected by several of the interviewees and were made available to the researchers. Excerpts from the most important of these messages are used to highlight the main events of the case in the following sections of the paper.

Interviews: In-depth interviews with 15 members of the organisation were a major source of data for this study. There were ten interviews with academics in the Department of Accounting. Of these, four were with senior faculty members (Associate Professors and Full Professors), three interviews were with junior faculty (Assistant Professor) and the remaining three interviews with teaching assistants. Two interviews were held with the Department of Accounting secretaries. From top management, the Provost, the personal assistant to the President, and the head of the Information Technology Division which installed e-mail at the Department of Accounting were interviewed. All interviewees had direct or indirect knowledge of the events that are described in the case.

In addition to gathering personal details (such as background, careers, and future plans), interviewees were asked to discuss quality of work life before and during the implementation of e-mail at the Department of Accounting. Although the questions varied from one interview to another, the same topics were covered in all. The taped open-ended interviews, which lasted about ninety minutes each, were transcribed and analysed by the authors.

Observations: Since most interviews took place on the premises of the university, there were additional opportunities for observation.

3.2 Case history

UOT (The actual names of organisations, people, and e-mail products are withheld to preserve their anonymity), is a small university, with about 6000 students, 250 academics, and 150 administrative staff. Located in a quiet suburb of a large city, it has not grown substantially since its inception in the early 1950's.

When Mr. Parson announced his resignation as Chair of Accounting in February 1992, accepting a position as Dean of the School of Business in a much larger university, the reverberations were felt in the community within and outside the University. The Department of Accounting is among the largest departments in UOT, attracting over 20% of the students at the University. The President of UOT, who was to chair the selection committee for the next Department Chair of Accounting, made it clear that only a person with proven superior leadership qualifications could be selected for the job.

After an intense but short selection process, in which ten candidates were interviewed, the job was offered to Mr. Jones, the head of a large accounting firm with many years experience as a part-time honorary professor at the Department of Accounting at UOT. The committee was aware that Mr. Jones had limited experience in research and publications but felt that his leadership skills and extensive links with local industry would more than compensate for his academic shortcomings. The committee was also impressed with his commitment to technological progress. In fact, his announcement that he would "bring technological efficiency to all aspects of managing the department" convinced some of the more reluctant members of the committee to agree to his appointment.

One of Professor Jones' first decisions was to make e-mail available to all academic and administrative staff at the Department of Accounting. Since the necessary communication lines were already in place, all that was required was to install communication software and hardware on all personal computers in the department. This was accomplished with the help of the Information Technology Division (ITD) within a few weeks after Professor Jones took office.

Professor Jones' first e-mail message to the members of the department was transmitted on the day the last computer was fitted with the new technology. His message was as follows:

> To: All members of the department of Accounting
> From: Professor Jones- Chair
>
> By now you must all be aware that we, the Department of Accounting have e-mail!! I am happy to say that it has just been installed on all computers in this department. E-mail will put us at the forefront of communication progress in this university. Other departments will be watching us and, before long, they will probably follow our example. I realise that it might be some time before we all know how to use this new technology. It will require some patience and some work, but master it we will. I wish us all the best of luck on the beginning of this new era in our history.

The first message from Professor Jones was soon followed by several others. In the first of these messages he indicated that he would be meeting with members of the department throughout the week in an attempt to learn how the department operated and how procedures could be improved. In particular, he announced that he will be looking at changing the structure of the department, making it flatter and more decentralised. Before long, another message, outlining the new structure, was transmitted to department members, again, on e-mail. The content of the message was as follows:

> To: All members of the department of Accounting
> From: Professor Jones- Head
>
> After a lengthy process of consultation with some ten members of this department, I have put together a plan which I would like us to discuss during our department meeting next week.
> To prepare you for the meeting, let me just say that I am suggesting a change into a matrix structure. We already have three individuals who are heading our major programs: the BA, the MBA, and the Ph.D. I am suggesting that these positions will be supplemented with three more, the head of corporate accounting, the head of small business accounting, and the head of public sector accounting.
>
> The proposed new positions will support the chair in decisions relating to teaching allocation. In the long term, the fact that we have organised ourselves in terms of these content areas, will also help us consolidate our research and consultancy activities. I am looking forward to hearing your views on these proposals.

Professor Jones opened the first of his monthly department meetings, which was held a few days after the above message was sent, with the announcement that he saw communication on e-mail as a major key to efficiency. "It is time", he said, "that this department join the rest of the world in using e-mail as the major media for intra-departmental communication".

He then proceeded to canvass department members' views on his plan to appoint three individuals as heads of the three new groups. Before long, the three most senior professors in each area were voted as the new groups' heads. These included Professor Lee, as head of Corporate Accounting, Professor Cole as head of Small Business Accounting, and Professor Jefferson, as head of Public Sector Accounting

Many faculty in the Department, who were not using e-mail prior to Professor Jones' appointment, actually welcomed his initiative. Attendance in training courses that he organised was high. Even members of the "old guard", who initially thought that e-mail was too difficult for them to master, were enthusiastic participants in the training sessions. Before long, staff members were all using the new technology, joining discussion groups, and browsing through international information databases.

However, it soon became apparent that Professor Jones had other uses for e-mail in mind. The secretaries were the first to become aware of the implications of his "technological policy". Their e-mail screens soon filled up with short messages from Professor Jones, many of which were left the night before, requesting immediate action. Following is an example of one such message.

> To: Ms. Carter
> From: Professor Jones- Head of Department
>
> It is 5.30pm now and I have just realised that I forgot to give you a letter that needs to be sent to the President tomorrow morning. I will be leaving a hand-written draft of the letter on your desk. Please have it typed and ready for my signature by 9.15 tomorrow morning.

Inability to provide the service that was requested early in the next morning resulted in complaints and reprimands from Professor Jones. During the day, Professor Jones developed a habit, which particularly infuriated the secretaries, of sending them e-mail messages containing requests for cups of coffee to be delivered to him and/or to his frequent industry guests. The "thank you" messages that followed the delivery of the coffee were not welcomed either. As put by the secretaries "a few words, or even a smile would have been much better".

The secretaries, who previously were rarely in the office at 8.30 AM, realised that not responding to Professor Jones' e-mail messages by 9.00 AM would be frowned upon. They also discovered that Professor Jones would send "urgent" messages around 2.00 PM in the afternoon to find out if they returned from their lunch break. Failure to respond to those was actually one of the factors that led to the dismissal of Ms. Smith, a young trainee who joined the Department shortly before Professor Jones appointment and was asked to leave a few weeks after he arrived.

As time went by, Professor Jones insistence that e-mail be used by all administrative personnel spilled over to include the academic staff as well. When the secretaries left "pink slips" on his desk from members of the Department who called and wanted him to call back, he routinely responded by e-mail. In one incident he actually exchanged five messages with Professor Carol, a junior member of faculty who wanted to see him, trying to solve a problem, that Professor Jones believed could be solved on e-mail. Following are the messages that were exchanged between the two during this incident.

> To: Professor David Jones- Head of Department
> From: Professor Michael Carol

I would appreciate it if you could meet with me today to discuss my teaching allocation for the next semester. I will be in my office today and will be able to see you when you are available.

To: Professor Michael Carol
From: Professor David Jones- Head of Department

Teaching allocations should be discussed with the head of your grouping first. Have you discussed your problem with Professor Lee? Please do. Once you do, please let me know if you still think you need to see me.

To: Professor David Jones- Head of Department
From: Professor Michael Carol

Yes, I did discuss my problem with Professor Lee, but was unable to reach a satisfactory solution. I am aware that you are busy today, but I really need to see you.

To: Professor Michael Carol
From: Professor David Jones- Head of Department

Can you provide me with some details about the meeting? Perhaps I should see Professor Lee before I meet with you. Further details will also make our meeting much more efficient.

To: Professor David Jones- Head of Department
From: Professor Michael Carol

I would have explained the problem here on e-mail, but it is simply too complex and too confidential. I would rather not put it in writing. The problem is also quite urgent and needs to be resolved by today. Can you please see me?

It was by late afternoon that day that Professor Jones agreed to meet with Professor Carol. The meeting was scheduled for several days later, because Professor Jones had to leave for a conference. The whole incident, which Professor Carol later discussed with other members of the department gave a clear signal that e-mail was the preferred way to approach Professor Jones.

Once back from the conference, Professor Jones did meet with Professor Carol. During the meeting Professor Carol shared with Professor Jones a series of problems that he has been experiencing with Professor Lee, the head of the Corporate group. The latest problem was related to teaching allocation within the group. Professor Carol, who was on the first year of his three year contract at the Department and therefore under pressure to publish, objected to Professor Lee's request that he teaches a large compulsory third year course that he had never taught before.

Professor Carol told Professor Jones that other professors within the group, including Professor Lee himself, had taught this course more than once in the past. He insisted that in view of his special situation, he should be allowed to teach the two courses that he already prepared for the first semester, rather than invest a large amount of time, which would take him away from his research, in preparing a new and difficult course. He requested Professor Jones' interference in what he saw as a case in which Professor Lee was abusing his position as head of the group. To support this claim,

Professor Carol mentioned several other members of the group who opposed Professor Lee and were in agreement with him on this matter.

Professor Jones explained to Professor Carol that the new structure that he introduced would not allow him to overturn Professor Lee's decision. This would send a wrong signal to the members of the department, suggesting that the new group heads were not truly in authority within their groups. He did promise, however, to look into the matter with Professor Lee and come back to Professor Carol with a final decision in a few days.

The following morning, Professor Jones sent the following e-mail message to Professor Lee, inviting him to a meet with him in his office.

> To: Professor Michael Lee
> From: Professor David Jones
>
> Enclosed please find a message that I just received from Professor Carol. As you can see, Professor Carol is concerned about his assigned teaching allocation for the second semester. I think we should meet to discuss it. Can you please contact my secretary to arrange a time for a meeting?
>
> <To: Professor David Jones- Head of Department
> <From: Professor Michael Carol
>
> <I would appreciate it if you could meet with me today to discuss my teaching allocation <for the next semester. I will be in my office today and will be able to see you when you <are available.

During the meeting that was held between the two professors later that day, it became apparent that Professor Lee was not going to change his decision regarding Professor Carol's teaching allocation. The meeting was concluded with Professor Jones' promising to see if he could solve the problem by discussing it again with Professor Carol. A few days later, the following message from Professor Jones was transmitted to the members of the department of Accounting on e-mail:

> To: All members of the Department of Accounting
> From: Professor Jones - Head of Department
>
> It was brought to my attention by several members of the department that decisions regarding teaching allocations within groups are not necessarily taken in consultation with the faculty members that are involved. In view of the fact that we have to submit our teaching schedule to central administration in three weeks and to maintain the principle of de-centralisation, I suggest that the three discipline groups would meet to discuss teaching allocations for the second semester. The meetings will be chaired by the three heads and will be attended by me. I will provide information about the dates and venues for the meetings once I have the matter cleared with Ms. Carter.

Within a few days, another e-mail message which outlined the dates and venues for the three meetings was transmitted by Professor Jones to the members of the Department. The three meetings were held within a week after the message was transmitted. While there were no particular problems with two of the groups, Professor Lee, the head of corporate accounting did not show up to his group meeting. None of the other members of the group was aware of Professor Lee's whereabouts and all attempts by Ms. Carter to locate him failed. After consulting with the other members of the group, Professor Jones announced that in view of Professor Lee's unexplained absence, he (Professor Jones) would chair the meeting. With Professor Jones as chair, the group decided that Professor Lee would teach the third year compulsory subject that he taught in previous years. It was also decided that Professor Carol would teach one of the two subjects that he taught on the first semester and another advanced seminar for a small group of graduate students. Within days after the meeting, Professor Jones sent the Departments' final teaching schedule to central administration.

In the next monthly staff meeting, in early June 1992, Professor Jones announced that those wishing to meet with him should let him know by e-mail what the meeting was to be about. This would ensure that all parties were prepared and the time spent in meetings efficiently used. Professor Jones followed his announcement by regularly informing staff on e-mail of the dates and agendas for meetings. Failure to read one's messages on any particular day could, thus, result in the faculty member not being aware that a meeting was to be held.

In early July 1992, immediately after the final teaching schedule for the second semester was printed and copies distributed to all faculty at UOT, Professor Lee, the head of the Corporate Accounting group and a recently elected Head of the Senate, called the President of UOT, requesting an urgent meeting. In the meeting Professor Lee complained about what he described as a "systematic marginalization of senior faculty members by Professor Jones". He listed several incidents in which senior members, including himself, were not informed in time of upcoming meetings and were consequently unable to attend those meetings. Motions passed in these meetings were then implemented, with little regard for missing faculty members' views and preferences.

The most recent and most disturbing incident which particularly infuriated Professor Lee was a meeting which was held only a week before and to which he, the group head, was not invited. During the meeting his teaching allocation for the next semester was decided in his absence. The decision would have required him to teach an undergraduate course that he did not consider himself qualified to teach even though he had taught it out of necessity in the past. According to Professor Lee, he never received the e-mail message that contained the date and venue for the meeting. Consequently, he scheduled another appointment, for that time and was impossible to reach by Ms. Carter when his group meeting was held.

Initially, Professor Lee was unaware that decisions regarding his teaching allocation and the teaching allocation of other members of his group were made in his absence. It was only when he saw the printed and final schedule for the second semester that he realised that Professor Jones, who chaired the meeting, actually overturned his previous decision, assigning one of his courses to a Junior Professor and expecting him, Professor Lee, to teach a large compulsory third year subject that he had not taught for years and did not feel qualified to teach. What infuriated Professor Lee the most was that the decision was made by Professor Jones in spite of the lengthy consultation they had on the matter. Professor Lee was convinced that the overturning of his decision was deliberate and reflected an attempt by Professor Jones to undermine his authority and destroy the unity of his group. He also saw the incident as reflecting a systematic strategy by Professor Jones to victimise and marginalise him and other senior members of the Department.

The President reassured Professor Lee that he would clarify the matters that he raised with Professor Jones. A meeting between the two followed a few days later. Even though the meeting took place behind closed doors, the rumour was that it developed into an ugly confrontation, culminating with Professor Jones' threat to resign. A letter of resignation from Professor Jones was submitted to the President the next day. By the end of the week, a formal announcement that the position of Chair of Accounting had been advertised was made by the President during a Senate meeting. Professor Lee was appointed as the interim Department Chair.

4 DISCUSSION

Technically, the diffusion and implementation of e-mail at the Department of Accounting was a great success. Within a relatively short period of time all members of the Department, including the "old guard" who were initially wary of the new technology, were using e-mail extensively. Thanks to Professor Jones' leadership, e-mail became the communication medium of choice, almost completely replacing all other communication technologies.

And yet what makes the case so interesting is that the technical success of e-mail was accompanied by unexpected political side effects. How can these political side effects be explained? Is there something that is inherent to e-mail which makes it particularly amenable to abusive political use by mangers? Was it a coincidence that by the end of the case study two individuals (the office trainee, and Professor Jones) were asked to leave the Department?

Earlier in the paper, at the end of the literature review, we proposed a series of assertions about the relationship between e-mail and petty tyranny. In the following sections we go back to these assertions and see to what extent they have been supported by the data in the case.

Assertion 1. - E-mail's features can lend themselves to different types of political mis-use by petty tyrants.

What features of e-mail were used politically in the case?

A recent publication by Romm and Pliskin (1995) outlines five distinct features of e-mail that can lend themselves to political usages. Applied to the case study in the previous sections, these features were manifested in the following ways:

Speed - Romm and Pliskin (1995) define this feature of e-mail as the fact that messages transmitted on e-mail can reach their destination, whether it is in the other room or the other side of the globe, in a relatively short period of time. They maintain that this feature can have significant political implications, particularly when communication with large groups of people is involved. In our case, the speed of e-mail made it possible for Professor Jones to convene meetings at short notice, including the one which Professor Lee was unaware of. The speed of e-mail was also the major feature which allowed Professor Jones to use e-mail to control his secretaries comings and goings.

Multiple Addressability - Romm and Pliskin (1995) define this feature as the capacity to send an e-mail message instantaneously and simultaneously to a large group of individuals within and outside an organisation. This feature too is considered of utmost political importance. In our case the multiple Addressability feature lent itself to several political uses. First, it enabled Professor Lee's secretary to organise meetings on his behalf at a relatively short notice, keeping all faculty members hooked to their computers in fear that they might miss an important message. As a result, this feature endowed Professor Jones with enormous power as the centre of most communication activities in the Department.

Recordability - Romm and Pliskin (1995) define this feature of e-mail as the capacity to store e-mail messages in a data base for transmission or processing at a later point in time. This feature allows political actors to collect e-mail messages (that may not have political significance when they are received) for future use when circumstances have changed to make the information politically useful. In our case, the recordability feature of e-mail was utilised by Professor Jones in his "campaign of terror" against the secretaries. Being able to record the exact time in which they responded to his messages (particularly the ones left late the previous night) made it possible for him to keep accurate track of their comings and goings. The e-mail "evidence" then allowed him to reprimand and even fire one of the secretaries for failure to meet his demands.

Processing - Romm and Pliskin (1995) define this feature of e-mail as the capacity to modify the content and structure of e-mail messages by the receiver prior to transmitting them to others. This feature allows political actors to add comments to data previously collected, thus turning neutral messages into highly politically explosive ones. In our case, the processing feature of e-mail was utilised when Professor Jones sent a copy of Professor Carol's message to Professor Lee, with an attachment that indicated that he took the matter seriously and was going to intervene on Professor Carol's behalf.

Routing - Romm and Pliskin (1995) define this feature of e-mail as the capacity of senders to transmit messages to selected groups of addressees whose names may or may not appear as receivers of copies. This feature allows senders to transmit slightly (but significantly) modified messages to individuals who supposedly receive the same message. It can also allow senders to re-transmit messages to individuals that the original sender did not wish to share the message with. These uses obviously have strong political implications. In our case, the routing feature of e-mail may have been exploited when Professor Lee was the only person in the Department not to receive a copy of the invitation to the group meeting. Our interviews with the different members of the Department failed to establish what actually happened to the message that Professor Jones claimed he sent to Professor Lee and Professor Lee claimed he never received. In theory, three explanations are possible. One is that Professor Lee lied about not receiving the message. Another explanation is that he deleted the message by mistake, without actually reading it. Finally, and most plausibly, considering the circumstances of the case, there is the possibility that the message was, indeed, never sent, reflecting a deliberate attempt by Professor Jones to "route" the message, whereby, excluding Professor Lee from the decision making process of his group.

Assertion 2. - Petty tyranny through e-mail can have devastating effects on subordinates.

What effects did the use of e-mail by Professor Jones have on his subordinates?

From the case we learn of several effects that Professor Jones abuse of e-mail had on his subordinates. First, Professor Jones used e-mail to keep a record of employees' comings and goings, particularly his secretaries. As a result of this practice the secretaries did improve their punctuality and productivity. However, this improvement was achieved at a high price. One of the secretaries, who was unable to adjust to the new work environment, was fired. The others worked under increased stress and were highly frustrated and resentful of their new boss.

Another abusive use of e-mail by Professor Jones involved the discouragement (through e-mail) of employees from using any other form of communication with him. As demonstrated by the incident with Professor Carol, e-mail was used by Professor Jones to create a "psychological distance" between himself and his subordinates. This ploy did not only annoy and frustrate employees but also caused a reduction in productivity as employees were forced to waste enormous amount of time on futile (but necessary) attempts to establish face to face contact with Professor Jones.

Finally, and most importantly, Professor Jones used e-mail in order to selectively screen information, making some of it available only to individuals that he wanted to share it with. Whether Professor Jones did or did not send the invitation to Professor Lee, it is clear from the case that he made full political use of the fact that Professor Lee was not in the room when the meeting was held. In the short term, this manipulation resulted in Professor Lee being out-manoeuvred, and if it were not for his own counter-attack, being forced to teach a course that he felt unqualified to teach. It was only Professor Lee's political clout in UOT that made it possible for him to turn the table on Professor Jones and eventually use the incident to force Professor Jones out of the Department.

Going back to the literature on petty tyrants, there is no question that Professor Jones uses of e-mail in this case and the devastating effects that these uses had on his subordinates are examples of petty tyranny. From the research on petty tyranny we learn that tyrannical behaviour by managers tends to have the following effects on subordinates(Ashforth, 1994):

Petty tyranny tends to be associated with low leadership endorsement. In our case, and perhaps because he was a new Chair, Professor Jones was definitely not endorsed by the majority of the members of his department, which led to his eventual dismissal.

Petty tyranny tends to foster employees' frustration, stress, and reactance. In our case, as indicated in the previous sections, Professor Jones' manipulations of e-mail have resulted in employees' frustration, stress, and at least in Professor Lee's case, reactance.

Petty tyranny tends to lead to employees' helplessness and work alienation. In our case, perhaps because Professor Jones was not around long enough, helplessness and alienation have not developed. Given more time, and considering Professor Jones' leadership style, it is most likely that such phenomena would have developed.

Petty tyranny tends to undermine employees' self esteem and consequently decrease performance. As indicated in the previous sections, our case contains several examples of the negative effects of Professor Jones' behaviour on employees' self esteem and consequently their performance.

Petty tyranny may undermine social unit cohesiveness. In our case, the conflict that erupted between Professor Lee and Professor Carol has been indirectly fuelled by Professor Jones. Under the guise of "the arbitrator", he managed to pit the two professors against each other, and indirectly undermine the unity of their group.

Assertion 3. - The use of e-mail for petty tyranny has far reaching implications for Information Systems research and practice.

What are the theoretical and practical implications from this research?

The first and most important theoretical implication is that e-mail should be considered a technology with **strong political potency**, possibly stronger than any other communication technology that is currently utilised in organisations. In this paper we have mostly discussed the potential that e-mail has for **negative** uses, i.e., uses that conflict with employees' welfare and as a consequence with the organisational long term productivity. There are, however, quite a few other, potentially beneficial and yet political uses of e-mail. Among these the most important are employees' individual political empowerment and coalition building. Sproull and Kiesler (1991) in a landmark research on e-mail's social effect in organisations listed the democratising effect of e-mail as one of its most socially promising features, asserting that through e-mail employees at the bottom of the organisation can gain immediate and unfiltered access to top management.

This study has described one incident in which e-mail was utilised for mostly negative political purposes. Based on one case, which occurred in a given organisational and cultural context, this paper is obviously unable to chart the range of political activities, negative or positive, that e-mail can lend itself to. It remains for future research to establish the boundaries of the political activities possible on e-mail across different industries and different cultural backgrounds. It also remains for future research to establish the effect of the merging of technologies (e-mail with Fax, e-mail with teleconferencing) on the political uses of office technologies.

Another important issue that is raised by this research is that e-mail, by virtue of its political potency can increase tensions between conflicting factions in an organisation. It should be noted that the data that has been presented here cannot conclusively **prove** that e-mail caused the events in the case. The tensions between Professor Jones, the new Department Chair, and the Department "old guard", represented by Professor Lee, may have existed before e-mail was introduced and abused. It is plausible to assume, however, that e-mail's presence brought the tensions that were already in existence in the Department to a head, with devastating results to all concerned.

The fact that e-mail's effect cannot be "proven" as the one factor explaining the events in the case is supported by recent theoretical assertions by Soh and Markus (1995) and by Robey (1995). As indicated by Soh and Markus (1995) cause and effect relationships are often impossible to demonstrate in IS research. Theories of process which focus on **necessary** conditions that bring about a given result are therefore preferable to theories of variance which focus on **sufficient** conditions that may or may not bring about a given result. A similar point is raised by Robey (1995, p. 61) who indicates that "Efforts to encompass contradiction in theory reveal the difficulty and futility of making simple predictions about the organisational consequences of information technology". Following this assertion, Robey advocates the adoption of less simplistic theories that put less emphasis on significant empirical associations between variables and more emphasis on plausible explanations of observed phenomena.

Finally, this study raises a series of intriguing ethical dilemmas for researchers and practitioners interested in the organisational implications of office technology. As indicated in the case, e-mail can be used by management to control and abuse employees. In extreme cases, such as the one described here, e-mail can be exploited to significantly affect employees' well being. What should be the role of IS practitioners in such cases? Should IS practitioners advise managers **against** the use of e-mail for abusive purposes? Should such advice be made part of managers' and employees' training on how to use e-mail? Should IS professionals interfere when e-mail is used for negative purposes? It remains for the IS profession and society as a whole to debate and perhaps legislate the use and abuse of e-mail in organisations.

5 REFERENCES

Adorno, T. W., Frenkel-Brunswik, E, Levinson, D. J. and Sanford, R. N. (1950) *The Authoritarian Personality*, Harper and Row, New York.

Ashforth, B. E. (1994) Petty Tyranny in Organizations, *Human Relations*, **47**, 7, 755-78.

Culnan, M. J. and Markus, M. L., (1987), Information Technologies: Electronic Media and Interorganizational Communication, In F. M. Jablin, L. L. Putnam, K. H. Roberts, and L. W. Porter (Eds.), *Handbook of Organisational Communication: An Interdisciplinary Perspective*, Sage Publications, Newbury Park, CA., pp. 420-43.

Eveland, J. D. and Bikson, T. K., (1988), Work Group Structures and Computer Support: A Field Experiment, *ACM Transactions on Office Information Systems*, **6**, 4, 354-79.

Feather, N. T. (1971) Value Differences in Relation to Ethnocentrism, Intolerance of Ambiguity and Dogmatism, *Personality*, **2**, 349-66.

Goffman, E. (1961) *Asylums: Essays on the Social Situation of Mental Patients and Other Inmates*, Anchor Books, New York.

Haney, C., Banks, C. and Zimbardo, P. (1973) Interpersonal Dynamics in a Simulated Prison, *International Journal of Criminology and Penology*, **1**, 69-97.

Hofstede, G. (1978) The Poverty of Management Control Philosophy", *Academy of Management Review*, **3**, 450-61.

House, R. J. (1988) Power and Personality in Complex Organizations, in B. M. Staw and L. I. Cummings (Eds.) *Research in Organizational Behaviour* (Vol. 10). Greenwich, CT: JAI Press, pp. 305-57.

Janis, I. L. (1982) Decision Making Under Stress, in L. Goldberger and S. Breznitz (Eds.), *Handbook of Stress: Theoretical and Clinical Aspects*. New York, Free Press, pp. 69-87.

Kets de Vries, M. F. R. (1989) *Prisoners of Leadership*. New York, Wiley.

Kipnis, D. (1976) *The Power holders*. Chicago, University of Chicago Press.

Kling, R. (1978) Automated Welfare Client Tracking and Service Integration: The Political Economy of Computing, *Communication of the ACM* (June), 484-93.

Kling, R. (1980) Social Analysis of Computing: Theoretical Perspectives in Recent Empirical Research, *Comput. Surv*, **12**, 1, 61-110.

Lee, R. T., and Ashforth, B. E. (1993) A Longitudinal Study of Burnout Among Supervisors and Managers: Comparisons Between Leiter and Maslach (1988) and Golembiewski et al (1986) models, *Organizational Behaviour and Human Decision Processes*, **54**, 369-98.

Markus, M. L., (1981) Implementation Politics - Top Management Support and IS Involvement, *Systems, Objectives, Solutions*, pp. 203-15.

Markus, M. L. (1983) Power, Politics, and MIS Implementation, *Communications of the ACM*, **26**, 6, 430-44.

Markus, M. L., (1994), Electronic Mail as a Medium of Managerial Choice, *Organization Science*, 5, 4, 502-27.

Markus, M. L. and Robey, D., (1983), The Organizational Validity of Management Information Systems, *Human Relations*, **36**, 3, 203-26.

Markus, M. L. and Robey, D. (1988) Informational Technology and Organizational Change: Causal Structure in Theory and Research, *Management Science*, **34**, 5 (May), 583-94.

Maslach, C. (1982) *Burnout: The Cost of Caring*, Prentice Hall, New York.

McGregor, D.(1960) *The Human Side of Enterprise*. McGraw Hill, New York.

Mintzberg, H. (1989) *Mintzberg on Management: Inside Our Strange World of Organizations*. Free Press, New York.

Mulder, M. De Jong, R. D., Koppelaar, L., and Verhage, J. (1986) Power, Situation, and Leaders' Effectiveness: An Organizational Field Study, *Journal of Applied Psychology*, **71**, 566-70.

Norton, R. W. (1975) Measurement of Ambiguity Tolerance. *Journal of Personality Assessment*, **39**, 607-19.

Pliskin, N., (1989), Interacting with Electronic Mail can be a Dream or a Nightmare: a User's Point of View, *Interacting with Computers*, **1**, 3, 259-72.

Pliskin, N., Ball, L. D., and Curley, K. F., (1989), Impediments to Proliferation of Electronic Mail: A Study from the Users' Perspective, *Human Systems Management*, **8**, 3, 233-41.

Pliskin, N. and Romm, T., (1990), Design of Charging Mechanisms According to the Interaction between Information Technology Type and Diffusion Life cycle Phase, Database, **21**, 3, 34-40.

Pliskin, N., Romm, T., Lee, A. S., and Weber, Y., (1993), Presumed versus Actual Organizational Culture: Managerial Implications for Implementation of Information Systems, *The Computer Journal*, **36**, 2, 1-10.

Ray, J. J. (1981) Authoritarianism, Dominance, and Assertiveness. *Journal of Personality Assessment*, **45**, 390-97.

Robey, D. (1995) , Theories that Explain Contradiction: Accounting for the Contradictory Organizational Consequences of Information Technology, in *Proceedings of the Sixth International Conference on Information Systems* (ed. J. I. DeGross, G. Ariav, C. Beath, R. Hoyer, and C. Kemerer), Amsterdam.

Romm, C. T. and Pliskin, N. (1995) Virtual Politicking: Toward a Theory of E-mail Use for Political Purposes Within and Between Organisations", forthcoming in *The Handbook of Administrative Communication* (Eds. J. L. Garnett and A. Kouzmin) Marcel Dekker, New York.

Romm, T., Pliskin, N., Weber, Y., and Lee, A. S., (1991) Identifying Organizational Culture Clash in MIS Implementation: When is it Worth the Effort?, *Information & Management*, **21**, 99-109.

Sproull, R., and Kiesler, S. (1991), (eds.), *Connections: New Ways of Working in the Network,* MIT Press, Cambridge, MA.

Soh, C. and Markus, M. L. (1995) How IT Creates Business Value, in *Proceedings of the Sixth International Conference on Information Systems* (ed. J. I. DeGross, G. Ariav, C. Beath, R. Hoyer, and C. Kemerer), Amsterdam.

Thompson, V. A. (1960) *Modern Organization.* Alfred A. Knopt, New York.

6 BIOGRAPHIES

Dr Celia Romm is an Associate Professor and Director of the HRM/OB specialisation at the Department of Management, the University of Wollongong, Australia. She received her Ph.D. in Applied Psychology from the University of Toronto, Canada. She has been a lecturer, consultant, and visiting scholar in Israel, Japan, Germany, Canada, and Australia. Her research interests lie in the areas of organisational power and politics, human resources decision support systems, the impact of communication technologies on organisations, and marketing of higher education. Dr. Romm published in such journals as Human Relations, Organisation Studies, Comparative Economic Studies, Information and Management, The Computer Journal, Database, The Journal of Information Systems Management, The Australian Journal of Information Systems, The Asia Pacific Journal of Human Resources, Higher Education, European Journal of Education, Interchange, and Management Education and Development.

Dr. Nava Pliskin is an Associate Professor at the Department of Industrial Engineering and Management at the Ben-Gurion University of the Negev, Israel. She holds a Ph.D. degree from Harvard University. Her research interests lie in the areas of management information technologies and the organisational implications of Information Systems' implementation (e.g. Power, Culture etc.). Dr. Pliskin published in such journals as Information and Management, Database, Human Systems Management, Information and Software Technology, Interacting with Computers, IEEE Transactions on Engineering Management, and the Journal of Information Systems Management.

20

Distributed work and client/server computing: issues from the field

S Sawyer
and
R . Southwick
School of Information Studies
Syracuse University
Syracuse, NY 13244-4100
Tel: 315-443-4473, Fax: 315-443-5806
Email: ssawyer@syr.edu, rmsouthw@syr.edu

Abstract

One of information technology's most alluring promises lies in its potential for enabling knowledge work. The evolution of distributed computing has created an opportunity for knowledge workers to customize their rapidly evolving computing environment. In this new environment, highly sophisticated information tools are being brought directly into the hands of the office worker. It is widely believed that client/server (C/S) is the technology which will enable the successful implementation of distributed computing infrastructures. However, C/S is not yet mature: tools and application are developing and adapting to client requirements as the process of building the C/S infrastructure occurs. Moreover, it represents a paradigmatic movement away from the traditional, centralized models of computing (i.e., the mainframe). These factors suggest that the implementation of C/S may bear a unique set of technical and organizational implications. In this paper we set forth some of the issues drawn from data collected in an ongoing, longitudinal study of information technology (IT) implementation at a mid-sized academic institution. This organization is in the midst of a multi-year project to migrate from a mainframe to a client/server computing environment. Issues derived thus far include the following: (1) C/S Implementation managers are currently 'straddling' the mainframe and C/S environments; (2) the C/S initiative appears to be primarily driven by technology; (3) the 'mindset' (mental models, cognitive processes) based on the mainframe model is still the basis for most clients (users), many developers, and some administrators; (4) there are unresolved issues of 'power' between IS managers, data custodians, and users; (5) there is a general trend toward distributed means of communication between members of the organization; and, (6) there is a growing awareness that end-user involvement is more time-consuming than expected.

Keywords

Organizational change, client/server, computing infrastructure

1 INTRODUCTION

One of information technology's most alluring promises lies in its potential for enabling knowledge work (Drucker, 1994; Sproull & Kielser, 1991). Dramatic advances in network technologies have made distributed forms of computing a practical reality for many of today's organizations (Hall, 1994). These distributed models have, in turn, spawned the development of new ways for members of organizations to accomplish their work: in forms of working together - individually and collaboratively - and in the types of work undertaken. Highly sophisticated information tools (for retrieval, storage, manipulation and communication) are brought directly into the hands of the office worker. In this rapidly evolving computing environment, knowledge workers are gaining increased levels of empowerment through their ability to access information, and control and customize their workplace.

Clearly, in this dynamic computing environment, there are a broad new spectrum of technical and organizational issues which will impact the management of work (Sproull and Kiesler, 1991). A considerable body of literature has accumulated which documents the ways in which information technology (IT) may affect both the physical forms and the work processes of organizations (Holsapple and Luo, 1995). Additionally, authors such as Orlikowski (1991) have pointed to the potential of IT to also enable cultural or social changes such as the redistribution of organizational 'power' or 'control'. She and others (e.g. Zuboff, 1988) portray this phenomenon as a 'flattening' of the traditional hierarchical organizational structure which results from a broadened access to strategic information among lower management and non-management organizational members. These literatures provide a basis for understanding the dynamic relationship between organizations and information technologies and may be extended to new distributed forms of computing.

In a distributed environment, data, hardware, software, and computer users form an interactive computing network - often across large geographic areas; computing functions are typically processed by more than one computer and control over processing is decentralized (Hall, 1994). In contrast to the traditional mainframe computing model, distributed models of computing seek to use the combined processing capability and storage of each computer that is connected to the network rather than giving exclusive control to a centralized master computer (i.e., the mainframe). The growth of the distributed environment is driven by the increased processing capabilities of desktop computers and the dynamic growth of network technologies.

The emergence of distributed models of computing may have important technical and organizational implications. First, it represents a paradigmatic change in the focus of computer technology. A "computer" must now be thought of as a network of components rather than as a singular piece of hardware. IBM's (a name synonymous with the mainframe) CEO, Louis Gerstner - in elaborating his 'network-centric' vision of computing, states:

The first wave of computing, 30 years ago, was driven by the technologies of host-based processors [mainframes] and storage devices. Twenty years later, we moved into a second wave, which was driven by microprocessors and simplified operating systems. The third wave [current wave] of computing is being driven by very powerful networked technologies that provide very inexpensive and very wide [communications] bandwidth. (Business Week, 1995, p. 152).

Second, as alluded to above, the inherent potential for a more 'democratic' access to information may create a unique set of management issues as distributed computing architectures are adopted by organizations.

It is widely believed that client/server (C/S) is the technology which will enable the successful implementation of distributed computing infrastructures. However, while C/S may represent the 'future' of computing, it is difficult to provide a precise definition. For the purposes of this paper we focus on C/S as software processes operating cooperatively, yet independently, in a peer-to-peer relationship. The client is the initiator of data interchange in this relationship, issuing requests for information as needed to the server or to other clients (Hall, 1994). In this view, C/S is one form of distributed computing.

Despite the rapid growth of client/server, little research has accumulated which highlights the issues inherent to implementing a C/S computing architecture. In this paper we set forth some of the issues, and our views, drawn on the data collected from our ongoing study being conducted at a mid-sized academic institution (pseudonym 'Mid-Sized University' or MSU). The primary goal of this three year, longitudinal, field-based study (in progress) is to chronicle the organizational activities related to the move from the existing mainframe architecture to a client/server architecture.

Because the technical aspects of C/S are in a dynamic state, we expect that there will be concurrent changes in the social environment of the organization (MSU) as well. There is little empirical data -- or even stories or anecdotes -- on organizational use of C/S as a computing infrastructure. And, as the technical constraints to access and distribution of data are removed, the social adaptations (organizational rules, departmental procedures, informal processes, and individual methods) to using C/S will be critical in forming the new ways of working in this interconnected environment. Thus, the change to a C/S infrastructure provides a unique perspective on how technology evolves, along with the social system in which it sits, as new ways of working arise. Stephen Barley (1986) said of his study of medical imaging technology: '...technology provides an occasion to structure.' We see the change to client server technology as an occasion to restructure at MSU.

Our focus in this research is on the reciprocal interactions and effects generated as a consequence of the change in computing infrastructure from mainframe-based to client/server-based, and the consequential changes within the organization. Our perspective on technology posits an interdependent relationship of negotiation between technology and the social structures within the organization. It is possible to adopt a framework for the study of organizational computing focusing on either of these perspectives independently. In other words, one may assume either a technological perspective in which technological change is viewed as driving the organizational structure, or an organizational perspective in which organizational needs determine technological innovation and implementation (Holsapple & Luo, 1995). However, we feel that change is best understood by viewing both in their interaction.

Following on the work of Goodman and Sproull (1989) we see any technology (such as client/server) as being a system best described by the social and structural, as well as the technological issues which it comprises. While the technical challenges to building a successful infrastructure are critical and often daunting (Desai, 1995), we have chosen to focus on the social and structural issues in this stage of research. Our emphasis on the social and structural issues stems from our desire to better understand the use of C/S. Technical issues, in this context, are the basis for organizational decisions. In this paper we address:

How the managers (administrators) are adapting to the organizational changes (intended and unintended) brought on by the new computing infrastructure.

How the technologists (those who support and run the system) are adapting to the new infrastructure's demands.

We do not actively portray the end-user's perspective. Instead, we focus on how the technologists and managers are adapting to the changes brought about by the C/S implementation. In doing so, however, end-user issues are revealed as central to both technologists and managers.

We believe that MSU's mainframe to client/server initiative offers a unique opportunity to study a phenomenon of relevance to the IT planning of many organizations. What follows in this paper is a brief historical background of the academic institution and a review of the theoretical and methodological bases for the study. We devote the bulk of this paper to some of the more salient issues derived from the data collected to this point. We also highlight our views on these issues.

2 THE RESEARCH SETTING - MSU

MSU is a private Carnegie Level II research school. It has a strong national and international reputation with high name recognition. MSU's administrative and organizational structures are typical for US universities of nearly 20,000 students. Employing nearly 3500 people, MSU is located on a large campus near the edge of a medium-sized city in the Northeastern US.

By 1993 three environmental factors created a context that demanded attention. MSU's vice-president for computing (CIO), who managed both research and academic computing systems, faced: (1) an increasing demand on the mainframe systems; (2) a restrictive reliance on outdated legacy systems; and (3) a nearly unmanageable tangle of administrative and academic networks with overlapping links and disparate technologies. The constant evolution of available technology, a given in the computing business, is a fourth factor implicitly reflected in these other three issues.

The MSU also has several long-term contracts with vendors who support their legacy database products. Over the nearly 20 years these systems have served the university (primarily the administrative side of the organization), the constraints of the database systems and the cost of their upkeep have grown ever more limiting. Since these contracts are on a fixed cycle, the CIO wanted to affect infrastructure changes to coincide with the next renewal (Fall 1997).

The constrained service provided by the administrative systems (mainframe-centered and database-specific) has contributed to a growth in local/departmental systems to support administrative computing. On the academic system side, the research computing network has always been decentralized at the school and departmental level. These local networks have been growing in number, expanding in size, and linking together. This has resulted in a systemic, but chaotic, expansion of departmental and research center computing infrastructure. This expansion, compounded with the increasing popularity of the Internet makes the strain on the computing infrastructure even more apparent. The proliferation of these local area networks is occurring even as the centralized administrative systems grow closer to being fully taxed.

MSU's issues with computing -- increasing demands on the mainframe, restrictive legacy systems, and explosive network growth -- are typical of most academic computing systems (Alpert, 1985). Facing this scenario MSU's CIO made the decision to revamp the computing infrastructure to take advantage of the new C/S architecture. As the CIO reflected this was, 'as much a decision on saving money as it was freeing ourselves from commitments we no longer wanted.' The steady rise in demand on the mainframes (processor time) was increasing faster than MSU could afford to upgrade. Since the software and service costs for MSU's mainframes were tied directly to the processors, any increase in processing power led to direct cost increases for existing software/services. In this period, MSU's IS staff was in regular contact with dozens of similar institutions that were facing the same issues. Regular contact between these organizations provided the CIO some of his information to aid in deciding on the C/S move. As he said, ' I am in regular contact with others in my same position, often on a weekly basis. We just decided to push ahead.'

The MSU's issues with computing also typify many non-academic organizations who face similar decisions about improving their computing infrastructure (Kling, 1990). Public entities such as governmental offices and utilities and for-profit organizations such as manufacturing and financial services are all confronted with constant pressure on the computing infrastructure. Moreover, the computing infrastructure of these organizations is an increasingly important aspect of the organizational operations. Recent estimates show that expenditures for computing systems average 8.4% of annual operating budgets. This percentage has been trending steadily upward since the inception of computer technology, and shows no signs of shrinking in the foreseeable future (Information Week, 1995).

As with many other mid to large organizations, much of the administrative work at MSU demands interaction between departments; the interdepartmental work is often an information intensive effort: for instance, as many as 12 views of a student's record may exist in disparate databases across MSU's campus; the work demands a high degree of knowledge and competency. Also, MSU's employees represent a mix of temporary and long-term employees. This arrangement, long an academic standard, is becoming increasingly popular with the modern organization. The core staff knows how to do their work -- and who to speak with to get that work done. With the changing computing infrastructure, the ways in which these workers accomplish their jobs will evolve as the C/S systems are understood and used.

3 CONDUCTING THE STUDY

3.1 Method and plan

The criteria which led to approaching MSU for this study center on the opportunity to observe the infrastructure change as it occurs. Since MSU has just begun this process, we can take the journey with the managers, technologists, and workers who are writing the story by their actions. In her book, In the Age of the Smart Machine, Shoshana Zuboff (1988, p.423) began the discussion of her methodology by saying: 'Behind every method is a belief.' Our belief is that in situ field work is an excellent method, well-suited for the type of research which seeks to understand the evolving process of implementing new technologies. This approach is becoming more common among present researchers. There has been an increased interest in longitudinal, field-based, and observer-centered research for the study of IT in organizations (Kling, 1980; Markus and Robey, 1988; Lee, 1995). This renewed interest has many reasons. Two of the most salient are (1) the limitations on what we know about technology's effects in organizations and (2) the speed at which technology changes. These issues echo the discussion by Ven de Ven and Huber (1990) as they introduce a special issue of Organization Science focused on longitudinal research methods. Our added focus is to use the change in technology (viz., implementation of C/S) as an opportunity to observe change in the organization.

We are pursuing a four-phased program of research (see Figure 1). The first stage has served to help us establish a context. This has included developing a history of the effort at MSU and of the people and organizational issues which have played a role in the genesis of the client/server initiative. It also serves as the context for interpreting the events and actions of the respondents as the infrastructure change occurs. The subsequent three phases are actually parallel tracks. Each of these phases centers on one group of participants. The first is the management team, which includes managers from across MSU. The second is the technology implementation team. This team includes both IS employees and users. This team also interacts with the management team and the work groups. The third team is a work group. This work group interacts with the technologists and is represented by their manager in the managerial group. The three follow-on phases of research focus on distinct levels and draw from the work of the first phase. Thus, the program of research provides the opportunity to triangulate findings across these three phases. In this paper we speak only of the data collected during our first phase.

3.2 Data collection

We have employed two primary methods for collecting data: interviewing and observation. Interviews vary by level of structure with most being semi-structured and open-ended. Typically these are taped and transcribed. Field notes are the data drawn from observation (as unobtrusive observer; as participant in committees and meetings; and through informal social interaction). There are two types of field notes for each period of observation: the first is a chronology of events and actions; the second is a more free-flowing account of perceptions, stories and anecdotes. The first serves as a record of observations. The second serves as a record of the observer's perceptions. We also have access to the formal documents and archives of the C/S change. This includes the email traffic, work records and archival memos and reports.

The mainframe to client/server project was initiated by MSU in February 1993. We began our research effort in February 1995. To date our activities have centered on participation with, and observations of, committees formed to work on specific aspects of the C/S initiative; ongoing interviews with managers (IS and other); and documentation collection. This includes more than 60 hours of meetings and over 20 interviews (averaging about 65 minutes each). We also have accumulated more than 180 documents (email, memos, handouts, and reports) and nearly 40 telephone conversations.

4 PRESENT ANALYSIS AND FINDINGS

As a result of these activities we have been able to conduct some preliminary analysis of the data. Our analysis has been developed through an iterative process of reflection and summarizing of the observations and interview notes. Source documents (memos, etc.) provided secondary support. In this section we describe some of our observations and discuss how each may be seen within the larger context of the organization and, more specifically, the C/S initiative (i.e., as 'issues').

4.1 C/S implementation managers are currently 'straddling' the mainframe and C/S environments

As with most IT implementations, the move from mainframe to C/S at the MSU involves a gradual transition from one system to the other with considerable system overlap and gray area (in contrast to 'pulling the plug' on one system and 'plugging in' the other). This duality in the computing infrastructure has the effect of creating parallel roles for the IS managers; especially for those who are most heavily involved in affecting the change. On the one hand they are actively involved in the strategic planning and various implementation issues of the C/S initiative. At the same time they must concern themselves with the day-to-day tactical decisions of the existing mainframe environment. A consequence of this added responsibility is that many of the high-level IS managers perceive that they are confronted with more work than they can handle. This is a matter of complexity as well as of work load. Not only is C/S technology new and rapidly changing, it also requires an alternative mode of thinking (i.e., new mental models) in problem solving.

Inherent in this dilemma is the risk that in focusing their efforts on the these technical issues, the IS managers may lose sight of their role as agents of change. For instance, this issue is apparent in the relationship between IS managers and their programming staff. It is important for the managers to both instill a sense of the importance in adopting C/S development techniques and at the same time to get the tasks at hand completed (largely mainframe related). Some IS managers have expressed a concern that some of their staff (i.e., some programmers) are reluctant to adopt the C/S model.

It is apparent that the amount of learning, the time to affect the transition, and the various sources of resistance are much larger and more persistent than expected. For instance, for those involved directly in the cross-over from mainframe to C/S, present roles include:

Learning new system(s) and the processes, methods, tools, applications, while building and maintaining this infrastructure. This is very close-to-home for some, looming as an issue for others, and tangential to a few.

Maintaining the present infrastructure. This varies from department to department. When (1) and (2) overlap it is the most difficult.

Acting as change agents with those who are involved in the transition at the present time. This seems to be more unexpected and difficult than anticipated.

Educating users of the new infrastructure.

The transition from mainframe to C/S has had differing effects on managers depending on their level of involvement and general attitude toward change. For many of the highly involved IS managers, enthusiasm for change at the outset (or soon after) has often given way to a sense of sisyphusian effort: the C/S rock never gets to the top of the change hill. Other IS managers have articulated that the changes will affect them at some point, but at present it has not. Their interest seems to be focused on minimizing the issues of change until they occur. Still other IS managers see this changeover as a way to expand and update the skills of their people and remain positive about the ultimate success of the new technology.

4.2 The C/S initiative appears to be primarily driven by technology at this point

As participants in meetings of the high level managers, we have observed that technical issues tend to predominate. This is not surprising, as C/S is a technology that is rapidly evolving, but also rapidly changing. Therefore, there is a high level of uncertainty inherent in all the decision-making, both at a tactical and at a strategic level. When asked to provide some definition or personal interpretation of C/S during interviews, IS managers were generally vague. We interpret this, first, to the inherent ambiguity that is found in even the technical definitions provided in the literature. However, we also believe that this also reflects a state of mind toward the C/S initiative that is, in a sense, pre-conceptual. In other words, concrete technical issues rather than the broader organizational issues are currently at the fore in the minds of IS managers.

The entire project is based on a strategic decision which assumes that C/S will become the predominant model (based on criteria which are largely technical). We perceive there to be a significant element of risk to the project if IS managers continue to be bogged down in technical issues and ignore user/organizational requirements. This risk is very real as we may expect the nascent C/S technology (i.e., the development tools and miscellaneous software) to lag behind the user requirements - at least in the near future. This problem is further complicated by the fact that many of these requirements have been previously established and structured within the culture of the mainframe model and may not match or be appropriate within the C/S model. Other requirements have emerged as part of the promise or mythology of the distributed model (of which C/S is a part) - e.g., distributed multimedia - and may be difficult to deliver given current technological constraints.

The IS managers have been willing to make project plans based on assumption that new tools will become available as they are needed. A project strategy ('official' or de facto) which makes such assumptions - i.e., a reliance on the marketplace - may bear a degree of risk. Relying on the market may ultimately be successful, but not within the hoped-for time-line. This demands a high level of flexibility and a constant change to project plans for staffing.

A more sinister outcome of such a strategy, may be a creeping loss of credibility toward the administration and the technology by the clients if the technology doesn't 'work' within the current organizational environment. In light of the current state of the (C/S) 'art', it is critical that administrators, managers, and developers not allow their focus to become so narrow that they are only concerned with fixing technology and not staying aware of user requirements and problems. It will be especially important to maintain good lines of communication between technologists and clients. In the same vein, we believe that training initiatives may be especially important in convincing clients to 'buy in' to the C/S initiative.

In sum, it is important that IS managers become active agents of change in their interactions with clients. This may present a challenge to them to the degree that it conflicts with their present identity within the organization (i.e., as technologist). It may require that they be much more interdependent, much more aware of the holistic issues with systems, and much less independent.

4.3 The 'mindset' (mental models, cognitive processes) based on the mainframe model is still the basis for most clients (users), many developers, and some administrators

This cognitive state has evolved through an ongoing (iterative) interaction between technology and people. As such, it has been strongly reified and is well established. C/S is disruptive to this world. This condition makes change difficult as people are 'speaking different languages.'

On the client side, this causes a problem with the 'requirements', which may be rooted in the mainframe model. For example, one of the many committees organized in response to the C/S initiative generated a list of recommendations intended to facilitate the seamless transition from mainframe to C/S at the organizational level. One of their recommendations was that printing continue to be done in a central location. This recommendation runs in direct conflict with the perceived (by IS) advantages of the C/S model - i.e., this (distributed printing) is the type of thing that C/S enables. This illustrates the inherent conflict between a new technology and the structured work practices of an organization.

4.4 There are unresolved issues of 'power' between IS managers, data custodians, and users

A tenet of distributed computing is that users (clients) become more 'empowered'. They are able to make greater use of their desktop computers. The desktop becomes 'smarter,' allowing the user a greater access to information. However, in such an environment, how will the user be 'controlled'? Will controls be implemented through technology or management? If a technology approach is taken (exclusively), by concentrating primarily on ways to restrict user access, there is a risk that users will not 'buy into' the program. In which case, they will try to circumvent controls (rules) whenever it is possible or convenient. This is a real possibility because: (1) There are significant issues with access, security and control which are presently unsolved in the current state of C/S software - it is less evolved and far more complex than mainframe solutions in maintaining controls (security); (2) it must be remembered that - first and foremost - the clients have a job to do and are likely to take the path of least resistance.

Bottom line: a management approach to control must accompany a technology approach. The way to implementing a management approach to control is through a process of making the clients adopt 'responsibility'. That is, they must be made aware of the risks involved, and be made responsible for the consequences (personally as well as administratively). Toward this end, a program of education and training would seem to be critical. However, it is remains unclear as to the level of financial support and general commitment the administration wishes to provide such an effort. Most key technical decisions about topology and infrastructure are still controlled by IS, and as we have discussed, the primary focus of attention remains on technical issues. Interestingly, it also is unclear whether the user community understands the implications of these decisions or has any ability to involve themselves in these decisions if they did.

Another aspect of control seems to be that, while the IS directors are quite comfortable in discussing and sharing issues and decision-making, this does not seem to occur at lowers levels in each department. Most issues are coordinated through the managers. The informal coordination at the lower levels -- across departments -- may be increasing. For instance, the various standing committees have cross-departmental membership. Often, though, this is the only time many of these people converse.

4.5 There is a general trend toward distributed means of communication between members of the organization

Despite the lower level of informal cross-departmental communication in the IS departments, the increased level of distributed communication (email, voice mail) is very noticeable. This may have several sources independent of the C/S effort (geographically distributed locations, more use of these communication media in general). However, three C/S-driven effects are noticeable. First, the increased interdependence between clients and IS demands more coordination and communication. Second, the increased reliance on vendors for products demands intra-organizational communication. Third, the rapidly evolving, and expanding, technologies demands tremendous communication and coordination. This creates an added level of bustle which is tied to the change in infrastructure. In fact, it is the direct consequence of the new infrastructure.

4.6 Growing awareness that end-user involvement is more time-consuming than expected

While this point can be subsumed under several others, our observations of several meetings encourages us to highlight this. While the concept of end-user involvement is central to much of the discussion in the IS manager meetings and in the interviews, the goals of this effort are less clear. User resistance to change based on technology, or to having more responsibility for their computing, is not as well-received as expected. Thus, the user 'pull' for this technology is less visible than the IS 'push' to implement.

5 EMERGING ISSUES FOR FUTURE RESEARCH

Our basic approach to conducting this research is generally inductive (e.g. Yin, 1984); we have carried a theoretic framework into the investigation (Glaser and Strauss, 1967). As we have stated in this paper, our focus is on the reciprocal interactions between the incipient technology (i.e., C/S) and the organization. This is defined by work practices, rules, norms, etc. That is, by it's 'structures'. Accordingly, it is within this framework that we have interpreted a common thread running through all of the issues listed above. We see the interaction between technology and the organization viewed in terms of a technological 'push' and an organizational 'pull'.

Technological Push. There is a drive - made manifest by administrative directive - to get to get the new C/S architecture up and running. This drive originates in the assumption - held by technologists - that innovation in computer technology may directly impact organizations by providing better means of accomplishing work. As such, we view this aspect as originating in the 'folklore' of the technology - a folklore constructed by the larger society and, therefore, originating outside of the organization (Jackson, 1987). Within the organization, this drive - which we refer to as the 'push' of organizational computing - is championed by various administrators and managers.

Organizational Pull. We assume that there also exist a set of needs which may be derived, based on the work processes of the organization. This view is based on the organizational (versus technological) perspective referred to earlier in this paper. We see this as the 'pull' of organizational computing. This aspect of the dynamic is largely theoretically derived (versus empirically) in our research thus far, as we have not yet had the opportunity to observe or interview system users. Moreover, we assume that organizational needs may be dynamic, complex, and difficult to derive (Holsapple & Luo, 1994).

Between these two forces lies the dynamic interplay. From our perspective the technological push should be counterbalanced by the needs of the technology users (organizational pull). In this view, it is not sufficient for a technology to merely possess a set of functionalities which may match the work processes of an organization. As we have illustrated in this paper, we feel it is necessary for the members of the organization to integrate the technology into their present social environment, and, ultimately, to restructure that environment and the technology until a proper fit is realized. In order for the technology users to integrate the technology, they must first embrace it. In order to embrace it, they must first understand it or at least be able to relate it to their work.

At MSU we see that the IS managers are currently preoccupied with technical issues in implementing C/S. Because they are unable to devote sufficient time or resources to their clients (or in the case of the IS managers, to their development staff), there is some question whether the C/S technology will be embraced by the organization. In this state, since a balance cannot be achieved between technological push and organizational pull a third force appears: 'social inertia' or resistance to change. Although we have not yet had the opportunity to observe or interview users, we imagine that such resistance exists and may increase as pressures to meet project time-line objectives elevate the push to get the technology implemented.

Finally, a notable exception to the imbalance between technological push and organizational pull is found in issue 4.5 (above). That is, we have seen a trend toward distributed means of communication between members of the organization. We attribute two reasons for this situation: (1) The transition of this aspect of the infrastructure between mainframe and C/S has been relatively smooth. Electronic communication which had been previously established in the mainframe environment has gone through the initial phases of the structuring interaction between technology and the organization. This carries over to, and is amplified by, the C/S environment. (2) The adoption of electronic communication has progressed to a point where the needs are salient enough in the mind of the users so that the organizational pull (defined by needs) is exceeding the technological push and there is minimal social inertia.

6 CONCLUSION

To close, we emphasize that in presenting these issues it is neither our intention to draw definitive conclusions nor to make long range predictions with regard to the ultimate success or failure of the C/S implementation, at MSU or any other organization. Our primary concern is to provide an accurate chronicle of the events as they unfold with the hope that our story may help to provide a 'road map' for this and other situations. As with any storytelling it is inevitable that certain 'themes' will emerge that help to guide the narrator toward the essential elements of the story - i.e., that which is 'important' (Van Maanan, 1995; Yanow, 1995; Barley, 1990).

In presenting these observations we hope to provide an indication of where we, as researchers, interpret the themes of importance to be in the MSU story. These will provide a guide for our future investigations in the present research. While guided by theory, we acknowledge that there may be as much intuitive artistry as science in our interpretations.

The six issues presented above appear to support one overlying theme. That is, technical issues -- critical and difficult as they arise, occur in a context much broader, across more interdependent levels, than was imagined at the outset of this implementation. The professional staff, their management, and the administrators and users involved in this change provide a view of change at a personal, structural, and technological level. It is this interplay that drives this research.

7 REFERENCES

Alpert, D. (1985). Performance and paralysis: The organizational context of the american research university. *Journal of Higher Education*, 56(3), 242-281.

Barley, S. (1986). Technology as an occasion for structuring: Evidence from observations of CT scanners and the social order of radiology departments. *Administrative Science Quarterly*, 31, 78-108.

Barley, S. (1990). Images of imaging: Notes on doing longitudinal field work. *Organization Science*, 1(3), 220-249.

Drucker, P. (1994). The age of social transformation. *Atlantic Monthly*, 53-80.

Glaser, B., & Strauss, A. (1967). *The discovery of grounded theory*. New York: Aldine de Gruyter.

Goodman, P., & Sproull, L. (1989). *Technology and organizations*. San Francisco: Jossey-Bass.

Hall, C. (1994). *Technical foundations of client/server systems*. New York: Wiley-QED.

Holsapple, C., & Luo, W. (1995). Organizational computing frameworks: Progress and needs. *The Information Society*, 11, 59-74.

Information Week, 25, September 1995, p. 20.

Jackson, B. (1987). *Field work. Urbana*, IL: University of Illinois Press.

Kling, R. (1980). Social analyses of computing: Theoretical perspectives in recent empirical research. *Computing Surveys*, 12, 61-110.

Kling, R. (1990). More information, better jobs?: Occupational stratification and labor-market segmentation in the United States' information labor force. *The Information Society*, 7, 77-107.

Lee, A. (1995). (Special Call for Longitudinal Research). *MIS Quarterly*.

Lou Gerstner on catching the third wave. (1995, Oct 30). *Business Week*, p. 152.

Markus, M., & Robey, D. (1988). Information technology and organizational change: Causal structure in theory and research. *Management Science*, 34(5), 583-598.

Orlikowski, W. (1991). Integrated information environment or matrix of control? The contradictory implications of information technology. *Accounting Management & Information Technology*, 1(1), 9-42.

Sproull, L., & Kiesler, S. (1991). *Connections: New ways of working in the networked organization*. Cambridge MA: MIT Press.

Van de Ven, A., & Huber, G. (1990). Longitudinal field research methods for studying processes of organizational change. *Organization Science*, 1(3), 213-219.

Van Maanen, J. (1995). Crossroads: Style as theory. *Organization Science*, 6(1), 132-143.
Yanow, D. (1995). Crossroads: Writing organizational tales: Four authors and their stories about culture. *Organization Science*, 6(2), 224-237.
Yin, R. (1989). Case Study Research. Beverly Hills, CA: Sage Publications.
Zuboff, S. (1988). *In the age of the smart machine: The future of work and power.* New York: Basic Books.

8 BIOGRAPHY

Steve Sawyer is an Assistant Professor at Syracuse University's School of Information Studies. His research interests are on how groups work together and how they use technology. Over the past several years he has done research to understand how software developers acquire and use information technology to support their work. Steve's present research seeks to understand some organizational issues behind the use of distributed computing systems from managerial, developer, and user perspectives. He is a member of ACM, IEEE, INFORMS and the Academy of Management.

Richard Southwick is a Ph.D. student at the Syracuse University School of Information Studies. His research interests focus on IT-based organizational change and information user behaviors.

21

Development decision centers - a strategy to improve development decision-making

D. Splettstoesser
Dept. of General Management, University of Dar Es Salaam
P.O. Box 35046, Dar Es Salaam, Tanzania
E-mail: splett@unidar.gn.apc.org

Abstract

Political, economic and social development requires 'good governance' and intelligent decision-making. Development decision centers (DDC) equipped with adequate information technology (IT) can help to improve development decisions, increase effectiveness and efficiency of decision conferences and support democratization and political stability.

DDC provide IT-based facilities for brainstorming, discussion, organization and evaluation of ideas, objectives, strategies, projects, etc. They can be integrated into community information centers which are recognized as a 'multisectoral concept' for improving development. They can also be established within government agencies, business corporations, universities and other institutions of higher learning to offer assistance in solving complex development problems that require close collaboration of management and expert teams.

The paper analyzes political, socio-cultural and economic development problems, and explains typical steps of development decision-making, using a group support system in the DDC, the author has established at the University of Dar es Salaam, Tanzania. It is believed to be the first such center in Africa.

In view of the increasing globalization of trade and international cooperation, DDC can play an important role in the concept of the *International Office of the Future*. They help to integrate developing countries into the world economy and enhance intercultural understanding while, at the same time, improving transparency, accountability and productivity of development planning.

Keywords

Development planning, management of development projects, development cooperation, group techniques, group decision-making, group support systems, group productivity, computer-supported collaborative work, electronic meetings

1 PROBLEMS OF DEVELOPMENT DECISION-MAKING

Development decision-making is concerned with political, economic and social progress in developing countries. Significant differences in problems and decision processes, depending on the political framework and socio-cultural background, exist in those countries. However, in general, there seem to be increasing difficulties in achieving development progress. Factors, such as lack of development-orientation and political stability, insufficient strategic planning, high level of official corruption, mass poverty, inadequate infrastructure, etc. affect almost all developing countries, particularly in Africa.

In view of these difficulties and the overall complexity of development, one may sometimes forget that most development problems are man-made and influenced by decisions that can be improved considerably. Information technology (IT) is expected to play a key role in implementing and sustaining such improvements in development decision-making, if appropriate strategies for exploiting its potential are found.

The subsequently discussed idea of development decision centers (DDC) appears to be a promising strategy. It is based on the author's experience as a lecturer, consultant and manager in East Africa since 1981. DDC are expected to substantially improve development decision-making, as they support the concept of 'good governance' through ensuring accountability, transparency, participation, productivity and decision quality. DDC may become a core facility within community information centers, providing an 'electronic meeting room' with notebook computers for each participant, a workstation for the meeting facilitator/chauffeur, a printer and a video projector to output the meeting results, network and communication software, and a group support system to assist in activities, such as brainstorming, discussing, organizing, evaluating and reporting of development programs, projects, funding, etc.

Development decisions are taken by governments, international financing institutions, non-governmental organizations, public and private corporations, foundations, communities, etc. in developing or donor countries. DDC can help in any such decision situation. In this paper, they are suggested as a strategy for developing countries, as they do not only assist in development decision-making itself, but also contribute to enhance a country's information infrastructure and affect the political, cultural and economic environs of development decision-making.

1.1 Political and Cultural Aspects

The Development Dilemma: 'Nation-Building' and National Disintegration

Development policy and decision-making started more than 30 years ago. It aimed at improving the economic and social situation of people in developing countries. In Africa, those countries typically had been colonies of European nations until the late 1950s or early 1960s. They had not only to overcome major problems from their colonial past, but also had to integrate numerous ethnic communities of different languages and cultures. To help these groups agree to a common development agenda, the newly independent governments considered 'nation-building' an important prerequisite for development.

At the same time, i.e. from about 1960 onwards, a number of West-European nations, including the former colonial powers that played a key role in shaping development policy, had begun to re-orient themselves from a narrow national view of development to a wider European perspective. This led to the establishment of the European Community. From the beginning of the 1980s, however, Europeans began to realize that neither the European Community nor the national governments were able to adequately fulfill the citizens' expectations with regard to growth, stability and employment. European administrative structures and procedures were increasingly criticized and considered an ineffective, unmanageable and costly bureaucracy. A gradual and rather unexpected renaissance of regions began. Other factors contributing to this shift were the rediscovery of original cultural values and identity, and, not least, 'glasnost' and the 'information revolution'. Among the consequences were not only decreasing enthusiam for European unity, but also the dramatic demise of communism, the Balkan tragedy, and increasing suspicion against all forms of central (national) administration.

Inevitably, these changes of political structures and cultural orientation also had an impact on development and developing countries. In North Africa, increasing tendencies for fundamentalism as evident in Algeria, Libya, and Egypt led to adverse development conditions. In Sub-Saharan Africa, civil war and irreconcilable conflicts between ethnic groups, living within national boundaries that were determined more than 100 years ago without regard to cultural differences, made reasonable development almost impossible. Examples for this can be found all over East and Central Africa, particularly in Somalia, Rwanda and Burundi. Hutus and Tutsis in Rwanda and Burundi will hardly ever be able to devise a common development strategy in a national context. Equally, national development efforts are unimaginable in Sudan, where the central government since more than 10 years fights a rebel movement that aims at establishing an independent state in the South. Even in Kenya, that appears in a relatively fortunate position when compared to its neighbors, national cooperation among the different ethnic groups is on the decline and 'majimboism' (regionalism) is growing.

Under these circumstances, sustainable economic and human development requires more efforts than national governments have been able to make. It requires particularly 'more local participation in the design and implementation of development programs', as the former president of the World Bank noted (WorldBank, 1992). This implies that development should ideally not be pursued as a national, government-initiated task, but as a community-initiated and locally managed effort, taking into consideration the accumulated knowledge and understanding of the people concerned.

Lack of 'Good governance'

Development requires 'good governance' which in essence means democratic decision-making, respect for human rights and the rule of law, efficiency, accountability, transparency in government and public administration. This is rarely achieved. While there is no one best way to 'good governance' and sustainable development (Blunt, 1995), there are universal best practices, like participative approaches to policymaking and decentralization, that deserve to be pursued.

Governments in many African countries have yet to reform decision-making processes that were devised under post-colonial, rather authoritarian regimes. There is frequently a considerable lack of political will and perhaps of understanding on the side of the ruling elites to do that. In recent years, several governments in Africa had to be pressed hard to accept more democracy and participation in policymaking. Frequently, there has been an attempt to preserve existing power structures and resist donor demands for changes. However, this resistance may have also been caused by different ideas about individual and collective freedom. In collectivist societies (Hofstede, 1983), where 'ingroups', for example tribes, play an important role, individual rights are usually less important than in individualist societies. This explains a rather hesitant position towards political demands for more individual freedom. The resulting lack of democratic structures and procedures, particularly the insufficient involvement of large parts of the population in development planning and program implementation, has most likely contributed to the fact that, despite all development aid, the economic and social gap between developed countries in Europe and North America and African developing countries has widened dramatically over the last twenty years.

Another factor hampering development, particularly in Africa, has been the rampant corruption on all levels of public life. While corrupt practices have become acceptable in many societies and have typically been acknowledged in taxation laws to the degree of deductibility of bribes from income tax, they could still be contained by strong mechanisms to ensure accountability and transparency of government and public institutions. Where such mechanisms are not yet in place or poorly enforced, like in many African countries, corruption spread like a contagious disease. Its devastating effects on development, resulting frequently from irrational and shortsighted development decision-making (Sabuni, 1996) are clearly visible. Despite the fact that codes of ethic for members of governments and civil service were introduced, and new laws to severely punish corruption were enacted in several countries, the practice went on unabated, since the underlying economic and societal conditions remained unchanged and sufficient controls, including a free press, were not firmly established.

As a legacy from colonialism, centralization of information and policymaking power is still high in most African developing countries. Decentralization efforts have started in some countries, but no acceptable level of participative policymaking and accessibility to public services, facilities and information has yet been reached. Most rural areas have been neglected in development efforts. This has led to huge information and communication deficits in these areas, further discrepancies between urban and rural living conditions and the resulting increase of migration to urban centers. Strategies to reverse this trend by strengthening rural development opportunities and allow rural dwellers to easily communicate not only with their own government institutions, legislative and judicial bodies, but also with other national and international partners will most likely facilitate 'good governance' and accelerate development.

Participative culture and 'Power distance'

Development decision-making requires involvement and participation of the main stakeholders. One could assume that this can be easily achieved in collectivist societies which have been typical for African developing countries. Such societies are characterized by tight integration of people who are supposed to look after the interests of the 'ingroup' and have no other opinions and beliefs than this group (Hofstede, 1983). Tribalism which is ubiquitous in Africa gives ideal examples for such a society. The resulting high level of integration is, however, inevitably restricted to the members of the 'ingroup'.

For development decision-making, members of all concerned communities would have to be integrated. This is much more difficult and has rarely been achieved. Intercultural cooperation is typically impeded by tribal prejudice. In Tanzania, for example, there are about 120 different tribes, speaking 108 different languages. While they have lived together relatively peaceful since independence, members of one tribe typically have misconceptions about other tribes. Cooperation is usually hampered by mistrust and anxiety. If methods can be found that support confidence-building, ease of involvement and equal participation of different communities, this will not only help to preserve cultural identities, but will also assist in solving intertribal conflicts and other community-related problems that hinder development.

In many developing countries, there are often enormous inequalities in power and wealth, resulting partly from the continuation of feudalistic structures. In African countries, the 'power distance', i.e. the degree of centralization of authority and autocratic leadership (Hofstede, 1983), is still large and widespread. Chieftainship has been one of the few stable and enduring institutions of the African society (Roberts, 1968) which has remained autocratic because its members permitted it and its leaders saw no reason to give up their privileges. There is no doubt that this power distance aggravated development.

One of its particularly negative effects has been its influence on maintaining the inequalities between male and female participation in education. Improving education for girls may be the most important element of development policy in Africa. It is 'a powerful cause of reduced fertility' (WorldBank, 1992). Women who have been able to complete a secondary education have, on average, only three instead of seven children. In Tanzania, for example, which shares with Malawi the lowest gross secondary school enrollment rate of only 5%, the percentage of female students in upper secondary school is only about 25%. The University enrollment rate of women has steadily declined during the last ten years from approximately 26% of all students to 17% (Mlama, 1995). Development chances will inevitably be adversely affected by this.

During the last ten years, development agencies have found that only approaches to decision-making that provided procedures to maximize involvement and participation of stakeholders led to acceptable planning and implementation of development projects. For long-term sustainable development, techniques and tools to enhance a participative culture, to minimize power distances, to foster development-orientation, and to reinforce equality and democratic procedures are of paramount importance. Without broad-based cooperation and sharing of responsibilities tangible development success will not be achieved.

Analogous to findings about resistance to implementation of information systems, one can assume that failure of development projects can be prevented by avoiding clashes between cultural presumptions and an actually existing culture (Pliskin, et al., 1993). Such clashes can be minimized and perhaps excluded completely by methods and tools that support cooperation by reducing inequalities, facilitating participation in decision-making, blocking domination or discrimination of individuals or minorities, and help to create a development-conducive atmosphere of tolerance and appreciation of cultural diversity.

1.2 Economic aspects

Harnessing the 'Information revolution'

While the idea of the 'information revolution' has almost become trivial among scholars, it was only in February 1995, that the first ministerial meeting of the G7 group of industrialized countries (Britain, Canada, France, Germany, Italy, Japan, USA) on the global information society took place. In their communique, the ministers agreed that 'the smooth and effective transition towards the information society is one of the most important tasks that should be undertaken in the last decade of the 20th century'. Governments seem to have realized now that IT is an essential development factor.

In an attempt to assist developing countries to 'harness the information revolution', i.e. make better use of IT for poverty alleviation and sustainable economic development, the World Bank has recently revised some of its objectives in this area and plans to give more support for:

- widespread and equitable access to communication and information services through accelerated deployment of national information infrastructure and effective integration into international communication and information networks;
- systemic improvements in the functioning and competitiveness of key economic sectors through strategic information policies and systems;
- new ways to use IT to help solve the most pressing problems of human and economic development - education, health, poverty alleviation, rural development, and care for the environment (Talero/Gaudette, 1995).

The emerging information society is characterized by substantial differences from the industrial society, such as more competition, more democracy, less centralization, etc. In the information society, 'trade and investments are global and organizations compete with knowledge, networking and agility on a global basis' (Talero/Gaudette, 1995). To cope with these changes requires structural adjustments, including regulatory and institutional reforms in all countries. Many developing countries are still hesitant or opposed to such reforms. They may not realize that they 'risk exclusion from the global economy and severe competitive disadvantages for their goods and services' (Talero/Gaudette, 1995), if they do not accept to reform their policies.

Productivity and competitiveness

Competitiveness and smooth organizational performance are critical success factors in an ever more closely linked global economy. They are also traditional weaknesses in many developing countries, particularly in African societies. It is obvious that this has contributed to the increasing marginalization of Africa within the last two decades.

Successful integration of developing countries into the world's communication networks requires adequate IT solutions which, in turn, represent an opportunity to accelerate development through:

- increased competitiveness for local industries in international markets,
- increased business opportunities through connections to trading networks,
- increased participation in research and development for local scientists,
- productivity increases in government services,
- major improvements in the delivery of services, such as education, health, agricultural extension, management of the environment, promotion of the private sector, etc.

Despite these prospects, only few governments have embarked on a systematic exploitation of IT for development. Particularly in Sub-Saharan Africa, IT strategies and national informatics policies are lacking.

Slow acceptance of IT has partly also been observed in industrialized countries and has been explained by discouraging results from analyzing previous IT investments. Several studies in the US came to the conclusion that the widespread use of IT had not resulted in tangibly increasing office productivity. One of the main reasons for that was the fact that most IT applications were simply automated versions of existing business processes. These processes had not been re-engineered before computerization. They reflected all weaknesses that existed before automation. IT cannot be blamed for this lack of strategic information systems planning. The observed lack of productivity increase, sometimes called the 'productivity paradoxon' of IT investment, has also been caused by:

- a generally insufficient use of IT for strategic decision-making,
- a typical underrepresentation of IT on the top level of an organization, with a chief information officer being an exception rather than the rule, and
- tall hierarchies in governmental and large corporate organizations with their extraordinary need for communication, coordination and control measures consuming many of the positive impacts of IT.

These observations demonstrate a rather limited validity of the productivity paradoxon of IT. Without adequate IT investment, developing countries will lessen their chances for productivity increases. More than any other technology, IT will prevent further loss of competitiveness and will help to reintegrate developing countries into the world economy.

Structural adjustments and reforms

On the macroeconomic level, structural adjustments have become a centerpiece of development and a prerequisite for development assistance. Without agreement on reforms of the public sector and the civil service, new multilateral loans are rarely given to governments in developing countries and even bilateral aid has been made dependent on such adjustments.

On the microeconomic level, structural reforms are equally required. Traditionally, corporate structures have been hierarchical. In recent years, however, more and more organizations have realized that obvious changes in human behavior require adequate structural adjustments as well. Reduced willingness to defer to authority and more demand for involvement in decision-making has contributed to flattening management structures and greater autonomy for staff (Lewis, 1994).

Hierarchical systems have proved unsuitable for rapid adaptation to changes required in a more competitive business environment. They cannot respond quickly enough to change because of the long time communication takes up and down the chain of command (Pava, 1982). Competitive organizations are characterized by high flexibility and responsiveness. Small, self-managed groups have been best in achieving such goals. Business re-engineering has during the last few years had a strong impact on creating such groups of managers and experts, collaborating through appropriate IT systems.

It is likely that the increase of group work will change the way corporations are organized and may accelerate the gradual 'demise of hierarchies'. There will be a shift of emphasis from financial to human capital (McNurlin/Sprague, 1989). Problems are becoming more complex and cannot longer be solved by individual managers or specialists. Teams must be formed since no one person has enough knowledge, experience or information. Organizations are becoming more dependent on workgroups to design problem solutions, take decisions and carry out the basic activities to meet organizational goals (Lewis, 1994). Workgroups will probably be an important part of an emerging organizational culture in the 'International Office of the Future' (Glasson, 1994) and will influence economic and social development anywhere in the world.

2 STRUCTURE AND PROCESSES OF DEVELOPMENT DECISION CENTERS

2.1 Goals and objectives

While the enormous difficulties of sustainable and human development for which there is no one-dimensional solution cannot be underrated, the view presented in this paper is that most problems are man-made and can be overcome through better decision-making and application of appropriate strategies. The strategy suggested here is the establishment of DDC within community information centers. DDC are expected to:

- accelerate development by decentralization and provision of facilities for demand-oriented, community-initiated and locally managed development programs
- enhance strategic development planning and decision-making capabilities by making optimal use of the emerging organizational culture of workgroups
- develop a culture of participative decision-making by enabling and improving approaches that minimize power distance and inhibit discrimination and domination of minorities
- improve the quality of decision-making, group productivity and motivation
- enable access to essential information services and offer new ways to solve development problems by educating decision-makers in IT based methods and tools

- contribute to a future-oriented information infrastructure
- support the concept of 'good governance' through enforcing democratic procedures, transparency and accountability
- assist in harnessing the 'information revolution' for development and enhancing competitiveness
- function as a hub for integrating developing countries into international communication, trade and cooperation networks
- reduce rural-urban migration.

A prototype of a DDC, providing an example for an 'electronic meeting room' that could be established within a community information center in a rural or urban area of a developing country, has been built up in the Faculty of Commerce and Management of the University of Dar es Salaam (UDSM). It serves the university community, government agencies, public and private organizations, and provides assistance for management and other groups of decision-makers in the process of developing, discussing and evaluating goals, plans, projects, strategies, etc. as well as access to decision-oriented information. The overall goal of the UDSM DDC is to help improve group decision-making through the application of adequate IT. Main objectives are to facilitate strategic decision-making, train decision-makers, enable research in group support and information systems.

2.2 Hardware and software configuration

The UDSM DDC is equipped with nine microcomputers, i.e. eight notebook PCs for the participants and one server. The participants' workstations have 80386 CPUs, 1 MB RAM and a VGA display. The chauffeur station has a Pentium CPU with 8 MB RAM, a fast harddisk drive and an SVGA display.

Notebook PCs have been chosen for the participants as these could be integrated into tables that have been designed to accommodate two computers each. The tables are arranged in U-shape which is well-suited for face-to-face discussions. The computers are placed in drawers and are thus less obtrusive, as the displays can be folded down and the drawers can be pushed back into the tables when not needed during a session. The drawers also contain the network cables connecting the participants' computers to the 'chauffeur' workstation which serves as the network controller and file server. The chauffeur workstation is also used to compute the results of the group work and display them through a video projector onto a common screen.

The group support system (GSS) used is called 'MeetingWorks for Windows'. It is based on ideas developed in the first doctoral dissertation on group decision support systems by Lewis (Lewis, 1982) who further developed it until 1992, and was then rewritten for the 'Windows' environment by Enterprise Solutions of Seattle (Enterprise Solutions, 1994). The system is designed for small groups engaged in face-to-face meetings. It is presently used at about 30 universities and between 60 and 100 public and private organizations in the US, Canada, Australia, New Zealand and Germany. The installation at the University of Dar es Salaam is the first in a developing country.

The GSS requires a network-based file system for communication between the chauffeur and the participants' workstations. The file system must support standard 'DOS' and 'Windows' file access over the network. In the UDSM DDC, 'Lantastic' has been installed for that purpose and configured for shared access in such a way that each station can read and write files on the network server disk, where the chauffeur files are installed.

2.3 Functions and results of DDC-based development decision-making

Meeting preparation

Preparing a development decision-conference or session requires thorough planning. This process is supported by the SCRIPTWRITING module which enables the facilitator of a meeting to define the meeting steps and allocate the appropriate tools to these steps, thus creating a suitable agenda. Figure 1 shows a script for a strategic development planning process, generated with this module. Preliminary session steps, such as clarifying the purpose and scope of the session and explaining the background and restrictions, as well as the creation of the final report of the meeting results are done without using the GSS. As the system is run under 'Windows', these steps can be supported by other 'Windows'-based software, such as a spreadsheet and wordprocessing system.

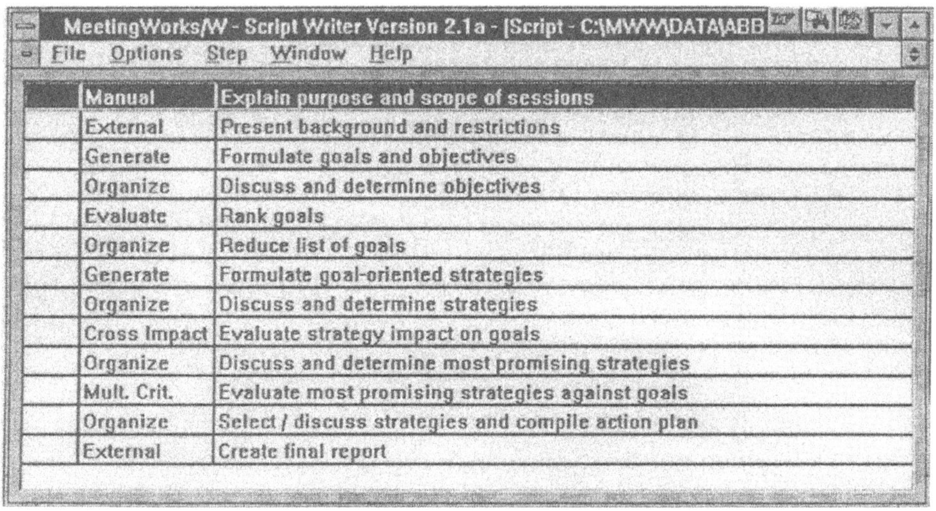

Figure 1 Script for a strategic development planning process

Idea generation

Strategic development planning typically starts with a brainstorming process. This is supported by the GENERATE module which ensures anonymity and thus protects minority viewpoints. All ideas entered into the participants' workstations are sent to a common file and displayed on the main screen at the front of the room, where everybody can read them (see Figure 2) without knowing who contributed the idea. Participants can use 'piggybacking' for maximum creativity. To avoid 'tunnel vision', which may occur if participants wait for one member to give some direction or guidance by entering his ideas first, switching on the front screen can be delayed until everyone has entered some ideas. With this approach, one has the advantage of initial independent idea generation, while retaining the possibility for 'piggybacking' later in the process. This also helps to overcome 'dispositional anxiousness' that may affect the generation of ideas when brainstorming in groups (Camacho/Paulus, 1995).

Brainstorming in the DDC is supported by providing access to internal and external databases through connections to the UDSM network and the Internet.

Idea discussion

On completion of a brainstorming session, a group typically proceeds to discussing and editing of the ideas generated. The DISCUSS module reads the list of items from a file created by GENERATE. It displays one item at a time and manages a timed discussion of the items, using the shared screen at the front of the room (see Figure 3). The group may set an appropriate amount of time to consider each item which is displayed along with the remaining discussion time. The timer can be interrupted at any time to either allow more discussion time or to proceed to the next item. The system, thus, helps to allocate each item adequate time and to avoid the frequently observed situation that the first few items of a list are discussed at length, and the ones at the bottom receive inadequate or no attention at all.

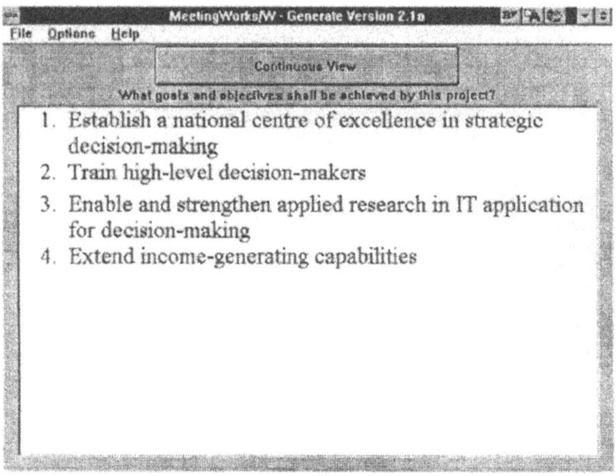

Figure 2 Common screen displaying brainstorming results.

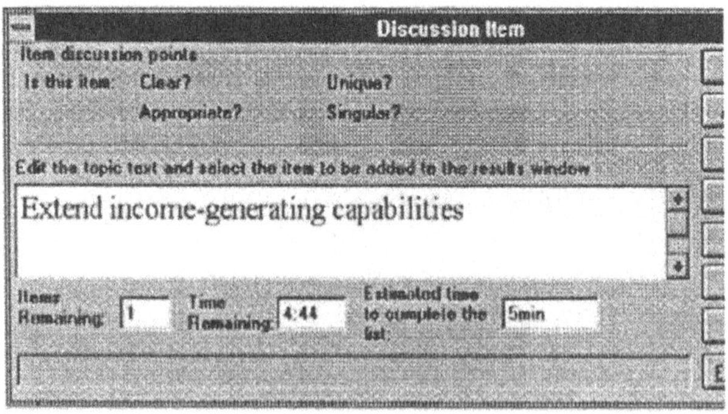

Figure 3 Discuss screen.

Idea organization

If a group has developed a complex list of ideas, where it is important to structure the list, the ORGANIZE module assists in building outlines. Different levels of an outline can be defined and displayed on the front screen, and ideas can be placed in the appropriate location in the outline following discussion by the group (see Figure 4).

The DISCUSS and ORGANIZE modules are usually run at the same time. The DISCUSS window displays the list of ideas, while the ORGANIZE window displays the outline. As each item comes up for discussion, it is entered into the outline at a position determined by the group.

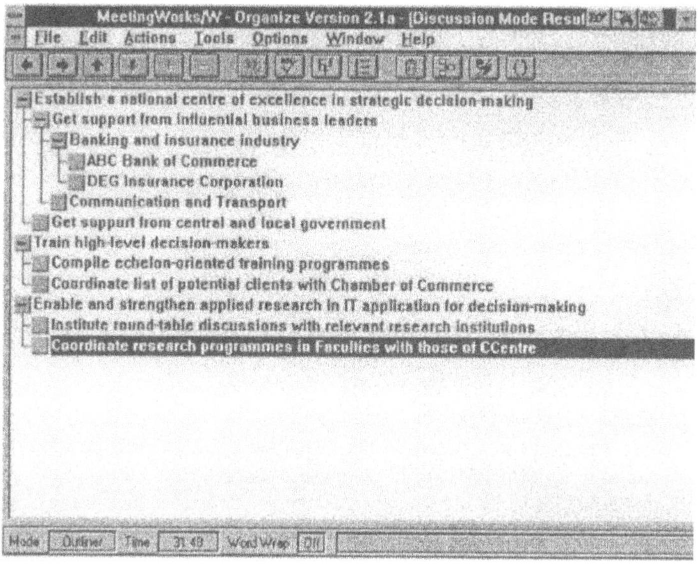

Figure 4 Organize screen

Item evaluation

To prioritize or decide on the items of a list, an evaluation tool is required. The software provides several modules for this purpose, such as CROSS IMPACT ANALYSIS, VOTE, RANK, RATE, MULTIPLE CRITERIA ANALYSIS. All of these modules guarantee that evaluations made by the participants remain anonymous and cannot be used against any individual or group.

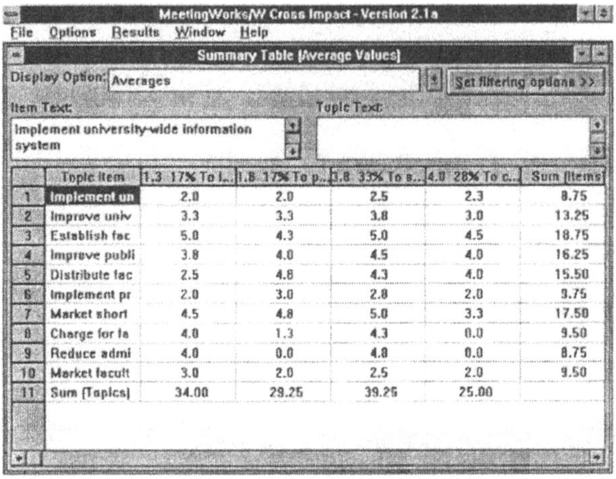

	Topic Item	1.3 17% To l...	1.8 17% To p...	3.8 33% To s...	4.0 28% To c...	Sum (Items)
1	Implement un	2.0	2.0	2.5	2.3	8.75
2	Improve univ	3.3	3.3	3.8	3.0	13.25
3	Establish fac	5.0	4.3	5.0	4.5	18.75
4	Improve publi	3.8	4.0	4.5	4.0	16.25
5	Distribute fac	2.5	4.8	4.3	4.0	15.50
6	Implement pr	2.0	3.0	2.8	2.0	9.75
7	Market short	4.5	4.8	5.0	3.3	17.50
8	Charge for fa	4.0	1.3	4.3	0.0	9.50
9	Reduce admi	4.0	0.0	4.8	0.0	8.75
10	Market facult	3.0	2.0	2.5	2.0	9.50
11	Sum (Topics)	34.00	29.25	39.25	25.00	

Figure 5 Results of a Cross Impact Analysis.

CROSS IMPACT ANALYSIS is used to compare any two lists of items. For example, a group may want to compare to what extent alternative strategies can help to achieve certain development goals, in order to prepare an appropriate shortlist for a final evaluation with multiple criteria analysis. The module allows participants to make YES/NO decisions or to rate items on a scale from +5 to -5. Figure 5 shows a table created by a Cross Impact Analysis of 10 strategies whose impact on 4 goals was evaluated. Based on the displayed results, it was decided that only those strategies with a total score of higher than 13 would be considered in the final evaluation process.

The RANK and RATE modules are similar in design and support a decision-maker in expressing preference for a certain item. The RANK module enables a participant to arrange the items in rank order, e.g. to allocate rank 1 to the goal or alternative he/she prefers or considers most important, etc. The RATE module allows participants to indicate their preferences on a 1 to 5, 1 to 7, or 1 to 10 scale. By using this program rather than the RANK module, decision-makers can express their opinion that there are two or more alternatives deserving the same judgment.

Each module provides a summary of the evaluation, indicating the average values and the variability as a percentage of the maximum standard deviation. The variability indicates agreement/disagreement among the participants. Figure 6 shows the results of a ranking decision.

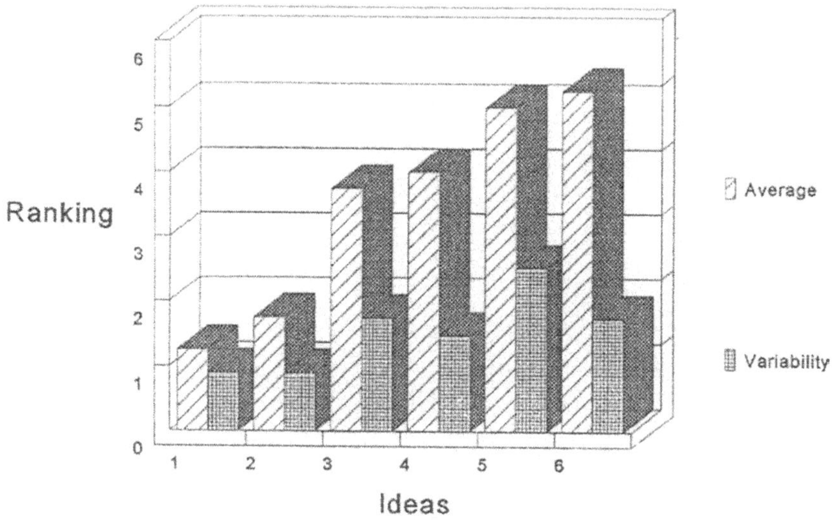

Figure 6 Results of a Ranking of Development Goals.

A useful feature for further analyzing agreement/disagreement is the possibility to display the distribution of the decision-makers rankings (see Figure 7). The distribution graph shows a separate small graph for each item evaluated. The Y-axis represents the total number of participants who assigned the same value for an item. The X-axis shows the actual values assigned. For example, the upper left graph indicates that the considered goal was ranked first by 3 participants and second by 1 participant.

The MULTIPLE CRITERIA ANALYSIS module is a multi-attribute tool, allowing a group to evaluate alternatives, for example development strategies, using a number of predetermined criteria. Each criterion is weighted by the group, i.e. it is assigned the average value of the individually assigned weights. Each participant rates how well each alternative meets each criterion. The product of the weight and rating determines the score for a given alternative on a given criterion. The scores are summed across all criteria for each alternative. The alternative with the highest score is considered the best. The individual evaluations are integrated into a results table and a final results graph, summarizing the mean of the participants' scores (see Figure 8).

The results window offers a number of options to further analyze the findings. By choosing the analysis method, the group can decide whether the 'group mean analysis' or the 'individual data analysis' method should be applied to compute the final results. By highlighting cells in the results table and clicking them on, detail bar graphs are displayed. Each of the displayed bars can be further analyzed with a mouse click. A detail graph may, for example, display the distribution of participant weighted scores for one alternative and one criterion. With another mouse click on each of the bars comments that may have been entered by the participants to explain their rationale for a particular rating can be displayed. Various filtering options can be used to show subsets of the results based on average values, variability or both. Weights and scores can also be easily re-evaluated.

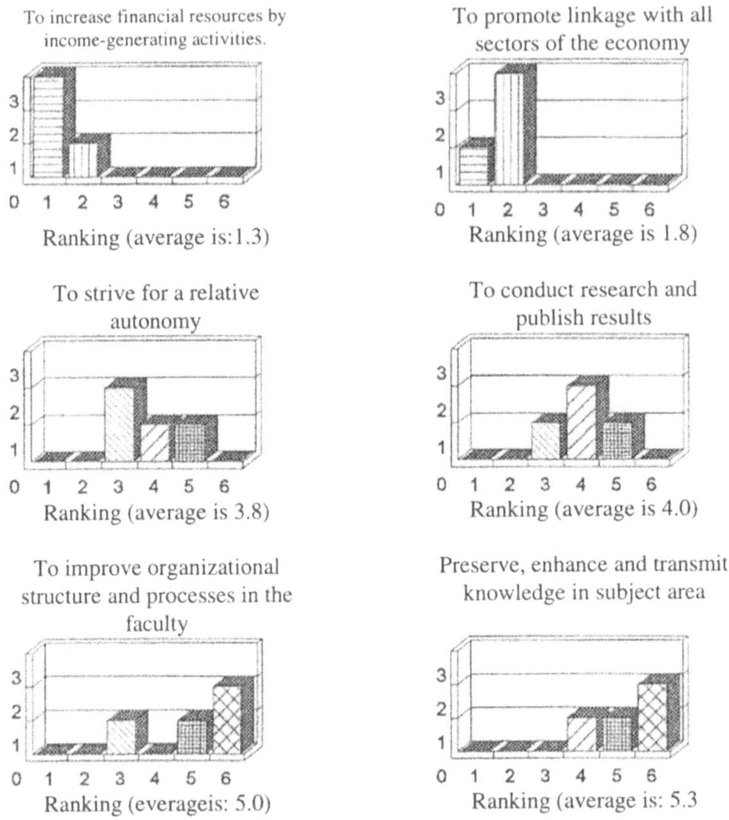

Figure 7 Distribution of ranking of 6 development goals by 4 participants.

At the end of a decision meeting, the results of the group's deliberations are typically summarized in a report. The system supports this process by providing a template, designed to make use of the MSWORD wordprocessor. A shell document containing macros to access the generated text and graphics files can be prepared. By integrating a report-writing phase into the script, the wordprocessor and the shell document are loaded. Running the macros then converts the shell into a professionally formatted report which can be ready for distribution within minutes of the completion of a session. Decision-makers will in this way not only receive a complete documentation of the group's work, but also a high-quality report including all tables and graphs produced during the course of the meeting.

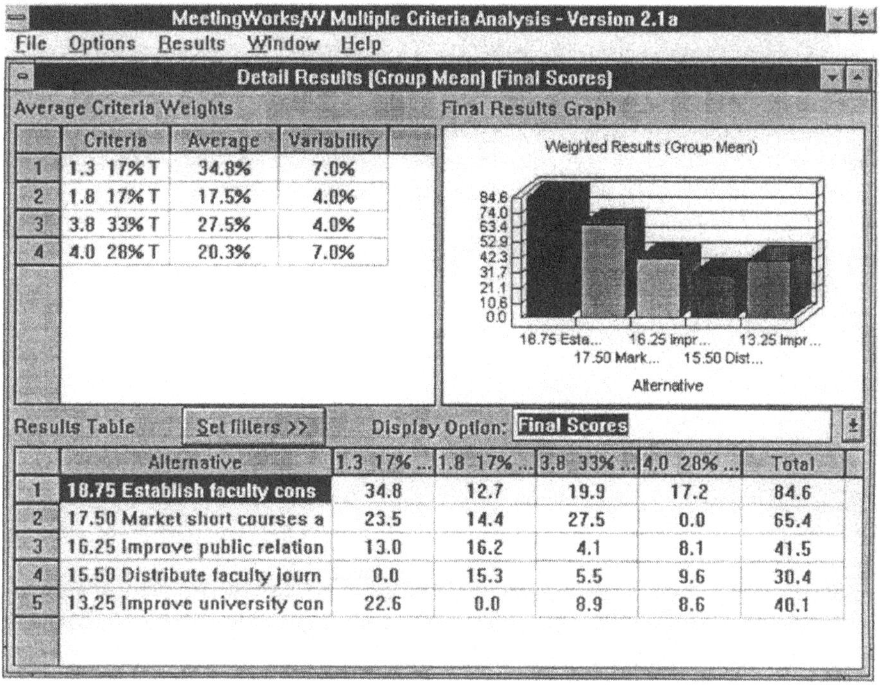

Figure 8 Results of a multiple criteria analysis of development strategies

3 BENEFITS OF DEVELOPMENT DECISION CENTERS

DDC can be seen as an example of 'culture-centered computing' (Hakken, 1991), particularly when installed within community information centers. They provide a strategy to enhance intercultural understanding and are likely to enhance creativity and originality of development planning. In a study involving mixed groups of introverts and extroverts and using traditional face-to-face meetings and a GSS to discuss scenarios, it was found that all participants contributed more original solutions using the GSS (Yellen et al, 1995). This is consistent with earlier findings in a different environment (Petrovic, 1993).

When established within institutions of higher learning, government agencies, public and private corporations, etc., to offer facilities for solving complex problems that require close collaboration of experts and policy-makers, DDC can contribute to making organizations more effective and efficient. Equipped with non-obtrusive hardware and with group support systems they achieve these improvements through the typical characteristics of computer-supported group work:

- Parallel and anonymous input of ideas, preferences, evaluations;
- Focussed discussion and easy organization of texts;
- Problem orientation instead of people orientation;
- Automatic preference analysis;
- Application of more sophisticated evaluation procedures;
- Automatic report generation.

DDC help to enhance strategic development planning and decision-making capabilities by making optimal use of human resources and IT. They improve the quality of decision-making in groups, as well as group productivity and motivation. They contribute to a culture of participative policymaking by minimizing power distance and preventing inequalities, discrimination and domination of minorities.

When integrated into community information centers, they help to create a future-oriented information infrastructure, facilitate access to essential information services and offer new methods to solve development problems. They provide a means to educate decision-makers in IT-based techniques and tools and support the concept of 'good governance' through enforcing democratic procedures, transparency, and accountability. They ensure that residents, non-governmental organizations, and businesses in rural and urban areas receive economical and easy access to service systems and networks for training, technical assistance, marketing, banking, government licensing, etc. This appears particularly relevant for small and medium enterprises that are recognized as 'vital engines' (Talero/Gaudette, 1995) of economic development and job creation. In this manner, they help to eliminate the typical development inequalities between rural and urban areas, and contribute to more evenly spread development chances.

As there seems to be strong evidence of a positive correlation between IT infrastructure and the level of development (Kraemer, 1992), it is likely that the combination of community information centers and DDC will contribute to accelerate development and to increase a country's participation in the world economy. This, in turn, is likely to have positive effects on the domestic growth rate (Talero/Gaudette, 1995) as well.

DDC assist in harnessing the 'information revolution' for development. For that purpose, developing countries frequently have to make structural adjustments, requiring substantial capital investments, whose benefits may take years or even decades to materialize. DDC, on the other hand, are innovations that need only very moderate investment and achieve an immediate positive impact on development decision-making and IT infrastructure. They help to integrate developing countries into international communication, trade and cooperation networks, and are likely to reduce migration to urban centers as they improve rural living and development conditions.

DDC can gather and disseminate development-relevant knowledge and best practices. They contribute to rationalize development planning and facilitate integration of the developing countries into the 'information society'. By providing methods and tools to accelerate decision-making and to generate comprehensive documentation of decision processes, they promote the idea of 'direct democracy' and challenge the typical bureaucratic rigidity and lack of responsiveness of public administration. In this manner, they also support political stability in developing countries.

4 REFERENCES

Aiken, M., Kim, D., Hwang, C., Lu, L.C. (1995) A Korean Group Decision-Support System. *INFORMATION & MANAGEMENT*, 28, 5, 303-310.

Blunt, P (1995), Cultural Relativism, Good Governance and Sustainable Human-Development. *PUBLIC ADMINISTRATION AND DEVELOPMENT*, 15, 1, 1-9.

Camacho, L.M. and Paulus, P.B. (1995) The Role of Social Anxiousness in Group Brainstorming. *JOURNAL OF PERSONALITY AND SOCIAL PSYCHOLOGY*, 68, 6, 1071-1080.

Enterprise Solutions Inc. (1994) *MeetingWorks for Windows. The Technology of Consensus.* Seattle.

Glasson, B.C. (1994) International Office of the Future: A Teaching and Research Facility, in *APPLICATIONS AND IMPACTS, Information Processing '94, Proceedings of the IFIP 13th World Computer Congress*, Hamburg, Germany, 28 August - 2 September, Amsterdam, North-Holland, 430-435.

Hakken, D. (1991) Culture-Centered Computing - Social-Policy and Development of New Information Technology in England and the United-States. *HUMAN ORGANIZATION*, 50, 4, 406-423.

Hofstede, G. (1983) The Cultural Relativity of Organizational Practices and Theories, *Journal of International Business Studies*, 14, 2, 75-89.

Kraemer, K., Gurbaxani, V., King, J. (1992) Economic Development, Government Policy, and the Diffusion of Computing in Asia-Pacific Countries, *Public Administration Review*, 52, 2.

Lewis, L.F. (1982) *Facilitator: A Microcomputer Decision Support System for Small Groups*. Unpublished doctoral dissertation, University of Louisville.

Lewis, L.F. (1994) *A Brief Introduction to Group Support Systems*. MeetingWorks Associates, Bellingham.

McNurlin, B.C. and Sprague, R.H. (1989) *Information Systems Management in Practice*, 2nd edition. Prentice Hall, Englewood Cliffs, New Jersey.

Pava, C. (1982) Microelectronics and the Design of Organization, *Working Paper No. HBS 82-67, Harvard Business School*, Division of Research, Soldier Field, Boston, Mass.

Petrovic, O. and Krickl, O. (1993) Traditionell-moderiertes vs. computergestütztes Brainstorming. Eine vergleichende Betrachtung. *Wirtschaftsinformatik*, 2, 120-128.

Pliskin, N., Romm, T., Lee, A.S., Weber, Y., (1993) Presumed Versus Actual Organizational Culture - Managerial Implications for Implementation of Information-Systems, *COMPUTER JOURNAL*, 36, 2, 143-152.

Roberts, A. (ed) (1968) *Tanzania before 1900*. East African Publishing House, Nairobi.

Talero, E. and Gaudette, P. (1995) *Harnessing Information for Development*. The World Bank, Washington.

WorldBank, (1992) *World Development Report 1992. Development and the Environment*. Oxford University Press, New York.

Yellen, R.E., Winniford, M., Sanford, C.C. (1995) Extroversion and Introversion in Electronically-Supported Meetings, *INFORMATION & MANAGEMENT*, 28, 1, 63-74.

5 BIOGRAPHY

Dietrich Splettstoesser is a Senior Lecturer in the Faculty of Commerce and Management of the University of Dar es Salaam, Tanzania. He holds an MBA degree from the University of Cologne, Germany, and a PhD degree from the University of Linz, Austria.

He has worked as consultant, lecturer, and manager in Europe, Australia and Africa, and has more than 25 years of experience in developing and implementing information systems. Since 1981 he has advised national and international organizations in Kenya, Uganda, and Tanzania, and has managed the development and implementation of several large-scale information systems.

22

Culture-building in action: developing a vision for Global Inc.

A. Whiteley
Graduate School of Business, Curtin University of Technology
Western Australia, Tel: +619 351 7714, Fax: +619 351 3368,
E-mail: A.Whiteley@info.curtin.edu.au

Abstract

This paper is written from an Organisational Behavior perspective. The paper reports on a set of activities that involved the collaboration of Organisational Behavior and Information Technology disciplines. The Organisational Behavior activities concerned culture building and the Information Technology concerned the use of Group Support Systems technology. The focus is using the values of key stakeholding groups in an organisation to build a strong and shared culture. The method being reported on is the core values model and method (Whiteley, 1995), although there seems no reason why other culture building methods would not work equally well. One of the objectives of the core values model is vision creation. The model and method were developed specifically for this purpose. They were developed over several years of workshops in Hong Kong and Australia, with ongoing critical feedback from manager, worker and customer groups. They have also been used for several years as part of MBA International Business teaching and have benefitted similarly in terms of critical feedback from a multicultural student group.

Keywords

GSS for Culture building, corporate culture, core values and GSS

1 INTRODUCTION

This paper describes the use of a well-trialled model or framework which helps groups create a shared vision in a Group Support Systems environment. Group Support Systems technology was first encountered by the author in a decision making environment. Although GSS is now acknowledged for its process as well as outcomes capabilities, it was tentatively adopted at first because of the emotional and imaginal requirements of vision-making in contrast to the mechanised properties of the GSS environment.

In the culture building situation the "efficiencies" leverage of GSS is not as important as the need to create a supportive and creative atmosphere. GSS is now being adopted with confidence for the sensitive and imaginative task of vision-making.

The paper will briefly describe the concept of corporate culture and its importance to managers, the anthropological notion of key organising principles, the epistemological basis of the core values model and a description of the method itself, as used practically, in organisations. GSS software incorporates properties that can help offset human frailties as they surface in meetings. These will be discussed. The paper will conclude by proposing a 'hands on' simulation of a vision making session at the 1996 IFIP conference.

2 CORPORATE CULTURE

Culture

The idea of culture is that it is an organising principle for the "we-ness" of a defined group of people bound together in a social setting. The deep generative moral, legal and social rules that prescribe acceptable behavior for the good of the group are implicit in the strategies structures and customs that are acceptable as 'normal', standards in daily life. As organised work is a feature of modern living it seems likely that this applies also to organisational life. Culture, unlike many of the other social systems that have to be flexible and malleable to survive change, evolves to form patterns of behavior that become embedded in the actions and reactions of group members. In other words whilst societies require many of their social systems to be flexible and responsive in the face of continuous change, cultural activities are directed towards becoming deeply held and valued anchors to hang on to in the face of turbulence and change.

From an organisational point of view, producing a strong culture could mean producing a stabilising factor in an otherwise seemingly unstable environment. The question is: Do organisations qualify as being 'cultures'? (The term culture is used in the 'definable group' sense rather than the sociological sense of sub-culture). If they do, can culture building serve the organisation as a key stability forming activity?

Adler (1993), drawing on the work of anthropologists, highlights some defining aspects of culture. Barnouw (1985) describes culture as "a way of life of a group of people...", Kroeber and Kluckholn (1952:181) write that "...the essential core of culture consists of traditional (*i.e.*, historically derived and selected) ideas and especially their attached values. Following his seminal work in the 1980's, Hofstede (1984:21) talks about culture as it 'determines the identity of a human group in the same way that personality determines the identity of an individual.'. He treats culture as "the collective programming of the mind which distinguishes the members of one human group from another". Although most writers in the corporate culture field acknowledge that culture is not readily captured or transparent there seems to be a consensus that corporate culture exists as an important organisational entity. Writers such as Schein (1985:51), Pugh (1993), Frost, *et al* (1991) make a convincing case for the existence of organisational or corporate culture (notwithstanding unresolved dilemmas and competing perspectives).

Key organising principles

Apart from making the diagnostic contribution to studying culture, with the now famous cultural dimensions of Power Distance, Uncertainty Avoidance, Masculine/Feminine, Individual/Collective frameworks, Hofstede (1984) coined the term 'Business Anthropology' and expressed the thought that this would be important for organisations (Hofstede, 1989). This led the author to adopt an anthropological approach when thinking about culture in organisations and the idea of key organising principles. This entails thinking about people at work as they go about developing the aspects of life they particularly value as being essential to successful living.

Central to any culture is its key organising principles. These are the 'designs for living' that have been worked out, over time, in such a way as to become a blueprint in terms of moral, social, legal patterns or value rules of behavior. Whilst each society or social group has different rules about, for example, educating, socialising, doing what is right, they all have rules. These rules have to be worked out by the group members as they find ways to 'live' and work together that feel comfortable and successful. In the organisational setting, each organisation develops its own rules (stated or unstated) about training and development, socialisation and distribution of status, and basically what it is 'OK to do around here'.

This anthropological approach guided the task of developing a process framework by which any business or organisation anywhere in the world could construct a shared vision. There is a premise that although the sort of values held by group members are different in each country, or indeed in each business, that each group holds values is a common factor. When presenting the core values process model to a multicultural group of people there is a high degree of agreement on its applicability in different cultural settings, although the method would vary according to things like the authority structures and systems in place.

Values, key constructs in understanding culture.

Put informally, each of us carries within ourselves the essence of our own culture. We usually know what we value as a group, whether this is independence, fairness, group companionship or, say, professionalism. We know what we believe in. These beliefs are closely related to our values. At work we may believe in fair play, promotion on merit, equality of contribution from colleagues and management alike, rewards when they are earned. These 'value rules' are best observed when they are infringed. Favouritism, unequal workloads, no recognition where it is due, all infringe the values of fairness, justice and equity. The values of different groups within the same organisation cannot be construed as being commonly held. Each group needs to articulate its own values and preferred value rules for operating. Effort will need to be made to select and test a set of values acceptable by both as harmonious. These values would become the guiding principles upon which future decisions and behaviors would rest:

> Values are among the most stable and enduring characteristics of individuals. They are the basis upon which attitudes and personal preferences are formed. They are the basis for crucial decisions, life directions and personal tastes, much of what we are is a product of the basic values we have developed through our lives. An organisation too has a value system, usually referred to as its organisational culture. Research has shown that employees who hold values that are congruent with their organisation's values are more productive and satisfied. Holding values that are inconsistent with company values, on the other hand, is a major source of frustration, conflict and nonproductivity (Whetton & Cameron, 1991:57).

Adler (1993), suggests that values are strong influencers of beliefs attitudes and behavior. They intuitively tell a person or a group if what is being done or suggested is right or wrong. This would apply for the most important of organisational activities such as the method of developing and communicating strategy, the design of structures and relationships down to the amount of personal authority accorded to each person in the organisation.

Constructivist paradigm

Culture is not a tangible entity. It cannot be counted as a fact, even a social fact. Culture cannot be discovered as 'a reality out there somewhere'. It is not observable, measurable and exists abstractly in the mind, rather than concretely in time and space. In other words, culture is a construct, a version of 'reality' produced by one or more individuals.

A collective construct can only be approximated but nevertheless, if it is produced by members of a group, working together, a shared understanding seems possible. An appropriate theoretical framework for designing culture-based work is the constructivist framework (Schwandt, 1994)

The constructivist way of managing would focus on those activities designed to encourage shared meaning. If 'personal reality' consists of what Senge (1992:5) calls mental models of how the world should work, then presenting or prescribing one 'authentic' reality to an individual or group of people would not be too convincing. This would apply to the company policy or manual, any documentation that represented a ready-made version of reality. Negotiating shared constructs seems a more effective way of working out desired ways of behaving and achieving the "we-ness" that makes for collective programming of the mind.

Theory of the core values model

It was this kind of constructivist thinking, together with many years of experience in diverse areas of organisational life, that led to the idea that an organisation would pull together more successfully if there was less prescribed reality from management and more negotiated reality between managers and workers. Figure 1 below, shows how each group needs to contribute to an area of shared meaning to the point that each other's values can be aligned to produce a set of shared value rules.

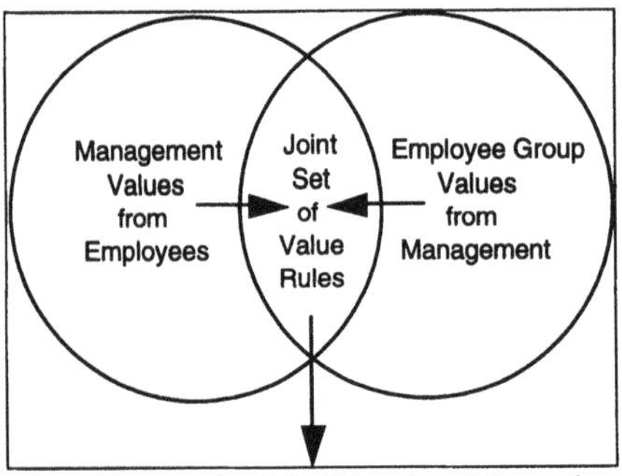

Figure 1 Internal core values (the way 'we' do things here) (reproduced from Whiteley, A. M. (1995) *Managing Change: a core values approach.* Macmillan Pub., Melbourne).

Negotiating the internal core values is not enough in an organisation though. Each organisation does not exist in a vacuum. Successful organisations exist to serve markets, customers and consumers as exemplified lessons in the literature from organisations such as Xerox (Kearns & Nadler, 1993). This goes for public and private sector organisations alike. Our experience suggests that there is usually one predominant characteristic that the customers in the marketplace value from the organisation. This value can be taken as a core value and inclusion of customers' core values is an essential part of culture-building. The business of aligning the three sets of core values, management, employee and customer, becomes the manager's major pre-occupation in the task of culture-building.

Although the vision making process may be started by management the contribution of each group is recognised as an integral part of the vision making process. Figure 2 shows management, employee and customer groups coming together to create shared values.

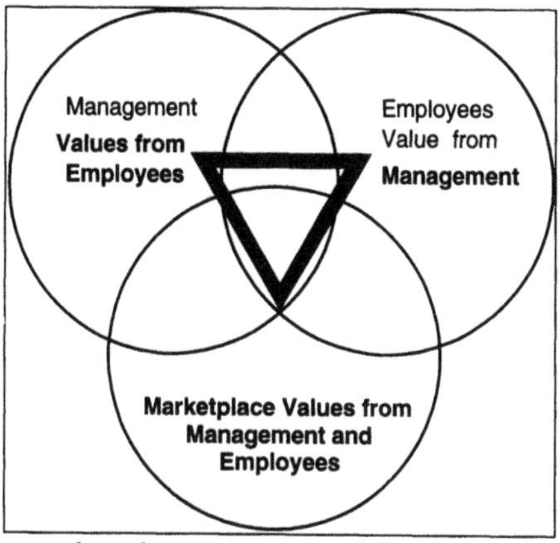

Figure 2 The three core value players (reproduced from Whiteley, A. M. (1995) *Managing Change: a core values approach.* Macmillan Pub., Melbourne.

The core values model is a framework for visualising the organisational process from a culture-building point of view. However, in this model there is a marked difference from the widely held view that vision making is the job of top management. An example of this comes out in recent research carried out in the U.K. (Aitken & Saunders, 1995) which reports that those organisations in the study that had outstanding performance felt a large part of their success was due to the vision of top management. To them the important task was to communicate the vision effectively. This idea is shared by writers such as Kotter and Heskett (1992). When the core values model was being developed, the idea that senior managers should develop vision and pass it down the line did not seem to overcome the problem of how to include the core values of workers in such a way that they could see their values, as they produced them, reflected in the vision statement. There was something abstract, once removed, in the idea of handing values and vision down to others. This was to be tested out over the next few years using an organisational workshops method that included employee groups. Overwhelming evidence from many different work sectors suggested that workers did have values, did think they were important and did wish to see them reflected in the vision statement (Whiteley and Atkinson 1995).

For the purposes of building the model, vision was conceptualised as a mental model of the way the organisation would organise for survival and success. It represented a mindset constructed by the people who play key roles in organisational life. It has become increasingly recognised that employees are to be included in these key roles (Eden 1992). The mindset is really a philosophical statement about the 'true' nature of the marketplace, management employee relationships, and of the contribution each makes to organisational success. Early in the stages of inquiring about vision it became evident that a developed vision by itself could be of little more than symbolic significance. Stories of framed vision statements where the tellers could not remember either what they contained or how they were developed led to the notion that visions really have to work for a living. The values have to be carried through into the organisational purpose or mission.

Organisational strategies have to be tested against the shared values for compatibility (at the time of writing, so many are found not to be in tune, so putting strategic implementation at risk). Structures and systems have to enable the strategies and also be in tune with the shared values, as do the policies and guidelines, processes. and people management styles. What this seems to do is to increase the sense of ownership not only of the good things but also of the problems and agreed ways of developing solutions. When introducing the workshop both to managers and employees, this is explained using the figure 3 below.

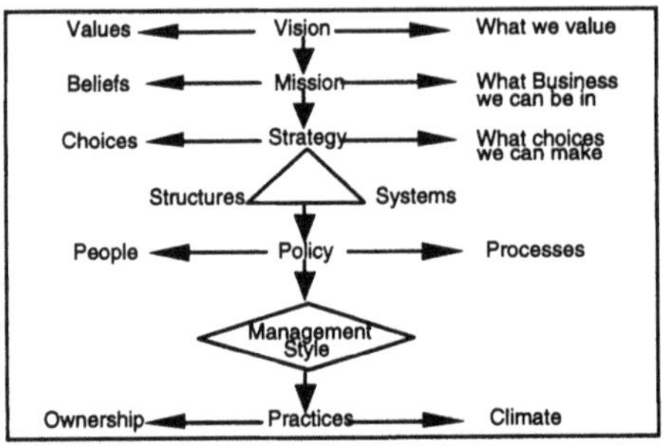

Figure 3 Vision and values carried through to daily practices (reproduced from Whiteley, A. M. (1995) *Managing Change: a core values approach.* Macmillan Pub., Melbourne.

3 THE CORE VALUES METHOD

During the development of the core values model, organisations most likely to be interested in the model and workshop method were those going through (sometimes drastic) change or faced with the prospect. Other organisations were those who needed to show improved performance and saw people as the key to this. Others were conducting strategic planning and were amenable to ideas on how to include vision making in this way.

The dominant groups were nearly always senior managers and/or human resource directors. Almost always the core values workshops were conducted with this group first, followed by the employee group. The ideal of accessing customer groups was not always achieved but in all cases work was done by the organisation to collect data on customer values and perceptions. The message that the core values method rests on the assumption that the most effective internal vision an organisation can have is one which is designed in collaboration with employees was a cornerstone of the workshops. The following narrative describes a core values initiative in a typical organisation.

There will be some preparation, perhaps over months for the sort of change which requires organisational renewal. Information about the organisation's future challenges and its state of readiness to meet them will have been communicated in such a way that the workforce can have opportunity to ask questions. During this time there will be a need to send clear signals that a new way of thinking or mindset is required. It may be a time for tough decisions. Those who can not commit to the internal model of genuine employee involvement may not feel that there is a role for them in the new organisational arrangements. Managers may have not had to rely on employee input and/or approval of decisions. They may need convincing that the realities employees construct about the organisation will be heavily influenced by management's structures, systems and methods of decision making.

Employees, especially those who are opinion leaders, whether formal or informal, will need to be prepared for the skills which are required in decision making such as planning, problem-solving, and communication. They will need to be convinced from the highest sources in the organisation that creating a shared vision is not a short-term crisis measure. They need to have some confidence that the energy they put into championing the new ways of thinking and operating will not be wasted when markets and economies improve. This sort of preparation will take varying amounts of time according to the existing relationships between management and employees.

When the climate is right and a reasonable amount of trust in management's and employees' intentions has been achieved then vision making sessions can be held to determine:

- an overarching vision
- internal visions for departments or groups.

As the task of leadership is to propose future direction, given that the senior management group have experience and access to environmental information this group will need to specify what it values from the workforce. Employee groups in turn will work out what they value from management. The shared values of each group will be extended to include the values of customers.

4 THE USE OF GROUP SUPPORT SYSTEMS TECHNOLOGY

One of the major drawbacks was conducting core values workshops in the same sort of meeting setting that previous battles have been fought and lost or won, friendships and enmities are at stake and it is the survival of the fittest in terms of being heard. These strengths of human nature work as frailties when trying to concentrate on issues rather than personalities, ensure equal opportunities for input and efficient capturing of a host of competing voices.

At the time of writing, core values workshops are still being conducted in both manual and GSS modes. The authentic work captured in the manual mode is conspicuously different from that using GSS. It is beyond the scope of this paper to go into detail, but major differences lie in the willingness of group members (manual) to clarify and make one person's idea their own. Another difference is the loss of focus in the manual mode particularly when favourite topics are aired.

Almost all management groups have used the vision making together with the first stages of strategic planning. There is still much to learn about GSS facilitation and the effect of GSS process variables on meetings (Jessup, Connolly & Galegher, 1990; Lewis & Whiteley, 1992; Nunamaker, 1991). This account recognises but does not deal with these in this paper as the focus is on the core values application. However one important facilitation activity, that of releasing the imaginal aspect of thinking, is necessary to vision making. So far the following imaginal releasing exercise is done manually. It is used both in vision making and strategic planning which also rests upon imagining a future.

Creating future scenarios

A simple method of releasing the imaginal (and the emotional is usually very prominent here) is to ask the visioning group members to close their eyes and imagine the organisation as it will be in five/ten years time. The scene they are imagining is bright and light. There is an air of prosperity. There is an aura of success. What sort of buildings do participants see? What sort physical layouts are in the workshops or other work areas? What can you tell about the human arrangements around the place? Who are the bosses and how can you tell? Are there any signs of the customer? Are there any symbols of how well the organisation is succeeding? How are the employees communicating? What sort of jokes and stories are being told? What values are evident in the scene you have just described?

Now the group members are asked to imagine a very different scenario. The brightness has faded away. A dullness has taken its place. There is an aura of "getting through the day as best as one can". They are asked things like these. What do the buildings look like here? How are things laid out? How are people relating to each other? How are managers and employees achieving goals together? How are the successes and failures communicated? What sort of stories are being told? What do you think the people here value?

Very often here one can see vision in the making. Even those participants who are metaphorically wedded to spread sheets begin the process of surfacing the inner workings of organisational life and in particular those aspects they value, feel are the right things to be doing. Although group members are invited to contribute tangible as well as intangible aspects there are always many more behavioral than substantive responses. It is not difficult to see that beliefs in the value rules governing the way people should behave are uppermost in the minds of people who are visualising themselves in a future at work.

5 GROUP SUPPORT SYSTEMS PROCEDURES

Following the core values method, the outcome of the first GSS step is a set of values generated by participants. Private comment enables each person to peruse the work of the group adding comments of support, agreement, disagreement, expansion to any of the contributions. Discussion and evaluation results in the adoption of one overarching or core value. The key and core values represent the value rules of the organisation from this group's point of view. Often with senior management groups, strategic planning follows the vision making, often requiring several sessions. Once the strategies are chosen, they are "tested" against the values for compatibility. A script for vision making would include:

'Warm Up' generate

Experience has shown that around thirty values can be facilitated such that each person's authentic work is processed by the group. A timed 'warm up' generate, inviting the group members to contribute a continuous list allows individuals to privately brainstorm. The use of private comment allows the usual piggy back and rethinking to further stimulate thinking;

Parallel interview process (PIP)

For the next step, observing the anonymity convention, individuals select and key in their three core values. The 'warm up' list is available in hard copy and time is given for informal discussions before choices are made. Group members are basically acting as individuals here contributions coming individually and in parallel.

Discuss/Organise

This step most closely resembles a manual workshop in that the individuals are free to talk, argue, listen, clarify and expand/contract without having to write things down, thereby identifying themselves and their particular point of view.

This is the step where the need for a constructivist paradigm is most visible. It is here one sees reality in the making. The combination of private comment and group endorsement of inputs offers more chance of commitment to the group process rather than a particular point of view.

Evaluate

The rate tool is often used so that the congruence or otherwise of individual thinking on values rated as important can surface. If there is too much dispersion then clearly more work would need to be done to see why this is so.

Because it is not possible to conduct GSS and manual sessions for this particular activity, it has not been possible to directly compare their relative effectiveness. More research will be conducted in this area so that a more critical view can be taken. Areas might include identifying ways of bringing more qualitative data into the GSS meetings to save time. An area that may not have been fully exploited is that of forward planning so that values can be incorporated into human resource systems and processes. This work is in its developmental stages.

6 THE CONFERENCE VISION WORKSHOP

This paper describes the way in which the core values model has been used together with GSS technology to build culture through a set of workshop activities in a number of organisations. Normally, a conference would not be an ideal environment for a demonstration because, although a conference has a unifying theme, it is not often an actionable one. However, the 1996 conference *The International Office of the Future:Design Options and Solution Strategies* leads up to the 1997 founding of an entity which, if we were giving it an organisational name, we could call "Global Inc." For all intents and purposes the conference workshop demonstrates a setting where the process of developing a vision and shared sense of purpose is begun.

The GSS workshop described earlier in the paper will be simulated at the 1996 conference. There are two purposes here. The first is to provide a setting for participants to think about the international office of the future concept in the company of their fellows. The second is to produce a tentative vision using the workshop mode. Members of the Organising Committee, Program Committee and Participants will represent three key stakeholding groups.

7 CONCLUSION

Since the late 1990's those working in the Information Technology field have recognised the qualitative aspects of meetings for which provision needs to be made.

> Today's organisations face a future of increasing turbulence and international competitiveness. Rapid adaptation to change is paramount. managers spend over half of their time in meetings addressing these and other important issues. Ironically, while we have provided considerable computer-based support for individuals and the organisation as a whole, we have historically provided virtually no such support for meetings. The situation is now beginning to change...

Vogel, D. R., Nunamaker, J. F. J., Martz, W. J. J., Grohowski, R., & McGoff, C. (1989) "Electronic Meeting Experience at IBM", *Journal of Management Information Systems*, **6** (3), 26.

For example, there are a range of activities where groups come together with the need to create shared understanding. Culture building is such an activity, dealing with the most fundamental of aspects of organisational life, values. A method for developing shared values in the form of vision statements was developed over several years, using manual rather than technical facilitation. For the last three years, Group Support Systems technology has been used for this purpose with effective results. There is a need for further work both in formalising responses to the technology and using the values results for strategic and organisational planning.

8 POSTSCRIPT - CONFERENCE FINDINGS

The task was to use the conference attendees to begin the process of creating a shared vision for the last event in the International Office of the Future (IOF) trilogy for which "Global Inc." was the metaphor. If Global Inc. was to "walk the talk" in terms of matching the values of community and global with

Table 1 Emergent Themes

Vision Statement

We see Global Inc. holding a global "round the clock conference" to enable knowledge exchange and shared experiences between individuals and groups interested in the international office of the future while meeting participant expectations with minimum risk, minimum complexity, and within the constraints of available resources

Emergent Themes

1. **Open participation: open sharing of information with global collaboration**
To conduct an open, information-sharing experience...intended for a wide diversity of participants and topics.
2. **People centered with technology as an enabling factor, not a controlling factor**
The conference should be people-centered, with technology as an enabling factor and NOT a controlling factor.
3. **Cooperative rather than competitive, synergistic where differences are valued**
The spirit should be cooperative rather than competitive, with a synergistic approach where everyone's contribution is valued and recognized from a team perspective.
4. **Multi-organizational structure adapted to different cultures**
In our case, we will have an opportunity to set up a multi-organization structure adapted to different cultures.
5. **High quality**
Quality sessions that incite discussions and new research ideas.
6. **Springboard for future ongoing research**
The conference should be a springboard for future ongoing research.
7. **Helping others to know more**
Be prepared to help others to know more - mentoring, assisting, tutoring, etc.
8. **Group focus**
dynamics of group relationships (within groups participating) building of group memory and studying of its dynamics.
9. **Outcomes (social, conference methodology, leadership)**
as a value the research should not only look at the task/production outcomes but also at the relationship/social outcomes including "would we want to do this again?"
10. **Innovation versus traditional**
The conference must be a trail-blazer in terms of multi-site conferences. The conference must also be a trail-blazer in terms of speaker audience interaction.

conference organisation, content and format, then the activity of constructing shared meaning was essential. The vision workshop was part of a design that included focused sessions. The output became the supporting data for the Design teams, whose brief was to advise on key conference aspects. The vision workshop was 'structured in sixes', with three pairs taking the role of the three stakeholding groups *program committee, organising committee and research opportunists.* The pairs convened to share their perspectives and combine them into a vision statement or a statement of values. Groups were invited to input the results electronically. One of the major uses of the vision data was to test the vision statement of the three pairs of conference coordinators, program chairs, organising chairs and research opportunist chairs for fit with those of the other groups. The fit was found to be a good one in terms of the sense of the other contributions. In addition a number of themes emerged (see Table 1 above).

The themes above were representative of the values to be preserved at the 1997 conference. As the participants said, "this really is the start of the 1997 conference". True to the values of participation and sharing, the data produced at the conference will provide the starting point for the wide dissemination of ideas, views and values that will help the conference be "a conference with a culture".

9 REFERENCES

Adler, N. J. (1993) "Do Cultures Vary?" In T. D. Weinshall (Ed.), *Societal Culture and Management,* New York: de Gruyter.

Aitken, A., & Saunders, I. (1995) "Vision only works if Communicated", *People Management* (December), 28-29.

Barnouw, V. (1985) *Culture and Personality.* (4th ed.) New York: Dorsey Press.

Eden, C. (1992) *Strategy Development and Implementation.* Paper presented at the 25th Hawaii International Conference on Systems Sciences, California.

Hofstede, G. (1984) *Culture's Consequences: International differences in work-related values.* Beverly Hills: Sage Publ.

Hofstede, G. (1989) "The Cultural Relativity of Organizational Practices and Theories". In J.N. Sheth & G. S. Eshghi (Eds.), *Global Human Resources Perspectives,* (pp. 3-19). Cincinnati: South-Western Pub. Co.

Jessup, L., Connolly, T., & Galegher, J. (1990) "The Effects of Anonymity on GDSS Group Process with an Idea-Generating Task", *MIS Quarterly*, **14** (3), 313-321.

Kearns, D. T., & Nadler, D. A. (1993) *Prophets in the Dark : How Xerox Reinvented Itself and Beat Back the Japanese.* New York: Harper Collins.

Kotter, J. P., & Heskett, J. L. (1992) *Corporate Culture and Performance.* New York: The Free Press.

Kroeber, A. L., & Kluckholn, C. (1952) "Culture: A Critical Review of Concepts and Definitions", *Peabody Museum Papers*, **47** (1 (Cambridge, Mass.: Harvard University)), 181.

Lewis, L. F., & Whiteley, A. (1992) *Initial Perceptions of Professional Facilitators Regarding GDSS Impacts: A study using the Grounded-Theory approach.* Paper presented at the Proceedings of the 25th Hawaii International Conference on Systems Sciences.

Nunamaker, J. J., and Vogel D. (1991) "Facilitation Issues", *Proceedings of the 24th Hawaii International Conference on Systems Sciences*, **4** (24).

Pugh, D. S. (1993) "Organizational Context and Structure in Various Cultures". In T. D. Weinshall (Ed.), *Societal Culture and Management.*, (pp. 425-435), Berlin: Walter de Grutyer.

Schein, E. (1985) *Organisational Culture and Leadership.* San Francisco: Jossey-Bass.

Schwandt, T. A. (1994) "Constructivist, Interpretivist Approaches to Human Inquiry". In N. K. Denzin & Y. S. Lincoln (Eds.), *Handbook of Qualitative Research*, (pp. 118 - 137). New York: Sage.
Weinshall, T. D. (Ed.) (1993) *Societal Culture and Management*. Berlin: Walter de Grutyer.
Whetton, D. A., & Cameron, K. S. (1991) *Developing Management Skills*. (2nd ed.). New York: Harper Collins.
Whiteley, A. M., & Aitkinson, D. (1995) *I.T. Tools Help the Management of Change*. Paper presented at the TIMS, Singapore.

10 BIOGRAPHY

Associate Professor **Alma Whiteley** is MBA Director at the Graduate School of Business, Curtin University of Technology. Alma has a PhD from the University of Newcastle-Upon-Tyne (UK). Alma's teaching areas include International Business Competitiveness, Critical Thinking and Human Resource Strategy. Alma consults to industry (public and private sector companies) in strategic planning and in the management of change. Group Support Systems has become a central support for this work.

23

Action learning: preparing workers for the international office of the future

Yoong, S.P.
Information Systems Group, Victoria University of Wellington,
P.O.Box 600, Wellington, New Zealand.
Office: +64 4 472 1000, Fax: +64 4 471 2200, Pak.Yoong@vuw.ac.nz

Abstract
This paper focuses on some organizational and social aspects of the International Office of the Future (IOF). In particular, it proposes an action learning model that could be used to prepare present generation office workers for the dynamic, complex, and turbulent IOF.

Keywords
Action learning, experiential learning, distributed facilitation, groupware.

1 INTRODUCTION

What is the nature of the International Office of the Future (IOF)? How would it affect the workplace and how should we prepare current generation office workers for it? To help answer these and other related questions, the IFIP WG8.4 working conference, *The International Office of the Future: Studies in Practice*, has chosen the following three themes as focal points for the multi-site conferences in September 1997: (a) Technology, (b) Business Processes and (c) Organizational, Cultural and Social Aspects. It is expected that each theme will be addressed at one of the three sites serving as major hubs: Tuscon, Arizona, U.S.A. (Technology), Delft, The Netherlands (Business Processes), and Perth, Australia (Organizational, Culture and Social Aspects). This and many other similar events like it are scheduled to be staged in the near future and these events require our immediate attention if the form and shape of the IOF are to be unravelled in a coherent and humane manner.

This paper focuses on some *organizational* and *social* aspects of the IOF. In particular, it proposes *action learning* as an approach to prepare present generation office workers for the IOF.

This paper is organized as follows. The first section summarizes some organizational and social aspects of the IOF relevant to this discussion. The summary is based on the book *The International Office of the Future: A Problem Analysis* (Bots 1995). The second section describes action learning and its relevance for the IOF. The third section proposes an action learning model to the IOF. The final section describes how action learning could be used to prepare present generation office workers for the *dynamic, complex, and turbulent* IOF.

2 ORGANIZATIONAL AND SOCIAL ASPECTS OF THE IOF

The International Office of the Future: A Problem Analysis (Bots et al., 1995) identifies a number of organizational and social aspects of the IOF relevant to this discussion. One message is clear: no matter what form the IOF infrastructure may finally take, the IOF will be a *dynamic*, *complex* and *turbulent* environment. Bots et al. (1995) have identified two basic organizational processes that need to be dealt with if the IOF is to be successful in this environment. These are:

1. to cope with the increasing complexity and turbulence (and with the resulting increase of unstructured tasks), organizations must adopt a dynamic, networked structure that allows them to get the most out of the knowledge and skills of its members . . .
2. to cope with the increasing hostility, organizations must adopt a process of 'ongoing improvement' . . . which means that they must create the appropriate culture and maintain this process, using short term gains as positive reinforcement to keep going and reap the long-term gains (p. 9).

Even though little is known about the exact nature of these 'coping' processes - as "it proves to be particularly difficult to predict *how* new technology will affect organizations, and also *when* this impact will actually take place" (Bots 1995; p. 7) - present generation office workers could increase their understanding by examining a number of possible IOF scenarios.

Bots et al. (1995) (citing Applegate 1988; Huber and McDaniel, 1986; DeLisi, 1980; and Charan, 1991) describe the IOF as a 'cluster organization' with a flat, flexible, dynamic, and networked structure. Dual structures will be put in place to manage structured and unstructured work and the latter is expected to have a dominating influence on the future workplace. Problem solving and decision making will be done by ad hoc project teams. These teams will be made up of individuals from several cultural and national backgrounds, with each team member choosing their preferred location and time of work.

A number of groupware tools could be used to support the various types of workgroups in the IOF. These products are designed to enhance, among other things, workflow automation, office conferencing and communications, information filtering, shared calendaring, electronic meeting support, and videoconferencing (Traunmuller, 1995) .

Given these possible technological and organizational scenarios for the IOF, what could be expected of the International *Workers* of the Future (IWOF)? One writer, Jacques (1995), expects the IWOF to be "a proactive problem solver, a self-managing team player, an abstract conceptualizer and a life-long learner" and since long-term employment is going to be a thing of the past, the IWOF is also expected to have a "mobile bundle of employable assets" (p. 20). This means that as well as being a subject-matter expert, the IWOF is also expected to be a 'process-oriented' worker with skills and knowledge that are easily transferable to, and applicable in, various unstructured tasks that might occur in different places, times, and cultures. As a member of various ad hoc computer-supported cooperative teams, the IWOF is expected to be able to coordinate and synchronize work, to collaborate with team members from diverse cultural backgrounds and opinions, and to make collective decisions and negotiations based on mutual trust (Traunmuller, 1995).

In summary, the IOF has been identified as a dynamic, complex, and turbulent environment in which workers are expected to adopt a flexible, collaborative, and open-minded approach to their work. Because very little is known about the exact nature and timing of the impact that technological infrastructure may have on the organization, workers are also encouraged to find out what 'works' and what doesn't as they proceed with life in the IOF. Specifically, they are asked "to create a suitable environment with incentives for spotting problems and opportunities and finding creative solutions" (Bots 1995; p. 14). The next section describes action learning and advocates its potential for developing the 'creative problem-solving' environment as described in the previous sentence.

3 THE NATURE OF ACTION LEARNING

The previous section describes a number of scenarios for the IOF. Given these scenarios, how do we assist present generation office workers (PGOW) to understand and prepare for the IOF? Perhaps a starting point is to acknowledge and take on board the suggestion given by Bots et al. (1995). They say that, in the dynamic, complex and turbulent IOF, the "office workers will more often have to define procedures as they proceed ... " (p. 6). This suggested approach aptly describes how PGOW can use *action learning* as a means of coping with the dynamic and turbulent workplace conditions of the IOF.

The term *action learning* was coined by Revans (1982) to describe the process in which groups of people work on real organizational issues and come up with practical solutions that may require changes to be made in the organization. Revans's original equation and concept for learning - L = P + Q (ie. learning equals programmed knowledge plus questioning insight) - have now been extended and applied in management education (MacNamara, 1982; Margerison, 1988; McGill et al., 1989), information systems education (Avison, 1989; Jessup and Egbert, forthcoming), and organisational development (Ramirez, 1983; Gregory, 1994).

In these contexts, action learning is both a learning and group problem-solving process in which people work on real issues and problems with the emphasis on self development and learning by doing. This group, known as the action learning 'set', meets regularly and provides the supportive and challenging environment in which members are encouraged to learn from experience, share that experience, listen to criticism and advice, implement that advice, and with group members review the action taken and the lessons learned (Margerison, 1988). In other words, both action and reflection-on-action (Schon, 1983) are essential processes in this approach to group problem-solving of real 'live' workplace issues. Associated with action learning is the notions of single-loop and double-loop learning (Argyris and Schon, 1974) . In single-loop learning, "we learn to maintain the field of constancy by learning to design actions that satisfy an existing governing variable" and in double-loop learning, we examine the underlying assumptions for the actions and therefore "learn to change the field of constancy itself" (p. 19).

Action learning is closely linked to action research. Cunningham (1993) describes action research as "a spectrum of activities that focus on research, planning, theorising, learning, and development ... a continuous process of research and learning in the researcher's long term relationship with a problem" (p. 4). By contrast, Carr and Kemmis (1986) emphasise the processes of 'improvement' and 'involvement' in action research :

> *There are two essential aims of all action research: to improve and to involve. Action research aims at improvement in three areas: firstly, the improvement of a practice; secondly, the improvement of the understanding of the practice by its practitioners; and thirdly, the improvement of the situation in which the practice takes place. Those involved in the practice being considered are to be involved in the action research process . . . As an action research project develops, it is expected that a widening circle of those affected by the practice will become involved in the research process.* (p. 165)

Zuber-Skerritt (1991) describes the relationship between action learning and action research. She says that action learning "is a basic concept of action research" (p. 214) and that action research is based on the "fundamental concepts of action learning, adult learning and holistic dialectical thinking" (p. 88).

Action learning provides a useful framework for the PGOW who are in the process of unravelling the nature and complexity of the IOF. Firstly, action learning focuses on tackling 'real life' organizational issues. Secondly, action learning promotes working and problem-solving in collaborative groups. The scenarios described in an earlier section suggest that the IWOFs need to be effective members of many ad hoc computer-supported cooperative teams. Action learning has the potential to prepare the PGOW for this. Thirdly, action learning is inherently a dynamic and adaptive process that promotes, among other things, 'ongoing improvement'. This process fits in with the notion that the IWOF will have to define procedures and find out what works and what does not. Finally, action learning is 'process oriented' and encourages the transferability of skills and knowledge between situations where tasks are unstructured. The nature of action learning and its potential for preparing the CGOW for the requirements of the IOF is therefore worth further examination.

Ramirez (1983) suggests that action learning is suited to organisations undergoing change in a turbulent environment while they are experiencing conditions of uncertainty and unpredictability because "action learning provides a 'how' that enables organizations continually and effectively to adapt the expectations upon which they base their strategies to the complex, rapidly changing outcomes that they face in turbulence" (p. 727).

The next section describes a proposed model of action learning and how it could be applied in the IOF. In particular, a scenario to prepare PGOW to be facilitators of 'distributed meetings' will be used to illustrate this model.

4 A PROPOSED MODEL OF ACTION LEARNING IN THE IOF

The proposed action learning model is based on the principles of 'collaborative group learning', 'commitment to improving workplace practice' (Kemmis and McTaggart, 1988), and 'learning from experience' (Boud, 1993). The model provides the following guidelines for the planning, design, and implementation of action learning projects by PGOW in their preparation for the IOF:

- PGOW are encouraged to learn in groups and to use the learning groups to:
  - work and gather data on real life issues and problems associated with working in the IOF,
  - reflect and improve on their workplace practice by the appropriate incorporation of groupware tools,
  - interlink their action and reflection, and
  - discuss their action and reflection with others.
- PGOW are encouraged to learn from experience and to:
  - use the experience as a foundation of and a stimulus for further learning,
  - discuss their prior experience and to recognize the effects and influence of prior experience on their learning,
  - use the knowledge, skills, and experience of other group members as resources for their own learning,
  - gain new experiences by testing new techniques and actions, and
  - invite group members to provide feedback, taking that feedback and implementing it, and reviewing with those members the action taken and the lessons learned.

While carrying out each action learning project, the action research spiral of *planning, acting, observing*, and *reflecting* (Figure 1) can be used to guide actual workplace learning and research (Zuber-Skerritt, 1995).

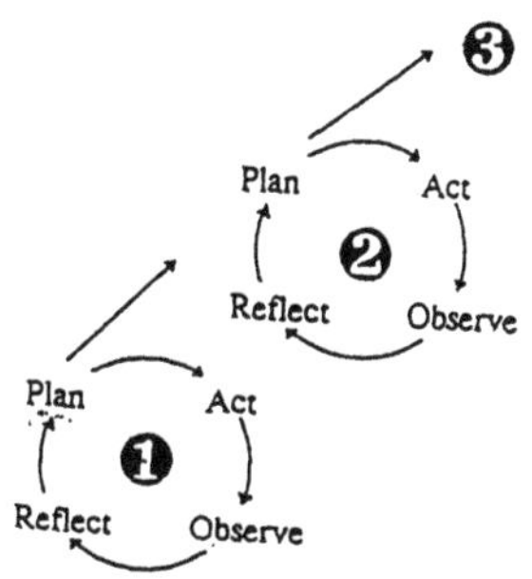

Figure 1 Action research spiral (Source: Zuber-Skeritt, 1995; p. 13)

This spiral, which is based on the work of Lewin (1948), indicates that a group of PGOW could seek out workplace issues (current or potential) that may have implications for the IOF and analyse and plan the first step for improvement, and devise ways of keeping a record of their collective experience and of monitoring their progress. As this first step is implemented, the PGOW will observe and reflect on their actions and share their findings with each other. Findings are then evaluated and appropriate suggestions for change are accepted and implemented before the next cycle of action learning activities begins. This 'ongoing improvement' cycle is continuous, allowing the PGOW to find out what works and what does not and to adapt their actions as the nature of the IOF unfolds.

This author has been using action learning and experiential learning approaches in training and accrediting facilitators for *electronic* meetings (Yoong, 1995(a); Yoong, 1995(b)) and has found an effective method for determining what works and what does not in the facilitation of electronic meetings. The method was particularly useful because, when the action learning projects were initiated, very little was known of GSS facilitation and what it takes to be a facilitator of electronic meetings. A body of professional skills and knowledge has now been developed and improvements of these skills are continually sought. To further these improvements, a network of GSS facilitators meets regularly to discuss and to exchange common experiences and to try out more effective ways of facilitating electronic meetings. The accumulated skills and knowledge are then passed on to the next generation of GSS facilitators (Yoong, 1995(b)).

In the next section, the scenario of PGOW learning to facilitate distributed meetings is chosen as a potential issue for the IOF, one for which creative solutions are required.

5 LEARNING TO FACILITATE DISTRIBUTED MEETINGS: AN ACTION LEARNING APPROACH

Literature on distributed meetings and their facilitation has been appearing in IS publications for a few years (for example, Dubs and Hayne, 1992; Niederman et al., 1993; Fellers et al., 1995; Knool and Jarvenpaa, 1995; Whitworth, 1995; Maaranen, 1995), and meeting support tools are also available (for example, VisionQuest, GroupSystems, RealTime Notes, and TCBWorks [a Web-based tool from the University of Georgia]). The practice of 'distributed facilitation' is relatively new and any activities that could build on what is already known will contribute towards an increased understanding of the IOF.

Imagine the following 1996 office scenario:

> *You are a member of the middle management group in the Head Office (HO) of a large international trading organization. The HO has GroupSystems (GS) and you are one of six in-house facilitators of face-to-face electronic meetings. Towards the end of the action learning programme for this facilitation role, you and the other five peer facilitators agreed to meet regularly and, among other things, to discuss any insights about the use of GS in new or innovative ways. You and your peers are also aware of the company's plans to add groupware tools to enhance computer-supported collaborative group work between some branch offices around the world. You have been given the task of devising procedures to promote this form of group work.*

The following action learning scenario - planning, acting, observing, and reflecting - is proposed as one approach to finding out procedures for facilitating distributed collaborative group work.

Planning (the following set of steps are not in a sequential order)

1. You and your peers have met to explore and analyse the problem. As a result of this discussion, your peer group has decided that the action learning model is an appropriate approach to solve the organizational problem. Your group has also decided to stay local and use only HO personnel for the first action learning cycle. This is because GroupSystems is

already available and also because there are experienced GSS facilitators in HO. You also want a quick result. You then plan the next series of learning cycles so that personnel from a selected overseas branches can be involved. The final make up of the project team includes three of the experienced GSS facilitators and three other participants from HO. These six members are selected to ensure a mixture of people from different business units, cultural backgrounds, and levels of experience with group facilitation and with the use of various groupware tools.

2. The project team then decides to deal with a 'real life' organizational issue and choose the planning of the next bi-annual company conference of middle and senior management groups. This is appropriate as the next action learning cycle can include some of the people who will be actually planning for the conference.

3. The project team also decides on the following ground rules: (a) each member must complete at least two learning cycles before their or his or her continuing involvement is discussed, (b) each member must enter an electronic journal after each meeting or learning activity, (c) the journal's data must include the member's description of the experience, his or her reflection on that experience, and anything useful for the group memory, and (d) the data from the electronic journal will be discussed and evaluated during the next scheduled face-to-face group meeting.

Acting and Observing

1. Members will take part in the distributed meetings from their preferred location (usually from their own office) and time. GroupSystems V will be used.

2. All members will take a turn at facilitating each meeting. Change overs could be at the completion of agenda items or at the end of 12-hour periods.

3. Each member, whether facilitating or not, will note their own behaviour and their observations of meeting co-ordination, monitoring, interaction, and feedback. The facilitator must also make sure that the time log is printed afterwards.

Reflecting

1. After the meeting, each member will enter their portion of the electronic journal and a first draft of the conference plan is completed before the scheduled face-to-face meeting.

2. During this meeting, comments from the electronic journal are read, discussed, and reviewed. Any improvements will be adopted at the next distributed meeting.

The project team's series of distributed meetings will end when the final conference draft is ready to send to the overseas branches. Now the details of the next action learning cycle, including the composition of the international project team, can be planned. The findings from the last action learning cycle and a list of what works and what does not will be included into the plan.

6 CONCLUSIONS

A model of action learning is proposed to prepare present generation office workers for the IOF. The model, which focuses on 'defining procedures as we go', can be seen as one of many 'coping' processes the IOF would need to formulate to successfully manage the dynamic, complex, and turbulent environment to come. By adopting this action learning approach, the opportunity "to create a suitable environment with incentives for spotting problems and opportunities and finding creative solutions" (Bots et al, 1995; p. 14) becomes a viable option. We must start now so that the form and shape of the IOF will be unravelled in a coherent and humane manner.

7 REFERENCES

Applegate, L., Cash, J., and Quinn Mills, D. (1988) Information technology and tomorrow's manager. *Harvard Business Review*, December.

Argyris, C. and Schon, D. (1974) *Theory in Practice: Increasing Professional Effectiveness*, Jossey-Bass Publishers, San Francisco.

Avison, D.E. (1989) Action learning for information systems teaching. *International Journal of Information Management*, 41-50.

Bots, P. and Uijlenbroek, J. (1995) Developing an international office of the future vision statement: workshop 1. in *The International Office of the Future: A Problem Analysis*, P. Bots, B. Glasson, and D. Vogel. (eds.) Faculty of Systems Engineering, Policy Analysis and Management, Delft University of Technology, Delft, The Netherlands, 57-64.

Bots, P., Uijlenbroek, J., and van der Herik, C. (1995) The international office of the future: a search for issues and challenges. in *The International Office of the Future: A Problem Analysis*, P. Bots, B. Glasson, and D. Vogel. (eds.) Faculty of Systems Engineering, Policy Analysis and Management, Delft University of Technology, Delft, The Netherlands, 1-17.

Bots, P., Glasson, B. and Vogel, D. (1995) *The International Office of The Future: A Problem Analysis.* Faculty of Systems Engineering, Policy Analysis and Management, Delft University of Technology, Delft, The Netherlands.

Boud, D. (1993) Experience as a base for learning. *Higher Education Research And Development* **12:1**, 33-44.

Carr, W. and Kemmis, S. (1986) *Becoming Critical: Education, Knowledge And Action Research*, Deakin University, Geelong, Australia.

Charan, R. (1991) How networks reshape organizations - for results. *Harvard Business Review*, September.

Cunningham, J.B. (1993) *Action Research And Organizational Development*, Praeger, Westport, Connecticut.

DeLisi, P. (1980) Lessons from the steel axe: culture, technology, and organizational change. *Sloan Management Review*, Fall.

Dubs, S. and Hayne, S. (1992) Distributed facilitation: a concept whose time has come? in *CSCW 92 Proceedings*, 314-321.

Fellers, J.W., Clifton, A., and Handley. H. (1995) Using the internet to provide support for distributed interactions. in *28th Annual Hawaii International Conference on System Sciences in Hawaii*, 52-60.

Gregory, M. (1994) Accrediting work-based learning: action learning - a model for empowerment. *Journal Of Management Development*, **13:4**, 41-52.

Huber, G. and McDaniel, R. (1986) The decision-making paradigm of organizational design. *Management Science*, **32:5**.

Jacques, R. (1995) The legacy of 'task-work': the office of the future meets the factory of the past. in *The International Office of the Future: A Problem Analysis*, P. Bots, B. Glasson, and D. Vogel. (eds.) Faculty of Systems Engineering, Policy Analysis and Management, Delft University of Technology, Delft, The Netherlands, 19-25.

Jessup, L.M. and Egbert, J.L. (forthcoming) Active learning in business education with, through, and about technology. *Journal of Information Systems Education.*

Kemmis, S. and McTaggart, R. (ed.) (1989) *The Action Research Planner (3rd ed.).* Deakin University, School of Education, Open Campus Program, Melbourne.

Knool, K. and Jarvenpaa, S. (1995) Learning to work in distributed global teams. in *Proceedings of the 28th Annual Hawaii International Conference on Systems Sciences in Hawaii,* 92-97.

Lewin, K. (1948) Resolving Social Conflicts. *Selected Papers on Group Dynamics* edited by Weiss Lewin, G. Harper and Brothers, New York.

Maaranen, P. (1995) Group video-distributed EMS for small groups. in *28th Annual Hawaii International Conference on System Science in Hawaii,* 1995, pp. 503-513.

MacNamara, M. and Weekes, W.H. (1982) The action learning model of experiential learning for developing managers. *Human Relations,* **35:10**, 879-902.

Margerison, C.J. Action learning and excellence in management development. *Journal of Management Development* **7:5,** 43-53.

McGill, I., Segal-Horn, S., Bourner, T., and Frost, P. (1989) Action learning: a vehicle for personal and group experiential learning. in *Making Sense Of Experiential Learning: Diversity In Theory And Practice,* S. Weil and I. McGill (eds.), Open University Press, Milton Keynes, 116-125.

Niederman, F., Beise, C., and Beranek, P. (1993) Facilitation issues in distributed group support systems. in *ACM SIGCPR in St. Louis, Missouri,* 299-313.

Revans, R. (1982) *The Origins and Growth of Action Learning,* Chartwell-Bratt, Bromley.

Ramirez, R. (1983) Action learning: a strategic approach for organizations facing turbulent conditions. *Human Relations,* **36:8**, 725-742.

Schon, D.A. (1983) *The Reflective Practitioner : How Professionals Think In Action,* Basic Books, New York.

Traunmuller, R. (1995) Enhancing office systems with CSCW-function. in *The International Office of the Future: A Problem Analysis,* P. Bots, B. Glasson, and D. Vogel. (eds.) Faculty of Systems Engineering, Policy Analysis and Management, Delft University of Technology, Delft, The Netherlands, 27-44.

Whitworth, B. (1995) The social psychology of distributed electronic task groups. *New Zealand Journal of Computing,* **6:1**, 171-179.

Yoong, P. (1995) Assessing competency in GSS skills: a pilot study in the certification of GSS facilitators. in *Proceedings of the 1995 ACM SIGCPR Conference,* Nashville, Tennessee, USA, 1-9.

Yoong, P. (1995) Training facilitators for electronic meetings: a New Zealand case study. in *Proceedings of the 6th Australasian Conference in Information Systems,* Perth, Australia. 503-516.

Zuber-Skerritt, O. (1991) *Professional development in higher education: a theoretical framework for action research.* Griffith University Centre for the Advancement of Learning and Teaching, Brisbane, Australia.

Zuber-Skerritt, O. (1995) Models for action research. in *Moving On: Creative Applications Of Action Learning And Action Research*, S. Pinchen and R. Passfield (eds.) ALARPM, Brisbane, Australia, 2-29.

8 BIOGRAPHY

Pak Yoong is a Senior Lecturer in Information Systems at the Victoria University of Wellington, New Zealand. He has recently completed a Phd on the question of how facilitators of conventional meetings make the transition to facilitating face-to-face electronic meetings. As part of this research he has helped establish the Group Decision Centre and trained many facilitators to manage and support electronic meetings. His current research focuses on the facilitation of distribued meetings and social aspects of the Virtual Workplace.

PART C

Extended Abstracts

24

Teamwork training for mobile interdisciplinary teams

Prof. Dr. F. Bodendorf, Dr. R. Seitz
Information Systems II, University of Erlangen-Nuremberg
Lange Gasse 20, 90403 Nuremberg, German
Tel.: +49 911 5302-450 (Fax: -379),
E-Mail:bodendorf@wiso.uni-erlangen.de

Extended Abstract

Successful management of business processes increasingly depends on flexibility and adaptability in the organization of work. In many cases you have to cope with ad-hoc-structured or ill-structured tasks. For virtual enterprises with frequently changing national or international partnerships this kind of processes will be the dominating one. More and more interdisciplinary or multicultural teams have to decide on their self-organization and self-management depending on the problem at hand. It is the university's task to train students in the management of teamwork as well as in modern techniques for cooperative and collaborative problem solving.

The training scenario is based on a team of three persons each playing a different role. Each of them contributes his know-how and skills acquired in different disciplines. The given task is to produce a compound document containing technical product information, cost data and marketing text. The product may be, for instance, a mountain bike (see Figure 1).

Figure 1 Teamwork Task.

The engineer is asked to improve the construction of a technical product. The cost calculator has to analyse the monetary effects of product variations. The marketing assistant adds information from a sales point of view. On the one hand each member of the team is responsible for a distinct part of the document. On the other hand all team members have to communicate and negotiate with one another in order to select the most appropriate product alternative and to harmonize the document. In this scenario students of different disciplines (engineering, cost accounting, marketing) have the opportunity to get a feeling for interdisciplinary collaboration. Using appropriate software and telecommunication equipment they conduct their teamwork in an asynchronous way independent of their location.

The teamwork process is shown in Figure 2. Subtasks assigned to the actors are outlined. Arrows represent trigger and information transfer functions.

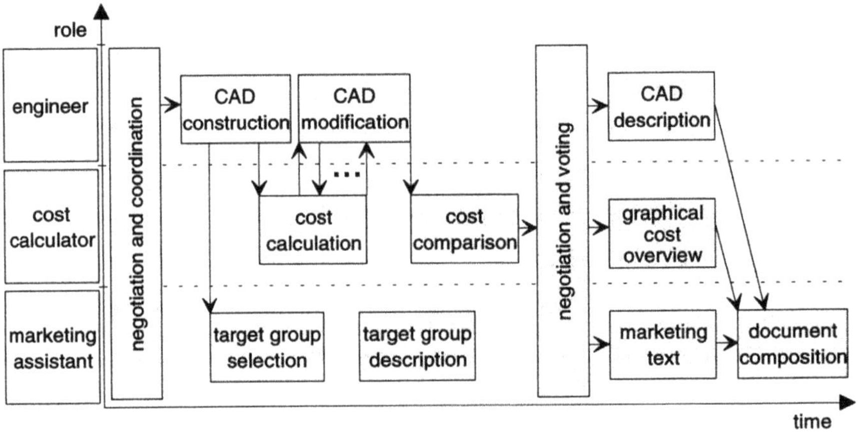

Figure 2 Teamwork Process.

The workgroup process begins with an electronic meeting involving all team members. They discuss distribution problems and decide to solve them by designing a new marketing initiative. Support is provided by an electronic meeting system offering assistance in the form discussion, brainstorming and voting facilities. The engineer begins to redesign parts of the mountain bike in accordance with the ideas and proposals worked out during the meeting. Evidently he uses a CAD system to achieve suitable results. When the engineer has completed his preliminary CAD sketch he informs the marketing assistant and contacts the cost calculator by sending him the construction file and the table of pieces. Using a spreadsheet application the calculator now estimates the effects of redesign on production costs. At this point feedback cycles may occur. If the price is obviously too high redesign and cost calculation are repeated until the product costs reach a realistic level. Meanwhile the marketing assistant produces textual information for the selected target group. Should more than one alternative prove to be feasible the cost calculator produces a table comparing the redesigned concepts. To do this he consolidates several spreadsheets into a larger one. The consolidated spreadsheet is the subject of a new conference. Independent of their current location the members of the team join the electronic meeting, discuss the available options and vote on the most suitable alternative. In the final step the marketing assistant assembles all aspects of the document: drawing of the redesigned product, technical description, calculation spreadsheet, graphical cost display, text of marketing proposals. A software agent automatically records all events (time of task completion, acting persons). Thus the current state of the process can be monitored by each member at any time.

25

Globalisation of information systems in Australian organisations

P. R. Cerotti, RMIT Business Higher Education
235 Bourke Street, Melbourne 3000, Australia
Telephone: 61 03 9660 5785, Fax:61 03 9660 5850
E-mail paulc@metro.bf.rmit.edu.au

J. Clifton, RMIT Business Higher Education,
235 Bourke Stree,t Melbourne 3000, Australia
Telephone: 61 03 9660 5786, Fax:61 03 9660 5850
E-mail judithc@metro.bf.rmit.edu.au

Extended Abstract

Introduction

Global communications technology offers those organisations that embrace it many strategic advantages in conducting business overseas; despite this however, it has not been a technology that Australian organisations have rushed to implement.

It was during the Eighties that discussions about the globalisation of business began; new markets were needed in order to sustain growth and to combat the number of foreign organisations entering the Australian marketplace and encroaching on existing business.

This paper investigates several Australian organisations and looks at their usage of global communications technology; the organisations chosen are a mix of those that are Australian owned and those that have their headquarters overseas. Some of the organisations have been exporting their products or services for a number of years, whilst others are new to business operations on a global scale.

The number of organisations researched is probably too small to provide a definite result. However, there does seem to be a clear indication that global communications is a technology that all the Australian organisations (included in the research) have investigated and have then proceeded to implement. *The proviso is of course that it does offer some definable form of competitive advantage when conducting business overseas.*

This paper describes an investigation into the use of global communications technology by Australian organisations paying particular attention to the following:

1. The long term information and management strategies organisations adopted when implementing global communications technology,

2. How information systems technology has been used to enhance the profitability of the organisations and also to contribute to the further expansion of the company's operations globally.
3. An evaluation of the role of global communications technology in sustaining a global competitive advantage for the organisation.

The Research Approach

A questionnaire was developed for use when conducting interviews with employees, holding a position in Management, in the selected organisations.

Six Australian organisations were selected for the research project; the organisations were selected for the following reasons:

- they were known to be conducting business on a global basis
- they had recently begun conducting business on a global basis,
- they were companies with their head offices overseas.

These organisations selected are listed below:

• **BHP**	Australia's Largest Company
• **BP Oil**	Multinational Oil Company
• **Ansett Airlines**	Major Australian Airline
• **Mattel Australia**	Multinational Toy Manufacturer
• **Carlton and United Breweries**	Australia's Largest Brewer
• **Knowledge Engineering Pty Ltd**	I. T. Consultancy

Conclusion

The relatively small number of organisations questioned prevents a definite conclusion being drawn, however, several similarities emerged from the answers provided.

The globalisation of business has become an important management strategy but only for those organisations who believe that some form of competitive advantage can be derived from such technologies. Most organisations began using global telecommunications in a rather ad hoc fashion however, management now play a more important role in deciding the future use of such technologies.

Those organisations that have been using global communications to conduct business for at least a few years state quite conclusively that being well informed of business opportunities worldwide does enhance profitability: the enhancement is derived mainly from cost savings. Several organisations believe that profitability was enhanced by global communications enabling them to be informed about business opportunities before their competitors but this advantage disappeared as soon as competitors improved their own global communications.

Manufacturing organisations indicate that the enhancement of their profitability is derived by being in touch with all markets and distributors around the world which enables them to optimise their production.

The competitive advantage gained by organisations is, again mainly through being better informed; as soon as information is available it can be acted upon which means that, despite the distances involved in competing for business in Europe, it can be accomplished much more easily than before.

26

DecisionWeb: a tool for asynchronous meeting support

P. Danyi
Rockefeller College of Public Affairs and Policy, University at Albany, S.U.N.Y.
135 Western Avenue, Milne Hall 300, Albany, NY 12222 U.S.A.
danyi@cnsunix.albany.edu

Extended Abstract

Among the many types of group activities that are supported by various group support technologies, perhaps the most widely studied is the group meeting. Meeting support systems have had two main goals in the past 20 years - *supporting* face-to-face (FTF) meetings and *replacing* face-to-face meetings with non-FTF meetings.

As FTF meetings first became supported by the use of computers, researchers developed a variety of software tools to assist the participants' activities. Group support and electronic meeting support systems were developed to create "electronic" communication instead of verbal communication, using structured problem-solving techniques to make the outcomes of meetings more efficient and effective.

In the 1980s, thanks to the local and wide area network infrastructure, more research was undertaken with non-FTF meetings, including computer-mediated communication. Although it has been argued that the most modalities for group communication are available at a FTF meeting, in some cases bringing people together is just too costly or logistically impossible. Our focus here is on *computer conferencing*, described by others as one of the three types of computer-mediated communication (besides electronic mailing and bulletin boards) used in *asynchronous, distributed* (or "any time/any place") context. It is increasingly apparent that a large variety of meetings, when properly supported by computer and by group facilitators, can be conducted asynchronously at least as effectively and efficiently as in a FTF context. This paper presents a meeting or conferencing system called *DecisionWeb*, designed for supporting such asynchronous, distributed problem solving and decision making.

Although DecisionWeb has been used, as have other computer conferencing tools, to replace at least some of the major activities that occur within FTF meetings (e.g., constructing lists of problems, opportunities, alternatives, or criteria), some situations demand that problem solvers must eventually meet together in the same room. In these cases, non-FTF meetings can be advantageous in the preparation and organization of FTF meetings. This is an important, third goal for meeting support systems developers - *preparing* for FTF meetings through asynchronous, distributed meetings.

Until recently, creating a meeting support system demanded fairly complex development work, including the establishment of appropriate hardware infrastructure for network communication, as well as composition of communications software for both hardware-related purposes and meeting-dependent procedures. Today, the situation has changed. Composite systems and methods can be built up from simple, pre-fabricated elements considered as *building blocks*. The emergence of basic group support tools (such as e-mail, World Wide Web, bulletin board, whiteboard, etc.) has created an important new opportunity for research and development, with the opportunity for constructing more complex systems. We have applied this building block principle to create a meeting support system, DecisionWeb, from existing groupware tools and problem-solving techniques that can be directed at the problem of providing more efficient and effective preparation for FTF meetings. The following criteria were defined as making the DecisionWeb system unique among other computer conferencing systems - reliant on any of the existing infrastructure of Internet facilities; usable in a variety of meeting/conferencing circumstances; facilitated, to insure more effective meeting outcomes; and inexpensive to initiate and routinely use.

As a groupware architecture, DecisionWeb connects participants in a *star-like* model. The basic communication channel is the Internet or any network including LANs or WANs. The sending and receiving of messages take place in one of many simple ways, using either (i) e-mail messages, (ii) e-mail attachments, (iii) file transfer by FTP, or (iv) file transfer by World Wide Web, depending on the user's easiest network access.

Each participant has the same "user" software to be able to read and write messages in a standardized way. Thus, the facilitator gets messages from every participant in the same format, and facilitator messages can be read easily by each participant. The system is also star-like with respect to group communication and interaction. The focus is not on intensive interactions among participants but on structured contributions to the group task. However, participants may send messages directly to each other at any time, though such interactions are not supported by structured way. The DecisionWeb software must be used for joining in any one of the *stages* of a meeting. A typical DecisionWeb conference moves through three stages: list building, categorization, and prioritization. These stages originated from non-computerized, structured problem-solving techniques of generating, organizing, and evaluating ideas.

The problem we illustrate here is *setting an agenda* which often is the responsibility of a group of people situated in geographically dispersed locations. This task is extremely important in the preparation of a FTF meeting. Since FTF meetings are relatively expensive when the organizers and participants arrive from different locations, there usually is a need to make FTF discussion as efficient as possible. One solution to achieve this result is creating a clear, properly scheduled agenda according to which each participant can prepare with information, questions, and concerns. The agenda setting situation can be well supported by DecisionWeb.

For this study, we chose the task of *setting discussion topics for a panel at an international conference*. Panelists were located in five cites and three countries. Altogether 28 categories of topics (culled from 66 separate proposals) were organized, rated, and ranked; 10 topics were selected which the entire panel deemed as important to address. The implication of this successful application is that complex asynchronous meeting support systems now are becoming available. Systems such as DecisionWeb will offer increasingly inexpensive and efficient means of convening "any time/any place" conferences world-wide with virtually no lead time for special arrangements or training requirements.

27

A culturally sensitive model of technology and groups: focus on group support systems

T. L. Griffith
University of Arizona and Purdue University, 1310 Krannert Bldg.
West Lafayette, IN 47907-1310 USA, 317/494-4485, 317/496-1778 (fax), griffith@mgmt.purdue.edu

D. R. Vogel
University of Arizona, McClelland Hall,
Tucson, AZ 85721 USA, 520/621-4016, vogel@bpa.arizona.edu

Extended Abstract

Technological research has arrived at an important nexus. At the same point that research is focusing on the enabling nature of technology in organizations, researchers are also acknowledging issues of culture for management, technology design, and use. The key is that technologies can enable new organizational forms, but the recursive nature of sociotechnical systems is riddled with opportunities for variation in outcomes as these technologies are used (and/or designed) across cultural boundaries. The focus of the current work is to outline a model of sociotechnical system outcomes given differences in culture. A group support system (GSS) context is used to communicate the vividness of cultural variation.

Group Support Systems (GSS) are one example of tools which link technology and groups of organizational participants into a sociotechnical system. In a GSS, users interact with and through computer-mediated communication systems to do collaborative work. Research suggests that GSS can reduce some aspects of process loss inherent in using groups and teams in organizations. Unfortunately, this outcome is predicated on research conducted solely in the U.S. In other cultures, processes losses may occur for different reasons, and/or process "losses" as defined for U.S. groups may not be "losses" in other cultures. The current work expands on these ideas by proposing a broad conceptual model for considering cultural issues in sociotechnical systems.

Definitions for the model's components follow. As noted above, for the purposes of this work technology means GSS. Hofstede suggests that culture is the collective mental programming which distinguishes one group of people from another. Group Process includes the methods of people working together to achieve a common goal. Group Outcomes are the extent to which the group achieves its goals and can include speed, full use of group resources (both task and process), and quality. This is by no means a complete list and would actually be the result of the group's own goals. The indicated links are the result of applying a variety of theories to this context. Connections from one box to another indicate direct effects. Connections from Culture to links between other boxes indicate moderating (interaction) effects. Western research has largely provided the support for the links between Technology, Group Process, and Group Outcomes. The links from Culture to Technology and other relationships are where explicit work is lacking.

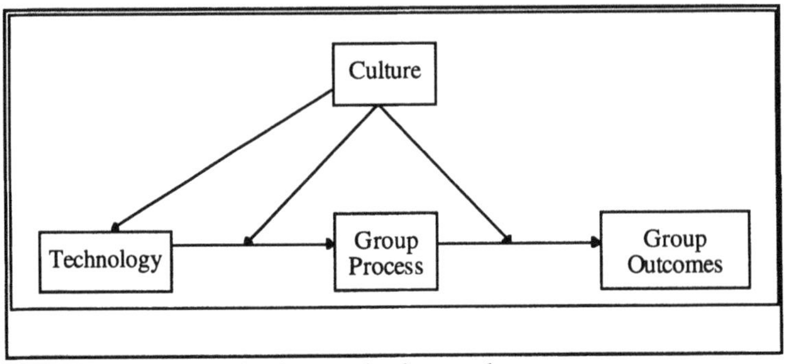

Figure 1 Effects of culture, technology, and group process.

This "white paper" is the beginning of a multi-cultural, longitudinal study using GroupSystems GSS as a focal technology. The long term use of the GSS in a wide variety of settings (GroupSystems is currently in place in over 30 countries) will be studied to consider each of the links in Figure 1. Working from Triandis' cultural dimensions of vertical and horizontal individualism and collectivism, GSS technology can be examined in terms of group process and outcomes. In the Horizontal cultures (HC and HI), features of GSS that promote equal participation (such as anonymous input) may not be needed. Equal participation is already the norm. However, in Vertical cultures (VC and VI), the GSS features that promote equal participation may have different outcomes depending on whether the culture is Collectivist or Individualist. In VI cultures (such as the US), the structural promotion of equal participation may be necessary and desirable. However, in VC cultures, the promotion of equal participation may have negative outcomes in terms of the disruption of basic social norms and values. VC cultures have learned to work with inequality in a way that maintains relationships. Task oriented technologies that promote information transmission for the betterment of the task may result in more important negative outcomes for the group's relationships.

We propose to use experimental and survey techniques in the examination of the above model. Both technological and group features will be manipulated (e.g., anonymity, status of group members) and measures will include both behavioral and attitudinal outcomes. The results should inform both sides of the sociotechnical model -- designers and implementers will learn the impact of different technology features in different cultural settings, and GSS facilitators will learn how to best utilize both their technological and group process options.

28

Subject areas for teaching GSS facilitation

R. B. Jarman
School of Information Systems, Curtin Business School
Curtin University of Technology, Perth Western Australia
E-Mail: bjarmanr@isis.curtin.edu.au

Extended Abstract

It has been proposed that 'strong facilitative and collaborative skills' will be required for the groupwork of the future, and that few institutions are offering training in these areas (Clawson & Bostrom,1995, p189). If research suggests meetings are an increasing part of business life (Mosvick & Nelson, 1987; Panko, 1992) and one in which substantial cost savings are available (Mosvick & Nelson, 1987) education and training in these areas are important. But what should be taught to students? Research described below is identifying knowledge, skills and abilities required by novice meeting managers (students) to effectively lead meetings where a face-to-face Group Support Systems (GSS) is available.

Research methodology

In summary, there are five main stages to this research project:

(1) establishing a body of subject material to be taught to students, defining the material and developing the course;
(2) teaching the course, observing and discussing the students effectiveness in leading meetings, and with the input of the students, evaluating the material included in the course;
(3) refining the subject areas to be taught;
(4) seeking comments from experienced GSS facilitators and educators on the subject areas; and
(5) revise and finalise the subject areas and course in accordance with these suggestions.

At the time of writing the research is at Stage 3.

Review of course development and evaluation

A single semester course was developed based on meeting management, facilitation and GSS literature using Clawson's 16 facilitator roles (Clawson, 1992; Clawson & Bostrom, 1995) as a starting point. The course contact was three hours per week over 14 teaching weeks. The structure was a 90 minute seminar followed by a 90 minute meeting. Areas covered included planning, designing and running meetings, communication skills, leadership, and problem solving and decision making processes. In the GSS area, results of the research were discussed including GSS effects such as anonymity and parallelism, and the factors which affect GSS meetings, and the effects on various processes and outcomes. There were eight students - five Asian, one African and two Australians. There were two females and six males. The multicultural background of the students is a factor of interest. Each student was part of a two-person facilitation team for two meetings. In these meetings, the students took turns in leading the meeting or being chauffeur. The GSS used in the meetings was GroupSystems V (for DOS).

The course has been evaluated both formally and informally. Formal evaluation was by questionnaire where students were be asked to evaluate the course based on what they learnt and how this equipped them to lead meetings. Informally, there was post-meeting evaluation and discussion. These evaluations, combined with the observations of the researcher, provide the basis for assessing how effectively the course achieved its objectives.

Outcomes

In summary, the students demonstrated they had acquired a variety of the facilitation skills but were not confident in actually administering the technology. In particular, the students were good at preparing and running the meetings, and ensuring there was an equality of participation, and that decisions were consensus decisions. The following points can be drawn from this phase of the research:

- the experience of running meetings is essential;
- in teaching students both facilitation skills and how to manage the tools careful consideration needs to be given as to how to achieve both within a single semester course;
- in brainstorming exercises some kind of arbitrary limit can be set to overcome information overload, and to ensure other aspects of meetings are also covered;
- teaching listening skills, and stressing the importance of the clarification of meanings is important to the idea organisation process;
- the importance of keeping to time versus the effects of rushing the group need to be highlighted;
- it may be beneficial to ensure the students are instructed in a number of specific process techniques rather than leaving it to their own reading;
- the stages of problem solving need to be emphasised so that problems are properly defined and criteria for evaluating solutions are developed before beginning the development of solutions;
- specific material on using 'questions' needs to be included;
- further methods for developing self awareness and self expression in a large group of students need to be examined, and included where appropriate;
- some students may require instruction on how to present information to a group;
- dealing with conflict appears a difficult area for teaching because of the experiential nature;
- inclusion of case studies where negotiation is required and with roles having conflicting interests is useful in highlighting where GSS may not be useful;
- subject material on GSS research does not appear to be relevant to facilitating;
- the opportunity to observe a variety of facilitator's would be beneficial;
- western facilitation, conflict management and feedback techniques may not be appropriate in Asian cultures

Next phase

At the time of writing, the course is being reviewed. A list of subject areas are being developed. When complete it will be sent to experienced GSS facilitators and educators for rating as to importance and comments. On return of the advice from more experienced facilitator's the subject areas will be finalised.

The impact of physical environment on performance and satisfaction in the white collar office: an overview of the literature

Daniel Mittleman
Center for the Management of Information
The University of Arizona
Tucson, AZ 85721
(520) 621-2932
danny@arizona.edu

Extended Abstract

Jean Wineman[1] provided a seminal review of research analyzing the relationship of white collar work environment to job satisfaction and productivity. While previous research had explored the relationship between physical environment and both performance and satisfaction in the industrial workplace, her work was the first summary of findings for that relationship among white collar knowledge workers. This presentation[2] updates and re-evaluates the status of current research that analyzes the relationship of white collar work environment on job satisfaction and productivity in office environments. This presentation describes the construction of both the independent and dependent measures used by Wineman, reviews recent research organized by Wineman's categories, and broaches the subject of how the physical environment impacts collaboration among knowledge workers.

Work environment is the range of requirements necessary for the health, well being and function of individuals in the workplace. This presentation organizes its evaluation of the work environment into three categories: PHYSICAL COMFORT; SYMBOLIC IDENTIFICATION; and EMERGING ISSUES. PHYSICAL COMFORT includes all factors of the environment which affect the contentment of workers and their ability to carry out work tasks. These factors include the ambient environment, ergonomics, lighting and view, privacy and social interaction, visual and acoustical privacy, and social interaction. SYMBOLIC IDENTIFICATION is the presence of status indicators and perceptions of status in the workplace. Finally several issues are lumped together under the rubric of EMERGING

[1]Wineman, J. D., 1982, "Office design and evaluation: an overview," *Environment and Behavior*, **14**(5), pp271-298.

[2]This presentation stems from: Mittleman, D. D., 1996, *Office Design and Evaluation: An Overview Revisited*, Working Paper, The University of Arizona.

ISSUES. Among these are office automation, collaboration, open office planning, control over the physical environment, and methodological concerns.

Satisfaction and performance are measured in several ways. Work environment satisfaction has been measured through survey instruments developed for the construct by several different researchers. While there is reasonable face validity for all of these measures, the lack of a consistent validated measure of construct of satisfaction with the work environment may contribute to differential findings among studies. Job satisfaction is a pleasurable or positive emotional state resulting from the appraisal of one's job or job experiences. Job satisfaction is one of the most established and studied constructs in the organizational psychology literature. While several different instruments have been used to measure job satisfaction in recent studies, most investigators have used well established and validated measures. Work performance is the amount of output produced by a worker. It can either be measured directly by counting output in some manner or perceptually by recording either the worker's own perception of performance or a supervisors perception of the worker's performance. Differing measures of performance is a serious threat to the external validity of many of the studies reviewed. Self measures and perceptual measures of performance may suffer from significant confounds with other perceptual or attitudinal factors.

In this presentation about 50 studies are reviewed and evaluated against the criteria set forth above. The state of the research literature is described. Opportunities for future research on these questions are explored.

Several emerging issues are discussed. They include: OFFICE AUTOMATION, COLLABORATION, OPEN OFFICE PLANNING, CONTROL OVER THE PHYSICAL ENVIRONMENT, and METHODOLOGICAL CONCERNS. Previous reviews of office automation as a moderator for the impact of physical environment impact on performance and satisfaction had occured prior to the ubiquitous arrival of personal computers in the office. Recent widespread usage of PCs has lead to heightened concerns such as VDT radiation and carpel tunnel syndrome. Current computer technology trends include audio, video, and data conferencing. These trends may impact issues such as privacy, social interaction and symbolic identification.

Open office systems planning, an absence of floor-to-ceiling walls and the use of systems furniture to landscape the workplace, was prevalent in the literature in the 1970s and became a common design strategy in the 1980s. Some are beginning to look beyond the basic systems furniture approach to team-based setting supporting group work. Research in the 1980s provided mixed success in its implementation.

Control over the workers physical environment consists of two related constructs. One is the amount of flexibility the environment affords for change to address the needs of an individual worker. Systems furniture, for example, that can be rearranged into different shapes might well afford much greater flexibility than systems furniture assembled so that it must remain in its initial shape. The other construct is the amount of control the worker has over the design or redesign of the work environment. Several studies have been undertaken during the past decade where workers have participated in the design of their workspace. Such a practice is slowly becoming more commonplace.

Wineman noted that relatively little field research has been conducted on behavioral responses to office settings and that the field research that has been conducted has usually been isolated case studies or surveys. However, most of the studies cited in this review have been survey or case studies. Only two are laboratory experiments and none are field experiments. Other advances in research methods are gradually making their way into workplace evaluation research including behavioral mapping and comprehensive post occupancy evaluations.

30

The virtual office in practice: a case study

Joseph Williams, Colorado State University,
Computer Information Systems Department

Extended Abstract

This research provides a case study and some empirical data for a small company running a virtual office today. Based on the lessons learned from thisvirtual office a look ahead is taken to what the virtual office of tomorrow will look likefor that company.

COSS is a geographically dispersed computer outsourcing company located in northern Colorado that has one unit specializing in network management and another that specializes in PC technical support. COSS has 9 clients in three cities located in two counties. COSS employs 14 permanent full-time employees, 5 permanent part-time employees, and as many as 20 temporary part-time employees on an as-needed basis. All of the temporary part-time employees are students at the local universities.

The initial strategy behind developing the virtual office was to leverage existing low-cost communication media into an effective virtual network that would function as efficiently as a regular office. Thus, the problem here was not to create a virtual office per se, but to create a virtual central office.

The economics of COSS's virtual office structure are described. This solution costs an average of 1.2% of monthly revenues, compared to a traditional office scenario that is estimated would average 3.8% of revenues. As importantly, the virtual central office solution has proven for COSS's clients to be more responsive and efficient than the traditional office solution.

The single most important difficulty with COSS's virtual office has been identified as the lack of credibility it engenders in some potential employees going through the recruiting process. However, clients report no credibility problems dealing with a company using a virtual office. A second problem is that employees report some loss of company identity.

The study of COSS's operation reveals at least two major areas in which new technologies are needed if their virtual central office is going to continue as the company grows. Today's technology of pagers and cellular phones is cumbersome and does not provide consistent access to the company's knowledge base. A cellular-level WAN or LAN is one solution.

The problem with cellular-level networks is that cellular costs could potentially be prohibitive. Consequently, COSS is extensively investigating the potential of the second technological area: intelligent agents. In fact, the COSS partners see intelligent agents as having the greatest potential of all "future technologies" to enhance their revenues and control their costs.

PART D

Panel Summaries

31

Making diffusion and adoption issues part of the design options and solution strategies for the international office of the future

Jan Pries-Heje, Copenhagen Business School, Denmark, Chair
Priscilla Fowler, Software Engineering Institute, Carnegie-Mellon University, USA
Karlheinz Kautz, Norwegian Computing Center, Norway
Gonzalo Leon Serrano, Universidad Politecnica de Madrid, Spain

1 INTRODUCTION

In the process of developing the Global multi-site conference for 1997 and especially in the time after that conference the issues of diffusion and adoption of IT become very important. The aim of this panel is threefold. First it will raise the diffusion and adoption issues. Second, it will overview the most important and salient diffusion and adoption issues from five different but complementary perspectives. Third it will enable discussion of these issues in relation to the International Office of the Future.

The panel members are active members of the new IFIP Working Group 8.6 on Diffusion and Transfer of Information Technology. The format of the panel will allow each panel member to briefly raise and address one of five key technology transfer and diffusion questions leading to open discussion from the floor.

2 TECHNOLOGY MATURATION REQUIRES INSTANTIATION (Priscilla Fowler)

Global Multi-Site Conference: Simulation Of What?

The futurist in me is enchanted with the idea of all that technology in the third conference of this exciting three-conference series. What an idea! An around-the-world conference "simulating the office environment of a globally distributed real or virtual organization." The pragmatist, veteran of many a failed technology adoption and implementation plan, is sceptical. All that technology (and all those technologists) simulating away! Where are the rest of us, with our human and organizational issues, and our desire to get "real" work done?

Technologies mature in context - in use. The best technologies have mechanisms for adaptation built right into them. For example, most organizations have used templates for word processors for years to encapsulate corporate forms, letterhead, etc. Most large-scale commercial suppliers of software routinely create language - or culture-specific versions of their products. What is the equivalent for the technological components of the office of the future? How will these technologies get adopted, adapted, and integrated? Will their use be codified by domain: medicine, aerospace, manufacturing?

The challenge of conference 3 will be to demonstrate, not generic technology like so many innovators and early adopters, but specific, adapted technologies for a typical modern business domain. When one can ring up a local supplier, specify a new business arrangement (eg. a virtual organization to install a new oil refinery) and readily get an environment configured to their own business requirements, then the international office of the future will have arrived.

3 CURRENT WISDOM ON DIFFUSION AND ADOPTION (Jan Pries-Heje) *How do you bring research on the International Office of the Future into the real office?*

There is no easy answer to that question but there is a lot current wisdom focusing on different parts of adoption and diffusion. One of the well known research schools is Diffusion of Innovation Theory. This theory can provide pragmatic guidance to the people facing the task of implementing the Office of the Future. Other theories focus on the role of learning, culture, context and human networking. All these theories can provide valuable contributions to the successful planning and diffusion of new IT within the future office. How and why this can be done will be explained.

4 THE DEVELOPER'S PERSPECTIVE (Karlheinz Kautz) *What will developers have to take into account when developing the International Office of the Future?*

The international office of the future has become more than a just a vision. The technology, at least in part, exists, but is not yet used in many commercial organisations. So what are the challenges for system developers in this field? From a technical point of view there still is some work to do. The necessary technical infrastructure is not in place everywhere. Neither are true distributed architectures which allow efficient use of the technical resources without the need to have all software to share applications at all physical locations. Cross platform connectivity has not been achieved either. For example there is still work to do making the UNIX and the PC world communicate with each other. These are technical challenges, but software engineers are already working on them and will come up with solutions. However, the real moment of truth will come when the office technology meets the users and the basic technology so far has been developed mainly in R&D departments with a long, long distance between the developers and the users. As one of my colleagues expressed it: "It is hard work to sell the idea of distributed cooperation to organisations to help them solve problems which they might not have discovered yet". So the distance to the users has to be diminished. Development projects which have not yet involved users should plan for and conduct structured, not incidental evaluation of their prototypes.

A general requirement for the technology going into the office of the future is that the communication support should be as invisible as possible. The users should still be able to concentrate on their work tasks and should not be distracted by the technology. But what this really means for all the different kinds of users can only be learned by involving them. This is however not that easy with users distributed over the whole world representing different cultures. And if user involvement is not possible system development should as an integral part include an introduction strategy. This also is part of the work of developers.

5 MANAGERIAL ISSUES (Jan Pries-Heje)
What steps should managers take to successfully integrate the Office of the Future into their organizations?

Business trends in the last years of the Twentieth Century emphasise the design and implementation of efficient and effective business processes, the establishment of core competencies, the divestiture of non-core activities, and the development of business relationships across organisational and geographic boundaries. The result is a leaner, more focused organisation with an external network of cooperative business relationships. They therefore require greater communication and coordination rather than direct, internal control. The office of the future, conceptualised as a means of coordinating across space and time, appears to address this need. It might be thought therefore that business managers would be keen to move to new forms of office.

The office of the future, however, is not a primary component of the value chain. It is an infrastructural concept and its constituent technologies are likewise infrastructural. Managers have too often burnt their fingers on IT infrastructural developments decoupled from concrete business benefits. Unless the strategic value and the near term benefits are evident and achievable managers are unlikely to be keen to invest heavily in the office of the future.

Research into the dynamics of IT-based organisational transformations has yielded some insights into the different paths which companies might take so as to obtain business value through exploiting the opportunities presented by the office of the future. The range of such paths is outlined. Of particular interest is the extent to which critical mass theory may apply to the office of the future and hence point to constraints on the range of successful paths available to managers.

6 ORGANISING THE ADOPTION PROCESS (Gonzalo Leon Serrano)
How can you do it?

The introduction of new IT in the office not only affects the way that the work is done; it also introduces a new dimension of the workplace and raises questions about the external recognition of new jobs. This section of the panel will analyze the way that the organization understands the innovation process and facilitates or complicates the introduction of a new technology. More specifically, we will present two conceptual tools for organizing the adoption process inside the company:

1. Circles of involvement: how to involve the company as a whole in the process to be sure that the new technology penetrates all levels of responsibility.
2. Adoption profiles: how to anticipate problems the company might encounter during the adoption process.

32

When we can't get together: how large is the value added of video-conferencing over computer-conferencing

J. Rohrbaugh, University at Albany, SUNY, U S A, Chair
C. Csaki, Bell-Northern Research Ltd, Canada
P. Danyi, Technical University of Budapest, Hungary
W.G. Hewett, Deakin University, Australia
S. Midkiff, Virginia Tech, USA

1 INTRODUCTION

When group members are unable to work together in the same room at the same time, there are at least five options currently available. The first is to wait as long as it takes until they can. The second is to add and subtract names from the original membership list to create a new group with one, overriding qualification: mutually convenient schedules. The third is to assign the responsibility to a smaller subgroup who can manage to be in one room at one time; at the extreme, this means one person can make all the key decisions. The fourth and fifth options are the subject of this panel.

Considerable developmental work on videoconferencing (option four) and computer conferencing (option five) has occurred over the past three decades, but it is only in the 1990s that communication networks have developed to the point that they can be used with relatively greater ease. Videoconferencing increasingly has been designed to simulate the intimacy and directness of face-to-face meetings, as if everyone were in the same room at the same time, for participants who actually may be thousands of miles away. Computer conferencing supports any time, any place meetings in which the interaction process is structured to completely connect all participants but without the immediate, give-and-take exchange of messages.

The proposed panel is prepared to address the question, "How large is the value added of videoconferencing over computer conferencing?" Two large and complex sets of issues will be examined during the session. First, the situational context of meetings may influence the appropriate selection of technology. Second, the resources expended to convene alternative forms of conferencing need to be considered. These two sets of issues, taken together, allow for an explicit accounting of the "value added" of videoconferencing.

2 SITUATIONAL CONTEXT

The situational context can be identified by

a) the organizational conditions
b)the problem domain
c) the meeting purpose.

Organizational conditions may include (but certainly are not limited to) the leadership and decision-making style to which the group is accustomed. The problem domain refers to the many dimensions that distinguish one type of problem from another (e.g., structured versus unstructured or creativity versus choice-making tasks). A meeting's purpose is defined by the limited or extensive goals (and associated objectives) that its convenors have established to define its success. Depending on organizational conditions, problem domain, and meeting purpose, the value added of videoconferencing over computer conferencing will vary.

3 RESOURCES EXPENDED

The resources expended include

a) communication infrastructure
b) computer hardware/software
c) start-up support

Resources devoted to communication infrastructure might comprise such categories as facility expenses (including non-computer equipment) and network costs. Hardware/software costs depend upon the extent to which an organisation must acquire additional computer technology beyond that which currently is available. Start-up support covers a broad array of training and facilitating services required to initiate first-time users. Depending on the system demands for communication infrastructure computer hardware/software, and start-up support, the value added of videoconferencing over computer conferencing will vary

4 PANEL FORMAT

After some introductory remarks from the panellists, the chair will raise a number of questions (see Table 1) as a prelude to open discussion.

Table 1 questions to motivate interventions and discussions:

Q1	Are there types of organizational conditions (e.g., leadership and decision-making styles) that are better suited to videoconferencing or computer conferencing?
Q2	Are there circumstances (e.g., crisis) that are better suited to one or the other?
Q3	What types of decision situations can be attacked efficiently?
Q4	What about group dynamics and team-building? How can they be supported?
Q5	How are different meeting goals supported?
Q6	What computing and communication infrastructure are required, and what is the availability of them?
Q7	What forms of communication can be supported, e.g. text, graphics, pictures? How easily?
Q8	What are the costs? Fixed costs (hardware, software, services) and variable costs (communication time, facilitator's time, etc.)?
Q9	What kind of preparation (including physical and mental) are the meeting participants required to make? And how much preparation is necessary on the facilitator's side?
Q10	What about first-time users? Can they use the system right away or do they need special training? How much?

33

The international office worker of the future

P. Yoong, Victoria University of Wellington, New Zealand, Chair
G. de Vreede, Delft University of Technology, The Netherlands
J. Gricar, University of Maribor, Slovenia
L. Jessup, Indiana University, U S A

1 INTRODUCTION

In the International Office of the Future (IOF), individuals will use a variety of technologies to assist them in communicating, in collaborating, and coordinating their activities across distance and time. These technologies are designed to enhance workflow automation, office conferencing and communications, information filtering, shared calendaring, electronic meeting support, data interchange, videoconferencing, etc.

Within the networked organization, dual structures will be put in place to manage structured and unstructured work. Business processes would thus need to be easily understood, analysed, diagnosed, and adapted. Problem solving and decision making will be done by ad hoc project teams made up of individuals from several cultural and national backgrounds, with each team member choosing their preferred location and time of work.

As there is great social and cultural diversity across the globe, the IOF also presents many potentially interesting opportunities for discovering and managing our differences and, subsequently, for enhancing global communications, collaboration, and coordination. For example, an individual from one country is likely to encounter difficulties in collaborating with someone from another culture. How things get done in the project teams is governed not only by the project requirements but by differences in languages, cultural norms, values, and expectations. If this cross-cultural collaboration is mediated by computer and communications technology, the difficulties become more complex.

As the IOF is expected to be a complex environment, characterised by turbulence and rapid change, in which individuals are expected to adopt a flexible, collaborative, and open-minded approach to their global work, we must start to find what 'works' and what doesn't as we proceed to create an IOF environment.

2 PURPOSE /AIM

The aim of this panel discussion is to explore the opportunities, challenges and issues of the IOF and how these would impact on the role of the International Office Worker of the Future.

3 FORMAT AND QUESTIONS

The final IOF multi-site conference in September 1997 has chosen the following three themes as the focal points for discussions: (a) technology, (b) business processes and (c) organizational, cultural and social aspects.

Using each of the three themes in turn, the panel will examine, among other things, the following questions:

1) What opportunities, challenges and issues of the IOF would impact on the role of the International Office Worker of the Future (IWOF)?

2) What is the likely impact?

3) What skills and knowledge do IWOF need in order to manage these impacts, and how can these skills and knowledge be acquired?

34

Round the clock work: the organisational issues

Bernard Glasson, Curtin University, West Australia, Chair
Dennis Bourque, Chevron Information Technology, USA

1 PANEL AIM

Global Inc., the 1997 IFIP WG 8.4 working conference, will operate "round-the-clock" and across the world. It will need a socio-technical infrastructure. Socio aspects include the organisation structure, the work flow, managing different time and different place work, synchronisation and version control, irregular working hours, multicultural teams, workplace management, and dealing with non-standard telecommunication interfaces and tool sets. If we call these the organisational aspects, then the aim of this panel is to surface the organisational issues associated with running Global Inc and to attempt to identify possible strategies for dealing with them. The "technical" aspects will be dealt with later in another panel.

2 SOME EXAMPLES

As an example let us consider work flow management and version control. In a distributed work environment it may be prudent to have one "region" (office or whatever) be responsible for a piece of work at any one time. Ownership may change as the work progresses (eg the problem is defined by one regional office, a solution to it is designed at another, the solution is built at a third and so on). Project ownership, albeit temporary, may bring with it rights and responsibilities. A right might be that of update. The other regions may read to project file, but the owner is the only one allowed to update it. And the responsibility might be to progress the work to a point where it can be handed on to the next region. At the hand-over of work from one region to the next the token or "baton" is passed to the next region which then assumes ownership rights and responsibilities. The "baton" may be one solution to an aspect of work flow management and an aspect of version control. The table below contains extracts from an earlier IFIP panel with a related theme which serve as further examples.

3 PANEL FORMAT

Dennis Bourque began proceedings with some short catalytic remarks. This was followed by a "brainstorm" session to surface the issues. Once the issues were raised and aired, the intention was to have open discussion in an attempt to identify possible solution strategies for dealing with the more significant of those issues. The intended outcome would be a list of issue statements and, hopefully, possible solution strategies which would be passed back to the Global Inc. design teams for their consideration.

Table 1 Extracts from the panel discussion "Round the Clock Engineering" IFIP WG 8.1 Working Conference, Trondheim, Norway, August 1995

"More and more professionals are able to perform their daily work independent of their employer. In brief, physical distances are to a lesser and lesser degree serious obstacles for personal and professional communication....Engineering and construction of complex installations requires a number of different skills, and usually a large professional staff, with a corresponding need for extensive co-ordination of activities. Engineering projects have therefore traditionally been executed by one team, preferably located at one site where all the required skills were available...(but) it is no longer realistic to carry out (all) projects with remotely located teams. The cost, both in economic and social terms, are prohibitively high....The scenario is therefore that several groups of people, maybe alien to each other, and located in principle at an arbitrary distance from each other, often with disjoint working hours, shall cooperate over several months in order to produce one consistent set of specifications....The challenge is to combine distributed human skills in a synergetic manner....In a practical working environment, exchange of information is qualitatively different from data transfer." *Helger Moen, Kvaerner Engineering, Norway*
"Shift work was and still is unpopular with most people....Today around the clock working has a new meaning. We have an office in Houston, which is six hours behind (London) and an office in Yokohama which is 8 hours ahead....The opportunity now exists for performing work in three centres around the clock. In concept it should be possible to begin work on a design in London and then pass the effort around the world for as long as it takes to complete that design.....In order for international around the clock working to be effective (we need to solve) a number of practical problems, some connected with the computer and others connected with ideas...the problems with communications of electronic documents are soluble, although transfer does take a considerable amount of time and must be carefully planned for. The problem that is less easy to solve is the transfer of ideas....for this we took advantage of the overlap in office times and teleconferencing facilities so that individuals could discuss matters face to face across a conferencing facility....It seems that there is nothing standing in the way of successful round the world engineering providing the economic will is there." *Ron T Duckling, M V Kellogg Limited, UK*
"A project management and engineering system designed for world-wide execution of multidisciplinary projects may cover a wide range of applications, systems and various organisations....the "time/activity/person" definition of ownership and responsibility for data becomes critical....Distribution of work may not only occur along the organisation, schedule and capability axes, but also along the time axis." *Jorgen Piene, Kvaerner a s, Norway*
"The distribution of the engineering process over multiple locations imposes additional requirements over those normally experienced at a single site operation: - Consistent language/terminology; consistent working practices and methods, including coding and numbering standards; consistency of tools and in particular software tools; efficient, reliable and secure voice and data networks; single source data; and efficient design change/revision control" *Steve Chatterton, Kvaerner H&G Offshore Ltd, UK*
"Now that the Engineering business is moving (..towards..) sending information back and forth across the Data Highway (..it..) creates a whole new set of problems: - What information do we have to send and in what format? What information do we receive back and in what format? How do we manage the outgoing and incoming information streams?....Our world has shrunk....and we better learn to speak the global language. We therefore....(must develop and fully adopt)....international standards for our information exchange". *Hans Teigeler, Fluor Daniel*

4 POSTSCRIPT - THE PANEL OUTCOMES

The thought-provoking input from Dennis Borque led to some the lively discussion between the 26 participants in the panel session. The outcome of that discussion was captured as eighteen "issues". These issues were then ranked in order of importance. There was not time to address the question of possible "solution strategies". The eighteen issues in order of perceived importance are summarised below along with one or two illustrative clarifying comments.

1 How do we maintain some form of coherence rather than disjointed disintegrated entries?

> "This is a problem in face-to-face groups. We exhort planning and project management but live on-the fly. Can we expect to behave better when separated by time and space? Or, will we just become better at flaming?"
>
> "encourage people to join in and see benefit - gain from this, don't throw the opportunity away"

2 How to create "focus" amongst people on different locations?

> "The problem with not being together in "ill structured" tasks is that there is no natural focusing circumstance such as being in the same room together. For the Global Inc. event, this introduces a risk of superficiality. Solution direction: reduce ill-structuredness (eg. using "formal" brainwriting facilities or setting specific tasks such as playing a role in a game). Any other ideas?"
>
> "Focus does not need to be just about location. What about drawing across several organisations? If a project team, working across time/space, is comprised of members from several organisations (or even several departments in one organisation), where is the loyalty when a paradox occurs between what is good for the project team, the person, and the organisation(s)? Time and space dislocation make this problem MORE critical than it is at this time."

3 How do you ensure everyone knows what they are supposed to be doing?

> "This comment relates to the mere mechanics of the work that has to be done. Roles and responsibilities need to be clearly defined. When you are working across cultures, time zones, etc., co-ordination becomes difficult. Also when you have multiple centres of "control," coordination is difficult. So there needs to be some process or coordinating mechanism in place for ensuring that work is done by the correct people at the correct time."

4 How do we create and subsequently manage the archives/results/"memory" of the conference?

> "Everyone who attends will have a different interpretation of what took place. How do we decide on what is the "official" record?.....Will all of the conference materials be available to anyone who wants to look at them, or will some of them have restricted access?....Who does the "memory" belong to?"

5 Should we (or do we want to) allow access to the conference from other than the 3 main sites? (e.g. voice/video/data)

"do we want to allow access to this conference to people at locations other than the three main sites - for example can I join the conference even if I am located at my home university?"

"I have a different (more nervous) point of view. This will be a first attempt for this community. We must ensure that what we tackle is achievable (eg organisers are volunteers, there is no obvious funding "pot of gold", must use the available technology etc.)"

6 How do we ensure that agreed tasks are done on time and what mechanisms do we need to ensure accountability?

"I think this comes under the same general topic as #3 above"

7 The value of conferences is the networking

"Whole new cultural dimensions are emerging as a result of interactions based solely on electronic contact. Is this necessarily a bad thing? How can we effectively leverage this new culture?"

"I find many of the issues I "want" to talk about regarding global companies inappropriate for a one-shot conference, where almost no institutional relationships will persevere"

8 "personal presence": the need to interact directly with your co-workers for subtle communication and simulations

"If workers around the world are limited to only computer-mediated contact, will coordination, communication of goals, strategies and other subtle messages suffer?"

9 How do I foster informal communication when there is no "down time?"

"I value informal communication. Through this I can evaluate my contributions, my value, and my understanding of the work we, as a team, are enacting. Research and practice on how can I do this across time and space is mixed. How will I work across time and space when (1) there is no "time off" and (2) the work is critical to me, my team, and our organisation(s)? That is, when someone is always going, and things are constantly being added, how can I chat? For example, if round-the-clock work is a relay team, passing a "baton," then when did we practice? When do we finish the relay and debrief? How do we share?"

10 I like to meet people

"One of the greatest benefits for me regarding coming to a conference is meeting the people I have electronically spoken with - it helps build bonds and get to know what they are like better"

11 How do we establish and maintain sufficient trust among strangers?

"A better formulation of the original question might be (at least as far as generic work settings are concerned): How can we design and use technology to establish and reinforce collaborative relationships between people distributed in space and time, i.e. transform strangers to collaborators?"

12 How do we overcome technical skill deficiencies? Proposal assumes a fairly high level of technical competence.

"Sounds like a good research topic right there :-)."

13 Nature of the work being done

"might itself raise challenges... might involve group discussion at times, information transmission, information exchange, etc..."

14 Work discipline

"If people are working at different places and times, it sometimes is very tempting to postpone activities you have to do for the `group goal'. How do you encourage the participants' discipline with respect to group work?"

15 How can we differentiate proprietary and public knowledge?

"we are talking about issues to do with ideas, experience, concepts, frameworks"

"Everything you submit to a conference ...becomes public knowledge"

"But I might wish to archive some of the informal communications that occur at a conference and not have them available to everyone"

16 How do individuals receive credit for the work?

"When individuals work in teams they do not always contribute the same. In fact, one individual may contribute the fundamental "concept or thing" that makes the whole team activity work. Should this individual get credit for his/her input or should we care?"

17 How will the global connectivity be done (e.g., Internet, etc.}?

"A technical issue!?"

18 Will Global Inc. lead to higher or lower quality "papers"?

"If the mode of work encourages folk to submit the number of submissions will go up making greater competition for fewer slots therefore (probably) the selected submissions will be of higher quality - conversely if it discourages submissions the "quality" might go down)"

"I think the quality of papers is one of the few things that won't be different for Global Inc. I mean, you're not going to sacrifice your current refereeing standards because we're getting global?? I think you should be careful to bring it to people's attention that paper quality is still one of the key factors that makes a conference a good conference."

35

Round the clock work: the technology issues

Doug Vogel, University of Arizona, Tucson, Arizona USA, Chair

1 PANEL FOCUS

The issues to be explored in this panel represent the technological challenges associated with effective and efficiently supporting the international office of the future distributed in time and space. The sampling presented is indicative of this broad spectrum. Key issues are grouped as audio/video, computer hardware, connectivity/data-telecommunications, control software, and application software. More emerged through discussion.

2 A SAMPLING OF ISSUES

2.1 Audio/Video

Audio and video technologies vary significantly in characteristics and impact on group dynamics. The options and choices are many, including: document cameras for transparencies and opaque materials; video tape recorders; audio cassettes and compact discs; videodisc; 35mm slides; television, satellite, or cable tuners; microphone pickup of all participant contributions for reinforcement at the same site and transmission to other sites; a stereo audio playback system for audio and video sources; large screen display of video and computer sources; scan conversion of computer text/graphics to video for recording; capture of video images for use by application software; life-size display of fixed cameras from other sites to give a "reach out and touch someone" effect. Which of these technologies and/or in what combination(s) provide the best return on investment given group and task characteristics is a perennial question.

2.2 Computer hardware

The hardware needs to effectively support the broader aspects of the IOF can become extensive. Multiple live video window capabilities integrated with the windowing of computer text/graphics may be needed to enhance users' interface with the system. Capture of textual documents through optical character recognition (OCR) is highly desirable, as is capture of graphic documents in a high resolution format. FAX transfer between sites or to other locations would aid in the incorporation of existing documents into some processes especially when other hardware is absent. When possible, the information FAXed should be in the form of a file rather than a physical document for ease of incorporation and highest resolution transfer. The capability to do "on-screen" annotation over computer graphics, text, or video facilitates the discussion of important issues.

2.3 Connectivity/Data-telecommunications

To robustly interconnect sites, a number of communications channels may be required. The types of information to be transmitted over the different channels include combinations of audio, video, and graphics in electronic meeting system (EMS) environments. For example, a configuration may include: a fixed wide-angle camera shot of all participants, a mix of all participants' audio contributions, participant close-up shots and accompanying audio, a high resolution graphics image, carry network data transmissions, and equipment control data transmissions. Easy access to external resources e.g., the World Wide Web, is imperative. Issues quickly extend beyond technological aspects to encompass coordination between multiple telecommunications formats and protocols that span international boundaries.

2.4 Control software

To realize a truly unified environment, tight integration of graphics and presentation software with computer and traditional video, audio, and other technologies is essential. What is needed is a consistent interface between integrated information technology software and the wide range of information and presentation technologies from a variety of vendors that potentially could be incorporated. From the user's perspective, examples of the types of interfaces that need to be considered are: keyboards, mice, touch screens, light pens, graphics tablets, and voice recognition. The type of interface used will vary with each individual's preferences. Executives, educators and other professionals, the primary users of these facilities, tend to prefer "low touch" and "no touch" interfaces. Providing these types of interfaces may be essential to productivity and wide-based multi-cultural acceptance.

2.5 Application software

Requirements for effective distributed support software in the IOF includes aspects of individual, group, project, and organizational support all built upon a communications infrastructure. Individual support needs include ready access to personal data sources and a degree of independence appropriate for personal exploration of topic areas. Group support includes the combination of session structure and process support seen in some groupware products. Project support includes presentation of the status and effective integration of information across sessions and between groups, thereby providing anelement of synergism and value added for a group engaged in a series of sessions. Organizational support includes access to internal organizational information as well as external information more commonly associated with executive support systems. This helps provide a level of information support that extends across projects.

3 PANEL AIM

The aim of the panel was to discuss these technological challenges associated with effectively and efficiently supporting the international office of the future and, in the process, identify others. With the set of technological challenges identified and understood, the panel discussion turned to strategies for dealing with them in different circumstances. The panel resulted in some early views as to appropriate technological infrastructures to support future work.

4 POSTSCRIPT - THE PANEL OUTCOMES

The audience involvement using GroupSystems and subsequent discussion developed focus on three primary areas of technological challenge: hardware/software platform, telecommunications, and dealing with time differences. Dialectics as well as consensus around key questions emerged as discussion not only involved dealing with issues associated with the IOF conference but extensions to use in broader organizational contexts.

4.1 Hardware/Software platform

Platform challenges focused on how to resolve different hardware platforms of different conference sites, different software platforms, and different communication facilities in different countries. It was especially noted that the same interface across software platforms and network connections is needed so that as people move from work to home to traveling to conferences they can log in and see the same interface and metaphors they are used to getting work done. Of concern was providing a ubiquitous interface to a dynamic group memory i.e., all participants need to have equal access to all media. The World Wide Web in general and Netscape in particular provide only part of the answer. Standard software suites are important as is consistency of technical formats e.g., all slides via PowerPoint, etc. Of particular concern, however, was the ability to cover a wide range of technological capability. A basic dialectic and tension emerges as, on the one hand, we want universal capability but, on the other hand, we recognize that tolerance for a wide range of technological capability creates a multitude of integration problems.

There are two dimensions to this issue, simplicity versus complexity and standardization versus accommodation. Some participants favored going for simple solutions given limited economic conditions at most universities stating that simple but high quality solutions are best for now e.g., a high quality conference phone. Others noted, however, that it is in our best interest to explore the forefront of technology. Standardization tended to favor Microsoft Windows. As one participant noted, "I would suggest: Windows machine, some similar software interface for downloading/viewing files, searching, adding/responding to comments, accessing information about event times, on-line "socializing", and Internet access." Other participants lamented the rigidity this brings about and the desire for a mix of high tech, low tech, and no tech solutions e.g., coexistence between conventional and electronic technology for presentations. The following matrix summarizes participant discussion around this key question of simplicity versus complexity and standardization versus accommodation.

simple - standardization [boring]	complex standardization [interesting - Bill Gates smiles]
simple - accommodation [workable - but limited]	complex accommodation [chaos]

4.2 Telecommunications

Multiple communications channels are required to not only support the more formal aspects of the IOF but also to support side conversations, spontaneous break-out sessions, etc. Unfortunately, the technology is not mature enough. As one participant noted, "the experiences trying to extend desktop videoconferencing systems to events distribution have been a complete failure when you transmit more that one face in 2B+D." At this point, true multi-point video is but a dream. Bandwidth limitations and their impact on communication richness remain an important research issue. Much conversation revolved around the question "Why don't we just give up on video conferencing?"

- Some participants noted that there "doesn't seem to be too much progress in the last 10 years" and that "video conferencing has been given a long time to develop with little perceived progress." Others noted that "it seems like the payoffs are questionable and the costs are large. Can't the `getting to know and trust you' phases be accomplished through computer conferencing? I hear all about these `Internet Relationships'. With the low cost systems and even high-cost systems the distractions can be worse than if you had only audio. Further the Internet community is taking over the videoconferencing standardization issues anyway."

- However it was that noted that "actually there is great progress in the areas of video compression and the ability to send video over the Internet. Also new capabilities like holographic images are opening up new possibilities." Further, "Getting to know and trust people can be done via the Internet only to some extent. Computing conferencing is ONLY one of several layers need to actually accomplish work. Conferences are usually too unstructured and ad-hoc to build working teams that can accomplish real tasks and develop a sense of team identity." Video conferencing not only helps in the development of trust and assuring presence but is an effective way of communicating with people that you already know.

The session participants had a number of suggestions and conclusions to this key question of audio versus video versus data. Among them was the need to insure that video conferencing quality is adequate to the task. As one noted, "Proshare does not suffice for most needs." A suggestion to "create the listener category for people that prefer to `attend' in a passive way" was responded to as follows: "This is a good idea. But rather than just one or several categories, there needs to be a continuum of control by the leader or leaders so that different options and privileges can be turned on and off for specific participants or subgroups of participants. Perhaps some of the features could be controlled by the participants themselves, at the discretion of the leader or the group as a whole through developing protocols that are appropriate to the nature of the task and the nature of the group."

4.3 Dealing with time differences

With a virtual conference, many time considerations become apparent e.g., "does the conference ever end and it can begin anytime, like now. "Participants need to apriori know the schedule of events so they can make plans to be involved in those activities that are motivating to them. There was a tension over how to schedule and degree of synchronous versus asynchronous interaction. One noted that "I find that with people in various time zones you do a lot of asynchronous work -- catching up on what was put in by the group while you were sleeping." There was a suggestion that we "may want to try ignoring time differences and let some participate on an adhoc basis. This is what happens in the real world." Participants especially noted the need for integration of synchronous and asynchronous tools and that "we are using new technology to implement an old process. The old process was developed from different motivating factors and using different technology. Lets take off our blinders and think outside the box" to address this key question of the balance of synchronous and asynchronous interaction.

Group memory was an especially important item of discussion. In response to a comment that group memory must be kept current and well organized, a participant noted "Yes, this is key. One method to do this is to organize the information as it is created by using tools that allow one to build tasks, subtasks, and categories for different ideas as they are generated. The idea of using some search engine to sift through huge amounts of data only takes you so far. We need tools that let you organize and synthesize as you go through a process to accomplish an objective." Another noted that "memory contains structured and unstructured information such as documents and video and audio. We need tools that do that." In response to "there is a big power in defining categories and structure for memories," it was noted that "Correct. Somehow, the group needs to get some consensus on what is stored in the memory and how it is stored." It was suggested to use Lotus Notes as a good organizer and document database and InterNotes to insure ubiquitous access.

5 CONCLUSION

Participants in general concluded that we need good planning, testing, rethinking, testing, rethinking, and then, maybe, the implementation will work and provide high quality. As one noted, "Remember - the conference is the network or at least highly effected by the capability the network provides." The control of this very heterogeneous communication infrastructure makes it more difficult to run the conference. A participant noted that, in organizational contexts, "You need tools that allow you to pose ideas, argue about them, and determine the level of group consensus before the meeting. This allows actual meaningful work to be done during the meeting, rather than wasting lots of time level setting and getting issues on the table for the first time. This also allows people to think through issues thoroughly prior to a meeting and gather relevant information which they can bring to the meeting and share with others in real time."

Comments also suggested that more meaningful, long-term working relationships are created through long-term electronic communication and collaboration than through casual talk at a cocktail party. There was, however, a plea that "couldn't we have some kind of on-line, real-time(?) social times for people with similar research interests to allow them to get acquainted?" Concluding comments reiterated the importance of the need for redundancy and backup and disaster planning to accommodate reliability problems and that tech support during the conference at each site is critical.

36

Future environments

J. F. Nunamaker, University of Arizona, Tucson Arizona USA, Chair

1 PREAMBLE

Given the high rate of change in technology and working environments, organizations are under tremendous pressure to improve their effectiveness. Many large organizations have evolved to the point where their structure and procedures are no longer in keeping with the needs of the future. Globalization of business, internationalization of trade and the increasing prevalence of multi-cultural interdisciplinary teams are beginning to redefine the nature of office work in general and decision making in particular. Organizations need to study themselves to determine what should be changed. Recognition must particularly be given to relationships between the organization and its external environment. The International Office of the Future (IOF) will be a dramatically different environment than that which exists in the majority of today's organizations. Imagine a meeting in the IOF:

2 A SCENARIO

As the participants arrive at their local conference room, the walls near the conference table light up with live video images from similar meeting sites at the location of the other participants. Camera angles and directional speakers give the illusion that the local conference table extends into the screen to the other sites, joining with the other tables forming a large single conference environment. Participants feel as if they are all present in the same room. They are able to converse with other group members and join various conversations at the other sites. Following introductions, the group leader assisted by a facilitator presents a decision making agenda that includes phases of problem framing, creative brainstorming, information organization, consensus formation and generation of action plans to achieve a value-added partnership complete with associated contractual obligations. Techniques and protocols are introduced and agreed upon to assist in managing the meeting process. The facilitator not only makes sure that the various cultures are respected but helps the group use its collective diversity to create a climate of creativity, synergism, and efficiency.

Group members are invited to present their opinions and participate in the discussions verbally as well as through use of a wide variety of technology interfaces including personal notepads and conventional laptop computers using electronic pens and voice recognition in addition to keyboards. Videowalls enable gestures and body language or remote participants to be recognized and acknowledged. Language translation is electronically supported, if needed, at least to the extent that exchanges are understandable, if not in the best grammatical form.

A wide variety of software tools are available to support group members. For example, an "electronic brainstorming" tool provides each group member with an electronic copy of a common question. Ideas entered by participants are simultaneously shared with other group members. The result is that everyone is able to electronically speak at once and participate in multiple conversations. Group members can also access a variety of external data sources and expertise. Electronic "agents" directed by group members seek out relevant information that may bear on the topic at hand.

As the meeting continues, artificial intelligence is used to cluster and display common elements and streams of thought. As appropriate, analytical models and simulations are introduced to assist in negotiation and decision making. At various times during the meeting, group members make presentations or draw attention to a particular set of issues. Other group members are free to capture public information at their own computer, annotate visuals, and save information for their personal use as well as comment verbally and electronically back to the group and presenter as appropriate. Group members can vote electronically and begin to see consensus emerge as well as get personal feedback on their level of agreement with the group.

As the meeting draws to a close, some participants record on diskette information that they want to personally retain. Other participants send meeting information directly to their office computers. In addition, public information is stored in a team memory to be accessed and used by other stakeholders and in future meetings. Action plans are electronically circulated for comment and implementation is initiated as appropriate. Participants leave the meeting with a sense of accomplishment, commitment, and personal satisfaction in the negotiation and decision making process and product.

As participants return back to their offices, the issues from the meeting and action plans continue to move forward as other stakeholders take responsibility with a sense of purpose and direction as appropriate. Team members stay in touch through electronic mail, bulletin boards, electronic "scoreboards", desktop videoconferencing, and customized shared databases. As appropriate, subgroups as well as the main group reconvene to summarize progress, redirect energies, and conclude phases of larger projects.

3 PANEL AIM

For the most part, the technological components of this multi-dimensional environment exist to be integrated. However, without benefit of organizational development and behavioral wisdom, technology will be wasted at best and most likely counter-productive.

The challenge exists to sensibly integrate technological and organizational components. The key is a reasoned mix of theory and application through establishment of environments that meet the needs of the future. The IOF is a space, not just a place. This panel will explore issues associated with this multi-faceted domain.

INDEX OF CONTRIBUTORS

KEYWORD INDEX

www.ingramcontent.com/pod-product-compliance
Ingram Content Group UK Ltd.
Pitfield, Milton Keynes, MK11 3LW, UK
UKHW020132290926
15471UKWH00003B/431
* 9 7 8 1 4 7 5 7 5 4 8 8 9 *